Privileged Precariat

White workers occupied a unique social position in apartheid-era South Africa. Shielded from black labour competition in exchange for support for the white minority regime, their race-based status effectively concealed their class-based vulnerability. Centred on this entanglement of race and class, *Privileged Precariat* examines how South Africa's white workers experienced the dismantling of the racial state and the establishment of black majority rule. Starting from the 1970s, it shows how apartheid reforms amounted to the withdrawal of state support for working-class whiteness, sending workers in search of new ways to safeguard their interests in a rapidly changing world. Danelle van Zyl-Hermann tracks the shifting strategies of the blue-collar Mineworkers' Union, culminating in its reinvention, by the 2010s, as the Solidarity Movement, a social movement appealing to cultural nationalism. Integrating unique historical and ethnographic evidence with global debates, *Privileged Precariat* offers a chronological and interpretative rethinking of South Africa's recent past and contributes new insights from the Global South to debates on race and class in the era of neoliberalism.

DANELLE VAN ZYL-HERMANN is a Postdoctoral Research Fellow in the Department of History at the University of Basel, Switzerland, and a Research Associate with the International Studies Group at the University of the Free State, South Africa. Her research on the entanglement of race and class and the politics of whiteness in Africa has been published in various international journals. She is the co-editor of *Rethinking White Societies in Southern Africa, 1930s–1990s* (2020), a regional history of poor and working-class whites during colonialism and white minority rule.

THE INTERNATIONAL AFRICAN LIBRARY

General editors
LESLIE BANK, *Human Sciences Research Council, South Africa*
HARRI ENGLUND, *University of Cambridge*
DEBORAH JAMES, *London School of Economics and Political Science*
ADELINE MASQUELIER, *Tulane University, Louisiana*
BENJAMIN SOARES, *University of Florida, Gainesville*

The International African Library is a major monograph series from the International African Institute. Theoretically informed ethnographies, and studies of social relations 'on the ground' which are sensitive to local cultural forms, have long been central to the Institute's publications programme. The IAL maintains this strength and extends it into new areas of contemporary concern, both practical and intellectual. It includes works focused on the linkages between local, national, and global levels of society; writings on political economy and power; studies at the interface of the socio-cultural and the environmental; analyses of the roles of religion, cosmology, and ritual in social organisation; and historical studies, especially those of a social, cultural, or interdisciplinary character.

For a list of titles published in the series, please see the end of the book

Privileged Precariat

White Workers and South Africa's Long Transition to Majority Rule

Danelle van Zyl-Hermann
University of Basel
University of the Free State

International African Institute, London
and

CAMBRIDGE
UNIVERSITY PRESS

University Printing House, Cambridge CB2 8BS, United Kingdom

One Liberty Plaza, 20th Floor, New York, NY 10006, USA

477 Williamstown Road, Port Melbourne, VIC 3207, Australia

314–321, 3rd Floor, Plot 3, Splendor Forum, Jasola District Centre, New Delhi – 110025, India

79 Anson Road, #06–04/06, Singapore 079906

Cambridge University Press is part of the University of Cambridge.

It furthers the University's mission by disseminating knowledge in the pursuit of education, learning, and research at the highest international levels of excellence.

www.cambridge.org
Information on this title: www.cambridge.org/9781108831802
DOI: 10.1017/9781108924702

© Danelle van Zyl-Hermann 2021

This publication is in copyright. Subject to statutory exception and to the provisions of relevant collective licensing agreements, no reproduction of any part may take place without the written permission of Cambridge University Press.

First published 2021

A catalogue record for this publication is available from the British Library.

Library of Congress Cataloging-in-Publication Data
Names: Van Zyl-Hermann, Danelle, author.
Title: Privileged precariat : white workers and South Africa's long transition to majority rule / Danelle van Zyl-Hermann.
Other titles: International African library.
Description: Cambridge, United Kingdom; New York, NY: Cambridge University Press, 2021. | Series: The international African library | Includes bibliographical references and index.
Identifiers: LCCN 2020046743 (print) | LCCN 2020046744 (ebook) | ISBN 9781108831802 (hardback) | ISBN 9781108927208 (paperback) | ISBN 9781108924702 (epub)
Subjects: LCSH: Working-class whites–South Africa–Social conditions. | Working-class whites–South Africa–Economic conditions. | Working-class whites–Political activity–South Africa. | South Africa–History–1994–
Classification: LCC DT1768.W55 V36 2021 (print) | LCC DT1768.W55 (ebook) | DDC 305.56208909068–dc23
LC record available at https://lccn.loc.gov/2020046743
LC ebook record available at https://lccn.loc.gov/2020046744

ISBN 978-1-108-83180-2 Hardback

Cambridge University Press has no responsibility for the persistence or accuracy of URLs for external or third-party internet websites referred to in this publication and does not guarantee that any content on such websites is, or will remain, accurate or appropriate.

To my family, at home.

Contents

List of table and figures	*page* viii
Acknowledgements	xi
List of abbreviations and acronyms	xv
Introduction: The return of the white working class	1

Part I   White workers and the racial state

1 Privileged race, precarious class: White labour from the mineral revolution to the Golden Age — 33

2 From sweetheart to Frankenstein: The National Party's changing stance towards white labour amid the crisis of the 1970s — 76

3 Race and rights at the rock face of change: White organised labour and the Wiehahn reforms — 116

Part II   White workers and civil society mobilisation

4 From trade union to social movement: The Mineworkers' Union/Solidarity's formation of a post-apartheid social alliance — 157

5 An 'alternative government': The Solidarity Movement's contemporary strategies — 198

6 Discursive labour and strategic contradiction: Managing the working-class roots of a declassed organisation — 241

7 'Guys like us are left to our own mercy': Counternarratives, ambivalence, and the pressures of racial gatekeeping among Solidarity's blue-collar members — 264

Conclusion — 303

Bibliography — 310
Index — 330

Table and figures

TABLE

1.1 Distribution of the Afrikaner labour force, 1946–70. *page* 69

FIGURES

1.1 Underground drilling in a gold mine on the East Rand, 1972. *page* 34
1.2 White and black mineworkers of the Witwatersrand in the early 1900s. 39
1.3 Hand hammer stoping in Crown Deep mine in the 1900s. 43
1.4 Members of the Newlands strikers' commando ride past supporters holding a banner with the Rand Revolt's famous slogan. 46
1.5 Mounted police sweep through central Johannesburg on 9 March 1922. 47
1.6 Jackhammer stoping in East Rand Proprietary Mines, 1938. 50
1.7 The crew that attained the world deep-level mining record in 1958 at East Rand Proprietary Mines. 62
1.8 Workers operating the four-stand tandem cold reduction mill at Iscor's Vanderbijlpark works, 1965. 65
1.9 Arrie Paulus (right) and Cor de Jager (centre-left) emerge smiling from a meeting with then Minister of Mines Carel de Wet (centre-right) in 1970. 73
2.1 Marais Viljoen, Minister of Labour, on the political stage. 88
2.2 Minister Viljoen meets members of the African workers' liaison committee of the Alusaf aluminium smelter in Richards Bay, 9 December 1974. 93
2.3 The new Minister of Labour, Fanie Botha, in conversation with Wessel Bornman (left) and Attie Nieuwoudt (right) at SACLA's 1976 congress. 104

3.1 The Wiehahn Commission. Front, left to right: C. A. Botes, Dr E. P. Drummond, A. I. Nieuwoudt, Professor N. E. Wiehahn (chairman), B. N. Mokoatle, C. W. H. du Toit. Back, left to right: R. V. Sutton, G. Munsook, Professor P. J. van der Merwe, J. A. Grobbelaar, D. van der Walt (secretary), C. P. Grobler, T. S. Neethling, N. J. Hechter, T. I. Steenkamp. 123

3.2 Attie Nieuwoudt (left) with Prime Minister John Vorster (centre) and Minister of Labour Fanie Botha (right) at a meeting of labour representatives in Pretoria, 1977. 127

3.3 Minister Fanie Botha and his secretary Jaap Cilliers (both centre) attend a meeting of the Wiehahn Commission, 1977. Dennis van der Walt and Nic Wiehahn consult in the background, with Chris du Toit and Errol Drummond attending in the foreground. 133

3.4 Minister Fanie Botha and chairman Nic Wiehahn present Part 1 of the Commission's report to Prime Minister P. W. Botha (centre) in his office, 19 February 1979. 143

3.5 Clamorous mineworkers disrupting a public meeting in Welkom, at which Minister Fanie Botha spoke, following the release of the Wiehahn report in 1979. 148

4.1 MWU organisers lead a Volksfront rally at Vanderbijlpark, 22 May 1993. 163

4.2 Cor de Jager and Arrie Paulus emerge from a meeting with Minister Fanie Botha, 1976. 173

4.3 Andries Treurnicht, leader of the Conservative Party, with Cor de Jager (left) and Peet Ungerer (right) at the MWU's 1993 annual congress. 181

4.4 MWU members from Evander on the East Rand protest against Eskom's decision to allow the desegregation of residential areas under its control, 1991. 183

4.5 Peet Ungerer (second from left) and Cor de Jager (right) flank General Constand Viljoen at the founding meeting of the Afrikaner Volksfront, 1993. 184

4.6 Flip Buys (left) acts as MWU signatory of the union's recognition agreement with Telkom, marking another significant expansion of the union, 1993. 187

4.7	Flip Buys (centre) leads a media conference following the MWU's Labour Court victory against affirmative action policies at Eskom in 1997. Among the MWU legal and union representatives is Dirk Hermann (far left). Note the MWU slogan 'Times have changed … you need the MWU now!'	192
5.1	Flip Buys and ANC general secretary Gwede Mantashe during a press briefing on the out-of-court settlement following the Malema hate speech case, 2012.	215
5.2	AfriForum legal spokesperson Willie Spies braves the crowd of Malema supporters outside the Johannesburg High Court during the hate speech case in 2011.	220
5.3	Dirk Hermann (left) and Flip Buys (right) meet with President Jacob Zuma as part of an anticrime campaign initiated by the Solidarity trade union, 2010.	230
7.1	MWU members at a protest meeting against Eskom's decision to desegregate its residential areas, 1991.	269
7.2	Peet Ungerer and Flip Buys (front centre) with other MWU representatives after presenting Eskom officials with a petition against the company's decision to desegregate its residential areas, 1991.	270
7.3	Some 2,500 MWU members protest against affirmative action policies at Iscor's Vanderbijlpark works on 15 March 1995.	271
7.4	MWU members protest at Telkom's head office about wage demands, 1995. Note the banners: 'White workers unite'.	275
7.5	MWU members protest at the Duvha power station near Witbank against Eskom's decision to phase out housing, transport, water, and electricity allowances for employees in 1995.	277
7.6	MWU members demand wage increases during a strike at Samancor Chrome in Krugersdorp in 1998.	283

Acknowledgements

It is a humbling and somewhat surreal experience to reflect on the vast amount of support I received over the course of this project. The research for this book was conducted between 2011 and 2018, and I would like to thank the archivists and staff members at the South African National Archives (Pretoria), Heritage Foundation (Pretoria), Archive for Contemporary Affairs (Bloemfontein), National Library of South Africa (Pretoria and Cape Town branches), and Stellenbosch University Library who graciously dealt with my requests and questions. In Pretoria, I was truly overwhelmed by the enthusiasm and generosity with which I was received at the Solidarity Movement. I am grateful to Flip Buys and Dirk Hermann for facilitating access to the trade union archives, granting me interviews and readily permitting my research at the Movement's head office. My heartfelt thanks to the Solidarity staff, who always assisted me in a friendly and professional manner. I salute the trade union veterans I interviewed at the union for so generously giving me their time and trusting me with their stories – their voices and experiences have humanised this study. I expect my interviewees will not agree with all the interpretations put forward here, but I trust they will find that I have represented them fairly. It is my hope that the story told here may perhaps widen their own understanding of their world. I was privileged to gain access to the personal archive of Naas Steenkamp in Somerset West for my research into the Wiehahn Commission. I am deeply saddened that Mr Steenkamp did not see the publication of this book, passing away shortly before the manuscript was completed. Even though he may not have supported all my arguments, I know that the finished product would have given him much joy, and it would have been my pleasure to debate it with him on his porch over a cup of rooibos flavoured, as it always was, with his witty banter. I am further indebted to Adam Ashforth, Hermann Giliomee, Deborah Posel, Naas Steenkamp, and Wessel Visser for kindly providing access to earlier interviews they had conducted with key actors. A big thank you, finally, to my students and assistants – Eleanor Born-Swart and Ruhan Fourie in Bloemfontein, Max Hufschmidt, and Oliver

Göhler in Basel – who tracked down obscure publications, checked missing references, and sent through scans. There would be many more gaps in this research if it wasn't for them.

It has been my privilege to enjoy the intellectual support of a number of extraordinary scholars in the course of this project. In what I now think of as its first phase, this book started as my PhD thesis at the University of Cambridge, where Megan Vaughan provided expert supervision, accompanied by much kindness and patience. She encouraged me to persevere through the messiness of primary research and turn the problems I encounter into productive opportunities. These are lessons I try to teach my students today. In the later stages of analysis and writing, Emma Hunter generously shared her time and considerable expertise, spurring me on with her enthusiasm and positivity. As this phase drew to a close, I received incisive comments from my examiners, Robert Ross and Saul Dubow.

I next moved to a postdoctoral position with the International Studies Group (ISG) at the University of the Free State (UFS), Bloemfontein. Being back in South Africa enabled me to pursue still unanswered questions in my work, while the wonderfully collegial and well-connected environment of the ISG allowed me to develop the emerging global dimensions of my study. All of this was facilitated by Ian Phimister, head of the ISG. Throughout this second and consolidating phase, I benefited from Ian's vast knowledge and networks, not to mention his good humour, generosity, and encouraging admonitions ('*Please* listen to me, Dr van Zyl!'). It is no exaggeration to say that this book would not have been completed without his support. I am thankful, also, for colleagues and staff who made working at the ISG enjoyable and easy. Ilse le Roux and Tari Gwena – always helpful, always friendly, always ready for a chat – deserve medals for the administrative feats they performed. Jackie du Toit and Neil Roos approached my work with attentiveness and enthusiasm, providing essential professional support and advice. Fellow ISG postdocs and UFS colleagues – Andy Cohen, Chris Holdridge, Tarminder Kaur, Philippa Kerr, Kate Law, Clement Masakure, Jared McDonald, Admire Mseba, Cornelis Muller, Lazlo Passemiers, David Patrick, Rory Pilossof, Ana Stevenson, Christian Williams, and Rosa Williams – generously shared ideas and life, enriching mine in the process. Meanwhile, Maureen and Gerhard Conradie, Ronél and Gideon van der Watt, and Phia van der Watt offered homes away from home in Bloemfontein, providing, with extraordinary flexibility and grace, the everyday care and encouragement essential to sustain both body and soul.

I never imagined this project would be completed, finally, in Switzerland. My warmest thanks to Julia Tischler who offered the

Acknowledgements   xiii

opportunity, and in many ways created both the professional and personal space for me to finish the manuscript. At the University of Basel, colleagues in the African History group and the Namibia and Southern Africa research group provided constructive and considered feedback on a number of chapters. As a newcomer in a very different academic context, I am grateful to Alexandra Binnenkade, Tanja Hammel, Heinrich Hartmann, Cassandra Mark-Thiesen, Laura Ritter, and Meike von Brescius in the Departement Geschichte for welcoming me into the fold, offering advice, support, and friendship. I would also like to thank my 2018 students who, on a dark December afternoon, humoured me and my enthusiasm for my subject by commenting on a chapter draft in the context of the coursework on twentieth-century South Africa. Their comments were impressively insightful and alerted me to a number of blind spots.

I am grateful for funding I received in the course of this project from, most notably, Gates Cambridge, the International Studies Group at the University of the Free State, the South African National Research Foundation, and the Swiss Federal Commission for Scholarships for Foreign Students. My sincere thanks, also, to the various archives and institutions that granted permissions to reproduce images from their collections. For their support in this regard, I am particularly grateful to Zabeth Botha, Jos Damen, and Gabriele Mohale, as well as the teams at the African News Agency and Gallo Images. All due efforts were made to trace copyrights for images.

As the manuscript crept towards completion, Maxim Bolt, Christian Williams, and Zoë Groves offered valuable publishing advice and encouragement. At the International African Institute and Cambridge University Press, I was greeted, and accompanied throughout the review and production process, with a wonderful combination of enthusiasm, professionalism, and patience. My heartfelt thanks to Stephanie Kitchen, who was always available to provide advice and answered scores of questions with clarity and kindness. Maria Marsh, Atifa Jiwa, Stephanie Taylor, and Niranjana Harikrishnan expertly guided the manuscript and its author through the various production phases. It was a pleasure to work with Judith Forshaw, as copyeditor, who approached my text with care and insight. *Baie dankie* to the gracious Sanet le Roux, who devised the index with great skill and efficiency. The fact that each of these individuals played their part in this impeccable way in the midst of the manifold challenges and anxieties produced by an unfolding global pandemic makes them all the more remarkable. My sincere thanks to each of them. Finally, I am honoured and truly thrilled to be able to use the work of one of South Africa's most eminent photojournalists, Greg

Marinovich, on the cover. This image captures not just the entanglement of race and class which this book is about, but our very co-constitution as South Africans, as human beings, that makes us who we are.

Of course, the phases and stations I've sketched were seldom clear cut and I treasure the connections, collaborations, and friendships which continue to stretch across projects and continents. In particular, I would like to thank Jacob Boersema, Lindie Koorts, and Duncan Money, each of whom has generously shared ideas and knowledge, networks, workload, struggles, and triumphs – not to mention drinks and meals. At various points in this project, they provided insightful and immensely helpful input. I have learned so much from them, while having so much fun. At Stellenbosch, I can always count on a kind of homecoming with long-time mentors and friends including Anton Ehlers, Chet Fransch, Albert Grundling, Bill Nasson, Schalk van der Merwe, and Wessel Visser, who continue to be models of integrity, creativity, and verve. In Cape Town, my joys and trials were shared and softened by Renate Asch, Alana Bolligelo, Rob and Laura Booth, and Melissa Melnick. My family, at home, always supported my choices, obscure as they must often have seemed, saying all that needed to be said with their 'thinking of yous'. The spiritual foundations lain by my parents, and the continued assurance of their prayers for me, are my daily comfort and strength. Finally, I consider myself uniquely blessed to be accompanied throughout it all by Clemens Hermann. Whatever achievement this book may represent is a testimony to his love, encouragement, and sacrifice.

Earlier versions of Chapters 4 and 5 appeared as articles in *International Labor and Working-Class History* (86, Fall 2014) and *Ethnic and Racial Studies* (41, no. 15, 2018), respectively. A chapter in *Rethinking White Societies in Southern Africa, 1930s–1990s* (Money and Van Zyl-Hermann, 2020) drew in part on research presented in Chapter 2.

Abbreviations and acronyms

AB	Afrikaner Broederbond (Collection) [Erfenisstigting, Pretoria]
AEU	Amalgamated Engineering Union
AFL-CIO	American Federation of Labor and Congress of Industrial Organizations
ANC	African National Congress
ARCA	Archive for Contemporary Affairs [University of the Free State, Bloemfontein]
AWB	Afrikaner Weerstandsbeweging (Afrikaner Resistance Movement)
CERD	Committee on the Elimination of Racial Discrimination [United Nations]
COSATU	Congress of South African Trade Unions
CP	Conservative Party
FAK	Federasie van Afrikaanse Kultuurvereniginge (Federation of Afrikaans Cultural Associations)
FF	Freedom Front
GDP	gross domestic product
GEAR	Growth, Employment, and Redistribution [strategy]
GVA	Gemeenskap Volk en Arbeid (Society of People and Labour)
HNP	Herstigte Nasionale Party (Reconstituted National Party)
ILO	International Labour Organization
Iscor	Iron and Steel Industrial Corporation
MP	Member of Parliament
MWU	Mineworkers' Union
NA	National Archives of South Africa [Pretoria]
NMC	National Manpower Commission
NP	National Party
NPA	National Prosecuting Authority

NUCW	National Union of Clothing Workers
NUM	National Union of Mineworkers
NUMARWOSA	National Union of Motor Assembly and Rubber Workers of South Africa
NUMSA	National Union of Metalworkers of South Africa
PANSAB	Pan-South African Language Board
PP	Progressive Party
PRP	Progressive Reform Party
RDP	Reconstruction and Development Programme
SACLA	South African Confederation of Labour
SACP	South African Communist Party
SACTU	South African Congress of Trade Unions
SAP	South African Party
SA/WD	Steenkamp Archive/Wiehahn Documentation [Somerset West]
SIC	Solidarity Investment Company
TMA	Transvaal Miners' Association
TUCSA	Trade Union Council of South Africa
UDF	United Democratic Front
UN	United Nations
UNISA	University of South Africa
UOA	Underground Officials' Association
UP	United Party

Introduction
The return of the white working class

'Class has never really been an Afrikaner thing, you know,' Flip Buys, general secretary of Solidarity, stated matter-of-factly during an interview.

It was September 2011, and I had recently started my doctoral research into white working-class experiences of South Africa's transition from apartheid to majority rule. I had come to Solidarity – the country's largest predominantly white trade union – hoping that the organisation would function as an entry point, enabling me to step into the world of working-class whites that historians of late and post-apartheid South Africa seemed to believe did not exist. Buys' assertion – that social inequality or class consciousness had never been significant factors within the white, Afrikaans-speaking community, and played little role in animating or explaining Afrikaner identities, experiences, and politics – thus seemed distinctly discouraging. Perhaps it was intended as such. However, as this book demonstrates, Buys' statement in fact alluded to a much more complex reality, intimately bound up not only with the history of Afrikaner class formation and South Africa's turbulent transition, but also reflective of much greater transnational trends and structural shifts reconfiguring the global political economy since the 1970s.

White[1] workers occupied a unique social position in apartheid-era South Africa, their privilege dependent on the Afrikaner nationalist, race-based social contract upheld by the regime. In the labour arena, this saw whites shielded from black labour competition in exchange for their support for the ruling National Party (NP). White workers

---

[1] Racial terminology and categorisations are problematic and continually contested, especially as apartheid-era labels have in many instances become accepted and widely employed indigenous categories. This book uses the term 'African' for South Africans who would have been classified as black (or 'Bantu') according to apartheid-era categorisations. 'Coloured' refers to those of slave, Khoesan, and mixed-race descent; 'Indian' to South Africans of Indian descent; and 'white' to those of European descent. 'Black' is used in the inclusive sense advocated by the Black Consciousness Movement to refer to African, coloured, and Indian South Africans collectively.

benefiting from these arrangements were deeply invested in the oppression of their black counterparts and the maintenance of the racial order. The white blue-collar workers organised in the Mineworkers' Union (MWU) exemplified this position of labour vulnerability concealed by race-based status – while the state sanctioned their position as members of a privileged race, they were keenly aware of being a precarious class. Through its focus on the MWU, this book offers the first study of how such white workers experienced and negotiated the dismantling of the racial state and the establishment of black majority rule under the African National Congress (ANC). Starting from the escalating economic and political crises confronting the white minority government from the 1970s onwards, it shows that late apartheid reforms amounted to the withdrawal of state support for working-class whiteness. This sent white workers in search of new ways to safeguard their interests in a rapidly changing world. In the process, the MWU shed its working-class identity and repositioned itself as a culture-based civil society organisation. By the new millennium, the union had been reinvented as the Solidarity Movement, a service-providing social movement expressing state-like ambitions. It presented itself as the voice of South African minorities, and white Afrikaans-speakers in particular, defending their rights and interests, which, it claimed, were being threatened in the context of majority 'domination'. In the 'new' South Africa, it seemed, the organisation no longer represented a vulnerable class but a precarious race.

This book seeks to foreground the shifts and intersections between structure and subjectivity, experience and representation, inequality and identity – whether expressed in terms of class, race, or ethnicity – inherent in this story. This invites a chronological and interpretative rethinking of South Africa's recent past. My focus on the MWU/Solidarity uncovers the longer chronology of white working-class formation and workers' search for a new patron, and shows how this process has shaped contemporary white minority politics. In this way, the focus is shifted away from 1994 – so often the fixation of scholarship on South Africa – to highlight a 'long transition' on the labour front with regard to the dismantling of the racial state and the adoption of neoliberal policies, and the enduring continuities between the late apartheid and post-apartheid periods. This provides new insight into the end of apartheid, and into the nature of the post-apartheid state, society, and its politics not captured by dominant 'elite transition' views.

The 'long transition' view, moreover, facilitates placing South Africa's white workers within the recent transnational history of capitalism and state formation. White workers' experiences during this period reflect broader global realities such as the rise of free market ideology, the decline of traditional industrial unionism, and the ascent of social movements and new populisms. Taking account of the global political and ideological context in which local labour reform and political change took place connects South Africa to a wider world, thus breaking away from the parochialism and ideas of exceptionalism that so often characterise scholarship on this country. This, in turn, contributes a view from the South to international debates on the political, social, and cultural consequences of global structural shifts since the 1970s and the making of race and class in the context of late capitalism.

The rise and demise of white workers as historical subject

The white labour movement and white working-class lives form the mainstay of a wide-ranging body of scholarship examining the workings of racial capitalism, the making of the racial state, and the entanglement of class struggle and racial identities in South Africa. Significant contributions in this regard were made by Frederick Johnstone, Robert Davies and Dan O'Meara. This generation of Marxist scholars, writing in the 1970s and 1980s, insisted on the analytical primacy of class over race and argued that racial policies served dominant capitalist interests.[2] White workers featured prominently in these analyses, which sought to explain the failure of a non-racial labour movement in South Africa.[3] In parallel, emerging social historians wary of the theoretical abstractions and determinism often characterising neo-Marxist scholarship started producing histories 'from below' to demonstrate the agency of ordinary people in the making of their own lives in the context of capitalist development. Charles van Onselen, most notably, produced a collection of studies which included white domestic workers, brick makers and prostitutes.[4] White working-class lives continued to be an important subject of

---

[2] F. A. Johnstone, *Class, Race and Gold: a study of class relations and racial discrimination in South Africa* (London: Routledge and Kegan Paul, 1976); R. H. Davies, *Capital, State and White Labour in South Africa 1900–1960: a historical materialist analysis of class formation and class relations* (Atlantic Highlands NJ: Humanities Press, 1979); D. O'Meara, *Volkskapitalisme: class, capital and ideology in the development of Afrikaner nationalism* (Johannesburg: Ravan Press, 1983).

[3] Other notable works include H. J. Simons and R. E. Simons, *Class and Colour in South Africa, 1850–1950* (Harmondsworth: Penguin, 1969); S. Greenberg, *Race and State in Capitalist Development: South Africa in comparative perspective* (Johannesburg: Ravan Press, 1980); H. Wolpe, *Race, Class and the Apartheid State* (London: James Currey, 1988); various contributions in E. Webster (ed.), *Essays in Southern African Labour History* (Johannesburg: Ravan Press, 1978).

[4] C. van Onselen, *New Babylon, New Nineveh: everyday life on the Witwatersrand 1886–1914* (Johannesburg: Jonathan Ball, 1982).

historical inquiry amid subsequent historiographical developments. The end of the Cold War saw a turn away from class analysis towards ideas of community, gender, and identity.[5] This resulted in a substantial literature on white working-class women, examining, for instance, their role in the Afrikaner nationalist movement or in non-racial trade unionism in the first decades of the twentieth century.[6] Around the turn of the century, the impact of the cultural turn, postcolonial theory, and the emergence of whiteness studies stimulated new attention to discourse and subjectivities. This inspired Jeremy Krikler's masterful work on the entanglement of class struggle, racial imaginaries, and cultural understandings in shaping white working-class organisation and psychologies during the 1922 Rand Revolt.[7] South Africa's white workers have also featured prominently in recent scholarly efforts to move away from the analytical confines of the nation state, thereby exposing processes of integration and difference between the local, regional, and global.[8] Jonathan Hyslop, in particular, has produced trailblazing work on the transnational dimensions of working-class formation and white subjectivities.[9] Throughout this existing historiography, scholars often approached white miners as proxies for the wider white working class in South Africa – an observation that underlies this book's choice of the MWU as its case study.

Historiographical developments since the 1960s have therefore generated a body of scholarship on white workers that is diverse in terms of approach, focus, and interpretation. Yet – strikingly – this vibrant scholarship has remained restricted to the early twentieth century. With the

---

[5] See, for instance, B. Bozzoli (ed.), *Class, Community and Conflict: South African perspectives* (Johannesburg: Ravan Press, 1987); L. Lange, *White, Poor and Angry: white working class families in Johannesburg* (Aldershot: Ashgate Publishing, 2003).

[6] C. Blignaut, 'Untold history with a historiography: a review of scholarship on Afrikaner women in South African history', *South African Historical Journal* 65, no. 4 (2013), pp. 596–617.

[7] J. Krikler, *The Rand Revolt: the 1922 insurrection and racial killing in South Africa* (Johannesburg and Cape Town: Jonathan Ball, 2005).

[8] M. Lake and H. Reynolds, *Drawing the Global Colour Line: white men's countries and the international challenge of racial equality* (Cambridge: Cambridge University Press, 2008).

[9] For instance, J. Hyslop, 'The imperial working class makes itself "white": white labourism in Britain, Australia and South Africa before the First World War', *Journal of Historical Sociology* 12, no. 4 (1999), pp. 398–421; J. Hyslop, 'The world voyage of James Keir Hardie: Indian nationalism, Zulu insurgency and the British labour diaspora 1907–1908', *Journal of Global History* 1 (2006), pp. 343–62; J. Hyslop, 'The strange death of liberal England and the strange birth of illiberal South Africa: British trade unionists, Indian labourers and Afrikaner rebels, 1910–1914', *Labour History Review* 79, no. 1 (2014), pp. 95–118.

exception of a handful of works,[10] including Wessel Visser's biography of the MWU, with which I deal extensively in Chapter 4,[11] scholars of the second half of the century have neglected white workers as a historical subject. Scholarship on the late apartheid period has focused either on the high politics of the apartheid state and its reform and repression from above, or on the crescendo of black resistance to apartheid and the liberation struggle from below.[12]

The neglect of white workers from the second half of the twentieth century may be attributed to popular perceptions and scholarly understandings of the effects of NP rule on the material position of whites. Building on existing policies, from 1948 the NP saw to the tightening and expansion of racially discriminatory labour legislation, a dramatic increase in state employment from the civil service to parastatal industries, the widening of the social security net, and privileged educational and employment opportunities. Such policies benefited whites in general and Afrikaners in particular, and, within the context of strong post-war economic growth, they are understood to have facilitated dramatic upward social mobility. The reigning consensus, therefore, is that white poverty was 'solved' under the apartheid regime and whites moved up and out of the working class.[13] This narrative of embourgeoisement sees the story of South Africa's white workers, so vividly portrayed for the first half of the century, fall silent from the 1950s.[14] The Afrikaner nationalist movement's foregrounding of ethnic identity and Afrikaners as a 'classless volk',[15] and – once in power – the regime's intensified

---

[10] F. Wilson, *Labour in the South African Gold Mines, 1911–1969* (Cambridge: Cambridge University Press, 1972); Davies, *Capital, State and White Labour*; M. Lipton, *Capitalism and Apartheid: South Africa, 1910–1984* (Aldershot: Gower, 1985); I. Berger, *Threads of Solidarity: women in South African industry, 1900–1980* (Bloomington IN: Indiana University Press, 1992); E. Webster, *Cast in a Racial Mould: labour process and trade unionism in the foundries* (Johannesburg: Ravan Press, 1985).

[11] W. Visser, *Van MWU tot Solidariteit: geskiedenis van die Mynwerkersunie 1902–2002* (Centurion: Solidariteit, 2008).

[12] This is evident in South African Democracy Education Trust, *The Road to Democracy in South Africa. Volumes 1–7* (Cape Town: Zebra Press, 2004–17); T. Lodge, 'Resistance and reform, 1973–1994' in R. Ross et al. (eds), *The Cambridge History of South Africa* (Cambridge: Cambridge University Press, 2011), pp. 409–91; S. Dubow, 'Closing remarks: new approaches to high apartheid and anti-apartheid', *South African Historical Journal* 69, no. 2 (2017), pp. 304–7.

[13] C. Bundy, *Poverty in South Africa: past and present* (Auckland Park: Jacana, 2016), p. 53.

[14] In fact, there is a lack of attention to ordinary whites' experiences and agency more broadly. N. Roos, 'South African history and subaltern historiography: ideas for a radical history of white folk', *International Review of Social History* 61, no. 1 (2016), pp. 117–50.

[15] D. O'Meara, *Forty Lost Years: the apartheid state and the politics of the National Party, 1948–1994* (Randburg: Ravan Press, 1996), pp. 164–6.

suppression and exploitation of the black population, may well have contributed to the shift in scholarly attention away from white labour.

This book contends that white workers did not unproblematically disappear into the middle class. No comprehensive economic analysis of the class structure of the white population exists for the apartheid and post-apartheid eras. What structural information is available is fragmented and problematic: it does not consistently focus on either whites or Afrikaners, and scholars utilise different occupational categories and different measures of social stratification, some looking at income, others at occupation or skill. For the 1960s, O'Meara records artisans and production workers – what may be called blue-collar workers – as the *largest* occupational category of Afrikaans-speaking white males and *one of the lowest earning* in relative terms.[16] This is supported by occupational data offered by Sadie, which shows a substantial blue-collar component to the Afrikaner population throughout the late apartheid period, with 31.5 per cent of Afrikaners in blue-collar jobs in 1980 and 29.1 per cent in 1991.[17] Focusing on income trends, Terreblanche notes that the poorest 40 per cent of white, 'mainly Afrikaner' households experienced a significant decline in income between 1975 and 1996. He suggests that this 'can perhaps be explained in terms of the rapid (perhaps too rapid) embourgeoisement of Afrikaners in the third quarter of the century, and the inability of many ... to maintain their income levels when economic conditions deteriorated'.[18] Of course, income is relative: Seekings and Nattrass categorise the vast majority of the white population as located in the top two income deciles of 'rich' or 'very rich' by the end of apartheid in 1993.[19] Crankshaw's quantitative study of African advancement in various South African industries is the closest we get to detailed information about the class structure of the white population. Echoing Sadie, he shows that substantial numbers of whites worked in routine white-collar, front-line supervisory, skilled, and semi-skilled occupational categories throughout the late apartheid period. By 1990, a total of 893,617 whites were employed in these working-class occupations, compared

---

[16] O'Meara, *Forty Lost Years*, p. 137. See also Chapter 1.
[17] J. L. Sadie, *The Fall and Rise of the Afrikaner in the South African Economy* (Stellenbosch: University of Stellenbosch Annale, 2002), p. 54.
[18] S. Terreblanche, *A History of Inequality in South Africa* (Pietermaritzburg: University of Natal Press, 2003), p. 391. He later comments that it would 'be a mistake to underestimate the traumatic experiences of many Afrikaners who had progressed from relative poverty in the first half of the twentieth century to substantial wealth during the third quarter, and then regressed to substantially lower standards of living in the last quarter.'
[19] J. Seekings and N. Nattrass, *Class, Race, and Inequality in South Africa* (New Haven CT: Yale University Press, 2005), p. 199.

with 676,227 whites in management, professional, and semi-professional jobs. Regrettably, Crankshaw's study only covers the period from 1965 to 1990.[20] Existing structural data therefore offers only an impressionistic view of the shape of the white working class from the second half of the twentieth century, suggesting the outlines of continued intra-racial inequality and fragile processes of class formation. The picture is not much clearer when we focus on the MWU/Solidarity as a case study. Precise membership information for the union is unavailable for most of the period under study here. The Chamber of Mines stopped publishing race-based employment information in 1986, and so subsequent records do not reflect the racial composition of the workforce.[21] Thereafter, the growing diversity of the union's membership as well as structural changes to the economy, shifting production methods, and changing labour policies mean that it is difficult to determine the exact positions and power of MWU/Solidarity members in the production process and their resulting social relations.

What is clear, however, is that throughout the late apartheid period, white workers – many of them Afrikaans-speakers – remained a significant part of the white population. We know little of how such workers reacted to efforts to reform apartheid from the late 1970s, or how the subsequent transition to majority rule impacted them. Where white workers are mentioned in the existing literature, it is typically as obstinate racists and supporters of conservative or hard-right political parties. While some labour-focused histories give some attention to white workers, acknowledging varying opinions within the white labour movement,[22] these insights have remained marginal to literature dealing with the fall of apartheid and South Africa's transition. Rather, the 'working class' in the scholarship on the period of reform and ensuing political transformation is typically African – and, to a lesser extent, coloured and Indian. White workers' experiences of the challenge to white minority rule and racial citizenship, increasingly emanating from the swelling

---

[20] O. Crankshaw, *Race, Class and the Changing Division of Labour under Apartheid* (London and New York NY: Routledge, 1997), pp. 141–51.
[21] Compare Chamber of Mines of South Africa, *96th Annual Report: 1985* (Johannesburg: Chamber of Mines, 1986) and Chamber of Mines of South Africa, *97th Annual Report: 1986* (Johannesburg: Chamber of Mines, 1987).
[22] These include G. V. Doxey, *The Industrial Colour Bar in South Africa* (Cape Town: Oxford University Press, 1961); M. Horrell, *South Africa's Workers: their organizations and the patterns of employment* (Johannesburg: South African Institute of Race Relations (SAIRR), 1969); Greenberg, *Race and State*; D. du Toit, *Capital and Labour in South Africa: class struggle in the 1970s* (London: Kegan Paul, 1981); J. Lewis, *Industrialisation and Trade Union Organisation in South Africa: the rise and fall of the South African Trades and Labour Council* (Cambridge: Cambridge University Press, 1984).

ranks of urban African labour after 1973, remain absent from the scholarly narrative. Indeed, white workers are absent in the scholarship on white minority-ruled Southern Africa more broadly in the second half of the century.[23]

Nor has post-apartheid South African scholarship remedied this omission. In terms of structural analyses, the post-apartheid era has seen some studies of the impact of racial redress on employment trends, but these are typically industry-specific.[24] More often, there is a general consensus that post-apartheid South Africa witnessed 'the remarkably successful material adjustment of whites ... despite their largescale departure from state employment and certainly from official preference'.[25] This, argues Freund, reflects the skills, education, and capital built up by white households during the apartheid era, as well as the fact that, after 1994, the state 'respected private suburban property, preserved pension funds and other private investments, and has not imposed punitive taxes to make white South Africans pay reparations for past injustices', thus further facilitating the maintenance of white wealth and privilege after apartheid.[26] Such observations, while undoubtedly accurate on the whole, perpetuate homogenising views of white society – views that continue to conform to ideas of comprehensive white embourgeoisement under apartheid. This is also the case in sociological and social anthropological research. Here, scholars have offered a range of critical analyses of how whites have sought to negotiate the 'identity crisis' spawned by their loss of political power and the collapse of the Afrikaner state.[27] This is exemplified by the work of Melissa Steyn, who identified a range of reactions among Afrikaans- and English-speaking whites respectively, cast as varying efforts to 'rehabilitate a whiteness disgraced' while safeguarding white power, privilege, and status within the new democratic context.[28] Further research pointed to physical, political, and

---

[23] D. Money and D. van Zyl-Hermann (eds), *Rethinking White Societies in Southern Africa, 1930s–1990s* (Abingdon: Routledge, 2020).
[24] A. Habib and K. Bentley (eds), *Racial Redress and Citizenship in South Africa* (Cape Town: HSRC Press, 2008).
[25] B. Freund, *Twentieth-century South Africa: a developmental history* (Cambridge: Cambridge University Press, 2019), p. 15.
[26] J. Sharp and S. van Wyk, 'Beyond the market: white workers in Pretoria' in K. Hart (ed.), *Economy For and against Democracy* (New York NY: Berghahn Books, 2015), p. 126.
[27] M. Vestergaard, 'Who's got the map? The negotiation of Afrikaner identities in post-apartheid South Africa', *Daedalus* 130, no. 1 (2001), pp. 19–44.
[28] M. Steyn, '*Whiteness Just Isn't What It Used to Be*': *white identity in a changing South Africa* (Albany NY: SUNY Press, 2001); M. E. Steyn, 'Rehabilitating a whiteness disgraced: Afrikaner *white talk* in post-apartheid South Africa', *Communication Quarterly* 52, no. 2 (2004), pp. 143–69; M. Steyn and D. Foster, 'Repertoires for talking white: resistant

psychological withdrawal into private 'comfort zones' and homogeneous cultural circles,[29] or announced the 'death' of Afrikaner nationalism.[30] In apparent contradiction, some scholars reported that Afrikaners were adopting a defensive and exclusivist ethnic identity through discourses of post-apartheid victimhood and second-class citizenship.[31] This included appeals to minority rights – although this strategy was also identified as being involved in mobilisations around a more inclusive Afrikaans identity focused on language.[32] I discuss this literature in further detail in Chapter 4. But, surveying this scholarship, the reader might well be tempted to accept Buys' assertion that 'class had never really been an Afrikaner thing'. In fact, the overwhelming focus on subjectivities and discourse in this period reflected not only the 'death' of class analysis and the growing dominance of identity debates, but also the widespread acceptance of ideas surrounding apartheid-era white embourgeoisement.

A welcome exception in this regard is provided in a recent ethnographic study of white working-class lives in post-apartheid Pretoria.[33] This research by John Sharp and Stephan van Wyk is restricted to the

whiteness in post-apartheid South Africa', *Ethnic and Racial Studies* 31, no. 1 (2008), pp. 25–51.

[29] J. van Rooyen, *The New Great Trek: the story of South Africa's white exodus* (Pretoria: Unisa Press, 2000); D. M. du Toit, 'Boers, Afrikaners, and diasporas', *Historia* 48, no. 1 (2003), pp. 15–54; R. Ballard, 'Assimilation, emigration, semigration, and integration: "white" peoples' strategies for finding a comfort zone in post-apartheid South Africa' in N. Distiller and M. Steyn (eds), *Under Construction: 'race' and identity in South Africa today* (Sandton: Heinemann, 2004), pp. 51–66; K. van der Waal and S. Robins, '"De La Rey" and the revival of "Boer heritage": nostalgia in the post-apartheid Afrikaner culture industry', *Journal of Southern African Studies* 37, no. 4 (2011), pp. 763–79.

[30] T. Blaser, *Afrikaner Identity after Nationalism* (Basel: Basler Afrika Bibliographien, 2006); T. Blaser, '"I don't know what I am": the end of Afrikaner nationalism in post-apartheid South Africa', *Transformation: Critical Perspectives on Southern Africa* 80 (2012), pp. 1–21.

[31] On whiteness as victimhood in sub-Saharan Africa more broadly, see D. van Zyl-Hermann and J. Boersema, 'The politics of whiteness', *Africa* 87, no. 4 (2017), pp. 651–61.

[32] R. Davies, *Afrikaners in the New South Africa: identity politics in a globalised economy* (London: Tauris Academic Studies, 2009); M. Kriel, 'A new generation of Gustav Prellers? The Fragmente/FAK/Vrye Afrikaan Movement, 1998–2008', *African Studies* 71, no. 3 (2012), pp. 426–45.

[33] Other scholars, too, have sought to varying degrees to account for the intersectionality of race, ethnicity, class, and gender. However, in contrast to Sharp and Van Wyk discussed here, these scholars continue to focus largely on issues of identity and subjectivity. See, for instance, J. R. Boersema, 'Between recognition and resentment: an Afrikaner trade union's brand of post-nationalism', *African Studies* 71, no. 3 (2012), pp. 408–25; I. du Plessis, 'Living in "Jan Bom": making and imagining lives after apartheid in a council housing scheme in Johannesburg', *Current Sociology* 52, no. 5 (2004), pp. 879–908; J. Smuts, 'Male trouble: independent women and male dependency in a white working-class suburb of Pretoria', *Agenda* 20, no. 68 (2006), pp. 80–7; Davies, *Afrikaners in the New South Africa*.

capital city, but the processes of deindustrialisation, rationalisation, and resulting livelihood struggles that form the backdrop to their ethnographies may be taken as suggestive of developments throughout the country's industrial centres. The west side of Pretoria had long hosted various parastatal industries. Most notably, it was the site of the first state-owned steel mill, set up in the 1930s under the parastatal Iron and Steel Industrial Corporation (Iscor) to create employment opportunities for impoverished, unskilled, and newly urbanised whites. Capital shortages in the midst of escalating economic and political crises saw the apartheid government privatise Iscor in the late 1980s. Under the ownership of the multinational Mittal Steel, the plant's labour force was systematically downsized until the Pretoria West works were closed down entirely in the mid-1990s.[34] This had detrimental knock-on effects for other industries in the city, particularly those producing armaments and munitions, which were already struggling to stay afloat amid the rapid decline in demand following the end of the apartheid regime's military interventions in Southern Africa and, after 1994, in South Africa's townships. In the space of just a few years, this reduction in industrial activity in Pretoria West left some 15,000 white workers unemployed. Those made redundant from state employment lost not only their jobs but also company-sponsored housing and amenities. These processes coincided with the transition to majority rule and the institution of policies of racial redress. For laid-off white workers, employment equity policies blocked access to alternative employment in the civil service or armed forces, both headquartered in Pretoria. While some were able to find other industrial employment, the majority were unable to do so. They resorted to the informal economy, trying their hand at self-employment, or became reliant on other household members.[35]

Sharp's and Van Wyk's research follows the fortunes of these whites. Rather than white subjectivities, they are interested in the economic and social strategies that individuals devise to adapt to their new

---

[34] Rationalisation processes, driven by technological change and intensified international competition in the global economy, continued at Mittal's other factories. See M. Hlatshwayo, 'NUMSA and Solidarity's responses to technological changes at the ArcelorMittal Vanderbijlpark plant: unions caught on the back foot', *Global Labour Journal* 5, no. 3 (2014), pp. 238–305; M. Hlatshwayo, 'Neo-liberal restructuring and the fate of South Africa's labour unions: a case study' in P. Vale and E. H. Prinsloo (eds), *The New South Africa at Twenty: critical perspectives* (Pietermaritzburg: University of KwaZulu-Natal Press, 2014), pp. 115–39.

[35] J. Sharp, 'Market, race and nation: history of the white working class in Pretoria' in K. Hart and J. Sharp (eds), *People, Money and Power in Economic Crisis: perspectives from the Global South* (New York NY: Berghahn Books, 2015), pp. 82–105; Sharp and Van Wyk, 'Beyond the market', pp. 120–36.

circumstances. Their research, respectively, investigates the attempts of an ex-steelworker to reinsert himself into the market, and the options available to former members of the white working class who remain unemployed and homeless – notably, charity and 'upliftment' initiatives run by other whites, or recourse to informal housing and the informal economy. This work highlights the economic and social pragmatism of blue-collar whites, including their openness to cross-racial support and intimacy. The authors contrast these responses to those of Pretoria's white middle classes, who continue to live in segregated worlds while paying lip service to non-racialism or even actively pursuing apartheid-inspired nationalist agendas. Sharp and Van Wyk include some of the Solidarity Movement's efforts in the latter category.

In important ways, their findings intersect and diverge with the research presented in this book. Crucially, like this book, these authors take seriously the reality of social class within the white population and its consequences for shaping experiences, strategies, and subjectivities. While they do not follow a historical approach, their ethnographies of 2010s Pretoria are firmly grounded in an understanding of the processes of deindustrialisation that have marked the city since the 1980s, as well as the changing labour and economic policies which accompanied the end of apartheid. In this sense, their findings support this book's argument that a focus on issues of class facilitates a shift in analytical emphasis away from 1994 to reveal the contours of a long transition. While Sharp and Van Wyk are concerned with the post-apartheid present, however, I seek to uncover the longer history of these experiences. And, whereas their research subjects are blue-collar individuals who lost the secure jobs they once held and who have little direct relation to the state, my research follows the fortunes and strategies of a section of white organised labour and its shifting relationship with the state since the 1970s. These divergent research approaches and foci mean that we deal with different sides of (un)employment and hence different realities and perceptions of precarity. Moreover, while Sharp and Van Wyk are interested in market strategies, I place more emphasis on political strategies. Yet our respective research projects articulate in productive ways. This includes demonstrating the real and perceived fluidity between the 'white poor' and the white working class: some have lost jobs and houses and are actively seeking to re-enter the market, while those employed and active in organised labour circles are uncomfortably aware of how little separates them from the slippery slope from unemployment to destitution. This is demonstrated in the chapters that follow. The arguments of labour representatives such as Attie Nieuwoudt and Arrie Paulus in the late 1970s revealed how the spectre of white poverty tormented blue-collar whites. Similarly, the fortunes of blue-collar individuals and communities, such as those studied by Sharp and Van Wyk, were foremost in the minds of the shop stewards I interviewed in 2011, and played a significant role in motivating their commitment to the Solidarity Movement's ideals. I will return to these intersections in Chapter 7. This work therefore presents crucial evidence countering existing studies' tendency to homogenise along lines of race and ethnicity and to remain oblivious of issues of class – despite repeated insistence that class is overtaking race as the chief determinant of social inequality in post-apartheid South Africa.[36]

Identity and inequality in contemporary debate

Returning the white working class to analytical prominence offers a productive opportunity to examine the interaction of inequality and identity. Attention to issues of class in this respect does not signal a return to the Marxian approaches so prominent during the 1970s and 1980s. The limitations of this scholarship have long been exposed, its arguments eroded by structural and social changes in production, the crisis of socialist politics, and an onslaught of postmodernist, feminist, and postcolonial critiques. At the same time, the turn to issues of identity following the 'death of class' has resulted in a regrettable – some would say dangerous – lack of attention to social inequality. In embarking on an analysis which seeks to take account of both structure and subjectivity, this book does not take 'class' – or, indeed, 'race' – to correspond to any objective reality. The acknowledgement that race is constructed, Hilary Pilkington explains, leads to the recognition that the social phenomenon with which we are dealing is not that of different 'races', but the culturally, socially, and historically contingent *racialisation* of different groups.[37] Similarly, as the *beau idéal* of social history E. P. Thompson long asserted, class is not a structure or category, but a social phenomenon expressing the relationships between people in historically specific circumstances.[38] Race and class may therefore be understood as perpetual projects-in-the-making 'through a dialectic of discursive labour and actually existing forms and relations'.[39] Nevertheless, despite being

---

[36] Seekings and Nattrass, *Class, Race, and Inequality in South Africa*.
[37] H. Pilkington, *Loud and Proud: passion and politics in the English Defence League* (Manchester: Manchester University Press, 2016), p. 5.
[38] G. Eley and K. Nield, 'Farewell to the working class?', *International Labor and Working-class History* 57 (2000), pp. 1–30; S. Todd, *The People: the rise and fall of the working class, 1910–2010* (London: John Murray, 2014), particularly pp. 1–4.
[39] Eley and Nield, 'Farewell to the working class?', pp. 21–2.

social constructions, race and class do have a certain 'social materiality'. Indeed, Kwame Anthony Appiah designates 'colour', 'class', and 'culture' as among those 'lies that bind'.[40] Whether real or imagined, these have very real consequences in terms of the ideologies, representations, and perceptions which surround them.[41] These need to be probed and historicised in terms of their production and lived experience[42] through an analysis that foregrounds attention to both structure and subjectivity.

To be sure, the entanglement of race and class is not a new historical subject,[43] and, in taking this approach, I am building on the work of the new labour history that emerged in the 1990s.[44] This scholarship diverged from earlier labour histories' focus on trade unions and working-class institutions by thematising the culture, communities, ideologies, and subjectivities of workers themselves, and taking seriously the role of race in the making of working-class identity.[45] In the United States – the birthplace of the new labour history – David Roediger's work is emblematic of this approach;[46] in the South African context, Krikler and Hyslop spearheaded the writing of nuanced histories which grapple with the complexities of white working-class experience and agency in local, national, and, most recently, transnational context. Whereas these

---

[40] K. A. Appiah, *The Lies That Bind: rethinking identity* (London: Profile Books, 2018).
[41] Pilkington makes this point with regard to race. Pilkington, *Loud and Proud*, p. 5.
[42] G. Valentine and C. Harris, 'Strivers vs skivers: class prejudice and the demonization of dependency in everyday life', *Geoforum* 53 (2014), pp. 84–92.
[43] This should be distinguished from historiographical debates of the 1960s–1980s around the analytical value of race and class. D. Posel, 'Rethinking the "race–class debate" in South African historiography', *Social Dynamics* 9, no. 1 (1983), pp. 50–66; C. Saunders, *The Making of the South African Past: major historians on race and class* (Cape Town and Johannesburg: David Philip, 1988); R. Ross, A. K. Mager, and B. Nasson, 'Introduction' in Ross et al., *The Cambridge History of South Africa*, pp. 1–16.
[44] For an overview, see B. Nelson, 'Class, race and democracy in the CIO: the "new" labor history meets the "wages of whiteness"', *International Review of Social History* 41 (1996), pp. 351–74; M. van der Linden, 'Labour history: the old, the new and the global', *African Studies* 66, nos 2–3 (2007), pp. 169–80; B. D. Palmer, '"Mind forg'd manacles" and recent pathways to "new" labor histories', *International Review of Social History* 62 (2017), pp. 279–303.
[45] D. Brody, 'Reconciling the old labor history and the new', *Pacific Historical Review* 62, no. 1 (1993), pp. 1–18; P. Bonner, J. Hyslop, and L. van der Walt, 'Rethinking worlds of labour: Southern African labour history in international context', *African Studies* 66, nos 2–3 (2007), pp. 137–67; G. Field and M. Hanagan, 'ILWCH: forty years on', *International Labor and Working-class History* 82 (2012), pp. 5–14.
[46] Most notably D. Roediger, *The Wages of Whiteness: race and the making of the American working class* (New York NY: Verso, 1991). See also J. Krikler, 'Re-thinking race and class in South Africa: some ways forward' in W. D. Hund, J. Krikler, and D. Roediger (eds), *Wages of Whiteness and Racist Symbolic Capital* (Berlin: Lit Verlag, 2010), pp. 133–60; J. Krikler, 'Lessons from America: the writings of David Roediger', *Journal of Southern African Studies* 20, no. 4 (1994), pp. 663–9.

authors have concentrated on early twentieth-century South Africa, this book examines the 1970s to the present.

The necessity of addressing these scholarly lacunae emerges with particular clarity at the current historical juncture, as the global surge in inequality, populist identity politics, and political fragmentation characterising the 2010s see the white working class sweep back into popular and scholarly debates, and class revived as an analytical category.[47] These developments have been a long time in the making. In the industrialised economies of the North Atlantic, the crisis of capital accumulation emerging in the 1970s forced politicians towards neoliberal, pro-business policies of deregulation, labour casualisation, and outsourcing. This severely undermined trade union organisation and brought an end to the historic class compromise between powerful unions, large-scale national employers, and social democratic governments on which the post-war political and economic order had been built.[48] The internationalisation of labour, production, and capital, the scaling back of state functions, and the advance of supranational authority proceeded apace throughout the next three decades. This created ever greater disparities in wealth, power, and control on local, national, and international levels. In particular, this included the normalisation of employment and working conditions marked by instability, insecurity, and insufficient protection. The term 'precarity' or 'precarious labour' was increasingly invoked to describe the social and economic vulnerability experienced by growing numbers of workers under these conditions. This insecurity was dramatically exposed when the 2008 financial crisis unexpectedly crippled national economies and heightened levels of labour insecurity, in terms of both 'the phenomenon of precarious work and its perception by social actors'.[49]

Whereas critics of neoliberalism had long been inhibited by its international hegemony and representation as beneficial for capitalist development, its dark underbelly had now been exposed. Soon, popular, policy, and academic forums were ablaze with debates on the nature, consequences, and possible responses to precarity. Here, precarity was

---

[47] B. D. Palmer, 'Reconsiderations of class: precariousness as proletarianization', *Socialist Register* (2014), pp. 40–62; C. L. Walley, 'Trump's election and the "white working class": what we missed', *American Ethnologist* 44, no. 2 (2017), pp. 231–6.

[48] E. Webster, 'South African labour studies in a global perspective, 1973–2006', *Labour, Capital and Society* 37 (2004), pp. 268–70; D. Harvey, *A Brief History of Neoliberalism* (Oxford: Oxford University Press, 2007).

[49] E. Betti, 'Historicizing precarious work: forty years of research in the social sciences and humanities', *International Review of Social History* 63 (2018), p. 274.

typically understood as a new phenomenon emerging in developed economies where job insecurity was becoming the norm. Flexibilisation certainly impacted different workers in different ways: high-wage and mobile professionals and members of the emerging 'creative class' often found flexible work advantageous; temporary, migrant, or low-wage workers, by contrast, were rendered vulnerable by short-term contracts offering no benefits. The global workplace offered 'nice work if you can get it', Andrew Ross concluded cynically.[50] An even bleaker assessment came in 2011 from Guy Standing, who identified the 'global precariat' as a new 'dangerous class' born of the insecurity wrought by neoliberal globalisation. While not uniform, the precariat formed a distinctive socio-economic group. In contrast to salaried workers and the Keynesian proletariats of old, the precariat had minimal trust relationships with capital and the state, and none of the benefits of the post-war social contract. The precariat represented an 'incipient political monster', Standing warned, whose 'anger, anomie, anxiety and alienation' made them susceptible to political radicalisation and disengagement from mainstream values.[51] Other observers pointed out that the realities of insecure labour and livelihoods under late capitalism impacted not only a 'new' precarious class, but also the 'old' industrial working class. In fact, argued Ronaldo Munck, 'the European and other emerging racist and fascist formations are appealing more to the "old" working class displaced by the ongoing economic crisis'. Munck and others criticised the concept of the 'new' precariat for reflecting a Northern-centric view of labour market developments which at best described 'a certain phase of Europe's post-Fordist working-class history'.[52] Writing as the financial crisis hit global markets, Brett Neilson and Ned Rossiter similarly argued that precarity is 'the common – and not the exception'.[53] Rather than regarding it as a new phenomenon, its recent emergence as a political platform in Western Europe could be explained by the relative longevity of the welfare state vis-à-vis neoliberal labour reforms in that context. A number of scholars have pointed out that the (re-)emergence of

---

[50] A. Ross, *Nice Work If You Can Get It: life and labor in precarious times* (New York NY: New York University Press, 2009).
[51] G. Standing, *The Precariat: the new dangerous class* (London: Bloomsbury, 2011), pp. vii, 1, 7–14, 19, 22.
[52] R. Munck, 'The precariat: a view from the South', *Third World Quarterly* 34, no. 5 (2013), p. 752.
[53] B. Neilson and N. Rossiter, 'Precarity as a political concept, or, Fordism as exception', *Theory, Culture and Society* 25, nos 7–8 (2008), p. 68.

informality and precarity in post-industrial societies in fact marked the global convergence of labour relations as 'the West followed the Rest'.[54]

These debates around Standing's provocative book, followed by Thomas Piketty's bestselling tome on the historical roots of the United States' and Europe's unequal distribution of wealth,[55] catapulted precarity and inequality into mainstream debate. The intensity and troubled tone characterising these debates marked the increasing public awareness of the dramatic and potentially destructive consequences of decades of state retreat, deindustrialisation, and growing inequality, compounded by post-2008 austerity. These observations seemed to ring chillingly true as right-wing populism gained traction throughout the 2010s. In the 2014 European Parliament elections, radical right-wing parties topped the polls in the United Kingdom, France, and Denmark and gained seats in Germany and Sweden.[56] In 2019, these results were repeated as political polarisation increased. Far-right and nationalist parties continued to draw votes while green and liberal blocs also saw a surge in support. At both ends of the political spectrum, these gains came at the expense of the traditional power wielders, the centre-right and centre-left, creating a more fragmented legislature.

An Open Society Foundations report soberly set out the reasons for the recent shift to the right: the deindustrialisation accompanying the move to a service economy, growing inequality amid challenges to the sustainability of social welfare, and the increasing ethnic and cultural diversity that had characterised Europe since the 1970s had produced dramatic demographic, social, and economic changes. On an official level, it was recognised that these developments posed challenges to social cohesion. Hence, 'as Europe's Muslims and other minorities became more visible and demographically larger, there has been a pursuit of policies to encourage integration'. However, the report points out that these were mostly directed at immigrant communities while neglecting the position of the majority population, many of whom experienced:

---

[54] J. Breman and M. van der Linden, 'Informalizing the economy: the return of the social question at a global level', *Development and Change* 45, no. 5 (2014), p. 920; see also S. Mosoetsa, J. Stillerman, and C. Tilly, 'Precarious labor, South and North: an introduction', *International Labor and Working-class History* 89 (2016), pp. 5–19. In addition to the scholars of the Global South, feminist and migration scholars also offered important critiques. See Betti, 'Historicizing precarious work'.

[55] T. Piketty, *Capital in the Twenty-first Century* (Harvard MA: Harvard University Press, 2014).

[56] Open Society Foundations, *Europe's White Working Class Communities. At home in Europe: a report on six European cities* (New York NY: Open Society Foundations, 2014), p. 8.

growing anxiety about migration, the perceived erosion of national identity, and the perception that communities from the majority population of European countries have been ignored and consequently disenfranchised ... For many this failure to address the concerns or anxieties created by changes in the economic and social structures of their neighbourhoods reinforces a sense of being ignored, left behind and demonised. In some cases, this has fed into resentment of mainstream political parties and the liberal political values they are seen to represent and increased the appeal of populist parties.[57]

These observations about the growing appeal of nationalist and protectionist politics were confirmed in June 2016, when the United Kingdom voted to leave the European Union. Five months later, Donald Trump was elected president of the United States on an anti-immigration, anti-establishment, and protectionist political platform captured by his election slogan 'Make America Great Again!' Across the world, electorates disillusioned by economic insecurity, the challenges of multiculturalism, and the decline in national sovereignty characterising globally interconnected societies seemed to be turning to populist politicians who promised to secure the national interests of 'the people' being threatened by self-serving elites and unscrupulous outsiders.[58]

After decades of neglect, these dramatic developments saw media and academic attention thrust back onto the working classes as the 'explanation for everything'.[59] The day after Trump's election win, the *New York Times* singled out Nancy Isenberg's *White Trash: the 400-year untold history of class in America*, Arlie Hochschild's *Strangers in their Own Land: anger and mourning on the American right*, and J. D. Vance's *Hillbilly Elegy: a memoir of a family and culture in crisis* – all published in 2016 – as key to

---

[57] Open Society Foundations, *Europe's White Working Class Communities*, p. 3.
[58] On defining populism, see R. Brubaker, 'Between nationalism and civilizationism: the European populist moment in comparative perspective', *Ethnic and Racial Studies* 40, no. 8 (2017), pp. 1191–226. Analyses of contemporary right-wing populism are concentrated on the North Atlantic and Western European world, but Central and Eastern Europe, Turkey, India, Brazil and Japan have received some attention. In addition to Brubaker, see, for instance, C. Mudde, *Populist Radical Right Parties in Europe* (Cambridge: Cambridge University Press, 2007); R. Ford and M. Goodwin, *Revolt on the Right: explaining support for the radical right in Britain* (Abingdon: Routledge, 2014); L. Panitch and G. Albo (eds), *The Politics of the Right: Socialist Register 2016* (London: Merlin Press, 2015); M. A. Hunter, 'Racial physics or a theory for everything that happened', *Ethnic and Racial Studies* 40, no. 8 (2017), pp. 1173–83; C. W. Hunter and T. J. Power, 'Bolsonaro and Brazil's illiberal backlash', *Journal of Democracy* 30, no. 1 (2019), pp. 68–82.
[59] D. Roediger, 'Who's afraid of the white working class?: On Joan C. Williams's *White Working Class: overcoming class cluelessness in America*', *Los Angeles Review of Books*, 17 May 2017, https://lareviewofbooks.org/article/whos-afraid-of-the-white-working-class-on-joan-c-williamss-white-working-class-overcoming-class-cluelessness-in-america/# (accessed 28 January 2019).

'understand Trump's win'.⁶⁰ In an echo of Munck, the white working class was identified as the key support base of the populist right. As those most likely to compete with foreign jobseekers and to bear the brunt of neoliberal rationalisation and austerity policies, white workers were the main victims of economic and social marginalisation, and they felt relegated to 'second class citizenship'.⁶¹ Employing survey data from Western and Eastern Europe, Gidron and Hall argued that working-class, low-educated men were the main supporters of populist right-wing parties. Since the 1980s, they argued, working-class men in particular have experienced a decline in their economic status. This resulted from the disappearance of decent jobs (often due to automation) and worsening inequality, and a decline in their social status due to perceived threats from immigrants, women, and others supported in drives for equality.⁶² As the national polarisation most vividly represented by Brexit and Trumpism translated into significant international disruption, the 'white working class' seemed to become a synonym for racism, bigotry, and ignorance.⁶³

But important critiques of these analyses soon emerged. Studies harnessing election data disputed the claim that a white working-class backlash underlay the unexpected 'taking our country back' victories of Brexit and Trump: in the UK, 59 per cent of those who voted 'Leave' were from the propertied, well-off (and often pension-age) white middle class; similarly, in the USA, Trump supporters in 2016 were largely middle-class, college-educated whites.⁶⁴ Christine Walley highlighted the 'confused' class narratives and 'demographic reductionism' of the media and academic studies that reinforced assumptions about working-class

---

⁶⁰ '6 books to help understand Trump's win', *New York Times*, 9 November 2016, www.nytimes.com/2016/11/10/books/6-books-to-help-understand-trumps-win.html (accessed 29 January 2019); N. Isenberg, *White Trash: the 400-year untold history of class in America* (New York NY: Penguin Books, 2016); A. R. Hochschild, *Strangers in their Own Land: anger and mourning on the American right* (New York NY: New Press, 2016); J. D. Vance, *Hillbilly Elegy: a memoir of a family and culture in crisis* (New York NY: HarperCollins, 2016).

⁶¹ Ford and Goodwin, *Revolt on the Right*; D. Edgar, 'The politics of the right: a review article', *Race and Class* 58, no. 2 (2016), pp. 87–94; Pilkington, *Loud and Proud*, p. 8, 11.

⁶² Hochschild, *Strangers in their Own Land*, pp. 261–3; N. Gidron and P. A. Hall, 'The politics of social status: economic and cultural roots of the populist right', *British Journal of Sociology* 68, no. S1 (2017), pp. 57–84.

⁶³ K. Malik, 'Elites still use the working class as an excuse for their own prejudices', *Guardian*, 22 April 2018, www.theguardian.com/commentisfree/2018/apr/22/elites-still-using-working-class-as-excuse-for-their-own-prejudices (accessed 28 January 2019).

⁶⁴ Bhambra notes a number of studies in this regard. See G. K. Bhambra, 'Brexit, Trump, and "methodological whiteness": on the misrecognition of race and class', *British Journal of Sociology* 68, no. S1 (2017), pp. 214–32.

bigotry while downplaying middle-class racism. Moreover, this obscured the growing severity of economic inequality, including the impact of stagnating incomes and casualisation for the increasingly precarious well-educated middle classes.[65] Gurminder Bhambra also criticised the 'methodological whiteness' of assumptions that unproblematically cast the left-behind working class as white, male industrial workers, thus negating the profound effects that neoliberal globalisation has had on ethnic minorities and women – the majority of whom did not support Trump or Brexit.[66]

There are clearly important differences between these contexts and that of the study presented here. First, whites have always been a minority in South Africa and the country is characterised by a very different politics of racial demography compared with white majority contexts. Second, South Africa was not exposed to neoliberal imperatives to the same extent as other industrialised economies from the 1970s onwards. While privatisation and processes of individual and community responsibilisation in the face of a weak state are realities in contemporary South Africa, the state continues to play a significant role in the economy.

Yet dramatic shifts did occur during this period – notably, the dismantling of racial capitalism and the demise of the racial state. A focus on white workers reveals how this mirrored parallel transnational processes. Embedding local white working-class experiences in wider global histories and globalisation debates offers a fresh perspective on the dismantling of the race-based order, the current historical moment, and the political possibilities of the future. This book reveals how white workers interpreted the drive for racial equality from the 1970s onwards – first in the labour sphere and subsequently in the political arena – as a direct threat to their position and status, and it connects this experience to expressions of cultural nationalism and populism in post-apartheid South Africa. These developments clearly have important contemporary parallels and, in our era of global interconnection, they function in connected contexts and discourses of race, culture, and nationalism. Existing scholarship on South Africa's transition has remained theoretically weak when assessing the role of class in white experience, relegating white workers to vague generalisations or ignoring them altogether. This book, in an effort to extricate South Africa's white workers from the historiographical oblivion into which they disappeared from the second half of the century,

---

[65] Walley, 'Trump's election and the "white working class"'; see also Pilkington, *Loud and Proud*, p. 5.
[66] Bhambra, 'Brexit, Trump, and "methodological whiteness"'; Walley, 'Trump's election and the "white working class"'.

offers a way to integrate South Africa's recent past with current global debates to unlock new perspectives on precarity and working-class experiences under late capitalism and on the growing appeal of separatist and nationalist politics.

Backdrop to the long transition

Our story begins in the 1970s, in the fading glow of the golden era of post-war economic growth and apartheid state hegemony. The slowdown in world production and trade alongside the escalating price of oil increased inflationary pressures on South Africa, which exposed the dysfunctionality of apartheid's economics. The country entered a downward economic spiral which continued into the 1990s. This was compounded by the eruption of African labour unrest in 1973 and country-wide community demonstrations against apartheid policies, starting with the 1976 Soweto student protests. The growing grassroots conviction that shopfloor oppression and capitalist exploitation could not be distinguished from political repression drew emerging African unions into the liberation struggle. This led, in 1985, to the formation of the Congress of South African Trade Unions (COSATU), a federation of unions representing some 650,000 predominantly African workers embracing liberation politics.[67] COSATU's close involvement in township struggles drew together workplace and community demands, working alongside movements such as the United Democratic Front (UDF) to pursue democratic citizenship as key to the social and economic rights its members were being denied. Scholars identified this as social movement unionism, a 'highly mobilised form of unionism [emerging] in opposition to authoritarian regimes and repressive workplaces in newly industrialising countries of the developing world' such as Brazil, South Korea and the Philippines in the 1980s.[68] This form of 'bread and roses' unionism, embedded in a network of community and political alliances, stood in stark contrast to the regularised negotiations mechanisms and institutionalised labour practices characterising the industrialised societies of the Global North – as well as South Africa's existing racially exclusive system of industrial conciliation.[69] In the year

---

[67] J. Baskin, *Striking Back: a history of COSATU* (Johannesburg: Ravan Press, 1991).
[68] K. von Holdt, 'Social movement unionism: the case of South Africa', *Work, Employment and Society* 16, no. 2 (2002), p. 285; E. Webster, 'The rise of social-movement unionism: the two faces of the black trade union movement in South Africa' in P. Frankel, P. Pines and M. Swilling (eds), *State Resistance and Change in South Africa* (New York NY: Croom Helm, 1988), pp. 174–96.
[69] Webster, 'South African labour studies'.

following its establishment, COSATU committed itself to the liberation struggle under the leadership of the ANC, and in 1990, when the liberation movements were unbanned, COSATU and the ANC entered into a formal alliance, along with the South African Communist Party (SACP).[70]

By the 1980s, South Africa boasted the fastest growing trade union movement in the world. Indeed, the vitality of labour movements in the Global South stood in stark contrast to the inimical impact that economic liberalisation and globalisation were having on labour in the Global North. The social movement unionism of the Global South was increasingly seen as a model of unionism to be replicated in an effort to regenerate labour in the North.[71] Black workers' engagement in the struggle to overcome apartheid earned the South African labour movement 'global acclaim' for its 'virtuous commitment to democratic organisation, membership participation, linkages with civil society and broader social/political goals'.[72] COSATU entered the transition period in a strong position. Its grassroots links made it an essential partner to the ANC during the years of township struggle, during the liberation movement's subsequent negotiations with the apartheid government, and eventually in helping the ANC to its election victory in 1994.[73] The prospect for organised labour as a member of the governing alliance is an important theme in post-apartheid labour studies. While this partnership gave the federation much scope to influence national policy debates in the new democracy, it has had only limited success in transforming workplace conditions and working-class lives, and the socialist order of its struggle-era pursuits has not been achieved. Shifts in the economy and employment patterns saw traditionally more militant union membership in mining and manufacturing decline, and COSATU's partnership in the alliance benefited union leaders with connections to political and business elites, at the cost of ordinary union members.[74] Observers lamented

---

[70] A. Beresford, *South Africa's Political Crisis: unfinished liberation and fractured class struggles* (Basingstoke: Palgrave Macmillan, 2016), pp. 8–10.
[71] Webster, 'South African labour studies', p. 259, 271.
[72] Beresford, *South Africa's Political Crisis*, p. 8.
[73] Beresford, *South Africa's Political Crisis*, p. 11. On the role of African workers' protest and labour union mobilisation in overthrowing authoritarian governments elsewhere on the continent, see J. Kraus (ed.), *Trade Unions and the Coming of Democracy in Africa* (Basingstoke: Palgrave Macmillan, 2007); B. Freund, *The African Worker* (Cambridge: Cambridge University Press, 1988).
[74] Von Holdt, 'Social movement unionism'; B. Freund, 'Labour studies and labour history in South Africa: perspectives from the apartheid era and after', *International Review of Social History* 58 (2013), p. 507; D. Pillay, 'Between social movement and political unionism: COSATU and democratic politics in South Africa', *Rethinking Development and Inequality* 2 (2013), pp. 10–27.

the erosion of South Africa's vibrant social movement union. In an analysis that could equally be applied to the white labour movement of early twentieth-century South Africa (see Chapter 1), Sakhela Buhlungu dubbed these developments the 'paradox of victory': a once powerful and militant mass labour movement now apparently rendered largely impotent through its co-optation into the structures of power.[75]

Meanwhile, the young democracy's integration into the global economy exposed it to the same neoliberal imperatives felt elsewhere – liberation was accompanied by liberalisation. Several studies have highlighted how only a section of the South African workforce – often employed in the public sector – enjoys the benefits of stable, secure employment and trade union membership. A significant group is in much more precarious employment due to practices of outsourcing, casualisation, insufficiently regulated working conditions, or, indeed, growing recourse to informal sector employment. This renders industrial unionism increasingly irrelevant. Meanwhile, some 40 per cent of the working-age population is unemployed.[76] Thus 'class struggle in South Africa no longer opposes capital and labour, but the employed and the unemployed'.[77] At the same time, there is 'little gap here between the working class and the immense so-called lumpenproletariat whose lives are intertwined'.[78]

Clearly, in the post-apartheid era, the tight entanglement of race and class which characterised the making of modern South Africa has started to loosen. The reconciliatory approach marking Nelson Mandela's presidency encapsulated hopes for overcoming the country's divisive past and building an overarching politically based national identity.[79] However, the veneer of the newly established 'rainbow nation' soon started to crack, revealing real limits to liberation. During the negotiations of the early 1990s, as the NP conceded simple majority democracy, the ANC largely lay aside its socialist priorities in favour of the free market path set

---

[75] S. Buhlungu, *A Paradox of Victory: COSATU and the democratic transformation of South Africa* (Pietermaritzburg: University of KwaZulu-Natal Press, 2010). See also C. Bassett, 'Labour and hegemony in South Africa's first decade of majority rule', *Studies in Political Economy* 76 (2005), pp. 61–81.
[76] Freund, 'Labour studies and labour history', pp. 508–10. See also E. Webster and K. von Holdt (eds), *Beyond the Apartheid Workplace: studies in transition* (Scottsville: University of KwaZulu-Natal Press, 2005); F. Barchiesi, *Precarious Liberation: workers, the state and contested social citizenship in postapartheid South Africa* (Albany, NY: SUNY Press, 2011).
[77] Barchiesi, *Precarious Liberation*, p. 22.
[78] Freund, 'Labour studies and labour history', p. 513.
[79] K. Bentley and A. Habib, 'Racial redress, national identity and citizenship in post-apartheid South Africa' in Habib and Bentley, *Racial Redress and Citizenship in South Africa*, pp. 3–32.

during the late apartheid years.[80] Leftist commentators branded this an 'elite transition' – a politico-economic compromise effectively clearing the way for a small black elite to enjoy the wealth, security, and power long held by the white minority.[81] While 1994 saw blacks enfranchised, this political liberation had little impact on the everyday lives of the majority of South Africans who remained trapped in apartheid-era living and working conditions. To be sure, the ANC's election platform policy, the Reconstruction and Development Programme (RDP), formulated with its alliance partners, had started to make important advances in dealing with the most pressing social problems relating to housing, sanitation, electricity, and healthcare. But, in 1996, fiscal and organisational constraints saw the RDP replaced by the Growth, Employment, and Redistribution (GEAR) strategy, which prioritised macro-economic stability, the creation of a favourable business environment, and reduced government spending. The ANC's overt embrace of such neoliberal policies severely impaired its ability to deliver on promises of economic and social justice.[82] South Africa's most vulnerable – often rural and overwhelmingly black citizens – bore the brunt of the consequences, with many households surviving only on state social grants.[83]

Recent years have revealed the extent to which state retreat in the face of an advancing market became entangled with and compounded by state failure resulting from patrimonial politics and crony capitalism in government ranks.[84] The presidency of Jacob Zuma – already a controversial figure by the time he came to power in 2009 after ousting

---

[80] H. Adam, F. Van Zyl Slabbert, and K. Moodley, *Comrades in Business: post-liberation politics in South Africa* (Cape Town: Tafelberg, 1997), pp. 51–65.

[81] P. Bond, *Elite Transition: from apartheid to neoliberalism in South Africa* (Scottsville: University of KwaZulu-Natal Press, 2005); H. Marais, *South Africa Pushed to the Limit: the political economy of change* (Claremont: UCT Press, 2010).

[82] F. Cheru, 'Overcoming apartheid's legacy: the ascendancy of neoliberalism in South Africa's anti-poverty strategy', *Third World Quarterly* 22, no. 4 (2001), pp. 505–27; G. Hart, 'The provocations of neoliberalism: contesting the nation and liberation after apartheid', *Antipode* 40, no. 4 (2008), pp. 678–705.

[83] Terreblanche, *A History of Inequality in South Africa*. On the survival strategies of South Africa's poor more broadly, see S. Mosoetsa, *Eating from One Pot: the dynamics of survival in poor South African households* (Johannesburg: Wits University Press, 2011). This is not to discount the ANC's achievements since 1994. For both sides of the coin, see T. Meyiwa, M. Nkondo, M. Chitiga-Mabugu, M. Sithole, and F. Nyamnjoh (eds), *State of the Nation: South Africa 1994–2014* (Cape Town: HSRC Press, 2014).

[84] Marais, *South Africa Pushed to the Limit*; T. Lodge, 'Neo-patrimonial politics in the ANC', *African Affairs* 113, no. 450 (2014), pp. 1–23; A. Beresford, 'Power, patronage, and gatekeeper politics in South Africa', *African Affairs* 114, no. 455 (2015), pp. 226–48.

Mandela's successor, Thabo Mbeki[85] – was characterised by a steady crescendo of allegations of mismanaged public funds, political patronage, personal enrichment, and efforts to undermine the independence of public institutions for the purpose of securing access to state coffers. The frequency of such allegations drove exasperated South Africans to concur that corruption had become 'a way of life' in their country,[86] and commentators to worry that democracy itself was at risk.[87] The shocking nature of such revelations was amplified by the fact that they often appeared alongside reports on the dismal state of public services and institutions, dilapidated infrastructure, and deepening inequality amid appalling levels of unemployment.[88] As critics denounced a 'degenerative' political elite running a 'predatory' state,[89] growing public frustration led to a surge of community uprisings. These have typically been seen to revolve around issues of service delivery, but Patrick Bond and others have pointed out that public protest is forged through the combination of 'entrenched social and economic inequalities, ecological degradation, indebtedness and corruption'.[90] The growing distance between ruling elites and the vulnerable black communities that formed the bulk of the voting and working public was graphically demonstrated in August 2012, when 34 striking mineworkers were shot dead by the police in Marikana. Such state violence perpetrated in the interests of multinational capital against a community suffering low wages and abysmal social conditions evoked global outrage.[91]

---

[85] T. Lodge, 'The Zuma tsunami: South Africa's succession politics', *Representation* 45, no. 2 (2009), pp. 125–41; R. Southall, 'Understanding the "Zuma tsunami"', *Review of African Political Economy* 36, no. 121 (2009), pp. 317–33.

[86] S. Powell, 'Corruption becoming endemic', Corruption Watch, 23 January 2012, www.corruptionwatch.org.za/corruption-becoming-endemic/ (accessed 5 December 2016). To be sure, corruption was nothing new to South African governments. On corruption in the apartheid regime, see O'Meara, *Forty Lost Years*, pp. 230–44; H. van Vuuren, *Apartheid, Guns and Money: a tale of profit* (Auckland Park: Jacana, 2017).

[87] R. Southall, 'Democracy at risk? Politics and governance under the ANC', *Annals of the American Academy of Political and Social Science* 652 (2014), pp. 48–69.

[88] A. Habib, 'State–civil society relations in post-apartheid South Africa', *Social Research: An International Quarterly* 72, no. 3 (2005), pp. 680–1; S. L. Robins, *From Revolution to Rights in South Africa: social movements, NGOs and popular politics after apartheid* (Woodbridge: James Currey, 2008), p. 172.

[89] P. Bond, 'South Africa's resource curses and growing social resistance', *Monthly Review*, 1 April 2014, https://monthlyreview.org/2014/04/01/south-africas-resource-curses-growing-social-resistance/ (accessed 5 November 2017); R. Southall, 'The coming crisis of Zuma's ANC: the party state confronts fiscal crisis', *Review of African Political Economy* 43, no. 147 (2016), p. 74.

[90] P. Bond and S. Mottiar, 'Movements, protests and a massacre in South Africa', *Journal of Contemporary African Studies* 31, no. 2 (2013), p. 283.

[91] Bond, 'South Africa's resource curses'; P. Alexander, 'Marikana, turning point in South African history', *Review of African Political Economy* 40, no. 138 (2013), pp. 605–19;

By the 2010s, South Africa was witnessing levels of public action unprecedented since the end of apartheid.[92] Few days passed in the Republic without protests, with the disillusionment and frustration of vulnerable communities often expressed through violence and the destruction of public property in great 'bonfires of discontent'.[93] Some analysts expressed the hope that such nascent social movements would see the fusion of 'labour, social, gendered, environmental and other interests',[94] forging a national movement for social transformation in the spirit of the Arab Spring. But in the absence of ideological coherence and sufficient interconnection, this has not come to pass so far. Meanwhile, political uncertainty and low business confidence saw already wilted economic growth rates shrink further. The country's international credit rating was constantly hanging in the balance – and this in a troubled global economic context in the wake of the 2008 financial crisis.[95] Flashes of racial tension and xenophobia demonstrated the strain these conditions placed on South Africa's already fragile social fabric.[96]

Chapter outline

Privileged Precariat seeks to reinsert white workers into this story of turbulence and transformation. It does so in two parts. Part I focuses on the white labour movement and the racial state. It opens, in Chapter 1, with a discussion of the structural and subjective formation

---

V. Satgar, 'Beyond Marikana: the post-apartheid South African state', *Africa Spectrum* 47, nos 2–3 (2012), pp. 33–62.

[92] Beresford, *South Africa's Political Crisis*.

[93] A. Eliseev, 'Analysis: bonfires of discontent, in horrifying numbers', *Daily Maverick*, 5 February 2014, www.dailymaverick.co.za/article/2014-02-05-analysis-bonfires-of-discontent-in-horrifying-numbers#.WEU_WvmGPIU (accessed 5 December 2016). See also P. Alexander, 'Rebellion of the poor: South Africa's service delivery protests – a preliminary analysis', *Review of African Political Economy* 37, no. 123 (2010), pp. 25–40; J. Brown, *South Africa's Insurgent Citizens: on dissent and the possibility of politics* (London: Zed Books, 2015).

[94] Bond and Mottiar, 'Movements, protests and a massacre', p. 283; see also P. Bond, 'Neoliberalism, state repression and the rise of social protest in Africa' in B. Berberoglu (ed.), *The Palgrave Handbook of Social Movements, Revolution and Social Transformation* (Cham: Palgrave Macmillan, 2019), pp. 213–31.

[95] Southall, 'The coming crisis of Zuma's ANC'.

[96] Southern African Migration Project, 'The perfect storm: the realities of xenophobia in contemporary South Africa', Migration Policy Brief no. 50 (Cape Town: Idasa, 2008), http://samponline.org/wp-content/uploads/2016/10/Acrobat50.pdf (accessed 13 October 2020); J. Hayem, 'From May 2008 to 2011: xenophobic violence and national subjectivity in South Africa', *Journal of Southern African Studies* 39, no. 1 (2013), pp. 7–97.

of the white working class in the context of South Africa's industrial and political development since the late nineteenth century, including an introduction to the MWU, whose history is embedded in these processes. The chapter suggests a much more complex reality than the accepted embourgeoisement view, arguing for a reinterpretation of the nature of white working-class privilege in the racial state. On the eve of the 1970s' crisis of capital accumulation and liberation struggle, there remained a materially more vulnerable group of whites whose social position and political priorities were defined by their class position. This structural and subjective position is crucial for understanding white workers' responses to reform efforts from the 1970s onwards and the ensuing dismantling of the racial state, presented in subsequent chapters.

Chapter 2 examines the changing politics surrounding white labour amid the emerging crisis of the 1970s. Employing parliamentary debates, media reports, and sources from the secretive Afrikaner Broederbond, this chapter demonstrates that the plight and power of white labour were central preoccupations shaping the political elite's response to the crisis. Observing widespread labour unrest in countries such as Britain, political power wielders were adamant that trade unions such as the MWU be made subservient to the 'national interest'. This would see the NP abandon its long-standing commitment to the protection of white workers. Going beyond conventional historical explanations, I argue that this shift was not simply a function of the changing nature of the NP's support base and priorities. Rather, this move towards reform marked important changes in the local political imaginary and mirrored global shifts in the relations between states, labour, and capital in this period.

The NP's appointment of a commission of inquiry into labour legislation in 1977 seemed to signal the elite's appetite for reform. Chapter 3 represents the first extensive utilisation of the Wiehahn Commission's documentation for historical research. It shows that white organised labour was at the forefront of the investigation, with unions testifying before and workers' representatives serving on the Commission. Close examination of these sources exposes the limitations of existing scholarship that views white labour as homogeneous and reform as a 'scheme' to safeguard white supremacy. Crucially, the chapter demonstrates how, for a vulnerable section of white labour, reforms emerging from the Wiehahn investigation constituted the withdrawal of state support for working-class whiteness and the dismantling of their racially privileged citizenship more than a decade before the end of apartheid.

This sent left-behind white workers in search of new ways to safeguard their race and class interests in a rapidly changing world. Part II follows this process through a focus on the MWU – the predecessor to Flip Buys' Solidarity – drawing on archival research and media sources, interviews and ethnography. In this second part, the analysis shifts from the white labour movement and its relation to the racial state to white workers and mobilisation in the civil society sphere. The blue-collar production workers of the MWU exemplified the position of labour vulnerability concealed by race-based status produced by the racial state. Chapter 4 examines the MWU's response to the dismantling of the racial state, from the late 1970s to the union's centenary in 2002, when it was re-established as Solidarity. The chapter brings established understandings of the MWU's post-apartheid 'reinvention', and of post-apartheid white and Afrikaner 'identity crisis' discussed above, into conversation with a discursive analysis of the union's response to the unravelling of workers' privileged position and the shifts in black status and citizenship born of reform and the transition to majority rule. The chapter acts as an important hinge in the overall analysis, demonstrating the shift – in the organisation, but also reflective of global political discourses – from class to culture. I argue that dramatic changes in the organisation's discourse from the late 1970s to the early 2000s reflected and facilitated the merger of cross-class Afrikaner experiences in terms of cultural identity, reflecting global trends in identity politics and social movement mobilisation during this period. The chapter therefore argues that the shifts in identity, politics, and organisation characterising the MWU's 'reinvention' as the broad-based social movement union Solidarity represented the formation of a new post-apartheid social alliance.

By the 2010s, the Solidarity Movement boasted over 300,000 members and claimed to represent, by extension, a million Afrikaners. In 2015, it overtly positioned itself as an 'alternative government' or 'state' for Afrikaners amid ANC-led majority rule. Chapter 5 investigates the discursive and organisational strategies that underlie the Movement's contemporary campaigns and assertions. It reveals how these reflected and inflected opportunities offered by the global hegemony of neoliberal policies, rationalities, and discourse amid the local specificities of majority rule. I place the Movement's strategies in conversation with social movement scholarship and theorisation on race and neoliberalism. Specifically, Solidarity's discursive and organisational strategies offer new insight into the opportunities for extra-parliamentary political mobilisation in the context of constitutional democracy and late capitalism and into the way in which race is refashioned in the neoliberal epoch. The chapter is based on participant observation and interviews with executive members, specifically Flip Buys, then general secretary, and Dirk Hermann, then deputy general secretary.[97]

In addition to my interviews with these executives, I interviewed several veteran blue-collar members and employees of Solidarity. This took the form of extensive personal and group-based interviews, as well as shorter telephone interviews. Embarking on my research at Solidarity, I had expected to enter the organisation as an outsider and to be met with professional reservation. Quite the opposite was true. I found I was welcomed at Solidarity, for the most part easily accepted by staff and respondents alike, readily accommodated in meetings, and included in informal conversations. During personal interviews, I was often astounded by how freely my interlocutors shared their stories and views. It was clear that, underlying this apparent ease of rapport, were assumptions made about my racial and cultural identity – and hence about my convictions. In the Afrikaner environment in which my research was taking place, I was accepted as an insider, often in an avuncular manner. This was evident in everyday exchanges. Once, a friendly staff member asked how I was finding interviewing Solidarity members. When I admitted I sometimes felt nervous when starting an interview, she spontaneously responded, 'Don't! These are our people, after all!' My acceptance thus stemmed largely from the very racial and ethnic identities, stereotypes, and understandings that the organisation propagated and which I was seeking to investigate. In this context, my white skin could be seen and my Afrikaans mother tongue could be heard, and this seemed to be sufficient to testify to my heart and mind.[98] Kathleen Blee describes encountering a similar ease of rapport, noting that 'oral historians are acutely sensitive to the meaning of silences in the narrative and to barriers to communication between us and our informants' – yet, in her interviews as in mine, 'it was the lack of silence and the ease of communication that revealed their worldviews'.[99] Despite the discomforts these assumptions often caused me personally, they clearly held advantages for my research. For this reason, like Blee, I did not 'violate the tenuous empathy that propelled [my research] along',[100] choosing to leave assumed shared understandings in place by not disclosing my own views.

---

[97] Despite the coincidental similarities in surnames, there is no relation between myself and Dirk Hermann.
[98] For a comprehensive discussion of the various intersectional dynamics that characterised my research at Solidarity, see D. van Zyl-Hermann, 'White workers and South Africa's democratic transition, 1977–2011' (PhD thesis, University of Cambridge, 2014).
[99] K. M. Blee, 'Evidence, empathy, and ethics: lessons from oral histories of the Klan', *Journal of American History* 80, no. 2 (1993), p. 605.
[100] Blee, 'Evidence, empathy, and ethics', p. 605.

Belinda Bozzoli acknowledges the productive analytical potential of intersubjective dynamics and information exchanged between an interviewee and 'insider' interviewer. Such interactions facilitate the analysis of 'hidden forms of consciousness' and identities revealed in that which is taken for granted – the supposed 'common universe' between interviewer and interviewee.[101] This is not to say that my interviewees were kept in the dark about the purpose of our conversations. The subject of my research was always made clear and I always secured explicit consent to use the information given to me.

All conversations took place in Afrikaans, my and my interlocutors' mother language, and all translations in the text are my own.[102] Throughout, I endeavoured to translate my respondents' words as directly as possible, except where this would have obscured what I took to be the intended meaning. Afrikaans idioms and expletives often resist translation – I selected what I deemed to be appropriate English equivalents, but opted to privilege meaning over eloquence. In the case of the stuttering or multiple repetition that sometimes marks the speech of a person formulating their thoughts aloud or struggling to express themselves, as with particularly emotional responses, laughter, or meaningful silences, I have conveyed these in my own descriptive terms. With the exception of Buys and Hermann – public figures regularly appearing in the media who agreed to being identified – all interviewees are quoted using pseudonyms and the text is deliberately vague about their positions in the organisation at the time of our conversations.

Whereas Chapter 5 examined the Solidarity Movement's contemporary discursive and organisational strategies, Chapters 6 and 7 uncover sub- and counternarratives within the broader organisation which contradicted its official discursive framing. In this sense, these two chapters act as counterpoints to Chapter 5. Chapter 6 examines classist subnarratives emanating from Solidarity's leadership. It reveals the discursive labour performed by the Movement's executives to reformulate working-class interests and identity so that these may be absorbed into the new social alliance as a vehicle for advancing ethnic and racial interests in the wake of the demise of the racial state. These discourses provide striking insight into the class-based understandings and tensions which persist within this section of the white population, begging revision

---

[101] B. Bozzoli, 'Interviewing the women of Phokeng' in A. Thomson and R. Perks (eds), *The Oral History Reader* (London: Routledge, 1998), pp. 145–56.
[102] In 2008, 80 per cent of the Solidarity trade union's members were Afrikaans-speaking, some 19 per cent English-speaking, and less than 1 per cent identified 'other' languages as their mother tongue. 'Solidariteit Lede-inligting 2000–2008', courtesy of Dawid Durie (10 November 2011).

of existing scholarship on post-apartheid Afrikaner identity construction and white subjectivities.

At this point, a word is needed on issues of gender. In both late and post-apartheid South Africa, the labour arena and, arguably, imaginaries of the citizen worker remain overwhelmingly male. The MWU/Solidarity, in its historical and contemporary guise, is decidedly androcentric. Its institutional framing, significant figures, and even the current leadership's representations of 'the marginalised Afrikaner' were male. As Buys insisted during an interview, the Solidarity member was 'under threat because *he* is white, not because *he* is a worker'.[103] While the chapters that follow do not explicitly address aspects of gender and masculinity,[104] these are necessarily entangled in the analysis by virtue of my particular subject matter. This is perhaps most clear in Chapter 7. In this final chapter, I return to the white workers' voices that originally led me to Solidarity. The workers' narratives demonstrate the persistent reality of class within the white Afrikaner population. This is revealed in deep personal and collective anxieties related to material security, masculinity, respectability, and the future, born of workers' experiences of various forms of state withdrawal since the late 1970s. These experiences led these men to hold considerably more ambiguous views on issues of race, ethnicity, and class than the executive, and to contravene discourses of respectability and modernity which prevail in the Movement at large.

Taken together, these findings not only place white workers into the postcolonial historical narrative, they also offer a white working-class perspective from the Global South on transnational debates on the insecurities and subjectivities born of late capitalism, and on the growing appeal of separatist and nationalist politics.

---

[103] Flip Buys, interviewed 25 October 2011, Kloofsig (my emphasis). For context, see Chapter 6.

[104] A rich and growing body of scholarship that focuses on gender has developed in the post-apartheid context, including a continuing interest in the intersection of gender and 'Afrikaner' ethnic identity under apartheid and after 1994. See, for instance, R. Morrell (ed.), *Changing Men in Southern Africa* (Durban: University of Natal Press, 2001); T. Shefer, K. Ratele, and A. Strebel (eds), *From Boys to Men: social constructions of masculinity in contemporary society* (Cape Town: UCT Press, 2007); C. van der Westhuizen, *Sitting Pretty: white Afrikaans women in postapartheid South Africa* (Durban: University of KwaZulu-Natal, 2018).

Part I

White workers and the racial state

1 Privileged race, precarious class
White labour from the mineral revolution to the Golden Age

In 1973, *Washington Post* journalist Jim Hoagland published a reportage on the current state of South African society, tracing how apartheid ideology facilitated the exploitation of black labour in the service of white economic prosperity and foreign capital. In his book, Hoagland recounted his observation of a typical work process in the industry that formed the backbone of the South African economy – gold mining:

> Willie, the white miner, crouched inside a four-foot high pit, or stope as it is called by the miners. He had already marked the face of the rock wall for drilling. A black labourer, known to the company not by name but by an identity number, sat on the floor of the pit, his arms and legs wrapped around a jack-hammer drill. As Willie dropped his hand as a signal, the black labourer started to drill. At the end of the eight hour shift, Willie would insert explosive charges into the hundred holes being drilled in the rock face, and the blasting apart of the gold and ore would begin. Willie ... earned about R300 a month. The black labourer (technically miner is a rank that only whites can hold in South Africa) made R20 a month. The work they did is not all that different, a mining supervisor ... conceded in response to a question. Then why the large gap in pay? 'Because Willie's skin is white', the (supervisor) replied matter-of-factly. 'It is the most valuable commodity you can have in South Africa. It is more valuable than this yellow stuff we blast out of the earth.'[1]

Although racially discriminatory practices and patterns of exploitation had long characterised life in Southern Africa, the mineral revolution of the second half of the nineteenth century and the resultant development of industrial capitalism were definitive in shaping the political, economic, and social order of modern South Africa. The economy's dependence on the availability of a large and exploitable labour force meant that issues of labour were always entangled with issues of race. This emerges with

---

[1] J. Hoagland, *South Africa: civilisations in conflict* (London: George Allen and Unwin, 1973), pp. 196–7, quoted in R. Davies, 'The white working-class in South Africa', *New Left Review* 82 (November–December 1973), p. 51.

Figure 1.1 Underground drilling in a gold mine on the East Rand, 1972.
Source: Chamber of Mines Annual Report, 1972

particular clarity in the position, politics, and subjectivities of white workers.

While the early decades of the twentieth century witnessed instances of fierce white working-class resistance to the interests of capital, by the interwar period white workers are understood by scholars to have entered a class compromise with the racial state and capital at the expense of black labour. This rendered them a 'labour aristocracy', enjoying the benefits of legislative race-based job reservation, inflated wages, and social security in exchange for political and industrial acquiescence. The concept of a labour aristocracy had its origins in mid- to late-nineteenth-century Britain. It sought to explain the appearance of a 'highly-skilled and (consequently) strongly-unionised stratum of the working class that was economically, socially and politically allied to the middle class of the time' and distinguish them from the true proletariat. Friedrich Engels scoffed at how such 'aristocrats of labour' were eager to perform their 'bourgeois respectability' in service of this alliance.[2] Later, in the context of the First World War, Lenin extended the notion to explain the nationalist and reformist character of European labour movements. He saw European workers as a 'privileged upper stratum of the proletariat in the imperialist countries [which] lives partly at the expense of hundreds of millions of members of uncivilised nations'. Lenin further pointed to the co-optation of union leaders and representatives into state-based structures, leading to their mollification as they come to share in the privileges and perquisites of power. The term was therefore deployed to explain the conservatism evident either within certain sections of a working class, or of a working class as a whole. The 1960s and 1970s saw it taken up by socialist historians in the United States and United Kingdom to explain dynamics within their respective organised labour movements at the time.[3]

During the same period, Africanists observing the unfolding of decolonisation on the continent adopted the term in an effort to explain why regularly employed, organised African workers seemed to play an important role in the liberation struggles of their countries, yet after independence fell in with ruling elites. In contrast to the Western industrialised context in which the notion of a labour aristocracy was

---

[2] P. Waterman, 'The "labour aristocracy" in Africa: introduction to a debate', *Development and Change* 6, no. 3 (1975), p. 57, 58.

[3] Waterman, 'The "labour aristocracy" in Africa', p. 58. See, for instance, E. Hobsbawm, *Labouring Men: studies in the history of labour* (London: Weidenfeld and Nicolson, 1964); G. Stedman Jones, 'Class struggle and the industrial revolution', *New Left Review* 90 (1975), pp. 35–69. Also E. J. Hobsbawm, 'Artisan or labour aristocrat?', *Economic History Review* 37, no. 3 (1984), pp. 355–72.

developed, most of the African labouring population worked in farming or in the informal economy. Urban wage earners and union officials formed but a small section of the workforce, most often employed in large capital-intensive foreign-owned industry or in the state sector. Scholars such as Giovanni Arrighi and John Saul regarded them as a privileged stratum. Invested in the political and economic status quo, these workers aligned their interests with those of international capital and local elites, rather than with migrant workers and peasants.[4] Such arguments were later criticised for taking too homogeneous a view of Africa's industrial working class when empirical studies revealed much more complexity and ambiguity in the conditions, values, status, and power of workers and their organisations vis-à-vis the state and other workers in different countries over time.[5]

Reflecting on the prospect of a workers' revolution in apartheid-era South Africa, leftist scholars invoked the labour aristocracy thesis to explain why white workers were unlikely to support such action. Robert Davies highlighted how white workers enjoyed high incomes and privileged employment opportunities, resulting in elevated status, in exchange for their support for the racial state and the interests of capital. This, he argued, meant that white workers participated in the exploitation of the black majority through the extraction of surplus value. In this way, they were bound in an alliance with the bourgeoisie that simultaneously detached them from the bulk of South Africa's proletariat. Davies, writing, like Hoagland, in 1973, concluded that since 'the white working class is a strategically necessary support for the settler bourgeoisie, the likelihood that the latter would sacrifice the former *en bloc* ... is minimal'.[6] Without white workers, the settler bourgeois state 'would be reduced to a relative handful of exploiters incapable of resisting the onset of indigenous black revolt, as elsewhere in the continent'.[7]

---

[4] G. Arrighi and J. S. Saul, *Essays on the Political Economy of Africa* (New York NY: Monthly Review Press, 1963); P. Werbner, 'Rethinking class and culture in Africa: between E. P. Thompson and Pierre Bourdieu', *Review of African Political Economy* 45, no. 155 (2017), p. 9.
[5] Waterman, 'The "labour aristocracy" in Africa', p. 63.
[6] Davies, 'The white working-class in South Africa', 56.
[7] Editors, 'Introduction', *New Left Review* 82 (November–December 1973), p. 38. Critique followed that, because white workers were mainly supervisors, they were not a labour aristocracy but a 'nonworking class'. H. Simson, 'The myth of the white working class in South Africa', *African Affairs* 4, no. 2 (1974), pp. 189–203; H. Wolpe, 'The "white working class" in South Africa', *Economy and Society* 5, no. 2 (1976), pp. 197–240. Davies later designated white workers in supervisory work as part of a 'new middle class', because they performed a function of capital. But those who still did actual productive labour, he maintained, were actual workers, albeit very privileged ones, and

Yet, as Hoagland's sketch reveals, the basis of the material and social privilege possessed by white workers such as Willie was paper thin. This chapter presents the structural and subjective formation of the white working class in the context of South Africa's industrial and political development since the late nineteenth century. In so doing, it argues for a reinterpretation of the nature of white working-class privilege. It shows that, rather than a labour aristocracy, white workers represented a privileged precariat – benefiting from the advantages bestowed by their white skin, but remaining precariously dependent on state benevolence to protect them from black labour competition. The members of the whites-only Mineworkers' Union, to which Willie undoubtedly belonged, exemplified this position of labour vulnerability concealed by race-based status. With this argument, the chapter lays the foundation for this book's assertion that the shape and legacy of white working-class formation are crucial for understanding white workers' responses to reform efforts from the 1970s onwards, and to the dismantling of the racial state from the 1990s.

The mineral revolution and the making of South Africa's racial order

From its inception in the mid-nineteenth century, the social landscape of mining was highly mobile and cosmopolitan and was shaped by the demands of its industry. The diamond fields of Kimberley and, later, the promise of gold on the Witwatersrand attracted hundreds of local and foreign fortune seekers. The capital-intensive nature of excavating the mineral deposits soon saw individual enterprisers displaced by larger companies. On the Rand, the first shaft was sunk in 1888, and by 1895 some 130 producing and working companies were in operation, controlled by some eight mining houses. These were dominated by European, mostly British and German, entrepreneurs and financiers who, from 1889, organised in Johannesburg as the Chamber of Mines. A 'unifying and cost-conscious institution',[8] the Chamber saw to the coordination of the various companies' labour and wage strategies in order to maximise profits. It also represented the industry's interests to

---

hence labour aristocrats. R. Davies, 'Mining capital, the state and unskilled white workers in South Africa, 1901–1913', *Journal of Southern African Studies* 3, no. 1 (1976), pp. 41–69. See also criticism of the 'labour aristocracy' concept in Lewis, *Industrialisation and Trade Union Organisation*, pp. 17–18; Greenberg, *Race and State*, pp. 276–7.
[8] N. Levy, *The Foundations of the South African Cheap Labour System* (London: Routledge and Kegan Paul, 1982), p. 28.

the state. Under the watchful eye and shrewd direction of the mining magnates, South Africa was producing a quarter of the world's gold supply by 1899.[9]

The chemical processes and machinery required for deep-level gold mining demanded substantial capital investment and a vast amount of manpower possessing a certain skills base. Skilled tasks such as blasting and surveying were initially performed by professional miners, drawn primarily from the mining regions of Britain and Australia. These men were persuaded to brave the dangerous working conditions and high cost of living characterising early South African mining life in exchange for high wages.[10] But the bulk of mining operations, constituting the daily drudge of shovelling tons of broken ore into skips for transportation to the surface and hand-drilling holes for the placement of dynamite, was performed by an army of African migrants from across the Southern African region.[11] Hailing from as close as the Basotho mountain kingdom to as far as present-day Tanzania, these men were typically recruited to the Rand on six- or nine-month contracts. By 1892, 25,000 were working the goldmines of the Witwatersrand, a figure that would soar to 200,000 by 1910.[12]

Gold mining on the Rand functioned within a set of structural economic conditions which would render labour a site of enduring struggle. High production costs, together with the price of gold being fixed internationally for extended periods of time, made minimising the cost of labour a central priority for mining companies.[13] The migrant labour system developed in direct response to the mines' insatiable demand for large numbers of cheap workers. The system allowed mining companies to drive down labour costs by calculating workers' wages around the level of subsistence required for a single individual, rather than a worker with a family of dependants. This allowed mining companies to effectively externalise the cost of social welfare and labour reproduction to

---

[9] R. Ross, *A Concise History of South Africa* (Cambridge: Cambridge University Press, 2008), p. 65; Van Onselen, *New Babylon, New Nineveh*, p. 1, 4, 12–13.
[10] S. Marks, 'Class, culture, and consciousness in South Africa, 1880–1899' in Ross et al., *The Cambridge History of South Africa*, pp. 125–6, 132, 136.
[11] A. H. Jeeves, *Migrant Labour in South Africa's Mining Economy: the struggle for the gold mines' labour supply, 1890–1920* (Johannesburg: Witwatersrand University Press, 1985), p. 23.
[12] T. D. Moodie with V. Ndatshe, *Going for Gold: men, mines and migration* (Berkeley CA: University of California Press, 1975), p. 1, 7; J. Crush, A. Jeeves, and D. Yudelman, *South Africa's Labor Empire: a history of black migrancy to the gold mines* (Cape Town: David Philip, 1991), p. 104.
[13] Jeeves, *Migrant Labour in South Africa's Mining Economy*, pp. 6–9; Levy, *The Foundations*, pp. 8–9, 16.

Figure 1.2 White and black mineworkers of the Witwatersrand in the early 1900s.
Source: Patrick Pearson collection of photographs, Historical Papers Research Archive, University of the Witwatersrand, South Africa

communities in the reserves, facilitating the exploitation of not only the wage earners' own labour, but also that of their rural kin.[14] In contrast to the mines of Katanga and the Copperbelt, moreover, most minework on the Rand did not require a skilled workforce. The unskilled nature of the work therefore rendered migrant labour more appealing than the expenses involved in sustaining settled labour communities.[15] Only in the 1970s would the makeup of mining's black labour force shift away from foreign peasant labour towards local, proletarianised workers.[16]

The economic imperative of a cheap and docile workforce, in combination with ideologies of racial superiority prevalent among local and foreign whites, served to justify not only this large-scale exploitation but also the authoritarian control of African workers. Black male migrants were housed in compounds for the duration of their contracts,

---

[14] M. Burawoy, 'The functions of migrant labour: comparative material from Southern Africa and the United States', *American Journal of Sociology* 81 (1976), pp. 1050–87; H. Wolpe, 'Capitalism and cheap labour power in South Africa: from segregation to apartheid', *Economy and Society* 1, no. 4 (1972), pp. 425–6.
[15] Levy, *The Foundations*, p. 29. [16] Moodie, *Going for Gold*, pp. 4–5, 40–2.

their movements closely monitored by compound police. Scope for similar control of white workers was politically more limited and constrained by European miners' experience of labour organisation against the interests of capital. By the first decade of the twentieth century, white miners with families earned 10 shillings per shift, while black migrants earned a maximum daily wage of 3 shillings.[17] Such divergent treatment served to reinforce existing social distance and racial prejudices. In time, mining's racialised patterns of labour were copied throughout the evolving South African economy.[18]

While the diamond fields were administered by the British-ruled Cape Colony, the rich goldfields of Witwatersrand lay within the jurisdiction of the overwhelmingly agricultural Zuid-Afrikaansche Republiek or Transvaal, under Paul Kruger. The Transvaal's defeat in the South African War (1899–1902) brought it under British rule, and legislative apparatuses were utilised to secure the mining industry's interests, not least where the supply and control of African labour was concerned.[19] When the Transvaal was granted self-government in 1907 under an Afrikaner-led administration, mining concerns remained hugely influential. The new government under Boer Generals Botha and Smuts courted both mining magnates and white workers, presenting itself as representing the interests of both English-speaking and Afrikaner whites.[20] Such conciliatory sentiments, in the context of shifting European realpolitik and waning British imperial power, underlay the merger of the Transvaal with the Cape, Natal and Orange River colonies to form the Union of South Africa in 1910. During constitutional negotiations, Smuts categorically rejected proposals for extending the Cape Colony's qualified non-racial franchise throughout the new Union, since this would unsettle the racial order, with lower classes of whites losing the vote to a handful of educated and prosperous blacks. The establishment of the new dominion on the basis of exclusive white citizenship thus saw the racial stratification of the mining economy mirrored in political arrangements, as power was consolidated at the expense of non-Europeans, similar to arrangements

---

[17] Ross, *A Concise History of South Africa*, pp. 61–3, 70–2; Marks, 'Class, culture, and consciousness', p. 132, 143; H. Giliomee, *The Afrikaners: biography of a people* (Cape Town: Tafelberg, 2011), p. 324.
[18] Jeeves, *Migrant Labour in South Africa's Mining Economy*, pp. 5–6.
[19] Marks, 'Class, culture, and consciousness', p. 107; Van Onselen, *New Babylon, New Nineveh*, pp. 27–42.
[20] S. Marks, 'War and union, 1899–1910' in Ross et al., *The Cambridge History of South Africa*, pp. 180–1, 188–9.

in other assertive 'white man's countries' such as Australia, New Zealand, and Canada.[21]

Structural insecurity and white working-class subjectivities

Yet in the early twentieth century, a 'white man's state' did not automatically translate into security for white workers. Studying white working-class demands and identities in early industrialising South Africa, Frederick Johnstone identified white workers' condition of extreme 'structural insecurity'. The exploitation and economic vulnerability suffered by African migrant workers, Johnstone argued, were partly ameliorated by the fact that they remained embedded in peasant economies and relationships. In the event of unemployment, they could return to the impoverished yet persevering rural communities of their places of origin, rather than face desolation in the cities.[22] In contrast, white workers were completely dependent on waged work. With no rural fallback, unemployment would relegate whites 'to the margins of a capitalist society where charity was in short supply and social contempt abundant'.[23] While Johnstone's assessment underestimated the degree of exploitation suffered by Africans, he correctly identified the manner in which the presence of a large and exploitable black labour force aggravated white proletarian insecurity. With mining interests 'dominat[ing] the state, the compound system, labour migrancy and pass laws ensured that black labour was both cheaper and more easily controlled than its white counterpart and that capital had every incentive to substitute it for white'.[24]

This perpetual threat of displacement would animate conflicts between white workers, capital, and the state in the first two decades of the century, as white workers pressed for a colour bar which would protect their jobs from black encroachment. In the Transvaal, underground blasting was reserved for white workers as early as 1893. In 1902, workers organised to form the Transvaal Miners' Association (TMA) – later renamed the Mineworkers' Union – to represent white miners' demands for race-based protection to employers and the state. The union reflected the socialist labour politics of the British craft union tradition, and the first trade union leaders were overwhelmingly of British or Australian

---

[21] Lake and Reynolds, *Drawing the Global Colour Line*, pp. 210–37.
[22] Johnstone, *Class, Race and Gold*, pp. 57–9, 64–82, 145–50.
[23] Krikler, *The Rand Revolt*, p. 32.
[24] Marks, 'Class, culture, and consciousness', p. 133.

origin.²⁵ In addition to organisational experience, these workers brought an ideology of 'white labourism' to the Rand, which meshed with local racist views. Jonathan Hyslop has argued that white labourism's synthesis of hostility to capitalist exploitation, racist visions, and white workers' 'aspiration to incorporation into the dominant racial structure' was an important source of working-class racism across the early twentieth-century British Empire and animated much of the radical labour militancy characterising this era.²⁶

The Rand's white workers instigated strikes in 1907, 1913, and 1914. Various factors brought on these industrial conflicts, including efforts by the Chamber of Mines to enforce tougher work regimes, mine managers' refusal to recognise unions, and the terrifying death rate among underground workers caused by silicosis. Yet the threat of encroachment by cheaper African (or, briefly, Asian) labour shot through each upheaval.²⁷ White workers articulated their demands in terms of racial identity, insisting that their interests as members of the ruling race be safeguarded. The 1907 strikers framed the upholding of their demands as a necessity for preserving 'white civilisation' in the Republic.²⁸ The 1913 dispute saw white workers protest not only against the perceived despotism of mine management but also against state suppression, as the strike saw basic civil liberties curbed in an effort to quash the workers' movement.²⁹ Reflecting the bitter sense of rightlessness prevalent among organised labour, the South African Labour Party admonished the country to treat white workers 'not with the intolerance by a "baas to a boy" but as a man and a citizen whose right to life, liberty and competence, is as important as his "master's"'.³⁰ During all three strikes, the government intervened in favour of employers, deploying the police and armed forces against the strikers.

At the same time, the state did adopt race-based labour policies. In 1911, the Mines and Works Act was promulgated to regulate the working

---

²⁵ J. Hyslop, 'The British and Australian leaders of the South African labour movement, 1902–1914: a group biography' in K. Darian-Smith, P. Grimshaw, and S. Macintyre (eds), *Britishness Abroad: transnational movements and imperial cultures* (Victoria: Melbourne University Press, 2007), pp. 90–108.
²⁶ Hyslop, 'The imperial working class', p. 418.
²⁷ Hyslop, 'The imperial working class', p. 404; Krikler, *The Rand Revolt*, pp. 35–8; E. Katz, *The White Death: silicosis on the Witwatersrand gold mines, 1886–1910* (Johannesburg: University of the Witwatersrand Press, 1994); E. Katz, *A Trade Union Aristocracy: a history of white workers in the Transvaal and the general strike of 1913* (Johannesburg: African Studies Institute, 1976).
²⁸ Krikler, *The Rand Revolt*, p. 36.
²⁹ Hyslop, 'The imperial working class', pp. 398–9, 404–5.
³⁰ *Worker*, 10 July 1913, quoted in E. Katz, 'White workers' grievances and the industrial colour bar, 1902–1913', *South African Journal of Economics* 42, no. 2 (1974), p. 144.

Figure 1.3 Hand hammer stoping in Crown Deep mine in the 1900s.
Source: Barloworld Rand Mines Archive at Historical Papers Research Archive, University of the Witwatersrand, South Africa

of mines across the new Union, and effectively extended the Transvaal's race-based restrictions across the country. After the First World War, the number of job categories officially reserved for whites were further extended.[31] The adoption of these policies amid conflict between white labour and capital demonstrate that the colour bar cannot be attributed to white workers alone. State mining engineers, convinced that only whites could maintain safety underground; the white-ruled state, wary of the political consequences of alienating white workers; and the Chamber of Mines, eager to impede cross-racial working-class action – these all played their part in entrenching a racial division of labour.[32]

As long as foreign miners retained their monopoly on skills, the threat of displacement was held at bay. But as early as 1901, the ever declining grade of ore saw mine owners introduce a number of technological innovations in order to expand production. These served to erode the skills of professional miners. In a pattern that would contribute to the industrial conflict of this period, the fragmentation of skilled trades into component parts that were subsequently redistributed to lesser-skilled,

---

[31] Visser, *Van MWU tot Solidariteit*, pp. 5–6; C. F. Feinstein, *An Economic History of South Africa: conquest, discrimination and development* (Cambridge: Cambridge University Press, 2005), pp. 74–7.

[32] Krikler, *The Rand Revolt*, pp. 32–4; E. N. Katz, 'Revisiting the origins of the industrial colour bar in the Witwatersrand gold mining industry, 1891–1899', *Journal of Southern African Studies* 25, no. 1 (1999), pp. 73–97.

often black workers saw whites rapidly become predominantly supervisors in the production process – although their skills remained important in directing operations and training the ever changing black migrant labour force over which they presided. In addition to the eroding effects of technological advances, white workers were keenly aware that skills could be learned – not only by the black workers alongside whom they worked, but also by untrained whites entering the industry. Economic depression and war around the turn of the century saw an influx of impoverished, mainly Afrikaans-speaking whites into the urban economy.[33] The racial attitudes of this newly urbanised proletariat reflected the racialised master–servant relations of their agrarian colonial roots. Many found employment in mining, especially after the defeat of the 1907 strike saw mine owners rush to replace militant immigrant miners. As the erosion of skilled work rendered the distinctions between skilled, semi-skilled, and unskilled work ever more ambiguous, it was possible for new white miners to obtain blasting certificates – qualifications of competency authorising them to handle dynamite – after only nine months' training. This allowed them to work as blasters alongside professional miners from abroad. Meanwhile, unskilled whites were also appointed to perform supervisory work, overseeing unskilled aspects of the production process performed by Africans. By 1913, these developments had effectively rendered the craft unionism of the TMA obsolete. As the ranks of immigrant and local miners increasingly merged, the TMA transitioned from an artisan union to an industrial union.[34]

White working-class anger and anxieties regarding displacement came to a head in the wake of the First World War. The ensuing events of 1922 warrant detailed discussion – not only as a backdrop to the historical formation of the white working class, but also in relation to my interpretation of the politics of labour in the 1970s, addressed in Chapters 2 and 3. To South African historians, the 1920s and 1970s may seem like entirely different eras meriting very different treatment. However, chronologically, they are not far apart – the upheaval of 1922 was within living memory in the 1970s. Today, it is commonplace

---

[33] On Afrikaner impoverishment on the land and subsequent proletarianisation, see Giliomee, *The Afrikaners*, pp. 320–5.
[34] P. Bonner, 'South African society and culture, 1910–1948' in Ross et al., *The Cambridge History of South Africa*, pp. 264–7; Van Onselen, *New Babylon, New Nineveh*, pp. 27–9; Visser, *Van MWU tot Solidariteit*, pp. 2–3, 6; Krikler, *The Rand Revolt*, p. 22, 24–6; Katz, *The White Death*, p. 40, 47–73; D. Yudelman, *The Emergence of Modern South Africa: state, capital and the incorporation of organized labour on the South African goldfields, 1902–1939* (London: Greenwood, 1983), p. 128.

for scholars to argue – as I do – that events of the 1970s such as the oil shock, the election of Reagan and Thatcher, and the ascendance of neoliberal economic ideology are crucial for understanding developments in the 2010s. These are as distant from us today as the events of 1922 were in the 1970s, but this does not make them any less pertinent.[35] Indeed, as Chapter 6 will show, 1922 continues to figure prominently for the MWU in its contemporary guise as the Solidarity Movement.

With many foreign miners enlisting in the armed forces, Afrikaners formed the majority of white miners in underground jobs by 1918. In December 1921, in the context of soaring post-war inflation, the Chamber of Mines announced its intention to replace some 2,000 white miners in semi-skilled work with cheaper black labour. The broader white mining labour force feared that it was simply a matter of time before they faced the same fate. Already battling rising living costs and now facing unemployment, they reacted with outrage. In January 1922, a major strike broke out in the gold and coal mines, soon backed by a general strike throughout the Transvaal. The strike turned into an armed rebellion, as 22,000 workers – the majority of them Afrikaners – challenged the power of mine owners and the legitimacy of the South African state that supported them. This revolutionary challenge took two main forms: on the one hand, many workers saw the strike as a revolt against British imperialism and, organising in commandos reminiscent of Boer tactics during the South African War, sought the formation of an independent republic. On the other hand, communist revolutionaries saw the strike as an opportunity to overthrow the capitalist order. These various expressions reflected the enmeshment of race and class militancy in the white labour movement, most dramatically demonstrated by the most infamous symbol of the 1922 rising: the strikers' banner reading 'Workers of the world unite and fight for a white South Africa'.

The strike reached its revolutionary climax in early March in a 'small-scale civil war', which saw Prime Minister Smuts supplement state forces with aerial bombardment, artillery, machineguns, and tanks.[36] Battles took place throughout central Johannesburg's white working-class suburbs of Vrededorp, Braamfontein, and Fordsburg, as well as in the east of the city in Germiston, Boksburg, and Benoni. For a short period at the height of the insurrection, the strikers turned to attacking blacks, murdering over 40 Africans. By mid-March 1922, government forces prevailed and the eight-week strike was crushed. In what has been called

---

[35] I am grateful to Duncan Money for alerting me to this.
[36] Giliomee, *The Afrikaners*, pp. 332–4.

Figure 1.4 Members of the Newlands strikers' commando ride past supporters holding a banner with the Rand Revolt's famous slogan.
Source: *Star, Through the Red Revolt on the Rand* (Johannesburg, 1922)/African News Agency (ANA)

the 'biggest and bloodiest upheaval in South African labour history',[37] more than 200 people were killed, some 600 wounded, thousands arrested, and four hanged for treason.[38]

The militancy and murderousness of the strikers expressed anxieties inherent in the formation of white working-class identity in the context of politicised racial imaginaries and intense class struggle. White workers, Jeremy Krikler has argued, had come to define themselves in relation to 'that which they were not: rightless, wageless, racially-despised, unfree blacks'. The Chamber's efforts to tamper with the colour bar were viewed as an assault on white workers' racial identity and privilege, which, if successful, would 'ground [them] down into poverty' and see them become 'white kaffir[s]'.[39] According to Krikler, the 'intense class

---

[37] W. Visser, 'From MWU to Solidarity – a trade union reinventing itself', *South African Journal of Labour Relations* 3, no. 2 (2006), p. 20.

[38] Bonner, 'South African society and culture', pp. 267–70; Feinstein, *An Economic History of South Africa*, p. 64, 77–81; Giliomee, *The Afrikaners*, pp. 332–5; Krikler, *The Rand Revolt*, p. 110, 130–2; Visser, *Van MWU tot Solidariteit*, p. 27, 33, 35.

[39] All quotes from Krikler, *The Rand Revolt*, p. 32, 149. 'Kaffir' is a highly offensive racial slur for blacks, commonly used by whites in colonial- and apartheid-era South Africa.

Structural insecurity and white working-class subjectivities 47

Figure 1.5 Mounted police sweep through central Johannesburg on 9 March 1922.
Source: Star, Through the Red Revolt on the Rand (Johannesburg, 1922)/African News Agency (ANA)

consciousness' and 'militant anti-capitalism' of white workers meant that the 'White South Africa' for which they were fighting was 'a particular organisation of state, society and economy' in which white workers would not be at the mercy of the industrial despotism of employers, but would be recognised as citizens of equal importance to other classes in the white community. For this reason, white working-class animosity and insurrectionary violence during the strike were overwhelmingly directed against white employers and the white state – those seen as infringing their rights, and towards whom workers directed their claims for full citizenship.[40] At the same time, the conflict of 1922 occurred as the trade union organisation of African workers was gaining momentum and African political leadership was becoming increasingly vocal.[41] Just two years earlier, 70,000 African mineworkers had staged a strike that, like earlier white working-class action, was crushed by state forces. The

[40] Krikler, The Rand Revolt, p. xi, 52–3, 112, 113, 119, 122, 292–3.
[41] J. Seekings, '"Not a single white person should be allowed to go under": swartgevaar and the origins of South Africa's welfare state, 1924–1929', Journal of African History 48, no. 3 (2007), p. 379.

racial pogrom of March 1922 formed part of broader incidents of violence during which white workers targeted African trade union organisation on the Witwatersrand.[42] Indeed, during neither the 1920 African mineworkers' strike nor the 1922 Rand Revolt did white or black workers display labour solidarity across the colour line – they understood themselves to be fighting separate battles.

White workers' incorporation into the racial state

The aftermath of the strike saw a significant shift in state policy towards white labour. Eager to avoid future industrial and political action of this scale and intensity, Smuts' South African Party (SAP) government enacted legislation that secured a privileged bargaining position for white workers. The Industrial Conciliation Act of 1924 established, for the first time, a system for industrial relations across the economy through which employers' organisations and trade unions could negotiate the peaceful resolution of industrial conflicts. By expressly excluding Africans from the legal definition of 'employee', and hence from joining legally registered and recognised unions, the Act barred Africans from these structures, thereby giving unionised workers – whites, but also other minority race groups – the power to negotiate via industrial councils for the racial allocation of the most favoured jobs and working conditions.[43]

But this was too little too late to redeem the Smuts government. In the 1924 general election, white workers used their political power to elect a National Party–Labour Party government perceived as sympathetic to their interests. The Nationalists represented the largely unskilled and recently urbanised Afrikaner population, as well as small property owners and small-scale Afrikaner farmers. Labour, in turn, represented much of the urban English-speaking proletariat, including white artisans and working-class immigrants. All were vulnerable to efforts to undermine the colour bar and looked to the state for protection.[44] Together, the two parties formed an electoral pact and campaigned on the platform of 'civilised labour'. This held that more systematic policies of racial discrimination were needed to ensure that 'civilised' persons, as distinguished from 'barbarous and underdeveloped' Africans, received employment and wages allowing them to maintain the appropriate

---

[42] K. Breckenridge, 'Fighting for a white South Africa: white working-class racism and the 1922 Rand Revolt', *South African Historical Journal* 57, no. 1 (2007), p. 230, 238–40.
[43] Horrell, *South Africa's Workers*, pp. 2–3.
[44] Feinstein, *An Economic History of South Africa*, pp. 81–2.

'civilised' lifestyle.[45] The very ambiguity of these labels allowed the Pact parties to appeal to Cape-based coloured voters.[46] Yet National Party leader General J. B. M. Hertzog's declaration during the election campaign that the position of white workers represented 'the most important issue for the survival and welfare of the country' reflected the coalition's true colours.[47]

Once in power, the Pact enacted legislation to privilege and protect whites in the workplace. While it was eager to partner with mining to grow the economy and stimulate job creation, it would no longer allow the Chamber of Mines to unilaterally decide to reduce the white labour force. Hence, it implemented the 1926 Mines and Works Amendment Act to safeguard white mineworkers from displacement. Moreover, it set out to uplift impoverished, unskilled, and newly urbanised whites by bringing them into employment and paying them 'civilised' wages. Often, jobs were created by replacing unskilled and semi-skilled African workers in state sectors.[48] Grace Davie observed that this represented the reversal of 'the tenet of the so-called civilising mission in Africa. Instead of anticipating gradual improvements in African society through education and religious conversion, the state declared its intention to elevate white living standards while announcing that Africans and Indians would indefinitely remain at a lower stratum.'[49] The most significant drive to transform poor whites into 'civilised labour' occurred in the railways, where between 1924 and 1933 unskilled whites rose from 9.5 per cent to 39.3 per cent of the labour force, while unskilled black labour was reduced from 75 per cent to 49 per cent. By the early 1950s, the railways would become the largest employer of white labour, with some 100,000 unskilled and semi-skilled whites on its books. The Pact sought to create further employment opportunities for whites by expanding the industrial sector. It founded the parastatal steel company Iscor – which started production at its first site in Pretoria West in 1933 with an exclusively white complement – and introduced import tariffs to protect local industries. Meanwhile, in the private sector, companies were offered benefits and incentives, such as preference for state contracts, for favouring white over black labour.[50]

---

[45] Government circular quoted in Feinstein, *An Economic History of South Africa*, p. 86.
[46] Giliomee, *The Afrikaners*, p. 334; Seekings, 'Not a single white person', p. 381.
[47] Quoted in Giliomee, *The Afrikaners*, p. 335.
[48] Horrell, *South Africa's Workers*, pp. 2–3; Feinstein, *An Economic History of South Africa*, pp. 86–7.
[49] G. Davie, *Poverty Knowledge in South Africa: a social history of human science, 1855–2005* (New York NY: Cambridge University Press, 2015), pp. 56–7.
[50] Giliomee, *The Afrikaners*, pp. 340–2; Seekings, 'Not a single white person', p. 383.

Figure 1.6 Jackhammer stoping in East Rand Proprietary Mines, 1938.
Source: Barloworld Rand Mines Archive at Historical Papers Research Archive, University of the Witwatersrand, South Africa

Scholars disagree over who truly benefited from the reconfiguration of relations between the state, capital, and labour under the Pact government. Merle Lipton views the legislative measures implemented from 1924 as a victory for white workers in the wake of their 1922 defeat, drawing a more or less straight line from workers' support for the Pact and its 'civilised labour' policy, through growing enthusiasm for Afrikaner nationalism in subsequent decades, to the NP's election on its apartheid platform in 1948.[51] But not all white workers benefited from these policies. By prioritising the employment of unskilled and semi-skilled whites, skilled workers paid part of the price of financing full white employment: under the Pact, their wages fell in real terms.[52] Eddie Webster has demonstrated the uneven impact of the Pact's policies in the steel and metal industry. He shows how 'civilised labour' policies posed a threat to the position of skilled workers, as it encouraged the dilution of craftsmen's trades and the redistribution of labour to cheaper, lesser-skilled workers. Webster also argues that the Department of Labour, set up after 1924 to promote these policies, was in fact a

[51] Lipton, *Capitalism and Apartheid*.
[52] Giliomee, *The Afrikaners*, p. 336, 341; Seekings, 'Not a single white person', p. 383.

'propagandist for scientific management' that sought to wrestle control of the labour process from skilled workers by transferring the mental labour of planning and organisation to management.[53] The 1924 Industrial Conciliation Act – introduced by Smuts but implemented under Hertzog – similarly represented a double-edged sword. It bolstered the position of white labour vis-à-vis other racial groups, but placed controls on organised labour. Strike action was limited, so that workers effectively sacrificed their most powerful weapon.[54] Moreover, the Act's conciliatory mechanisms facilitated the institutionalisation of working-class struggles and the bureaucratisation of trade unions, co-opting white labour into state-controlled structures of power. This, according to Phil Bonner and Eddie Webster, saw white unions 'degenerate' into 'little more than benefit societies'.[55] Viewing the state as an instrument of capital, Davies argues that these measures represented efforts to divide the working class along racial lines and thereby diffuse any challenge to the existing conditions of capital accumulation. The state's accommodation of white workers during this period, says Davies, brought about 'the almost complete political capitulation' of the white labour movement.[56] Yudelman quotes the dramatic decline in white strike action after 1922 as evidence of this co-optation.[57] Coloured workers sat uneasily within the new labour dispensation. They did not enjoy the privilege bestowed on whites, but they were not excluded from the industrial relations machinery in the same manner as Africans, and therefore they enjoyed a measure of protection. In many instances, white, coloured, and Indian workers organised in the same trade unions.[58] The very ambiguity of 'civilised labour' suggested their inclusion in the benefits of the policy, but in practice it functioned to favour whites.[59] While employers were certainly frustrated by the new legislation forcing them to employ and negotiate with expensive white labour, African workers ultimately paid the price for white workers' security – their wages were suppressed even further in an effort to reduce labour costs, and they were restricted to performing unskilled labour.[60]

---

[53] Webster, *Cast in a Racial Mould*, p. 35, 38.
[54] Krikler, *The Rand Revolt*, pp. 291–2; Giliomee, *The Afrikaners*, p. 335.
[55] P. Bonner and E. Webster, 'Background', *South African Labour Bulletin* 5, no. 2 (1979), p. 3.
[56] Davies, *Capital, State and White Labour*, pp. 194–5, 198.
[57] Yudelman, *The Emergence of Modern South Africa*, p. 25, also 35, 190–213.
[58] Horrell, *South Africa's Workers*, p. 6.
[59] Giliomee, *The Afrikaners*, p. 343; Seekings, 'Not a single white person', p. 381, 394.
[60] Feinstein, *An Economic History of South Africa*, pp. 111–12; Breckenridge, 'Fighting for a white South Africa', p. 230, 243.

The election and policies of the Pact government inaugurated two important shifts in South Africa's political economy during this period. First, it demonstrated the political power of white workers and marked the overt politicisation of the colour bar.[61] By favouring poor whites for employment, paying them an inflated 'civilised wage', and institutionalising white labour's industrial power, the legislation of this period sought to separate and distinguish white workers from their African counterparts, to mark them out more clearly as citizens and as 'civilised' by conferring on them race-based privilege and status. This applied to white men as well as women. In the context of the Great Depression, particularly young, unmarried white women were increasingly drawn into the industrial workforce, with the garment industry in particular developing into a largely female sector.[62] It is no coincidence that white women were enfranchised in 1930. A year later, as the Depression swelled the ranks of the white poor, property and literacy voting qualifications for all white men over the age of 21 were also removed.[63] From this time onwards, white workers 'began to see their salvation not in independent organization as a class or in aggressively expressing their interests, but in developing a symbiotic relationship with the state'.[64] Second, under the Pact government, the state started to play an active role in the functioning of the economy – a trend which continued under subsequent governments. In a recent historical analysis, Bill Freund identified the Pact's policies as forming part of a trajectory of state-driven developmentalism in South Africa.[65]

White poverty and workers as the vanguard of whiteness

Reverberating through the industrial conflicts and labour politics of this period were broader social anxieties regarding the maintenance of South Africa's racial order. These became concentrated on the issue of white poverty. This was not a new phenomenon – a substantial population of

---

[61] Feinstein, *An Economic History of South Africa*, pp. 80–9, 120–6.

[62] See, for instance, Berger, *Threads of Solidarity*; J. Mawbey, 'Afrikaner women of the Garment Union during the Thirties and Forties' in Webster, *Essays in Southern African Labour History*, pp. 192–208; L. Vincent, 'Bread and honour: white working-class women and Afrikaner nationalism in the 1930s', *Journal of Southern African Studies* 26, no. 1 (2000), pp. 61–78.

[63] L. Vincent, 'A cake of soap: the *Volksmoeder* ideology and Afrikaner women's campaign for the vote', *International Journal of African Historical Studies* 32, no. 1 (1999), pp. 1–17. On the rights of white women before their enfranchisement, see H. Giliomee, '"Allowed such a state of freedom": women and gender relations in the Afrikaner community before enfranchisement in 1930', *New Contree* 59 (May 2004), pp. 29–60.

[64] Giliomee, *The Afrikaners*, p. 336.   [65] Freund, *Twentieth-century South Africa*.

impoverished proletarianised whites had long been present in colonial South Africa. But historians have convincingly argued that it was only from the late nineteenth century, in the context of depressed economic conditions and white middle-class anxieties about the future of the colony, that white poverty gained prominence and political traction as a major social problem.[66] South Africa's industrial heartland became the focal point of these anxieties, as impoverished rural Afrikaners spilled into the urban economy. The white population of Johannesburg swelled from 40,000 in 1899 to 250,000 in 1914, accompanied by the proliferation of unsanitary and crowded slums in suburbs such as Fordsburg and Vrededorp – the very neighbourhoods where mineworkers would clash with state forces in 1922.[67] Growing perceptions of the threat which these conditions posed to health, and of the preponderance of criminality, miscegenation, and racial mixing in poor communities, mixed with prevailing social Darwinist understandings to cast poor whites as a danger to continued white supremacy. One Social Welfare Department worried that 'the weak members of a superior race too readily adopt the lower mental and moral standard of a contiguous and inferior race',[68] while a prominent economist labelled poor whites 'a menace to the self-preservation and prestige of the white people'.[69] Such views mirrored concerns about racial degradation and the future of white rule in other European colonies.[70]

State efforts to address the 'poor white problem' and secure the racial order through racial segregation and labour protection are crucial to this chapter's discussion of the formation of the white working class. From 1910, the SAP government enacted urban reforms, clearing racially mixed slums and arranging segregated rehousing. The Pact introduced much more forceful interventions for safeguarding the racial hierarchy. The urban workplace was regarded as a key battlefront: poor unskilled

---

[66] C. Bundy, 'Vagabond Hollanders and runaway Englishmen: white poverty in the Cape before poor whiteism' in W. Beinart, P. Delius and S. Trapido (eds), *Putting a Plough to the Ground: accumulation and dispossession in rural South Africa, 1850–1930* (Johannesburg: Ravan Press, 1986), pp. 101–28; V. Bickford-Smith, *Ethnic Pride and Racial Prejudice in Victorian Cape Town: group identity and social practice, 1875–1902* (Cambridge: Cambridge University Press, 1995), pp. 127–9.
[67] Bundy, *Poverty in South Africa*, p. 47; Giliomee, *The Afrikaners*, p. 316, 325.
[68] Quoted in Davie, *Poverty Knowledge*, p. 46.
[69] Quoted in Giliomee, *The Afrikaners*, p. 346.
[70] A. Stoler, 'Sexual affronts and racial frontiers: European identities and the cultural politics of exclusion in colonial Southeast Asia', *Comparative Studies in Society and History* 34, no. 3 (1992), pp. 514–51; J. McCulloch, *Black Peril, White Virtue: sexual crime in Southern Rhodesia, 1902–1935* (Bloomington IN: Indiana University Press, 2000); W. Jackson, 'Dangers to the colony: loose women and the "poor white" problem in Kenya', *Journal of Colonialism and Colonial History* 14, no. 2 (2013).

whites forced to compete with cheaper African workers ran the risk of sinking below the level of blacks.[71] Hence, in addition to its 'civilised labour' policy, the Pact launched an ambitious programme of public works, employing poor whites in the construction of irrigation schemes, roads, dams, and railway lines. It also expanded government services in housing, education, and health, and instituted non-contributory old-age pensions. Whites – and, to a lesser extent, coloureds – were the beneficiaries of this state support; Indians and Africans were excluded.[72]

Despite these measures, the Great Depression exacerbated the material and symbolic dimensions of white poverty. Large numbers of rural poor – often Afrikaner *bywoners* (tenant farmers) who had not benefited from the Pact's urban-focused policies – washed up in the cities as the economic downturn was compounded by a prolonged drought.[73] Following a familiar pattern, these unskilled whites accumulated in multiracial neighbourhoods, struggling to find work amid a large body of cheap black labour. In 1929, a commission of inquiry, funded by the Carnegie Corporation of New York, embarked on the first research-based investigation into white poverty in South Africa.[74] In its highly influential 1932 report, the Commission put the number of poor whites at 300,000 (17 per cent of the white population), of which 250,000 were estimated to be Afrikaners. Members of the Commission reported evidence of a 'spirit of dependency' fast approaching 'national pathology' among the country's white poor. They recommended the improvement of education among poor whites and the provision of employment opportunities to address the problem.[75]

Grace Davie has demonstrated how the researchers involved in the Carnegie Commission were influenced by Western progressivist views, scientific racism, and everyday popular understandings of poverty and social health. These understandings of the possibility of white degeneracy now came to function alongside environmental and structural understandings of poverty.[76] The white poor were no longer simply dangerous

---

[71] L. Koorts, '"The Black Peril would not exist if it were not for a White Peril that is a hundred times greater": D. F. Malan's fluidity on poor whiteism and race in the pre-apartheid era, 1912–1939', *South African Historical Journal* 65, no. 4 (2013), pp. 560–1, 563.

[72] Seekings, 'Not a single white person', p. 381, 390–4.

[73] Seekings, 'Not a single white person', p. 393.

[74] Davie, *Poverty Knowledge*; T. Willoughby-Herard, *Waste of White Skin: the Carnegie Corporation and the racial logic of white vulnerability* (Oakland CA: University of California Press, 2015).

[75] Quotes from Giliomee, *The Afrikaners*, p. 348, 349; see also Bonner, 'South African society and culture', pp. 259–60.

[76] Davie, *Poverty Knowledge*, pp. 61–9.

but deserving and in need of protection: they formed a fragile barrier between racial suicide and racial purity that had to be bolstered. Afrikaner nationalists, who were mobilising aggressively in the 1930s, hijacked the Carnegie report, steering its impact and public uptake.[77] They used it to lobby for forceful state-led redistribution under an Afrikaner government to uplift poor whites. In the process, 'environmental explanations partially displaced notions of innate racial difference'.[78]

The political triumph of Afrikaner nationalism is discussed later in this chapter. Here, I wish to highlight two crucial points emerging from this period. First, poor whites and white workers did not form clearly distinct communities. Interventions raising poor whites into work, racially segregated rehousing efforts, and shared state dependence meant that a fluidity existed between poor whites and white workers in terms of both social relations and lived experience that did not always make them easily distinguishable. As we have seen, the white strikers of 1922 were very aware of this – they earnestly feared slipping (back) into the ranks of the white poor and becoming 'white kaffirs'.[79] 'Workers called white and classes called poor' were never, as Jon Hyslop remarks, simple sociological categories.[80] Second, this fluidity meant that, as most impoverished whites moved into work and the poor white problem was 'solved', the white working class came to represent the bulwark upholding the racial order, the vanguard of whiteness. As racially mixed slums were cleared and society increasingly segregated, the workplace, where white and black continued to labour shoulder to shoulder, became the key battlefront for maintaining the racial order. Chapter 2 shows how the idea that white workers formed the vanguard of white society against the *swart gevaar* (black peril) remained current on the eve of the political and economic crisis of the 1970s. At the same time, residues of popular understandings of white degeneracy, racial shame, and inferiority associated with poor whiteism never faded completely and continued to cling to the working class. This, too, would be revealed in contestations emerging around late-apartheid reforms.

---

[77] J. Tayler, '"Our poor": the politicisation of the poor white problem, 1932–1942', *Kleio* 24, no. 1 (1992), pp. 40–65; Davie, *Poverty Knowledge*, p. 91.
[78] Davie, *Poverty Knowledge*, p. 95. Koorts, 'The Black Peril would not exist' offers a similar argument.
[79] Krikler, *The Rand Revolt*, p. 149.
[80] J. Hyslop, 'Workers called white and classes called poor: the "white working class" and "poor whites" in Southern Africa 1910–1994' in Money and Van Zyl-Hermann, *Rethinking White Societies*, pp. 23–41.

The rise of Afrikaner nationalism and the triumph of apartheid

A party split in 1934 had left the NP significantly weakened when the majority of its members merged with Smuts' SAP to form the United Party (UP) and take power. In their new capacity as the official opposition, the Nationalists sought to mobilise support by rallying around white poverty as encapsulating Afrikaner economic and cultural subordination. To be sure, by the 1930s, the economy was dominated by people of British or Jewish descent, and English was the dominant language of commerce and the state. Afrikaners' educational levels were low and they were overwhelmingly concentrated in low-paid working-class jobs. This, Nationalists felt, saw Afrikaners exploited and excluded, their language and traditions treated with disdain, relegating them to cap-in-hand second-class citizenship. In response, Afrikaner intellectuals and politicians offered a Christian Nationalist reworking of Afrikaner history which framed Afrikaners as a cohesive and divinely ordained people, destined to unite against the dual threats of British foreign hegemony and the uncivilised natives, and to assume their 'rightful place' in their land of birth.[81] In his landmark study *Volkskapitalisme*, Dan O'Meara explained the rise of Afrikaner nationalism during the 1930s and 1940s by pointing to the material, rather than political or ideological, basis of this movement. Specific petty bourgeois class forces, he argued, sought to secure a base for capital accumulation by mobilising all Afrikaans-speakers – including workers – around an ideological redefinition of Afrikaner nationalism which would act as the vehicle for establishing an Afrikaner class alliance in order to capture economic, and later political, power.[82]

The 1938 centenary of the Great Trek presented a felicitous opportunity for propagating the Nationalist message. Nationwide celebrations, culminating in the laying of the cornerstone of Pretoria's colossal Voortrekker monument, attracted mass popular enthusiasm as Afrikaners came together to celebrate what was increasingly imagined as the volk's heroic history in its battle for survival and freedom. A speech by NP leader D. F. Malan presented the workplace as a battlefront between the races when he likened the Voortrekker pioneers of old

---

[81] T. D. Moodie, *The Rise of Afrikanerdom: power, apartheid, and the Afrikaner civil religion* (Berkeley CA: University of California Press, 1975).

[82] O'Meara, *Volkskapitalisme*, p. 103, 108. See also H. Adam and H. Giliomee, *Ethnic Power Mobilized: can South Africa change?* (New Haven CT and London: Yale University Press, 1979).

holding their own against black hordes in the interior to present-day Afrikaners facing black job competition in the urban economy. The difference, Malan claimed, was that:

> the task to keep South Africa a white man's land, which has become ten times heavier than before, [now] rests on the shoulders of those who are the least able to bear it. Our Blood River lies in the city and our Voortrekkers are our poor who, in the most difficult of circumstances, have to take up the cudgels for our nation against the swelling dark tidal wave.[83]

Such ideas encapsulated and transmitted understandings of the white lower classes – whether in work or seeking employment – as the front line of whiteness, not marching confidently but a desperate, socially precarious group in need of support.[84] *'n Volk red homself* (A people rescues itself) became the popular call to Afrikaners to use their financial resources in service of their people, supporting new Afrikaner businesses which would in turn employ (especially poor) Afrikaners, and promoting national pride in their language and culture. This form of mobilisation – what scholars have called the Afrikaner cultural and economic movement – acted as a vehicle for the popularisation of Afrikaner nationalism from the 1930s onwards. To a great extent, the movement was engineered and driven by the Afrikaner Broederbond (Brotherhood), a secretive Christian Nationalist organisation founded in 1918 by a handful of Afrikaans-speaking teachers, clergymen, and politicians – those petty bourgeois forces identified by O'Meara – to promote the 'welfare of the Afrikaner nation'.[85] Over the next decades, the Broederbond covertly developed and directed a gamut of interlocking political, cultural, educational, religious, and other organisations and initiatives – often with overlapping leadership – with a shared vision of capturing control of the state as a vehicle for Afrikaner advancement. This saw cultural mobilisation become entangled with economic and political ambitions. Through its subsidiary, the Federasie van Afrikaanse Kultuurvereniginge (Federation of Afrikaans Cultural Associations or FAK), for instance, the Broederbond engineered the large-scale coordinated promotion of the Afrikaans language and culture as white, nationalist, and politically coherent. Simultaneously, it was involved in setting up an Afrikaans savings bank, finance house, and chamber of commerce with the purpose

---

[83] Quoted in Koorts, 'The Black Peril would not exist', p. 573.
[84] These were not unique to South Africa but a feature of race-based societies in the context of the Great Depression. E. V. Meeks, 'Protecting the "white citizen worker": race, labor, and citizenship in south-central Arizona, 1929–1945', *Journal of the Southwest* 48, no. 1 (2006), pp. 91–113.
[85] Giliomee, *The Afrikaners*, p. 400.

of mobilising Afrikaner capital, in turn to finance the expansion of Afrikaner businesses and employment and see Afrikaners gain a foothold in trade and industry vis-à-vis established English business.[86]

For many white workers, developments during the Second World War caused great concern. Wartime industrial growth, particularly in semi-skilled positions, stimulated large-scale African urbanisation as workers flocked from the rural areas to job opportunities in the cities. Eager to attract black workers, anglophone manufacturing and commerce called for the loosening of segregationist labour and influx control. As Africans were absorbed into industry, the colour bar was regularly breached. The 1940s saw average African industrial wages rise more rapidly than those of white workers (although the former still lagged far behind), the emergence of an increasingly assertive black labour movement, and more vocal demands for black political rights. The UP government struggled to respond to black urbanisation, its influx control system 'overwhelmed' to the 'point of rupture'. In the run-up to the 1948 general election, it could only put forward modestly reformist and ambiguous proposals for affecting labour stabilisation and addressing African demands, and it was widely viewed as accepting mass African urbanisation as irreversible.[87]

The NP, by contrast, seemed to offer the white electorate a clear solution for safeguarding its interests: apartheid. As both an immediate political intervention and a long-term policy, apartheid promised more rigorous controls on Africans' movements and position in the labour market, and expressed commitment to the restoration of a racial order threatened by white poverty and black social mobility.[88] In contrast to the UP, which was closely identified with the interests of capital, the NP cast itself as the party of the 'working man' and the economically disadvantaged Afrikaner people, running on 'an explicitly anti-capitalist and (Afrikaner) populist platform'.[89] It promised state intervention in and regulation of the economy and labour market, including the nationalisation of mines, banks, and land companies. At the same time, in the post-war context of growing Cold War tensions and increasing African and multiracial labour organisation, it accused the UP of failing to defend whites against the threat of (non-racial) communism. Not content with appealing to workers in this way, the Broederbond launched covert attempts to gain control of unions with substantial Afrikaner

---

[86] Giliomee, *The Afrikaners*, p. 401, 432–7.
[87] O'Meara, *Forty Lost Years*, pp. 24–7, 31–2, 42, 48.
[88] D. Posel, 'The apartheid project, 1948–1970' in Ross et al., *The Cambridge History of South Africa*, p. 326.
[89] O'Meara, *Forty Lost Years*, p. 36.

membership through the infiltration of leadership structures and the exploitation of racist sentiments among white workers.[90] This met with varying degrees of success.[91] Despite measures implemented by the Pact government to co-opt white workers, organised labour still harboured a range of political and ideological sympathies in the 1940s. The flourishing of the manufacturing sector in this period saw the emergence of a new generation of industrial unions that were non-racial and socialist in orientation. Indeed, historians have interpreted the 1940s as a historical moment when real opportunities for multiracialism existed in the organised labour movement as the new industrial unions sought to mobilise alongside African workers.[92]

Nevertheless, the Nationalists' 'ideology of racism and mythology of black, Anglo and communist threats' directed white, particularly Afrikaner, workers towards 'adopting an ideology that neatly justified their exploitation and replaced class consciousness with race anxieties'.[93] By the late 1940s, notes O'Meara, 'most white workers had been persuaded that potential competition from cheaper African labour posed a greater threat to their interests than did the bosses'.[94] These developments contributed to the delegitimisation of working-class identification in the post-war years, making class identification harder to sustain.[95] Furthermore, it is perhaps unsurprising that the Nationalists' explicit ideological inclusion of poor and working-class whites in the body politic of the volk appealed to these constituencies, given the manner in which the Smuts administration was perceived to be in league with the very Anglo and capitalist interests which were seen to threaten white working-class citizenship.

---

[90] Giliomee, *The Afrikaners*, p. 427; Visser, *Van MWU tot Solidariteit*, pp. 55–101; Horrell, *South Africa's Workers*, pp. 10–11; D. O'Meara, 'Analysing Afrikaner nationalism: the "Christian-National" assault on white trade unionism in South Africa, 1934–1948', *African Affairs* 77, no. 306 (1978), pp. 45–72. See also below on the MWU.

[91] On the nationalist struggle to win the allegiance of white women in the Garment Workers' Union, see L. Witz, 'A case of schizophrenia: the rise and fall of the independent Labour Party' in Bozzoli, *Class, Community and Conflict*, pp. 261–91; Berger, *Threads of Solidarity*.

[92] R. Fine with E. Davis, *Beyond Apartheid: labour and liberation in South Africa* (Johannesburg: Ravan Press, 1990); P. Alexander, *Workers, War and the Origins of Apartheid: labour and politics in South Africa 1939–1948* (Oxford: James Currey, 2000), p. 2; S. Dubow and A. Jeeves (eds), *South Africa's 1940s: worlds of possibilities* (Cape Town: Double Storey Books, 2005).

[93] C. van der Westhuizen, *White Power and the Rise and Fall of the National Party* (Cape Town: Zebra Press, 2007), pp. 31–2.

[94] O'Meara, *Forty Lost Years*, p. 78.

[95] B. Kenny, 'Servicing modernity: white women shop workers on the Rand and changing gendered respectabilities, 1940s–1970s', *African Studies* 67, no. 3 (2008), p. 374, 377.

In 1948, the NP's apartheid platform won it significant support in the urban mining and industrial constituencies of the Witwatersrand, as well as among steelworkers and lower middle-class constituencies in Pretoria. Beyond the cities, farming communities – especially the maize farmers of the Transvaal – had become alienated from the UP government by its wartime suppression of agricultural prices. Deeply worried about the threat African urbanisation posed to the stability of the rural labour force, farmers also threw their weight behind the NP. Thus, when it came to power in 1948, the NP stood at the head of a broad social alliance of petty bourgeois Afrikaner political and cultural entrepreneurs, workers, and farmers.[96]

The apartheid state and the organised labour movement

In the decades following 1948, the NP intensified and expanded existing provisions for ensuring white domination on the basis of racial separation. The large-scale state intervention this required was not unusual in the post-war context. War-weary populations, governments, and businesses desired stability, growth, and broad-based social welfare, and centralised state planning presented a vehicle for achieving full employment and the reduction of economic inequality alongside industrialisation, modernisation, and rising production and foreign trade.[97] This international enthusiasm for large, regulatory states was given 'its own particular twist' by the NP. Posel explains that the NP 'harnessed the broadly Keynesian notions of statecraft ... to its own particular – and distinctive – project of "modernising" racial domination. Imagining a bigger, more interventionist and regulatory state as the agent of large-scale social transformation made it possible to envision a society in which constructs of race would become the all-embracing, ubiquitous basis of the social order.'[98]

These ambitions were clearly reflected in labour legislation designed to extend discriminatory provisions. The 1953 Native Labour Act cemented the exclusion of Africans from existing industrial conciliatory mechanisms by setting up a separate system centred on factory-level 'works committees' to represent African workers. These were largely powerless, leaving Africans no effective or legal avenues through which

---

[96] O'Meara, *Forty Lost Years*, p. 30, 35–6.
[97] E. Hobsbawm, *Age of Extremes: the short twentieth century, 1914–1991* (London: Michael Joseph, 1994), pp. 270–3.
[98] D. Posel, 'Whiteness and power in the South African civil service: paradoxes of the apartheid state', *Journal of Southern African Studies* 25, no. 1 (1999), p. 103.

to express their grievances.[99] The 1953 Act, claimed then Minister of Labour Ben Schoeman, would see African trade unions 'die a natural death'.[100]

Coloured and Indian workers continued to be included in the formal labour relations machinery alongside whites, but here, too, efforts were made to regulate the labour market for the benefit of white, enfranchised workers. The 1956 Industrial Conciliation Act broadened the discriminatory measures laid down in 1924. Its notorious Section 77 made statutory provision for the racial allocation of jobs across the economy through direct government intervention. The Act officially delineated this form of job reservation as 'a protective measure of the Whites, Coloureds and other Non-White groups against racial competition'.[101] Yet, when introducing the Act in Parliament, the Minister of Labour explained that Section 77 would serve to 'safeguard the standards of living of the White workers of South Africa and ensure ... that they will not be exploited by the lower standards of any other race'.[102] While white poverty is broadly considered to have been 'solved' by this point, such statements reflected the persisting conviction that white workers required protection if they were to continue upholding the vanguard of whiteness.

The 1956 Act also sought to bolster white working-class dominance in industrial relations. While the 1924 Act had allowed white, coloured, and Indian workers to organise in multiracial unions, the new legislation forbade the registration of new multiracial trade unions and ordered existing multiracial unions to split into separate branches or unions according to race. It further determined that only whites could serve on union executives, thus securing the leadership of the organised labour movement for whites and weakening the bargaining position of other workers. Doxey suggests that these provisions sought to obstruct the development of a united and potentially left-leaning multiracial labour movement – and, in the process, served to reduce the collective bargaining power of organised labour as a whole.[103] The NP had already dealt organised labour a heavy blow with its 1950 Suppression of Communism Act. This intentionally broad and ambiguous law subsumed all manner

---

[99] A. Lichtenstein, 'Making apartheid work: African trade unions and the 1953 Native Labour (Settlement of Disputes) Act in South Africa', *Journal of African History* 46, no. 2 (2005), pp. 293–314; N. L. Clark and W. H. Worger, *South Africa: the rise and fall of apartheid* (Harlow: Pearson, 2011), pp. 75–6.
[100] Bonner and Webster, 'Background', p. 4.
[101] Department of Labour, 1960, quoted in Department of Labour and of Mines, *Report of the Commission of Inquiry into Labour Legislation Part 1 (Key Issues)* (Pretoria: Government Printer, RP49/1979), p. 40.
[102] Hansard, 23 January 1956, col. 276, quoted in Doxey, *The Industrial Colour Bar*, p. 140.
[103] Doxey, *The Industrial Colour Bar*, pp. 148–9.

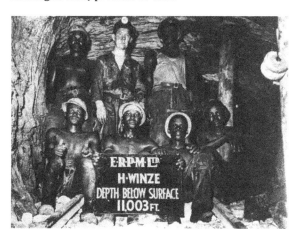

Figure 1.7 The crew that attained the world deep-level mining record in 1958 at East Rand Proprietary Mines.
Source: Barloworld Rand Mines Archive at Historical Papers Research Archive, University of the Witwatersrand, South Africa

of political dissent. Several hundred trade unionists were removed from their positions under the Act, stifling leftist sympathies within organised labour. According to Fine, this defeat of socialist ideas and independent trade unionism among white workers made them a 'prop for the apartheid state'.[104]

It is important to understand the profound impact of this legislation on organised labour, as it would significantly shape the nature of workers' responses to reform efforts from the 1970s. To be sure, factionalism had long characterised the South African labour movement – but this new legislation saw racial and ideological divisions become more pronounced. Despite the NP's success in purging socialist tendencies, different views about cross-racial solidarity remained within the labour movement. In October 1954, 61 unions – mostly open industrial and craft unions – formed the Trade Union Council of South Africa (TUCSA) as a coordinating body intended to bolster labour unity in anticipation of the divisive new Industrial Conciliation Act. Membership was restricted to registered unions, but TUCSA liaised closely with unregistered African unions outside the formal system. For some, this did not go far enough towards the goal of labour unity. In March 1955, unions opposing TUCSA's unwillingness to accept African affiliates

---

[104] Fine, *Beyond Apartheid*, p. 94.

formed the South African Congress of Trade Unions (SACTU), which afforded white, multiracial, and African unions equal rights. For others, TUCSA's fraternising with African workers and its new industrial unions' acceptance of 'non-white' members went too far. Thus, a number of predominantly Afrikaner craft unions in construction and state employment joined with racially exclusive industrial unions to form the Co-ordinating Council of South African Trade Unions. Together with white railway unions, they subsequently formed the South African Confederation of Labour (SACLA). Following the promulgation of the 1956 Act, TUCSA advised its multiracial affiliates to split into separate branches, not separate unions, in order to retain some unity. By contrast, SACTU encouraged coloured and Indian workers to break away from mixed unions and form their own organisations, lest they continue to be governed by white workers. At the same time, there was a strong movement of white workers into exclusive unions, and by the mid-1960s, white membership of mixed unions had virtually halved.[105]

The organised labour landscape remained tumultuous. SACTU's association with the liberation movement soon incurred the wrath of the government. By 1967 it had been immobilised, its organisational capacity depleted by the detention or banning of its leaders. TUCSA, meanwhile, wavered in its stance on the exclusion of African unions. Throughout the 1960s and 1970s, it variously moved to allow or disallow African membership. These oscillating efforts saw virtually all craft unions leave TUCSA. By the 1970s, TUCSA represented around 223,000 workers, of whom the majority were coloured, some were Indian, and about 58,000 were white. As per the determinations of the 1956 Act, TUCSA was white-led, even though the complexion of its leaders was representative of only 27 per cent of its members. SACLA also faced difficulties – racial homogeneity clearly did not guarantee unity. In the course of the 1960s, there were growing doubts among the artisanal affiliates about state policies, and in 1966 the Railroads and Harbours Staff Associations stated that the utilisation of labour resources needed to be reassessed in order to maintain economic growth. This brought it in direct conflict with the Co-ordinating Council's commitment to the status quo.[106] Various craft unions – including the Railroads associations – subsequently disaffiliated. By the mid-1970s, SACLA

---

[105] Horrell, *South Africa's Workers*, pp. 19–25, 30, 39; Greenberg, *Race and State*, p. 296, 300–1.
[106] Horrell, *South Africa's Workers*, pp. 26–7, 29–41; Greenberg, *Race and State*, pp. 301–2.

represented some 200,000 white workers, or 31 per cent of the organised labour force.[107]

The NP's labour legislation, which sought to promote the position of white workers and to distinguish them as a clear category of privileged citizens from other sections of labour, therefore did not go uncontested within organised labour. The main disagreement between – and, indeed, as Chapter 3 will show, within – these labour federations revolved around the inclusion of African workers in the labour movement. White workers were represented across the spectrum of these divided opinions, including forming a minority of SACTU members.[108]

Moreover, it is important to note how apartheid labour legislation sought to secure protected privilege for white workers. This was primarily done by keeping other races down – excluding coloured and Indian workers from leadership positions, barring Africans from participating in the mechanisms of industrial governance, and blocking 'non-white' access to certain jobs and skills – rather than by legitimately strengthening white workers' skills and bargaining positions. Iscor, for instance, adhered to state requirements for the employment of 'civilised labour' while excluding black workers – yet the measures taken in this regard were designed to preserve and reproduce the white labour force, rather than promote its upward mobility. Indeed, Iscor devised a range of measures – offering credit facilities to encourage homeownership, providing sport, recreational, and medical facilities to workers, recruiting successive generations from the same families – to ensure that it retained its workers.[109] Similarly, the NP's legislation fostered a certain kind of white labour movement – acquiescent, nationalist, and not anti-capital. The Suppression of Communism Act facilitated the removal of the best black and white trade union leaders, while the 1956 Industrial Conciliation Act deepened fragmentation throughout organised labour. Thus, Alexander argues, white workers, like blacks, were the victims of apartheid – their organisations crushed and their exploitation secured under the NP, leaving them reliant on the state.[110]

The race-based dualism of the labour regime – conferring rights and protection on the white minority and excluding the African majority – also extended to the NP's other legislative endeavours to enshrine a social hierarchy in which racial identity formed the basis of inclusion

---

[107] SAIRR, *A Survey of Race Relations in South Africa 1976* (Johannesburg: South African Institute of Race Relations (SAIRR), 1977), p. 313; SAIRR, *A Survey of Race Relations in South Africa 1977* (Johannesburg: South African Institute of Race Relations (SAIRR), 1978), p. 288; Horrell, *South Africa's Workers*, pp. 141–2.
[108] Horrell, *South Africa's Workers*, p. 26. [109] Sharp, 'Market, race and nation', p. 92.
[110] Alexander, *Workers, War and the Origins of Apartheid*, pp. 125–6; see also Fine, *Beyond Apartheid*, pp. 92–4, 100.

Figure 1.8 Workers operating the four-stand tandem cold reduction mill at Iscor's Vanderbijlpark works, 1965.
Source: *Iscor News*, January 1965

and exclusion in every aspect of political, economic, and social life. The 1950 Population Registration Act divided the South African population by race. Africans were additionally subdivided into 'distinct' ethnic groups. In the course of the 1950s, the creation of separate homelands for each of these 'nations' became NP policy. Enacting the Promotion of Bantu Self-government Act in 1959, Prime Minister H. F. Verwoerd explained in Parliament that the new law would see whites retain sovereignty in South Africa, while the 'black nations' would be led to 'full development' and 'full authority' in their 'own areas'.[111] In the context of worldwide decolonisation, this provided a convenient instrument for depriving Africans of their citizenship, thus cementing the convergence of race and rights in South Africa. This policy of separate development, explains Dubow, saw apartheid evolve 'from the pronouncement of white domination – *baasskap* – to an elaborate and obfuscatory ideology of "multi-national" development'.[112] The Transkei, identified as a Xhosa homeland, was the first territory to be granted self-government in 1963.

[111] Quoted in H. Giliomee, *The Last Afrikaner Leaders: a supreme test of power* (Cape Town: Tafelberg, 2012), p. 76.
[112] S. Dubow, *Apartheid 1948–1994* (Oxford: Oxford University Press, 2014), p. 105.

The scheme made no provision for Africans residing in South Africa's 'white' cities, or for the country's coloured and Indian communities.[113]

Capitalism and white society under apartheid

Western policy priorities at this time reflected the alliance between states, capital, and labour born of the post-war context. In this triangular arrangement, governments effectively oversaw institutionalised negotiations between capital and labour to reach deals acceptable to all sides – typically, high wages and good benefits in exchange for high profits and labour predictability; as well as a steadily expanding welfare state and state participation in the economy in return for political stability, the suspension of communist sympathies, and a predictable macro-economic environment. By the 1970s, notes Eric Hobsbawm, all advanced capitalist states had become welfare states in the sense that the majority of state employment and expenditure was concentrated in social security. This social consensus and the arrangements it produced were fundamentally dependent on the sustained economic growth characterising the post-war Golden Age.[114] In South Africa, the NP's efforts to shore up a distinctive racial and nationalist order were 'inseparable from efforts to sustain and regulate practices of capital accumulation and economic growth, along with the class interests and conflicts associated with those'.[115]

Thus, the statism evident in post-1948 labour legislation extended to all spheres of South Africa society, reflecting the broad-based social alliance represented by the ruling party. The implementation of stricter influx control attempted not only to stifle African urbanisation but created the rural reserves of cheap black labour that white farming required. Generous subsidies and inflated prices for agricultural products further benefited the sector, with white farmers' real incomes growing by 7.3 per cent per year between 1960 and 1975. This growing prosperity concealed white agriculture's deepening state dependence, with an estimated 20 per cent of farmers' incomes deriving from various forms of state support by 1972.[116]

For white workers, the discriminatory sanctions of apartheid labour legislation protected 'their narrow niche of privilege' by insulating them from black labour competition and guaranteeing employment in reserved jobs, often with inflated wages. The first five years of NP rule witnessed a

---

[113] Giliomee, *The Last Afrikaner Leaders*, p. 76, 81.
[114] Hobsbawm, *Age of Extremes*, pp. 282–4.   [115] Posel, 'The apartheid project', p. 322.
[116] O'Meara, *Forty Lost Years*, p. 77, 143.

10 per cent rise in real white wages in construction and manufacturing, while African wages shrunk by 5 per cent. Yet, as O'Meara notes:

while the NP government thus clearly improved both the living standards and job security of white workers, it conspicuously failed to implement the 'new economic order' it had promised them. Malan's government speedily abandoned its commitment to take a controlling interest in the mines and other strategic industries, to introduce effective state control over banks and other monopolies, and to impose a statutory system of profit sharing.[117]

What the NP did offer working-class whites, in addition to statutorily protected employment in industry, was privileged educational opportunities as well as expanded employment options as avenues for upward social mobility.[118] The creation of a range of new state and semi-state institutions saw Afrikaner employment in public administration expand by 98.5 per cent between 1946 and 1960, and the state become the country's largest employer. The civil service in particular shed its segregation-era English character to become an assertively Afrikaner domain.[119] Under the NP, the size and number of state bureaucracies grew rapidly – from 26 government departments in 1948 to 41 by 1970.[120]

For workers, however, state employment fostered dependence. Often public service employees were those who had failed in more competitive and lucrative private sector labour markets – to the extent that internal government observations noted that the civil service employed 'factory rejects'. And if the government bestowed jobs, it could just as easily revoke them – a realisation that often produced labour acquiescence. The civil servants' Public Service Association was a toothless organisation throughout the apartheid period, unwilling to bite the hand that fed it. As Posel argues, this dependency was magnified by the politics of job reservation: 'The prospect of having to compete for their jobs against a huge black labour pool must have been a rude reminder to white civil servants [and other protected workers] that their meal tickets remained with the National Party.'[121]

---

[117] O'Meara, *Forty Lost Years*, p. 78.
[118] Indeed, Seekings argues that the post-1948 NP was less ideologically statist than its Pact antecedent – it preferred supporting the white population through privileged opportunities in the labour market and education, rather than direct welfare provisions. J. Seekings, 'The National Party and the ideology of welfare in South Africa under apartheid' *Journal of Southern Africa Studies* 46, no, 6 (2020), pp. 1145–1162.
[119] O'Meara, *Forty Lost Years*, p. 62, 76.
[120] Posel, 'Whiteness and power in the South African civil service', pp. 101–4.
[121] Posel, 'Whiteness and power in the South African civil service', p. 108, 115.

Crucially, the expansion of state capacity also offered important opportunities to those petty bourgeoise Afrikaner elements which, in O'Meara's analysis, first initiated the reformulation of Afrikaner nationalism with the goal of capturing economic and political power. Many found favourable career prospects in the public service, where bureaucrats enjoyed 'security of tenure, cradle-to-the-grave social welfare, and handsome study opportunities'.[122] Most NP Members of Parliament hailed from Afrikaner petty bourgeois ranks and were members of the Broederbond. For Afrikaner businessmen, meanwhile, the expansion of state capitalism offered employment opportunities in the top management and advisory positions of state and semi-state enterprises such as the South African Railways and Harbours, Iscor, the national electricity provider Eskom, and the oil-from-coal energy and chemical company Sasol. State benevolence towards Afrikaner business also saw government accounts and contracts transferred to Afrikaner financial institutions and enterprises. From just 6 per cent in 1948, Afrikaner control of private industry rose to 21 per cent by 1975.[123]

The NP's statism was supported by strong post-war economic growth. South Africa's GDP showed an annual average increase of 5 per cent between 1948 and 1957, 3 per cent between 1957 and 1961, and a flourishing 6 to 8 per cent between 1962 and 1974, earning the latter period the label 'the golden age of apartheid'.[124] Supported by such consistent growth, NP policies facilitated dramatic upward social mobility among white South Africans. According to Davies, 'between 1946 and 1960 the number of whites described in censuses as labourers ... decreased by 61 percent while the numbers in the new petty bourgeoisie increased by some 74 percent'.[125] Within the Afrikaner population, the absolute and proportional number of males in the lowest-income categories shrunk, while their presence in the higher-income sectors of the economy swelled rapidly, leading to the establishment of an urban Afrikaner middle class of white-collar workers and managers.[126] Broad occupational data, meanwhile, shows the percentage of Afrikaners in blue-collar employment remaining remarkably stable in the first decades of NP rule (Table 1.1). By contrast, the same period saw a significant decline in the percentage of Afrikaners in agriculture, offset by the spike in those in white-collar employment.

---

[122] Quoted in O'Meara, *Forty Lost Years*, p. 77.
[123] O'Meara, *Forty Lost Years*, pp. 79–80.   [124] O'Meara, *Forty Lost Years*, p. 82, 116.
[125] Davies, *Capital, State and White Labour*, p. 351.
[126] O'Meara, *Forty Lost Years*, pp. 136–7, 140.

Table 1.1 *Distribution of the Afrikaner labour force, 1946–70.*[127]

	1946(%)	1960(%)	1970(%)
Agriculture	30.3	16.0	10.1
Blue-collar employment	40.7	40.5	38.3
White-collar employment	29.0	43.5	51.6

These local trends mirrored international developments. The dramatic decline of the peasantry alongside the rise in higher education opportunities during the Golden Age saw similar shifts in the population segments involved in agriculture and white-collar employment in industrialised countries. But the size of the industrial working class remained relatively constant at about one-third of the population in these countries, while it grew in Eastern Europe and the 'Third World', where industrialisation was expanding. Hence Hobsbawm stresses that 'the idea that the old industrial working class died out during this time of economic boom is statistically mistaken on a global scale' – this would not be the case until the 1980s.[128]

In the 1930, advocates of the Afrikaner economic movement had rallied around the slogan *'n Volk red homself*. When they reconvened in the 1950s, it was in a 'mood of self-congratulation'.[129] The poor white problem was considered solved, and Afrikaner businesses were establishing a firm foothold in the economy. With the rescue action accomplished, this section of NP supporters could now focus on making money. By the 1960s, writes Beinart, it was 'the best of times, materially, for white South Africans'; they had 'never had it so good'.[130] In this way, too, South Africa echoed global realities. Globally, the prosperity of the post-war era was not just visible in retrospect but consciously experienced by the populations of increasingly prosperous 'developed' countries. British Conservatives fought the 1959 general election on the slogan 'You've never had it so good', winning Harold Macmillan the premiership for a second time. Industrial expansion throughout the capitalist, socialist, and 'Third' world made this a Golden Age of impressive economic growth – and increasing labour shortage. Full employment and the burgeoning consumer society placed at least some affluence within most working-class people's reach, with

---

[127] Sadie, *The Fall and Rise of the Afrikaner*, p. 54.
[128] Hobsbawm, *Age of Extremes*, p. 302.   [129] Giliomee, *The Afrikaners*, p. 439.
[130] W. Beinart, *Twentieth-century South Africa* (Oxford: Oxford University Press, 2001), pp. 180–1.

workers in the industrialised West enjoying a universal and generous welfare state, paid annual leave – even the luxury of owning a car.[131]

Yet while apartheid was, in O'Meara's words, 'good for every white's business', the actual material advantage of the NP's pro-white policies was spread very unevenly. The new class of urban Afrikaner financial, industrial, and commercial capitalists emerged as the major beneficiaries; they 'blossomed from an embattled infancy to potent adulthood under the benevolent care of the NP government'.[132] Apartheid-era legislation drove down the cost of African labour and shielded local industries, creating favourable conditions for capital accumulation for Afrikaner business. The period 1946 to 1960 witnessed growing stratification within the white Afrikaans-speaking population, as Afrikaners became overwhelmingly concentrated in three distinct occupational categories: 'professional, managerial and executive (i.e. the upper middle class); clerical, sales and administrative (the middle to lower levels of the middle class); and skilled and supervisory workers'. O'Meara argues that:

> Rigid occupational criteria, educational barriers and different lifestyles together rendered very difficult any mobility *between* these strata. The apartheid policies of the NP government performed the crucial function of partially ameliorating the earnings gap between these strata normally found in free market economies, thus at least partially sustaining the old myth of a classless *volk*. It likewise consolidated the relatively privileged and protected position of Afrikaner skilled and supervisory workers. Nevertheless, the stratification was real, and ... the income gap between these categories would grow wider in the 1960s.[133]

Considering the position of economically active Afrikaans-speaking white males in 1960, O'Meara identifies those in 'administrative, managerial and executive' positions, representing only 4.2 per cent of this working population, as the highest-income category, earning an average monthly income of R3,308. Artisans and production workers, by contrast, are recorded as the largest occupational category of Afrikaans-speaking white males at approximately 27 per cent of the population. Yet with a median monthly income of R1,473, they were one of the lowest earning in relative terms, ahead only of 'manual labourers' with a median monthly income of R931 and the 'unemployed'.[134] Embourgeoisement was uneven and often shallow. By 1964, some 60 per cent of the unionised whites in the employ of the Chamber of

---

[131] Hobsbawm, *Age of Extremes*, pp. 257–9, 261, 264, 267, 276, 307.
[132] O'Meara, *Forty Lost Years*, p. 81, 139.
[133] O'Meara, *Forty Lost Years*, p. 137 (emphasis in original).
[134] O'Meara, *Forty Lost Years*, p. 137.

Mines were so-called day's pay men. By far the largest number of them were production workers represented by the all-white Mineworkers' Union.[135]

The Mineworkers' Union

The establishment of the MWU in 1902 came amid the intense conflict between workers and employers characterising the early twentieth-century industrialised and industrialising world. For most of the century, the MWU's membership covered non-artisanal underground employees – those whites at the lowest end of the mining skills and supervisory hierarchy, working in the production process directly alongside African workers. MWU members played a central role in the 1922 Rand Revolt. White miners who were organised in the MWU – totalling some 15,000 by 1922 and by then including immigrants as well as unskilled Afrikaans-speaking whites who had entered the mines during the war – shared both the republican and the revolutionary sentiments that animated the revolt. The MWU is said to have warned that the Chamber's reorganisation of labour would see 'the Kafir [sic] ... take up the place of the white man and then we are doomed to national annihilation'.[136] The strikers' banner reading 'Workers of the world unite and fight for a white South Africa' was carried by the Newlands commando, led by I. J. Viljoen, an MWU member.[137] According to the union's biographer Wessel Visser, the 1922 strike became 'embedded in the historical psyche and collective consciousness of MWU members'.[138] As subsequent chapters will show, the salience of this strike turned insurrection would reverberate through the union throughout the twentieth century and remains an evocative reference point in the present.

MWU members were major beneficiaries of the civilised labour policies instituted by the Pact government – in particular the 1926 Mines and Works Amendment Act, which entrenched white job reservation in mining by reserving certificates of competency in certain skills, such as blasting, for white and coloured workers.[139] By the 1930s, as the Carnegie Commission was undertaking its investigation into white poverty, newly proletarianised and often unskilled Afrikaners constituted the overwhelming majority of MWU members. The union's leadership,

---

[135] Wilson, *Labour in the South African Gold Mines*, p. 170.
[136] Simons and Simons, *Class and Colour in South Africa*, p. 285.
[137] Visser, *Van MWU tot Solidariteit*, p. 33, 35.
[138] Visser, *Van MWU tot Solidariteit*, p. 27 (my translation).
[139] Visser, 'From MWU to Solidarity', p. 20.

by contrast, remained largely English-speaking.[140] Afrikaner nationalists saw this situation as reflecting the overall disempowerment of Afrikaners under Smuts' pro-British UP and set their sights on gaining control of the MWU. They set about branding established labour leaders as communist agents and exploiting antisemitic and racist sentiments among white workers. In the context of falling workers' wages and corruption among union leaders, the nationalists successfully turned MWU members against their Labour Party-oriented executive. By 1948, Afrikaner mining constituencies – previously Labour strongholds – displayed strong support for the Nationalists and were instrumental in voting the NP into government. A few months later, the MWU elected a new NP-oriented executive. The union subsequently developed an assertively Afrikaans and Christian identity. Visibly more nationalist in character, its mouthpiece condemned communism and working-class consciousness as threatening the unity of the volk.[141]

The first decades of apartheid witnessed the race-based social alliance in action: South African businesses and the NP government benefited from the industrial discipline and political loyalty of white workers, while workers in turn enjoyed the protection and benevolence of the state and employers.[142] In addition to material benefits, white workers' new-found social security as full members of the white body politic and key partners in Afrikaner political power must have gone some way towards ameliorating the real and subjective class and race insecurities long associated with white proletarianisation and poverty. The MWU in particular wielded great influence within government – its representatives enjoyed direct access to ministerial offices and even the Prime Minister, with some serving on the executive of the Transvaal NP.[143] And on the labour front, MWU representatives drove hard bargains in the interests of their members. Particularly from the 1960s, as shortages of white labour and technological advances in mining techniques saw the Chamber of Mines press for the reorganisation of the racial division of labour, MWU general secretary Arrie Paulus jealously guarded his members' privilege and power. Paulus, known for his brashness and brinkmanship, negotiated improved wages and benefits in exchange for uncertified African workers

---

[140] Visser, 'From MWU to Solidarity', pp. 20–1; Davies, *Capital, State and White Labour*, p. 286.
[141] Giliomee, *The Afrikaners*, p. 427; Visser, *Van MWU tot Solidariteit*, pp. 55–101, 123–4; Horrell, *South Africa's Workers*, pp. 10–11; O'Meara, 'Analysing Afrikaner nationalism'.
[142] Visser, *Van MWU tot Solidariteit*, p. 121.
[143] Visser, 'From MWU to Solidarity', p. 21; see also O'Meara, *Forty Lost Years*; Davies, *Capital, State and White Labour*.

Figure 1.9 Arrie Paulus (right) and Cor de Jager (centre-left) emerge smiling from a meeting with then Minister of Mines Carel de Wet (centre-right) in 1970.
Source: *The Star*, 24 October 1970/African News Agency (ANA)

being given greater responsibility in the blasting process.[144] Government and mining capital alike regarded Paulus with wary reverence, with mining giant Anglo American recognising the firebrand unionist as 'the most powerful labour leader in the country'.[145]

Labour aristocracy or privileged precariat?

Understandings of white workers as historically unproblematically privileged and secure within the context of the racial state still prevail. In his opening to *The Rand Revolt*, Krikler admits that he started the study considering white workers 'something of a labour aristocracy – deserving infinitely less sympathy than the black workforce below them'. He records his bewilderment when his sources revealed these aristocrats of labour 'announc[ing] themselves rightless, [in a world] in which one sensed acute pain and fear, a jolting internal dislocation'. Krikler was

---

[144] Moodie, *Going for Gold*, p. 72; Crankshaw, *Race, Class and the Changing Division of Labour*, pp. 58–61.
[145] W. Visser, 'Arrie Paulus en Peet Ungerer – Twee gedugte leiers van die SA Mynwerkersunie', 30 September 2015, https://blog.solidariteit.co.za/arrie-paulus-en-peet-ungerer-twee-gedugte-leiers-van-die-sa-mynwerkersunie/ (accessed 17 January 2017). See also D. van Zyl-Hermann, 'Race, rumour and the politics of class in late and post-apartheid South Africa: the case of Arrie Paulus', *Social History* 43, no. 4 (2018), pp. 509–30.

writing, of course, about 1922 – and we must recognise that, after the economic boom of the 1950s and 1960s, the position of apartheid-era white workers was certainly different to that of their ancestors on the Rand one or more generations earlier. In the early decades of the twentieth century, 'the privileged position of this "labour aristocracy" of white workers ... was real relative to the black working class, but non-existent when set against the status of the wealthy whites who despised them'.[146] The powerful social and economic engineering of the state, the suppression of black resistance, and steady economic growth under apartheid seemed to cement white prosperity and the myth of the classless volk – even if the well-heeled sections of the volk drove the latest model ivory-coloured Mercedes while others rolled through life in Ford Zephyrs and Cortinas.[147]

Yet, as Krikler realised with regard to 1922, and as this chapter has shown for subsequent decades, things were distinctly more complex than this veneer of white workers' wealth suggested. While on the surface it might have been all bonuses and *braaivleis*, this ostensible privilege and security were a smokescreen held up by the state. It was the very nature of this artificial protection that rendered many white workers vulnerable and dependent on the racial state.

The workers of the MWU represent a case in point. By the 1970s, these white miners' role in the underground production process had progressively diminished. Blasting – formally reserved for whites – had become semi-skilled work, effectively rendering the holding of a blasting certificate superfluous. While there continued to be real skill involved in this job, concessions negotiated by the union saw black workers take on much of the actual work while the white blaster simply supervised – as the opening vignette about Willie demonstrates.[148] This made white miners completely dependent on racially discriminatory legislation to safeguard their superior position and privileges in relation to African workers. Without the protection of the racial state, these workers were simply under-skilled, overpriced, and expendable. Moreover, their mining-specific skills bound them to these precarious positions: MWU members – in contrast to craftsmen and maintenance workers in the mining industry – did not have a trade, making employment outside

---

[146] Krikler *The Rand Revolt*, p. ix, x.
[147] On cars and class in apartheid-era Afrikaner society, see A. Grundlingh, '"Are we Afrikaners getting too rich?" Cornucopia and change in Afrikanerdom in the 1960s', *Journal of Historical Sociology* 21, nos 2–3 (2008), pp. 148–50.
[148] See descriptions of the production process in Davies, 'The white working-class in South Africa'; Simson, 'The myth of the white working class in South Africa'.

mining unlikely.[149] This exacerbated the economic vulnerability of these white miners. In Posel's formulation, referring to workers in the apartheid-era civil service, the power and privilege conferred on workers dependent on the racial state were not unproblematically about the benefits of the 'wages of whiteness', but rather like a 'golden handcuff' – 'a mix of costs and benefits, pleasures and pains'.[150]

Thus, rather than seeking to categorise white workers during the apartheid era as either genuine proletarians or the lackeys of bourgeois capital, I propose that a more complex picture emerges from the history of white working-class formation over the course of South Africa's industrial and political history. This results in an understanding of white workers that places less emphasis on their relations to production and more on their relation to and position in the racial state. In this sense, they were certainly privileged, particularly from 1924 – and we may point to the same evidence offered by Marxists such as Davies and Simson on employment, status, and income. At the same time, however, white workers' position was precarious; often, what stood between them and material and subjective cataclysm was state legislation protecting them from black labour competition and exclusion from the white body politic. Would this ever come about? Would the likelihood that bourgeois interests could sacrifice the white working class remain as minimal as Davies supposed? How would white workers respond, and what would the impact be on their forms of organisation, their politics and subjectivities? The following chapters seek to answer these questions.

---

[149] Department of Manpower Utilisation, *Report of the Commission of Inquiry into Labour Legislation Part 6 (Industrial Relations in the Mining Industry)* (Pretoria: Government Printer, RP28/1981), p. 9.
[150] Posel, 'Whiteness and power in the South African civil service', p. 119.

2 From sweetheart to Frankenstein
The National Party's changing stance towards white labour amid the crisis of the 1970s

Introduction

The Minister gave a dismissive shrug. 'If at some future time circumstances alter, well, we might consider changing our labour laws, but we see no reason to do so now. We think our legislation is working well. The people are happy.' Marais Viljoen, Minister of Labour and Member of Parliament for the east Rand town of Alberton, leaned back in his chair, untroubled, as he spoke these words to the *Rand Daily Mail*'s labour correspondent. The reporter had raised the issue of improving negotiating machinery for African workers. But it was late in the year in 1972, things were slowing down around the Department of Labour's headquarters in downtown Pretoria as the summer break neared, and as far as the Minister was concerned, all was quiet on the labour front.[1]

Viljoen's insouciant confidence was reflective of global sentiments. A 1972 UN report stated that 'there is no special reason to doubt that the underlying trends of growth in the early and middle 1970s will continue much as in the 1960s',[2] while America's *Fortune* magazine reported that South Africa was 'one of those rare and refreshing places where profits are great and problems are small'.[3] But the rosy view from behind Viljoen's signature heavy-framed glasses would fade rapidly in the course of the new year, along with the dissipating glow of the Golden Age. Globally and in South Africa, the end of the 1960s saw the balance between the growth of productivity, earnings, and profits, which underpinned the post-war social alliance between states, labour, and capital, become increasingly unsettled. When a succession of international shocks hit in the early 1970s, the world economy tumbled into a full-blown crisis, dragging post-war consensus politics down with it.

---

[1] As recounted in J. Imrie, 'This was the year of the bursting labour bubbles', *Rand Daily Mail*, 28 December 1973.
[2] Quoted in Hobsbawm, *Age of Extremes*, p. 259.
[3] Quoted in A. Ashforth, *The Politics of Official Discourse in Twentieth-century South Africa* (Oxford: Clarendon Press, 1990), p. 198.

Introduction

By the late 1960s, full employment was steadily giving way to intensifying labour shortages. This caused a spiral of rising wages, rising demand, and, inevitably, rising prices. As productivity sagged, it became increasingly difficult to keep inflation in check. Any central attempt to overcome these problems 'ran into the seemingly immovable force of deeply entrenched working-class power'[4] as a generation of workers who had grown accustomed to the regular wage increases of the Golden Age stepped up their demands for higher wages and better conditions. This resulted in a wave of strikes, revealing the increasingly dysfunctional nature of Keynesian relations of power and reciprocity between labour, capital, and the state. Meanwhile, accelerating inflation and growing state debt saw America's international economic hegemony start to slip. While in the immediate post-war decades, US dominance had functioned as a stabilising force in the world economy, particularly through the international monetary system, which tied the dollar to a specific quantity of gold, this system now fell into disarray. In 1971, the USA abandoned the system of fixed exchange rates, introducing further volatility into the world economy.[5] This was exacerbated in 1973 when Arab oil-producing countries imposed an embargo on Western nations seen to be supporting conflict in the Middle East. The economic expansion of the Golden Age had been driven by the availability of cheap energy, particularly fossil fuels. Now, the skyrocketing price of oil sparked a crisis for production and profitability in a number of sectors, further aggravating inflation. The two years immediately following the oil shock saw a 10 per cent reduction in developed countries' industrial production and a 13 per cent contraction in international trade. While during the rest of the 1970s and 1980s economic growth did not stop altogether in the industrialised West, it slowed to a crawl, interspersed with short periods of stagnation. Instability, unemployment, and poverty returned to the West, inaugurating a period of widening social and economic inequality. In Western Asia, Latin America, and Africa, GDP growth per capita ceased completely, and these regions were caught in a severe depression throughout the 1980s.[6]

From this crisis, a return to economic policies resembling pre-war laissez-faire capitalism emerged as the antidote to the failure of Keynesian economic management.[7] A dramatic reordering of national

---

[4] D. Harvey, *The Condition of Postmodernity: an enquiry into the origins of cultural change* (Cambridge MA: Blackwell, 1992), p. 142.
[5] Hobsbawm, *Age of Extremes*, pp. 284–6, 301; Harvey, *The Condition of Postmodernity*, p. 142; Harvey, *A Brief History of Neoliberalism*, p. 12.
[6] Hobsbawm, *Age of Extremes*, p. 262, 286, 405–7.
[7] Harvey, *A Brief History of Neoliberalism*, pp. 13–63.

economies from state-led to market-driven policies and practices ensued, marked by widespread privatisation, deregulation, and reduced public spending on social provision. The implementation of free market policies inevitably led to the reconfiguration of power relations between labour, capital, and the state. Efforts to jumpstart the economy by creating a favourable and competitive business climate meant that working-class power had to be disciplined or even destroyed – a process that involved a full-blown assault on organised labour in the most resolutely neoliberal regimes such as the USA and the UK.[8] Such efforts, alongside the state's withdrawal from industrial policy, rising unemployment, and inflation, severely weakened the position of labour to the advantage of business.[9]

The 1970s and 1980s would see South Africa faced with similar upheavals – but here they exhibited a distinctive local hue. The country's creeping shortage of skilled labour was gaining momentum, stimulated by discriminatory policies reserving skilled work for whites while restricting blacks' educational opportunities. The 'never had it so good' 1960s saw ever more white entrants to the labour market choose high-status white-collar and professional careers over manual work. In the course of the decade, the skilled labour shortage became increasingly acute, even in the context of continuing economic growth. One desperate personnel manager in the motor industry summed up the situation: '[A]ny genuine white worker who presented himself at your gate and … hadn't been to prison for six or seven months in the last two years, you said, "Okay, give him a try. He's white."'[10] This situation caused a variety of responses. In some industries, organised white labour used the shortage to its advantage, negotiating with management to devise shop-floor alternatives to overcome the constraints imposed by apartheid policies. This saw white labour and employers strike industrial council agreements which allowed Africans to take on aspects of traditionally reserved work in exchange for benefits for organised labour – as in the case of the agreement negotiated by MWU general secretary Arrie Paulus in the mining industry.[11] In other instances, often with the support of white workers, businesses

---

[8] D. King and S. Wood, 'The political economy of neoliberalism: Britain and the United States in the 1980s' in H. Kitschelt et al. (eds), *Continuity and Change in Contemporary Capitalism* (Cambridge: Cambridge University Press, 1999), pp. 371–97; N. Brenner, J. Peck, and N. Theodore, 'Variegated neoliberalization: geographies, modalities, pathways', *Global Networks* 10, no. 2 (2010), pp. 182–222.

[9] Harvey, *A Brief History of Neoliberalism*, p. 3, 75; Hobsbawm, *Age of Extremes*, p. 415.

[10] Quoted in Posel, 'Whiteness and power in the South African civil service', p. 107. Posel shows that labour and skills shortages also affected the civil service.

[11] As discussed in Chapter 1. See also SAIRR, *A Survey of Race Relations in South Africa 1973* (Johannesburg: South African Institute of Race Relations (SAIRR), 1974), pp. 240–1. Evidence of such practices was also presented before the Wiehahn

applied to the Department of Labour for official concessions or amendments to job reservation determinations, so that work reserved for whites might be relinquished to blacks.[12] In still other instances, official legislation was simply contravened. In the construction industry, for instance, a Section 77 determination reserved trowel work for whites – but with ever decreasing numbers of whites seeking employment in construction, employers were faced with acute labour shortages. In their desperation, companies would buy hand forks used for gardening, beat them flat and have African workers use these as makeshift trowels as a way of circumventing the legislation.[13]

Skills shortages remained within bounds as long as the economy was driven primarily by the mining sector, which required a relatively small skilled labour force supported by an army of unskilled labour. Yet, as the manufacturing industry – with its much greater demand for skilled and semi-skilled workers – overtook mining during the middle part of the century as the main contributor to GDP, the skilled labour deficit increasingly inhibited economic expansion. Also, the overall low quality of labour meant that South African industry never displayed satisfactory levels of productivity, which, alongside the existing structural challenges, did not bode well for the prospect of becoming a competitive exporter. Indeed, manufacturing was heavily dependent on foreign imports, particularly capital goods. Again, as long as mining remained lucrative, bringing in large export earnings, this situation remained tolerable.[14]

Yet the early 1970s saw these longer-term structural weaknesses compounded by more immediate shifts in the local and global contexts, sending the South African economy into a period of decline which continued into the 1990s. The slowdown in world production and trade alongside the escalating price of oil increased inflationary pressures on South Africa. The country's dependence on imported capital goods further meant that it was particularly vulnerable to inflation, the rising exchange rate, and international fluctuations. While the dollar's uncoupling from gold reserves initially effected a rapid rise in the price of the precious metal, gains were soon overtaken by the drop in international

---

Commission. See, for instance, Steenkamp Archive/Wiehahn Documentation (SA/WD), Testimony Meeting 23, Johannesburg, 21 February 1978, p. 3300.

[12] M. Mariotti and D. van Zyl-Hermann, 'Policy, practice and perception: reconsidering the efficacy and meaning of statutory job reservation in South Africa, 1956–1979', *Economic History of Developing Regions* 29, no. 2 (2014), pp. 197–233.

[13] Piet Nieuwenhuizen, interviewed 11 August 2012, Bellville. Witnesses before the Wiehahn Commission testified to similar incidences of circumvention, and of factory inspectors turning a blind eye to them. See, for instance, SA/WD, Testimony Meeting 23, Johannesburg, 21 February 1978, p. 3308, 3300.

[14] Feinstein, *An Economic History of South Africa*, pp. 188–92, 230.

demand alongside rapidly rising costs in mining production.[15] Thus, poor economic performance, the contraction of the mining industry, and the tendency to replace labour with capital resulted in a crucial shift in the South African economy. As Feinstein explains, 'For three centuries since settlers arrived in South Africa, the dominant theme in all economic discourse had been a shortage of manpower ... But by the 1970s ... the central problem was no longer the inability of employers to find workers, it was the inability of workers – especially those who were unskilled – to find jobs.'[16] For the first time, therefore, labour supply started to outstrip demand. In addition to skills shortages, rising unemployment now also loomed. With growth ever more dependent on the uncompetitive secondary industry, the prosperity that had characterised post-war minority-ruled South Africa was replaced by economic stagnation, surging unemployment, and inflation. The eruption of African labour unrest in 1973 and nationwide community demonstrations against apartheid policies, starting with the Soweto student protests in 1976, demonstrated the dysfunctionality of apartheid's economics. Black demands for labour rights and political freedoms readily flowed together, threatening political and economic instability that the country could ill afford.

By 1977, the NP government recognised that, for its established economic policies, the writing was on the wall. In an effort to revive conditions favourable to economic growth and forestall the labour crisis from spilling into the political sphere, it initiated a reconsideration of South Africa's labour relations system. Prime Minister Vorster appointed a commission of inquiry headed by Nic Wiehahn, a professor of labour law at the University of South Africa (UNISA) and a man praised in Parliament by no less than the Progressive Reform Party (PRP) for his democratic convictions.[17] Expectations were high that a major overhaul of apartheid's labour dispensation was on the cards.

Existing scholarship typically attributes the NP's shift towards reform from the late 1970s to the changing social base and priorities of the party. The NP had come to power in 1948 as the champion of the 'small man' and uplifter of the white poor, but the 1960s saw it transformed into a party of white middle-class suburbanites and businessmen. According to Grundlingh, the NP increasingly presented itself as a bourgeois party, emphasising the importance of economic growth rather than ethnic

---

[15] Marais, *South Africa Pushed to the Limit*, pp. 28–32.
[16] Feinstein, *An Economic History of South Africa*, p. 237.
[17] Hansard Vol. 68 Column 7495–6, 12 May 1977, as discussed below.

Introduction 81

priorities, and portraying whites as a modernising and adaptive elite.[18] At the same time, ideological tensions emerged within the party between the so-called *verkramptes* – dogmatic and conservative Verwoerdians unwilling to countenance a shift in the NP's priorities – and more reformist and accommodating *verligtes*.[19] These divisions sparked two splits in the NP, leading to the formation of the Herstigte Nasionale Party (Reconstituted National Party or HNP) in 1969[20] and the Conservative Party (CP) in 1982. The former split had little impact on the NP, but the CP posed a serious threat to the Nationalists' political hegemony. Scholars understand the 1982 split as marking the end of the Afrikaner *volkseenheid* (unity of the volk) forged in the 1940s.[21]

The white working class is consistently connected to these *verkrampte* political parties, even though there is no agreement on whether the split in Afrikaner ranks was primarily material or ideological in nature.[22] As Chapter 1 showed, white workers remained a substantial part of the white populace by the 1970s. The majority of CP supporters, by contrast, were 'clergy, academics, teachers, doctors or professionals', thus making it a party representing 'a considerable cross-section of the Afrikaner establishment'. The CP concentrated on ethnic rather than labour-related appeals.[23] Indeed, it did not split from the NP in the wake of the government's acceptance of labour reforms, but only some years later in objection to constitutional reforms.[24]

Existing understandings of the NP's move towards labour reform therefore do not adequately account for the position and interests of white workers in the Nationalist movement and the white body politic

---

[18] Grundlingh, 'Are we Afrikaners getting too rich?', p. 159.
[19] Adam and Giliomee, *Ethnic Power Mobilized*, pp. 217–21; O'Meara, *Forty Lost Years*, pp. 289–303; Dubow, *Apartheid*, pp. 150–4.
[20] O'Meara, *Forty Lost Years*, pp. 310–11; Van der Westhuizen, *White Power*, p. 92; G. Leach, *The Afrikaners: their last great trek* (London: Macmillan, 1989), p. 88; J. van Rooyen, *Hard Right: the new white power in South Africa* (London: I. B. Tauris, 1994), p. 18, 20–2.
[21] O'Meara, *Forty Lost Years*, pp. 289–303.
[22] See specifically C. Charney, 'Class conflict and the National Party split', *Journal of Southern African Studies* 10, no. 2 (1984), pp. 269–82; Hermann Giliomee's rebuttal in '"Broedertwis": intra-Afrikaner conflicts in the transition from apartheid', *African Affairs* 91, no. 364 (1992), pp. 339–64. Also Van der Westhuizen, *White Power*, pp. 117–18; O'Meara, *Forty Lost Years*, pp. 295–312; Terreblanche, *A History of Inequality in South Africa*, p. 355.
[23] Van Rooyen, *Hard Right*, p. 32, also 34–5; O'Meara, *Forty Lost Years*, pp. 307–8, 311–12; J. Hyslop, 'Why was the white right unable to stop South Africa's democratic transition?' in P. F. Alexander et al. (eds), *Africa Today: a multi-disciplinary snapshot of the continent in 1995* (Canberra: Humanities Research Centre, Australian National University (ANU), 1995), p. 148.
[24] See Chapter 3.

during the 1970s. This chapter investigates the political establishment's relationship with its historically crucial white working-class voters against the backdrop of the decade's unfolding crises. Using a range of archival sources,[25] it examines sentiments expressed in public and behind closed doors by NP politicians and elite powerbrokers in the Afrikaner Broederbond. This reveals that, at the opening of the decade, the NP still presented itself as the champion of white workers, and political elites continued to advocate ethnic interests over economic ones. As the crises of capital accumulation and political legitimacy gained momentum, the plight and power of white labour were central preoccupations shaping the political elite's response. The chapter investigates how the NP moved from the commitment to protect white workers that it still maintained at the beginning of the decade to commissioning a reconsideration of the very legislation designed to protect white labour by 1977. In a period characterised globally by a breakdown in the post-war social alliance between the state, labour, and capital, this marked an uncoupling of the generations-old project of white survival from the fortunes of white workers.

Before Durban: the National Party's commitment to white labour amid emerging economic problems

The mounting urgency of apartheid-induced constraints on the economy is clear from parliamentary debates of the early 1970s. Yet prior to the outbreak of African labour unrest, these debates were not about discontent within the exploited African labour force. Rather, the focus was the growing problem of skills shortages created by restrictions on the utilisation of black labour, designed to safeguard white workers. '[T]here is no doubt that the problem of the shortage of labour ... is the most important internal problem in South Africa today,' claimed Marais Steyn, UP MP for Yeoville.[26]

Statutory job reservation stood at the centre of the House of Assembly's labour rows. While, in its narrowest sense, job reservation referred to the infamous Section 77 of the 1956 Industrial Conciliation Act, which reserved certain jobs for certain racial groups – particularly to the advantage of whites – the concept also often served as a shorthand for

---

[25] With the bulk of the NP's archival material uncatalogued and inaccessible at the time when this research was conducted, the analysis relies on parliamentary debates, NP pamphlets, the collections of labour ministers Marais Viljoen and Fanie Botha, caucus and Cabinet minutes, and documentation on labour matters from the Afrikaner Broederbond Collection.
[26] Hansard Vol. 30 Column 3283, 3 September 1970.

the maintenance of a rigid colour bar in South African industry more broadly.[27] The official Opposition UP viewed job reservation as the main cause of skills shortages, condemning it as an 'ideology-informed' policy that frustrated economic growth and aggravated inflation by excluding the majority of the workforce from doing higher skilled work.[28] Hence, the UP advocated better utilisation of black labour through the removal of job reservation and through large-scale training programmes. Nationalist MPs denounced the Opposition's policies as 'integrationist' efforts to undermine South Africa's established social order in service of capitalist interests. Theirs was '[t]he hand of Esau and the voice of Oppenheimer,' warned J. P. A. Reyneke, NP MP for working-class Boksburg, 'those people who, for the sake of bigger profits and enriching themselves, want to disturb our traditional labour pattern and racial harmony here in South Africa.'[29]

Of course, the UP did not oppose race policies per se. In fact, it expressed its commitment to racial separation as a fundamental principle in South Africa, declared its opposition to trade union rights for Africans, and stated clearly that the reorganisation of labour should continue to see whites occupy the top rungs of the labour hierarchy – it was, in effect, simply advocating the floating of the colour bar.[30] But the UP did regard economic growth as crucial to safeguarding white rule. Opposition leader De Villiers Graaff therefore challenged the NP to recognise that, with race-based policies such as job reservation undermining economic growth, the government would never have the economic strength to fully implement separate development. Graaff stressed the importance of economic growth for maintaining prosperity and hence 'harmonious race relations', and for ensuring sufficient military strength to secure 'us the freedom and the power to make our own decisions in respect of our race problems'.[31]

But Minister Viljoen accused the UP of taking a 'materialist' approach to labour issues while disregarding social considerations.[32] Economic considerations, he insisted, had 'never been decisive'[33] for the NP, for which 'the continued existence of separate White people' was far more

---

[27] See Mariotti and Van Zyl-Hermann, 'Policy, practice and perception'.
[28] Hansard Vol. 29 Column 2052, 19 August 1970.
[29] Hansard Vol. 30 Column 3398, 4 September 1970.
[30] Hansard Vol. 29 Column 2058–65, 19 August 1970; Vol. 30 Column 3289, 3 September 1970.
[31] Hansard Vol. 29 Column 2056, 19 August 1970.
[32] Hansard Vol. 34 Column 6991, 18 May 1971. See also Vol. 34 Column 6986, 7007, 18 May 1971; Vol. 39 Column 6722, 8 May 1972.
[33] Hansard Vol. 34 Column 6991–2, 18 May 1971.

important than 'temporary' economic benefits.[34] The UP retorted that the government was following a 'poor but white' economic policy[35] – referring to the Verwoerdian economic aphorism of 'better poor and white than rich and mixed'.[36] This NP rhetoric certainly challenges observations in the scholarship that by the 1970s the NP had become the party of business, emphasising the importance of economic growth and prioritising the interests of corporate Afrikanerdom over those of working-class whites.[37] Viljoen did appeal to workers to reflect seriously on further wage demands, for the sake of curbing inflation.[38]

Central to the NP's defence of its labour and economic policies was the imperative of protecting white labour as a fundamental prerequisite for the survival of the white race in South Africa. In defending job reservation policies, Viljoen insisted that protecting white workers was a matter of 'national honour' that took precedence over economic growth, and that whites' position in South Africa could not be maintained without job reservation.[39] Meanwhile, W. S. J. Grobler, Nationalist MP for the mineworkers' constituency of Springs, castigated the UP's call for the abolition of job reservation as a murderous readiness 'to hang the white man and the white worker from the gallows of labour integration'.[40] The terms in which the NP expressed its commitment to South Africa's traditional labour pattern – of which job reservation constituted the 'statutory pedestal'[41] – testified to its view of white labour as integral to safeguarding white power and identity at large.

Such Nationalist rhetoric – which reflected the established wisdom of workers as the vanguard of whiteness in South Africa – was closely connected to the ruling party's much more pragmatic awareness of white working-class power. It is clear that white labour was seen as commanding significant industrial muscle in this period. The NP repeatedly

---

[34] Hansard Vol. 34 Column 7006, 18 May 1971. See also Vol. 30 Column 3312, 3 September 1970; Vol. 34 Column 6986, 6990, 18 May 1971; Vol. 39 Column 6721, 8 May 1972.
[35] Hansard Vol. 32 Column 1447, 23 February 1971; Vol. 39 Column 6693, 8 May 1972.
[36] O'Meara, *Forty Lost Years*, p. 266.
[37] O'Meara, *Forty Lost Years*, pp. 78–9, 120, 139–40; S. Terreblanche, *Lost in Transformation? South Africa's search for a new future since 1986* (Johannesburg: KMM Review Publishing Company, 2012), p. 54; Grundlingh, 'Are we Afrikaners getting too rich?', p. 159.
[38] Hansard Vol. 32 Column 214, 3 February 1971.
[39] Hansard Vol. 39, Column 6655–6, 5 May 1972. NP speakers consistently emphasised the close connection between labour relations and race relations in this manner. See Hansard Vol. 30 Column 3416, 4 September 1970; Vol. 34 Column 6965, 17 May 1971.
[40] Hansard Vol. 30 Column 3303, 3 September 1970.
[41] Hansard Vol. 34 Column 7001, 18 May 1971.

insisted that forcing change on white workers would lead to debilitating strike action – variously expressed as an 'explosion',[42] 'chaos',[43] 'racial tension',[44] and 'revolt'[45] on the scale of '1922'[46] – leaving the country facing ruin.[47] The UP seemed to share this wariness, at least early in the decade, and insisted that none of the changes it was proposing would be implemented without consulting white unions, thus ensuring that white workers' position in industry would be maintained.[48] If such statements are to be believed, there is a sense in which the power to determine the nature and pace of any changes in labour patterns or legislation lay not with politicians but with white workers in the early 1970s.

But it was not only white workers' industrial power that loomed large in parliamentary debates. The NP showed a distinct awareness of white workers' political power at the ballot box. It took care to portray itself as 'the worker's party', insisting that white workers consistently voted for it 'because they trust the NP'[49] and that its labour policies sprung from the political mandate it had received from white workers.[50] MPs from working-class constituencies affirmed this in Parliament, urging the NP on behalf of white workers to continue to entrench their privileged position in law.[51] Indeed, on the eve of a by-election in Brakpan, the NP MP for Stilfontein reminded the Party that it had been brought to power in 1948 on the back of white workers' votes.[52] For its part, the NP sought to leverage the weight of white working-class political opinion against the Opposition. NP politicians often challenged the UP to explain the practical implications of its proposed labour changes, pointing out that white workers were 'entitled' to be given clarity on what a future under the UP would look like.[53] This revealed a political power balance in which parties were understood to be answerable to white labour. The UP, in turn, accused the NP of fearing white workers and being held

---

[42] Hansard Vol. 30 Column 3290, 3 September 1970.
[43] Hansard Vol. 30 Column 3293, 3 September 1970; Vol. 34 Column 6957, 17 May 1971.
[44] Hansard Vol. 30 Column 3393, 4 September 1970.
[45] Hansard Vol. 34 Column 6935, 17 May 1971.
[46] Hansard Vol. 34 Column 6950, 17 May 1971.
[47] Hansard Vol. 34 Column 6989, 18 May 1971.
[48] Hansard Vol. 30 Column 3290, 3 September 1970; Vol. 30 Column 3403, 3414, 4 September 1970.
[49] Hansard Vol. 34 Column 6989, 18 May 1971.
[50] Hansard Vol. 30 Column3396, 4 September 1970; Vol. 32 Column 1459, 23 February 1971; Vol. 34 Column 6956, 17 May 1971.
[51] Hansard Vol. 32 Column 1446, 23 February 1971.
[52] Hansard Vol. 39, 6696–8, 8 May 1972.
[53] Hansard Vol. 29 Column 2074, 19 August 1970; Vol. 34 Column 6934, 17 May 1971; Vol. 39 Column 6691, 6727, 8 May 1972.

hostage to working-class demands.[54] In addition to their industrial power, white workers' political clout and historical role in the social alliance thus continued to carry considerable weight in the early 1970s.

Indeed, this decade saw working-class power figure as a formidable force across the Western world – of which white South Africa considered itself a part. At the time, the USA and several European countries were plagued by confrontations between powerful labour movements and governments. Britain in particular saw widespread industrial action rapidly develop into a real political crisis for consecutive Conservative and Labour governments.[55] In South Africa, this international labour turmoil served as a constant reminder to those on the government benches of the industrial and political power that organised labour commanded, particularly in times of economic trouble. NP MPs were therefore quick to point out how, compared with the rampant strike action and growing unemployment characterising other parts of the world, South Africa was enjoying unparalleled industrial peace. This was attributed to NP labour policies that provided white workers with statutory protection and hence ensured working-class contentment.[56] Viljoen labelled South Africa's labour legislation the 'best in the world today', adding that if Britain had the same calibre of labour legislation, it would not be facing its umpteenth strike. 'At this very moment, Mr Heath is engaged in drafting legislation similar to our Industrial Conciliation Act,'[57] Viljoen boasted in 1971, in reference to the British Prime Minister's bitter struggle to appease British unions.[58] Speaking on the subject of worldwide inflation, Graaff also acknowledged the power of trade unions, musing that 'no government that wishes to stay in power dares either to disappoint the worker, or ... to demand that he lives within his country's means'.[59]

The NP made sure that its commitment to white workers was also communicated outside Parliament. In a 1970 pamphlet issued by the Party's Information Service – probably for distribution in white working-

---

[54] Hansard Vol. 32 Column 1478, 23 February 1971; Vol. 34 Column 6960, 6972, 17 May 1971.
[55] D. Childs, *Britain since 1945: a political history* (London: Routledge, 2006); D. Reynolds, *One World Divisible: a global history since 1945* (London: Penguin Books, 2000), p. 455, 404–7; D. Powell, *British Politics and the Labour Question, 1986–1990* (London: Macmillan, 1992), pp. 115–46; D. Clawson and M. A. Clawson, 'What has happened to the US labor movement? Union decline and renewal', *Annual Review of Sociology* 26 (1999), p. 97.
[56] Hansard Vol. 30 Column 3293, 3317, 3325, 3 September 1970; Vol. 32 Column 1446, 1469, 23 February 1971; Vol. 34 Column 6926, 17 May 1971.
[57] Hansard Vol. 32 Column 1476, 23 February 1971.
[58] See Childs, *Britain since 1945*, pp. 162–78.
[59] Hansard Vol. 29 Column 2057–8, 19 August 1970.

class constituencies – it asserted that white workers 'determine the security and welfare of our country'. Revealingly, this statement was immediately placed in the context of labour unrest in Europe, where, it was claimed, workers' perceptions of insecurity had led them to 'paralyse' their national economies. The NP reaffirmed its commitment to the statutory protection of whites' position in industry and mining from undermining by 'non-white' workers with a lower standard of living.[60] Protecting white workers was clearly deemed in the national interest.

Such assurances were repeated on public platforms. Speaking in industrial Vereeniging in October 1972 in support of the NP's new local candidate, one F. W. de Klerk, Marais Viljoen rejected UP and Progressive Party (PP) calls for the reorganisation of labour. Viljoen emphasised that the NP would allow non-white workers to perform semi-skilled work only if there was not enough white labour available, and then only with trade unions' consent, because 'we will not permit our traditions and way of life to be eroded'.[61] Vereeniging's white workers were clearly listening. The next day, Wessel Bornman, general secretary of the South African Iron, Steel and Allied Industries Union, wrote to Viljoen to congratulate him on his Vereeniging speech. His union was heartened by the Minister's views on job reservation, Bornman wrote, and encouraged to know that Viljoen's unambiguous assurance regarding white displacement 'amounts to an open door for us.'[62]

Bornman's claim to government favour was not out of step with the NP's own statements in Parliament about its partiality for conservative white workers' interests. The Minister saw the all-white SACLA and its right-wing constituent, the Co-ordinating Council of South African Trade Unions (to which Bornman's union belonged), as the true voice of white workers – and these bodies demanded job reservation.[63] Viljoen provided explicit reassurance to the MWU, another union affiliated with the Co-ordinating Council, that protection of its members in the mining industry would be maintained.[64] As a powerful union in the key economic industry, the MWU was known for wielding influence in the

---

[60] Archive for Contemporary Affairs, University of the Free State, Bloemfontein (ARCA), Pamphlet Collection, P1.15, H. H. Smit, 'Security of the white worker' (Cape Town: Information Service of the National Party, 1970).
[61] As reported in F. Day, 'Whites won't lose jobs to Blacks – Viljoen', *Rand Daily Mail*, 18 October 1972.
[62] ARCA, PV14: Marais Viljoen, 11/1/17 Scrapbooks – General 1972-5, Wessel Bornman to B. M. F. Hall, 18 October 1972.
[63] Hansard Vol. 32 Column 1446, 1459–60, 23 February 1971. Viljoen noted that the Co-ordinating Council represented some 200,000 white workers.
[64] Hansard Vol. 34 Column 6929–30, 17 May 1971; Vol. 34 Column 6998, 18 May 1971.

Figure 2.1 Marais Viljoen, Minister of Labour, on the political stage.
Source: *Die Vaderland*, 9 December 1975

corridors of government power.[65] Meanwhile, Viljoen consistently expressed his suspicion, and later open rejection, of the multiracial TUCSA, which supported the scrapping of job reservation and advocated affiliated union rights for African workers. TUCSA did not represent the majority of white workers, and certainly did not have their interests at heart, claimed Viljoen, who branded it 'so liberal that they are actually pink'.[66]

Skills shortages remained foremost on the labour agenda throughout 1972. By this point, the UP had shifted its position, and now, like TUCSA, it advocated affiliated membership of existing white unions for black workers alongside the abolition of job reservation.[67] The UP argued that incorporating black workers into the fold of organised labour in this manner would bring them under white control.[68] The maintenance of industrial peace and economic growth, rather than a concern for black workers, motivated this new policy position. Indeed, black workers and their interests remained largely absent from labour debates in this

[65] Visser, *Van MWU tot Solidariteit*, p. 121.
[66] Hansard Vol. 34 Column 6934–5, 17 May 1971. Also Vol. 30 Column 3403, 4 September 1970; Vol. 34 Column 6955–6, 17 May 1971; Vol. 34 Column 7001, 18 May 1971; Vol. 37 Column 3107, 3 February 1972; Vol. 39 Column 6682–3, 8 May 1972.
[67] Hansard Vol. 39 Column 6698, 6723, 8 May 1972. For shifts in UP policy and the struggles in its own ranks, see T. Eksteen, 'The decline of the United Party, 1970–1977' (MA thesis, University of Cape Town, 1982).
[68] Hansard Vol. 39 Column 6723, 8 May 1972.

period. Minister Viljoen's statements on labour matters typically took only white workers into account – and occasionally coloured and Indian workers – reflecting the NP's denial of the integral role African labour played in the South African economy.[69] The PP's only MP, Helen Suzman, was the lone voice warning the political establishment that they disregarded the majority of the labour force at their own peril.[70] For the ruling party, however, white survival remained dependent on a strict commitment to the racial order through the maintenance of the colour bar and the exclusion of African workers from industrial citizenship – even if this came at the cost of economic growth. Hence Nationalist MPs assured white workers that, as long as the NP governed South Africa, job reservation would remain on the statute book.[71]

Of course, as we have seen, the NP's obstinate rhetorical adherence to job reservation did not mean that the policy was not being eroded in practice. But even this process reflected the power of white labour. The suspension or circumvention of job reservation determinations typically came about through negotiations that saw white workers bargain for financial and other benefits in exchange for their willingness to fragment the labour process to allow for the greater utilisation of black labour. But the policy remained in place, and there is evidence that, even where job reservation was not being applied, white labour's recourse to it kept employers in check.[72] Of course, this recourse depended on favourable relations between white labour and the government and Minister of Labour.

Debates around job reservation in the early 1970s were a reaction to the emerging contradictions of apartheid policy in the context of the stalling economy. The NP–UP political establishment may have held opposing views in this regard, but their parliamentary swords crossed without anyone calling into doubt the racial order on which South Africa's labour regime was built. These were the last debates of a white-only world in which white interests – whether those of white workers or of the 'white race' in South Africa more broadly – remained a legitimate priority. It was a world that, for the most part, had not yet

---

[69] Viljoen stated, for instance, that there was 'no unemployment' in South Africa – a declaration hardly applicable to the African labour corps in the face of a growing oversupply of labour. Hansard Vol. 29 Column 2068, 19 August 1970.
[70] Hansard Vol. 30 Column 3406, 4 September 1970. See also her warnings in Hansard Vol. 34 Column 6949, 17 May 1971; Vol. 39 Column 6718, 8 May 1972.
[71] Hansard Vol. 32 Column 1482, 23 February 1971; Vol. 39 Column 6656, 5 May 1972; Vol. 39 Column 6703, 6721, 6739, 8 May 1972.
[72] Mariotti and Van Zyl-Hermann, 'Policy, practice and perception'.

realised that black workers were also 'human beings with souls'.[73] Durban 1973 would change this.

The Durban strikes and emerging tensions

On 13 February 1973, Frederick le Roux, NP MP for the working-class constituency of Hercules, rose in Parliament to introduce a motion on labour. With the country caught up in a great upsurge of African labour unrest, his proposal that the House 'express its appreciation to the government for its labour policy and the machinery it has created to bring about and maintain industrial peace'[74] must have been greeted with dropping jaws on one side of the House and stiff upper lips on the other. From early January 1973, starting in Durban and spreading to other industrial centres, African labour rose in a series of strikes that ripped through the country's manufacturing sector. Some 160 strikes involving over 60,000 workers took place in the first three months of 1973. The issue of union recognition and labour rights loomed large alongside workers' demands for improved wages. By the end of the year, some 100,000 black workers had engaged in industrial action, and 229,000 shifts had been lost – over seven times the number lost through African strikes in the eight preceding years. Whereas in the past strikes had readily been quashed and unruly workers replaced, the growth of manufacturing by this time had seen African workers acquire skills vital to the running of industry. Dramatic displays of black industrial action and the re-emergence of African trade unions rapidly became a feature of the South African labour arena over the course of the 1970s. African grievances could no longer be suppressed or ignored – internal as well as international economic confidence in the country was at stake.[75] 'I think we all realise that a new era in industrial relations in South Africa has been rung in as a result of what has happened,' the leader of the Opposition told Prime Minister Vorster in response to the Durban strikes.[76]

---

[73] As Prime Minister John Vorster was to tell the House of Assembly on 9 February 1973. Giliomee, *The Last Afrikaner Leaders*, pp. 99–100.
[74] Hansard Vol. 42 Column 529, 13 February 1973.
[75] A. Lichtenstein, '"A measure of democracy": works committees, black workers, and industrial citizenship in South Africa, 1973–1979', *South African Historical Journal* 67, no. 2 (2015), pp. 114–15; S. Friedman, *Building Tomorrow Today: African workers in trade unions 1970–1984* (Johannesburg: Ravan Press, 1987), pp. 37–40; Du Toit, *Capital and Labour*, pp. 244–53, 327; Clark and Worger, *South Africa*, pp. 75–7.
[76] Quoted in Du Toit, *Capital and Labour*, p. 325.

The UP scoffed at Le Roux's 'ironic' motion, condemning the government's labour policy and its failure to ensure decent standards of living for all workers in South Africa.[77] The NP's stance towards blacks was misguided and hypocritical – regarding them as strangers in the white economy who were responsible enough for self-government in the Bantustans, but not for trade unionism.[78] The Opposition warned of the danger black discontent posed to white survival: failure to address the fundamental problems revealed through the Durban strikes would see the country face extended industrial strife, 'bedevil[ling] our race relations' and even 'trigger[ing] off a holocaust'.[79] Without the 'peace and the goodwill of the Bantu in the labour pattern of South Africa, there is no future for the White man in this country,'[80] UP MP for Maitland, Tony Hickman, argued. The Opposition demanded Viljoen resign and that a commission of inquiry be appointed to conduct a complete reappraisal of the labour scene and devise new labour policies.[81] For its part, the UP now advocated a tiered system of negotiating rights for black workers based on class and skill rather than race: the 'urbanized, sophisticated' African in 'civilized', skilled work should receive union rights alongside whites, but the unskilled majority should make use of works committees.[82]

The Nationalist labour establishment did its best to downplay the extent and significance of African industrial unrest. Behind closed doors, the Cabinet agreed that the strikes were mainly due to rising living costs, and resolved to look into how the USA and UK were dealing with this problem.[83] In Parliament, however, Viljoen and NP MPs from working-class constituencies portrayed the Durban strikes as little more than a wage dispute between workers and employers, or the work of external 'agitators' looking to disrupt South Africa's traditional labour pattern. They maintained that black workers wanted improved wages but were otherwise essentially satisfied and not interested in trade union recognition.[84] Nationalist MPs reproached the Opposition for exploiting

---

[77] Hansard Vol. 42 Column 534, 13 February 1973.
[78] Hansard Vol. 42 Column 540–1, 552–3, 13 February 1973.
[79] Hansard Vol. 42 Column 578, 13 February 1973.
[80] Hansard Vol. 42 Column 539, 13 February 1973.
[81] Hansard Vol. 42 Column 1074, 20 February 1973; Vol. 43 Column 5450, 5437, 5446, 1 May 1973.
[82] Hansard Vol. 42 Column 1051, 1054–5, 20 February 1973.
[83] National Archives of South Africa, Pretoria (NA), SAB (National Archives Repository – Public Records of Government since 1910), CAB 1/1/5, Kabinet: Notuleregister 1973, 28.3.73.
[84] Hansard Vol. 42 Column 1072, 20 February 1973; Vol. 43 Column 5484, 5507, 5547, 1 May 1973. This also reflected the attitude of employers, says Lichtenstein, 'A measure of democracy', p. 121.

the strikes to further its agenda of labour 'integration' and affiliated trade union membership for black workers in coordination with the 'leftist' TUCSA.[85] While the UP argued that black labour discontent posed a threat to white survival, the NP insisted, as before, that the real danger lay in provoking white labour. P. R. de Jager, NP MP for Mayfair, warned of a repeat of 1922 should white workers' feeling of security be undermined;[86] P. Bodenstein, representing industrial Rustenburg, predicted that any change to labour patterns would cause industrial upset in South Africa that would be worse than the current 'chronic' strikes in England;[87] while Vereeniging's young new MP F. W. de Klerk spoke damningly about how any concessions to UP labour policy would leave white workers feeling that there was 'no future for them any more'. This, he predicted, was sure to result in the greatest labour unrest the country had ever known.[88]

But there were also sections of the NP, including Prime Minister Vorster, who realised that the black workforce's demands had to be taken seriously, at least in as far as they pertained to the improvement of what were recognised as starvation wages. Historian Hermann Giliomee suggests that Vorster was aware of the threat black workers' discontent posed to state security and white rule.[89] Indeed, the display of African labour power had clearly unnerved the ruling party. This was revealed in two important concessions made in 1973. The first saw Viljoen act swiftly to raise the minimum wage for unskilled workers, while the second saw the NP amend the 1953 Native Labour Act to provide African workers with limited strike and negotiation rights. Specifically, the amended Act sought to revitalise the existing system of factory-based committees as forums in which black workers could meet with employers to discuss their grievances and interests. These committees had little actual bargaining power and were often employer-controlled. But the NP championed them as effective negotiation structures for African workers, thus legitimising blacks' continued exclusion from the organised labour movement and its collective bargaining mechanisms.[90] This attempt to

---

[85] Hansard Vol. 42 Column 532, 13 February 1973.
[86] Hansard Vol. 43 Column 5483, 1 May 1973.
[87] Hansard Vol. 43 Column 5539, 1 May 1973.
[88] Hansard Vol. 43 Column 5521-2, 1 May 1973.
[89] Giliomee, *The Last Afrikaner Leaders*, pp. 99–100. See also Friedman, *Building Tomorrow Today*, p. 50.
[90] Friedman, *Building Tomorrow Today*, pp. 53–4, 66–7; Lichtenstein, 'A measure of democracy'; Giliomee, *The Last Afrikaner Leaders*, p. 100; A. Lichtenstein, '"We do not think that the Bantu is ready for labour unions": remaking South Africa's apartheid workplace in the 1970s', *South African Historical Journal* 69, no. 2 (2017), pp. 215–35.

forestall further unrest and demands for workers' rights reveals a new awareness in the NP of the potential threat black labour posed to white power – even though it is less clear whether this threat pertained to the damage African industrial action would do to the economy (as with the UP), or the threat African labour rights posed to white workers' position. Apprehension at the slumbering power of black workers occasionally surfaced in Nationalist MP's statements. Some pointed to the way in which black workers, if allowed to unionise, would affiliate themselves with the ANC and with 'communists'. This would lead to a push for black industrial rights which would undermine white supremacy and South Africa's 'traditional national policy', and eventually culminate in 'one man one vote'.[91] Even though reverence for white working-class power still overshadowed NP statements during labour debates, the government was increasingly realising that it was facing a powerful black labour force *as well as* a formidable corps of white workers.

Figure 2.2 Minister Viljoen meets members of the African workers' liaison committee of the Alusaf aluminium smelter in Richards Bay, 9 December 1974.
Source: Archive for Contemporary Affairs, University of the Free State, South Africa

[91] Hansard Vol. 42 Column 1057, 1046, 20 February 1973.

The general election year of 1974 saw Minister Viljoen eager to exalt the NP's efforts to diffuse the country's labour problems. He claimed that South Africa had 'virtually no unemployment' and that it enjoyed industrial peace because the NP made 'necessary and appropriate' negotiations machinery available to both black and white workers. In the process, productivity had been improved and skills shortages no longer constituted a serious bottleneck. While such claims sought to portray the apartheid economy as back on track, the Minister's statements revealed the shifts that had occurred in the ruling party's position: Viljoen now boasted that the NP was encouraging adjustment of the traditional labour pattern to facilitate black advancement into more skilled work in white areas. Crucially, however, these statements were always carefully and deliberately bracketed by assurances to white workers that the NP would continue to protect their position.[92] Indeed, Viljoen still represented white workers' industrial cooperation and loyalty as the highest prize in the labour arena. Had it not been for the NP's commitment to the white worker's security, adjustments to the labour pattern could have seen him 'resorting to the strike weapon in order to safeguard his position'.[93] An NP pamphlet issued around the time of the election similarly sought to convince white workers of the ruling party's commitment to their interests. In simple bullet points, the pamphlet proclaimed the government's dedication to racial separation and white supremacy in the workplace and in trade unions. The pamphlet confidently claimed that 'the white worker's security is guaranteed' – but in contrast to the NP pamphlet issued in 1970, no mention was made of job reservation, nor of keeping blacks out of white jobs.[94]

When the electorate returned the NP to power, Viljoen interpreted this as white workers' continued endorsement, telling opposition parties that '[t]rade unions are today those forces which can cause governments to fall or, if they have mercy on them, allow them to remain in office. I think Mr Heath and Mr Wilson could both testify to this. The political power of trade unions is a world-wide phenomenon today.'[95] Indeed, in the wake of continuing disputes between Heath's Conservative government and trade unions in the UK, the Tories had fought the February

---

[92] Hansard Vol. 47 Column 273–81, 6 February 1974; Vol. 51 Column 3015, 16 September 1974.
[93] Hansard Vol. 47 Column 276, 6 February 1974.
[94] ARCA, Pamphlet Collection, P1.41, R McLachlan (NP MP for Westdene)/Federal Council of the National Party: 'Die Nasionale Regering sorg vir die Blanke Werker' (Johannesburg: Brill Broers, n.d.).
[95] Hansard Vol. 51 Column 3023, 16 September 1974.

1974 general election under the slogan 'Who governs Britain?' The outcome saw the Conservatives replaced by Harold Wilson's Labour.[96]

Viljoen continued, boasting that 190,000 white workers represented by SACLA benefited from the government's policy of job reservation.[97] When the UP claimed to have consulted with white unions on the matter of blacks being included in the organised labour movement, the Minister challenged the UP to consult with the MWU and the steelworkers' association, the right-wing Co-ordinating Council's two heavyweights.[98] He warned the UP and the PP that they were ignoring the voices and interests of these white workers at their peril, pointing to these workers' industrial power. Although white workers formed a minority in the mining industry – only 85,000 white workers against 641,000 blacks – if whites were to withdraw their labour and go on strike, the mines – and South Africa's economy with them – would come to a standstill, and the country would 'experience a disaster ... which would make you shudder'.[99] The NP's commitment to maintaining job reservation and the colour bar meant that 'the workers of this country will ensure that it [the NP] will govern this country for all eternity',[100] Viljoen concluded in a megalomanic flourish. Meanwhile, opposition parties called on the government to stop trading on working-class anxieties and instead re-educate white workers to remove their 'mental bloc' on black advancement that the NP had created.[101]

Jood Henning, MP for the steel-producing Vanderbijlpark, became NP labour whip and leader of the Party caucus's labour group from 1975, and his statements may be seen as reflecting discussions in this forum.[102] Henning spoke at length about the government's steps towards improving the utilisation of labour, pointing in particular to the expansion of black work in the building industry and coloured workers being trained as mechanics. Denouncing the Opposition's portrayals of job reservation as 'shackles' restricting the utilisation of available labour, Henning expressed his commitment to Section 77 of the Industrial Conciliation Act. It was due to such protective legislation that the government was able to adjust labour patterns while maintaining industrial

---

[96] M. Clapson, *The Routledge Companion to Britain in the Twentieth Century* (Abingdon: Routledge, 2009), p. 98, 121; Powell, *British Politics and the Labour Question*, pp. 132–3.
[97] Hansard Vol. 42 Column 1097, 20 February 1973; Vol. 43 Column 5501, 1 May 1973.
[98] Hansard Vol. 51 Column 3028, 16 September 1974.
[99] Hansard Vol. 51 Column 3115, 17 September 1974; Vol. 51 Column 3028–31, 16 September 1974.
[100] Hansard Vol. 51 Column 3031, 16 September 1974.
[101] Hansard Vol. 43 Column 5565, 1 May 1973; Vol. 42 Column 1038–9, 20 February 1973.
[102] ARCA, PV408: National Party Caucus, 'Swepery 1975', 29-1-75.

peace and the confidence of its labour force. In its 'multinational' context, NP labour legislation 'give[s] every worker in South Africa peace of mind'. Job reservation protected all workers, not only whites, from 'unnecessary competition', he explained, pointing in particular to coloured workers of the Western Cape's furniture, building, and clothing industries, who, he claimed, would long have been displaced by black labour without Section 77.[103] As usual, opposition politicians scoffed at such views. Gideon Jacobs, UP spokesman on labour and MP for Hillbrow, tabled a private member's motion calling for the establishment of a commission of inquiry into labour relations, with specific reference to the labour requirements of the mining industry. The UP, like the PP, now showed itself in favour of full union rights for Africans. The PP's Alex Boraine derided the government's claim that its newly instituted committee system for African workers was equal to the mechanisms in place for white workers: Arrie Paulus's MWU, he scoffed, 'would certainly not for one moment agree to disband that union and form a works committee or liaison committee'.[104] Yet the NP continued to insist that its labour legislation was sound and ensured that the country enjoyed 'peace, prosperity and development', while Europe languished in strike action, lawlessness, unemployment, and bankruptcy.[105]

But there are indications that the NP's greater willingness after Durban to adjust the traditional labour pattern was causing tension in its relationship with conservative white labour. This is revealed in a letter from the MWU's general secretary to the Prime Minister. In it, Paulus pointed to the increasing tendency for traditionally white jobs to be performed by 'non-whites' and expressed his union's concern about the implications for white employment – specifically for unskilled whites. Paulus impressed on Vorster the need to consider his letter in a 'serious light', warning that he had been instructed by his union to inform the Prime Minister that, if the government failed to change its current course, the MWU would withdraw its support for the NP. 'We hope and trust that we can continue to build on the MWU and Government's established relationship of cooperation, and that the Government will still act as patron of the white worker,' Paulus concluded.[106]

Developments beyond Parliament provide further insight into how parts of the NP-aligned Afrikaner elite responded to the emerging

---

[103] Hansard Vol. 55 Column 3117, 21 March 1975.
[104] Quoted in F. Fisher, 'Parliamentary debate on labour', *South African Labour Bulletin* 2, no. 1 (1975), p. 48.
[105] Hansard Vol. 55 Column 3117, 21 March 1975.
[106] ARCA, PV14: Marais Viljoen, I A23/3 Mineworkers 1968-1975, P. J. Paulus to B. J. Vorster, 27 February 1975.

economic and political crisis. Behind closed doors, the Broederbond's Executive Council established an ad hoc committee for labour matters at its 6 June 1975 meeting to study the implications of the country's changing labour scene and make recommendations for action.[107] The Broederbond's operation as a closed society whose meetings took place in secret and with a strict commitment to confidentiality gave it the ability to freely express opinions and discuss scenarios that could not be mooted in public. Indeed, during its first sittings, the labour committee resolved to deal only with labour issues that needed addressing on a 'confidential level', leaving the rest to public debate or for government departments to address.[108] The Broederbond material therefore often contrasts sharply with the uncompromising obstinacy that the NP had to maintain in Parliament.

Although the archival record is fragmented, this Broederbond documentation provides valuable insight into how this section of the Afrikaner elite – with its close connections to the ruling party – saw the developing labour situation and considered white workers' position within it. With Broederbond members including Afrikaners in influential positions in all sectors of society, these were sure to be well-informed discussions. Indeed, the labour committee's founding members included Attie Nieuwoudt, president of SACLA, Wim de Villiers, managing director of General Mining, and F. W. de Klerk, NP MP for Vereeniging, who by 1978 would be a member of the cabinet.[109] More members were added to the committee over the following two years.

While the NP's quick-fix Bantu Labour Relations Amendment Act sought to paper over widening cracks in the functioning of the apartheid labour regime, the Broederbond's labour committee aimed to deal with the fundamental problems revealed by the Durban strikes. In contrast to the NP in Parliament, the secret committee could admit to the tensions between apartheid's political-ideological and economic imperatives. In its meetings, it acknowledged that certain apartheid policies mitigated against economic growth in order to maintain white identity. At the same time, it recognised that insufficient economic growth would have disastrous political and social consequences as far as black unemployment was concerned, making it impossible to pursue policies not focused on

---

[107] Erfenisstigting Argief, Pretoria (Erfenisstigting), Afrikaner Broederbond Collection (AB) 1/1/23, 1975/6-7, URanotDB, Notule van 'n UR-vergadering, 6 June 1975; AB 1/1/23, 1975/1-5 URanotDB, Notule UR-Dagbestuurvergadering, 2 May 1975.
[108] Erfenisstigting, AB 10/7, 10/7/3, 'Verslag van 'n vergadering van die komitee i.v.m. arbeidsaangeleenthede', 16 July 1975; 'Verslag van 'n vergadering van die komitee i.v.m. arbeidsaangeleenthede', 3 September 1975.
[109] Erfenisstigting, AB 10/7, 10/7/3, N. B. to T. A. Conradie, 23 June 1975.

facilitating economic expansion.[110] The committee's minutes show that this conundrum converged on the issue of workers' rights, privileges, and status in South Africa, as discussions on white workers and existing discriminatory legislation spontaneously slipped into debates about black workers' rights, negotiating mechanisms, and industrial action. An early discussion on the reasons for the 'delicacy' of South Africa's labour situation saw the committee point specifically to early twentieth-century white proletarianisation in the context of competition with black labour as shaping whites' struggle for survival in South Africa.[111] It was therefore understood that the fortunes of white and black labour were fundamentally entangled.

While, in Parliament, debates on white labour revolved mainly around workers' ostensible support for or resistance to changes in established labour patterns, the Broederbond's discussion of white workers took quite a different turn to focus on negotiating mechanisms. This saw the committee pursue two revealing ideas: namely, the infiltration of white trade union leadership, and works committees as alternatives to white unions.

The issue of white trade union leadership emerged early in the committee's discussions in response to a memorandum on the state of white trade unionism prepared by Broeder De Klerk. The document emphasised the importance of white unions in South Africa, highlighting their role in facilitating changes to the traditional division of labour and in combating inflation. Drawing on communication with 'responsible persons' in industry, however, it questioned whether current trade unionists constituted the 'right kind of leader' who would 'at all times play their key role in the country's economy with responsibility and balance, in terms of properly founded principles which accord with the Afrikaners' Calvinist life- and worldview'.[112] Clearly, in this assessment, not all white union leaders were supporting what were deemed to be desirable goals for ensuring white survival: changing existing labour patterns and combating inflation, most probably by curbing wage demands. De Klerk called on the Broederbond to take action and ensure that a 'substantial number of responsible and competent Afrikaners become involved *in all levels of trade unionism* to take the lead and fill key positions'.[113] Despite

---

[110] Erfenisstigting, AB 10/7, 10/7/3, 'Verslag van 'n vergadering van die komitee i.v.m. arbeidsaangeleenthede', 8 October 1975.
[111] Erfenisstigting, AB 10/7, 10/7/3, 'Verslag van 'n vergadering van die komitee i.v.m. arbeidsaangeleenthede', 8 October 1975.
[112] Erfenisstigting, AB 10/7, 10/7/3, 'Blanke Vakbonde', Arbeidskomitee, 1 December 1975.
[113] Erfenisstigting, AB 10/7, 10/7/3, 'Blanke Vakbonde', Arbeidskomitee, 1 December 1975 (emphasis in original).

assertions that he was not advocating union infiltration and takeover, subsequent proposals for how this might be achieved clearly suggest otherwise. De Klerk proposed that the Broederbond actively draws more organised workers into its fold, and ensured that 'positive Afrikaners' found their way into leadership positions in trade unions. He also raised the option of establishing a 'separate organisation', 'like the erstwhile "GVA"' – but he later dismissed the idea, as the '"GVA" … was abandoned in the past'.[114] The GVA (Gemeenskap Volk en Arbeid/Society of People and Labour) had been the secret labour wing of the Broederbond. It had been founded in 1962 in response to the awareness – similar to that expressed by De Klerk in 1975 – that 'fellow Afrikaners in the industrial sector' (read: workers) were not well represented in the organisation's ranks. This was seen as impairing the Broederbond's ability to exercise its leadership and influence at 'all layers of national life' – and the GVA was established to remedy the situation.[115]

The labour committee's acceptance of De Klerk's memorandum reveals a conviction that white labour needed to be brought under control – not unlike emerging African unions at the time.[116] The committee often framed this in terms of the idea that Afrikaners had not yet 'developed' very far along the path of trade unionism and required support[117] – a language strikingly similar to that used by Verwoerdian politicians to describe black workers' ostensible unsuitability for industrial citizenship.[118] This notion resurfaced time and again in the committee's discussions until its dissolution sometime after 1978, and was consistently connected to the ambition of placing more 'positive Afrikaners' in control of white unions.[119] There are few explicit indications in the committee's discussions of which trade unionists were deemed not of the 'right kind'. The economic goals outlined by

[114] Erfenisstigting, AB 10/7, 10/7/3, 'Blanke Vakbonde', Arbeidskomitee, 1 December 1975.
[115] Erfenisstigting, AB 3/1/3/ 3/65/arbeid 'Gemeenskap volk en arbeid, Jaarvergadering 1965; J. H. P. Serfontein, *Brotherhood of power: an exposé of the secret Afrikaner Broederbond* (London: Rex Collings, 1979), p. 108, 127. On the Broederbond's elitist membership by the 1970s, see also Adam and Giliomee, *Ethnic Power Mobilized*, pp. 247–9.
[116] Erfenisstigting, AB 10/7, 10/7/3, 'Verslag van 'n vergadering van die komitee i.v.m. arbeidsaangeleenthede', 1 December 1975.
[117] Erfenisstigting, AB 10/7, 10/7/3, 'Raamwerk vir 'n studie van die arbeidsituasie in die RSA', 1 July 1976; 'Verslag van 'n vergadering van die komitee i.v.m. arbeidsaangeleenthede', 17 September 1976; 'Verslag van 'n gesprek i.v.m. arbeidsaangeleenthede', 4 October 1978, p. 13, 17, 22.
[118] Lichtenstein, 'We do not think that the Bantu is ready for labour unions'.
[119] Erfenisstigting, AB 10/7, 10/7/3, 'Blanke Vakbonde', Arbeidskomitee, 1 December 1975.

De Klerk were most likely to have elicited resistance from conservative, lesser-skilled white workers, many of whom would have been organised in unions affiliated to SACLA. Indeed, the only trade union explicitly identified as a cause of concern was the MWU. A separate memorandum on the union noted that it was the 'strongest Afrikaner-controlled union' but expressed concern over its leadership's tendency to rally its members against the government by claiming that mineworkers could not rely on government protection. This held the danger that this 'crucial' body of workers and their families might have become 'suspicious' of and 'alienated' from Afrikaner cultural, political, and employers' organisations. Hence, the memorandum recommended that a concerted effort be made to draw the MWU's leaders and organisers into local Broederbond-controlled cultural bodies. The need to address miners' resistance to the 'more effective' utilisation of black labour in particular was highlighted.[120] The committee may well have had Arrie Paulus and the mineworkers he led in mind when their discussion noted the immense power and influence that a small group of organised unionists could exert, thus acknowledging the delicacy of the matter in the light of white workers' industrial power.[121]

The Broeders' critical stance towards the MWU's resistance to labour change indicated a shift in some Afrikaner elites' attitudes towards labour matters after Durban. In 1970, the Broederbond – like the NP – had expressed its commitment to maintaining the traditional pattern of labour in South Africa. It had argued that any adjustments to this pattern would be 'fatal to the welfare of the white worker and the survival of the Afrikaner', and it stated unequivocally that it was the white unions' task to *'increase* their resistance' to integration and concessions.[122] Only five years later, in the context of stalling economic growth and a rising black labour movement, the consensus on white survival had shifted – at least in Broederbond quarters – in favour of labour change. Upholding white working-class interests had once been considered paramount to white survival – by 1975, these committee discussions suggested that class interests were to be subjugated to broader national interests such as economic growth.[123]

---

[120] Erfenisstigting, AB 10/7, 10/7/3, 'Die Mynwerkersunie', document marked 'A', n.d. It is likely that the memorandum was drawn up in late 1975; see N. B. to J. G. H. Botha, 23 February 1976 in the same file.

[121] Erfenisstigting, AB 10/7, 10/7/3, 'Verslag van 'n vergadering van die komitee i.v.m. arbeidsaangeleenthede', 1 December 1975.

[122] Erfenisstigting, AB 3/1/3, 3/70/1/arbeid, 'Benutting van nie-blanke arbeid', 2 November 1970 (my emphasis).

[123] Not that there was unanimity in the Broederbond – the organisation was by definition plagued by the same *verligte–verkrampte* tensions as the NP. Contradictory opinions are

As the year's parliamentary session drew to a close, Minister Viljoen expressed the NP's satisfaction with its achievements on the labour front: yes, South Africa was battling inflation, as were all countries in the world, but it also enjoyed labour peace and full employment. Black workers had made great advances: they now enjoyed works committees – the 'most ideal system for South Africa' – benefited from improved wages, and were being employed as artisans in a variety of jobs recently still performed by white workers, thanks to the reclassification of jobs as well as the retraining of white, Indian, and coloured workers.[124] Most importantly, the NP enjoyed the support of white workers and never lost a by-election, thus reaffirming its mandate from voters.[125]

But all was not as well as the Minister sought to suggest. The re-emergence of African industrial action from 1973 had confronted the government with a new reality: the power to disrupt industry that NP politicians so readily attributed to white labour was being displayed by African workers. The result was a constellation of contradictory and mutually exclusive interests: conservative white labour insisted on the maintenance of the status quo, black workers demanded improved wages and industrial citizenship, and reformist sections of the NP and Afrikaner political elite sought ways to stimulate economic growth that required labour subservience. These emerging tensions would come to a head in 1976.

The turning point for labour: Soweto and the appointment of Wiehahn

It was with a sense of expectation that MPs assembled in the House on 14 June 1976. Their attention on that Monday morning was focused on the new Minister of Labour Fanie Botha, who was set to make his first speech as part of the labour vote. Marais Viljoen had announced his retirement to become President of the Senate late in 1975,[126] and the appointment of the Minister of Forestry and Water Affairs in his stead had come as a surprise – including to Botha himself.[127] The UP's Jacobs

---

evident in the labour committee, although the minutes rarely attribute statements to specific committee members, making the fault lines difficult to identify.
[124] Hansard Vol. 57 Column 8427, 16 June 1975; also Vol. 56 Column 4952–8, 5008, 28 April 1975.
[125] Hansard Vol. 56 Column 5004, 28 April 1975; Vol. 57 Column 8429–30, 16 June 1975.
[126] '43 jaar in politiek, maar geen klag teen koerante: Marias Viljoen kyk terug', *Die Vaderland*, 9 December 1975.
[127] Erfenisstigting, S. P. Botha Collection, Vol. 13, Scrapbook 6.8, 1976–8, letters collection; Fanie Botha interviewed by Wessel Visser, 27 May 2002. Botha, like his

opened the floor with a damning overview of the previous Minister's 'pedantic and stereotyped' approach to labour, which left him 'no room for manoeuvre'. Jacobs quipped that this was probably why Viljoen had received his recent 'Irish promotion'. Turning to Fanie Botha, Jacobs called on the incumbent to bring fresh and flexible solutions to the labour debate, and to act in the country's economic interest rather than continue his predecessor's strategy of using labour as a 'political playball' for securing votes.[128]

The UP's major concern was with the 'dangerous' growth of unrecognised black unions. It was imperative the government address this issue to secure what must be its primary aim: namely, economic growth.[129] In contrast to earlier in the decade, the importance of consulting with white unions to avoid provoking industrial action no longer featured as a UP concern. The newly constituted PRP similarly pointed to black labour representation and economic growth as the main issues demanding the new Minister's attention. Alex Boraine, PRP MP for Pinelands, warned that the government's continued denial of black labour rights was 'creating tension at a growing and alarming rate'. He reiterated opposition calls for the appointment of a commission of inquiry to address change in order to avoid 'confrontation'.[130]

Even before Botha's speech, a certain shift in tenor could be detected among NP MPs. MPs representing white working-class constituencies were still the main participants in the labour debate. While some, such as the representatives from Welkom and Hercules, stuck to the old refrain of the NP's commitment to white workers and their statutory protection,[131] statements by Vanderbijlpark's Jood Henning showed a change of emphasis. Henning, still chairman of the NP's labour group, emphasised that the ruling party was 'not ashamed to say that we shall make better use of black people' in jobs traditionally occupied by whites – in fact, this was already being done in 18,000 railway posts. Such statements may have been considered politically perilous in earlier years, given the NP's own statements about the need to protect the traditional labour pattern and the threat of white industrial and political vengeance if this were upset. But such statements were now noticeably absent from Henning's speech. Instead, he now stressed white unions' ostensible

---

predecessor, was a Broederbond member. I. Wilkins and H. Strydom, *The Super-Afrikaners: inside the Afrikaner Broederbond* (Johannesburg and Cape Town: Jonathan Ball, 2012), p. A11, A133.
[128] Hansard Vol. 63 Column 9069–70, 14 June 1976.
[129] Hansard Vol. 63 Column 9070–9, 14 June 1976.
[130] Hansard Vol. 63 Column 9089–97, 14 June 1976.
[131] Hansard Vol. 63 Column 9110–12, 9119–121, 14 June 1976.

willingness to assist in the process of black advancement and the reclassification of jobs, given their sense of responsibility towards the national interest and economic growth: 'the white worker of South Africa does not lack sense, nor are the trade unions unreasonable, and if the employers consult with them and co-operate with them properly, then we shall be able to utilize [black labour] better'.[132]

Fanie Botha's opportunity to respond arrived during the afternoon sitting, and his maiden speech proved revealing. On the one hand, it seemed to attest to a minister out of his depth, clinging to established NP policy for dear life. Starting off on a timid and hesitant note, Botha admitted to finding his new position 'a little strange', since he was a labour novice without the advantage enjoyed by Viljoen, who 'had a personal interest in this technical field'.[133] Despite trying to sound decisive, Botha's statement on his approach to the labour portfolio was empty and fumbling, stating nothing but his commitment to the party line:

> I want to state at once what my policy will be. In the years which lie ahead my policy will be to do what I am doing so fairly and to be so just that what has to be done – and I think that a great deal still has to be done within the framework of the NP policy – will be done cheerfully and with the support and active co-operation of the workers and employers in South Africa.[134]

Botha proceeded to insist on the continued importance of job reservation and to dismiss calls for the recognition of black trade unions. He repeatedly stated that solutions to whatever labour problems the country faced should be sought within the NP's established framework. Contrasting South Africa with other countries, he lauded local labour stability, dismissing the Durban strikes as a mere 'ripple'.[135] In this sense, his speech showed little trace of a major reformer – which is how he would later be hailed.[136]

Yet, on the other hand, Botha's speech, like Henning's, contained new elements with important implications. It no longer linked white workers' position to white survival; rather, it focused more on white labour's responsibility to cooperate with government priorities than on workers'

---

[132] Hansard Vol. 63 Column 9083–5, 14 June 1976.
[133] Hansard Vol. 63 Column 9183, 14 June 1976.
[134] Hansard Vol. 63 Column 9190, 14 June 1976.
[135] Hansard Vol. 63 Column 9187, 14 June 1976.
[136] 'Tribute by F. W. de Klerk on the death of Fanie Botha', Politicsweb, 7 September 2010, www.politicsweb.co.za/contact/fw-de-klerks-tribute-to-late-fanie-botha (accessed 17 September 2015); 'Former minister Fanie Botha dies', News24, 4 September 2010, www.news24.com/SouthAfrica/News/Former-minister-Fanie-Botha-dies-20100904 (accessed 17 September 2015).

Figure 2.3 The new Minister of Labour, Fanie Botha, in conversation with Wessel Bornman (left) and Attie Nieuwoudt (right) at SACLA's 1976 congress.
Source: Die Transvaler, 4 June 1976

right to statutory protection. Referring to other countries wracked by conflict between government and organised labour, Botha agreed with Henning that South Africa's workers displayed 'responsibility' – they were 'still good South Africans'.[137] Spoken in the context of the necessity of better manpower utilisation, such statements had a distinct Broederbond echo to them in terms of putting national interest before class concerns. Moreover, in contrast to Viljoen's 'poor but white' talk, Botha was clearly convinced of the necessity of economic growth. He stressed that growth was particularly important in the face of increasing international pressure – in the future, he stated ominously, South Africa would need to be able to function independent of outside assistance. Economic growth was also seen as crucial in order that the NP might present a 'positive image' to the outside world and prove that it sought to create prosperity for all, not just whites. Thus, it needed the economic power to fully implement separate development and establish independent African homelands.[138] In contrast to Viljoen, Botha therefore not

---

[137] Hansard Vol. 63 Column 9189, 14 June 1976.
[138] Hansard Vol. 63 Column 9189, 9197–8, 14 June 1976.

only displayed an awareness of foreign criticism, but also seemed to link the survival of white rule in South Africa to economic growth.

While Minister Botha was getting a grip on his new portfolio, the Broederbond continued its labour investigation. The first months of 1976 saw two further Broeders join the committee: Nic Hechter, senior legal draftsman in the Department of Labour, had been co-opted by February, while the law professor Nic Wiehahn was nominated to the committee in April.[139]

The year also saw the emergence in Broederbond discussions of the idea of establishing works committees for whites, or incorporating white workers into the existing committee system. This was again connected to the idea that Afrikaners had not yet 'developed' very far or were not 'completely adapted' to trade unionism. Although the minutes do not offer verbatim accounts of committee discussions, there is sufficient detail to show that works committees as bargaining forums for white workers were always raised in the context of the broader debate on industrial rights and trade unions for black workers.[140] In other words, these sources reveal that the organisational forms and negotiation powers of the *entire* labour movement were being reconsidered at this time, and this involved unprecedented proposals for what may have been conceived as an equally unprecedented unitary bargaining system in South African industry. Moreover, in as far as the expansion of the works committee system for black workers in fact embodied an effort to subdue or gain control over this section of the workforce, the extension of this idea to white workers further indicates efforts to bring under control the white labour movement as well – especially if read alongside planned efforts to infiltrate the leadership of conservative white unions.[141]

Such schemes for taming the power of white unions during this period are perhaps unsurprising. By mid-1976, the MWU was increasingly a source of concern for the government. The union had on occasion called for a five-day working week for miners. In 1975, it renewed this campaign and was soon locked in dispute with the Chamber of Mines. By

---

[139] Erfenisstigting, AB 10/7, 10/7/3, N. B. to N. Hechter, 23 February 1976; N. B. to Prof. N. E. Wiehahn, 12 April 1976. Wiehahn had joined the Broederbond in 1970. Wilkins and Strydom, *The Super-Afrikaners*, p. A138.

[140] Erfenisstigting, AB 10/7, 10/7/3, 'Verslag van 'n vergadering van die komitee i.v.m. arbeidsaangeleentded', 2 June 1976; 'Raamwerk vir 'n studie van die arbeidsituasie in die RSA', 1 July 1976; 'Verslag van 'n vergadering van die komitee i.v.m. arbeidsaangeleenthede', 17 September 1976; 'Verslag van 'n vergadering van die arbeidskomitee', 2 November 1976.

[141] Friedman notes a further effort to weaken the white labour movement in the form of a bill, released by Minister Botha in 1977, which would have denied miners their legal right to strike. The bill failed. Friedman, *Building Tomorrow Today*, p. 164.

threatening strike action, the MWU compelled Minister Botha to institute a conciliation board. When negotiations here also reached a deadlock, the union balloted its members on strike action, returning an 89 per cent favourable result and setting a seven-day ultimatum. The downward economic trend of the first half of the year had developed into a full-blown recession by 1976.[142] Despite Botha's appeals to Paulus to consider the damage a mining strike would do to the struggling economy, the mineworkers could not be moved. It took an intervention by Prime Minister Vorster himself to avert strike action in August 1976. A commission of inquiry was appointed to investigate the five-day week, while mineworkers received interim financial benefits.[143]

It would be the last time the government would intervene on behalf of white miners. The dramatic developments of June 1976 would see white workers definitively lose their position in the public – and secret – labour debate. Just two days after Fanie Botha's maiden speech as Minister of Labour, with Parliament recently in recess, some 20,000 African students took to the streets of Soweto in a mass demonstration against education policies. The protests soon turned violent as marching schoolchildren clashed with the police. Rioting spread to townships across the country, marking the start of broad-based black resistance to white minority rule, including large-scale worker stay-aways. The extreme force employed by the state evoked widespread international condemnation, while the government's inability to regain control exposed the vulnerability of white power in the face of black fury. Soweto marked a dramatic shift in the internal balance of forces determining the country's fate, evoking 'a new consciousness of the fragility of the social order in South Africa amongst legislators and their officials and amongst influential capitalists'.[144] Moreover, it finally pushed the debate on white survival beyond a narrow focus on apartheid's economic contradictions towards its political and moral implications.[145]

This shift was certainly evident in the Broederbond discussions. Prior to the Soweto protests, the Broeders' discussions had centred on the labour crisis as a primarily economic problem, their focus on bargaining mechanisms occasionally expanding to discuss the importance of regulating economic developments in such a way as to secure 'white

---

[142] O'Meara, *Forty Lost Years*, p. 171.
[143] NA, SAB, CAB 1/1/6, Minute Book 1976, 2.8.76; Visser, *Van MWU tot Solidariteit*, pp. 207–8.
[144] Ashforth, *The Politics of Official Discourse*, pp. 199–200.
[145] See also H. Giliomee, '"Survival in justice": an Afrikaner debate over apartheid', *Comparative Studies in Society and History* 36, no. 3 (1994), pp. 527–48.

survival'.¹⁴⁶ By August 1976, however, the committee had come to see South Africa's labour issue in a much wider context, noting 'how intertwined the total labour situation is with the political situation in this country and that the one cannot be addressed in isolation from the other'. Whites, it now noted, were embroiled in a broad 'struggle for survival' on demographic, ideological, and political fronts.¹⁴⁷ The committee's focus was now on urgently devising a labour solution that would pacify black workers and forestall the politicisation of their demands. It emphasised that the government must retain the initiative.¹⁴⁸

As controversial as the Broederbond's ideas about white works committees may have been, it must be noted that they were never the labour committee's main preoccupation, and the minutes show that after Soweto less and less time was spent discussing white workers' position in industry, while black workers' bargaining mechanisms, demands, needs, and power increasingly preoccupied debates. Indeed, the Broeders noted that, in considering action on the labour front, national interest was the 'only measure which counted' – and this dictated that legislative amendments urgently be made. By November 1976, the committee's concerns regarding white unions were decisively placed on the back burner in favour of first resolving the issue of a bargaining system for Africans. At the same meeting, the Broeders discussed the appointment of a state commission of inquiry and by all indications had already raised the matter with Minister Botha.¹⁴⁹ Indeed, the sources indicate regular interaction between committee members and the Minister and his department.¹⁵⁰

After Soweto, caucus discussions also displayed a new urgency and anxiety. Here, too, discussions shifted to a broader view of the challenges facing South Africa – which Vorster labelled a 'total onslaught'¹⁵¹ on the white state, with the goal of black majority rule.¹⁵² This idea would later

---

¹⁴⁶ For instance, Erfenisstigting, AB 10/7, 10/7/3, 'Raamwerk vir 'n studie van die arbeidsituasie in die RSA', 5 February 1976.
¹⁴⁷ Erfenisstigting, AB 10/7, 10/7/3, 'Die arbeidsituasie in die RSA', 9 August 1976.
¹⁴⁸ Erfenisstigting, AB 10/7, 10/7/3, 'Verslag van 'n vergadering van die komitee i.v.m. arbeidsaangeleenthede', 6 October 1976.
¹⁴⁹ Erfenisstigting, AB 10/7, 10/7/3, 'Verslag van 'n vergadering van die arbeidskomitee', 2 November 1976.
¹⁵⁰ Erfenisstigting, AB 10/7, 10/7/3, 'Verslag van die komitee insake arbeidsaangeleenthede', 23 March 1976; 'Verslag van 'n vergadering van die komitee i.v.m. arbeidsaangeleenthede', 6 October 1976; 'Verslag van 'n vergadering van die arbeidskomitee', 2 November 1976; 'Verslag van 'n samespreking van die komitee i.v.m. arbeidsaangeleenthede', 9 September 1977.
¹⁵¹ Vorster's words: ARCA, PV408: National Party Caucus, 'Koukus 2.2.77', 'Koukus 20.4.77'; also Louis Nel, 'Koukus 16.2.77'.
¹⁵² ARCA, PV408: National Party Caucus, 'Koukus 20.4.77'.

become the object of Vorster's successor P. W. Botha's infamous battle cry of 'total strategy'. Helgaard Muller told his NP colleagues that black trade unions were out to paralyse the South African economy, while the goal of black community uprisings was to sully the country's international image and thus sabotage its foreign alliances. International trade unions and the United Nations were all looking for ways to bring South Africa to its knees.[153] Prime Minister Vorster emphasised that steps must be taken to 'do what is right, and what will ensure domestic peace'.[154] 'We will have to open some doors, but at the same time, there are certain positions we cannot relinquish,' said the Prime Minister.[155]

NP speeches during the 1977 budget vote on labour thus show a clear departure from previous debates, revealing a real sense of urgency and willingness to reform established labour conditions that had not been present in the aftermath of the Durban strikes. Perhaps inevitably, this was accompanied by a clearer re-emergence of opposing views within the party.

When Henning opened the debate for the NP, MPs on the other side of the House would have been forgiven for checking twice whether they were indeed listening to the member for Vanderbijlpark. His speech concentrated on job reservation and revealed an NP on a new course. In the light of labour shortages, Henning argued that employers' request for the removal of Section 77 was 'logical': while job reservation had a historical basis in South Africa and had been 'absolutely essential' in the past, it had now 'perhaps become out of date'. Given the NP's staunch commitment to its policy of race-based job reservation up to this point, the public expression of such statements on the main stage of political power represented a historical departure for the ruling party. But, in a sense, Henning's suggestion that job reservation be reassessed came after the event: Minister Botha had already appointed an Industrial Tribunal investigation into all existing job reservation determinations earlier that year. It is more likely that Henning's call for the reconsideration of job reservation was a pretext for what came next. He proceeded to submit a 'very serious plea' to Minister Botha to appoint a commission of inquiry composed of stakeholders from across the labour spectrum – including 'other ethnic groups' – to make a thorough investigation of all labour legislation. While Henning's speech paid lip service to the NP's existing policy on black unions, his call included a reconsideration of the industrial rights of African workers. Aware that such a reconsideration

---

[153] ARCA, PV408: National Party Caucus, 'Koukus 20.1.1977'.
[154] ARCA, PV408: National Party Caucus, 'Koukus 20.1.1977'.
[155] ARCA, PV408: National Party Caucus, 'Koukus 16.2.77'.

would evoke consternation among sections of the established labour movement, he quickly added that no worker in South Africa 'regardless of race or colour' need worry that he would be 'edged out', as 'we are dealing with a responsible Government'. Henning concluded by expressing his appreciation for Nic Wiehahn's appointment as labour adviser to the Minister and the Department of Labour – perhaps a less than subtle attempt to prepare the way for Botha's own speech later the same day.[156]

It is instructive that Henning's speech also included him thanking the 'responsible trade union leaders of South Africa', a category in which he now included TUCSA alongside SACLA, for the two federations' appeal to workers to keep their wage demands 'realistic and reasonable' in the context of the country's economic difficulties.[157] This revealed a remarkable change of heart towards the multiracial federation and its politics, which Marais Viljoen had once disapprovingly characterised as the liberal shade of 'pink'.

A bristling Francois le Roux, NP MP for working-class Brakpan, spoke after Henning. Although he refrained from directly challenging his colleague for Vanderbijlpark, Le Roux expressed his refusal to accept that job reservation had become obsolete or constituted discrimination in favour of whites. He insisted that 'the white man is fully entitled to demand this [protection] from the Government', and maintained that job reservation represented the single most important reason for industrial peace in South Africa, thus continuing to point to the industrial threat of white working-class power.[158] Such opposition to reformist tendencies surfacing in the NP testify to *verligte–verkrampte* tensions already manifesting in the party. Indeed, in 1982 Le Roux would resign from the NP alongside 15 other MPs led by Andries Treurnicht to form the Conservative Party. Le Roux would hold Brakpan as a CP seat up until the country's first democratic elections.[159]

Opposition parties had already caught on to the new reformist tune in the NP. UP and PRP speakers indicated their expectation that Minister Botha would make an important announcement in the course of the debate – both parties seemed to expect that this would have something to do with the Industrial Tribunal investigation.[160] Neither the UP nor PRP had anything to say about white labour, expect for UP assertions that job reservation did not protect the white worker 'because there is, in

---

[156] Hansard Vol. 68 Column 7481–8, 12 May 1977.
[157] Hansard Vol. 68 Column 7481, 12 May 1977.
[158] Hansard Vol. 68 Column 7489–90, 12 May 1977.
[159] R. Weide and S. Weide, *Die Volledige Verkiesingsuitslae van Suid-Afrika, 1910–1986* (Pretoria: Private Publication, 1987); Hansard Vol. 38, 1993, p. xiv.
[160] Hansard Vol. 68 Column 7477–8, 7497, 12 May 1977.

fact, no real danger'.[161] Opposition speakers pointed again to the instability and loss of business confidence the labour situation was causing South Africa, and this amid rampant inflation, escalating unemployment, and the crescendo of international criticism.[162] The PRP's Boraine devoted valuable minutes to singing the praises of the Minister's new labour adviser. Boraine quoted Wiehahn as describing South Africa's present labour system as 'most unsuitable' and its dualistic characteristics as potentially 'disastrous' for the economy, and calling for the replacement of this structure with a uniform system based on fundamental democratic labour rights. Boraine expressed the hope that that this would be the kind of advice the Minister's new 'right-hand man' would be giving him.[163]

There was no sign of the fumbling new minister of 1976 when Fanie Botha rose to speak. He declared unequivocally that labour in South Africa had reached a 'watershed'. Perhaps intentionally, Botha echoed his predecessor in emphasising that South Africa's labour legislation was shaped by social considerations – but in contrast to Viljoen, for whom this was a motivation to maintain the status quo, Botha saw this as a reason for change. South Africa was currently 'moving rapidly', he said, and so labour legislation demanded 'constant consideration' as the domestic situation developed. Taking the leap his party had long balked at, Botha announced the appointment of a commission of inquiry under the chairmanship of Wiehahn to investigate and make recommendations regarding existing industrial legislation, including the Bantu Labour Act.[164]

Botha's announcement constituted a historic admission that the existing labour system had become untenable. It revealed a government now more nervous of the power of black labour than of white workers – a government eager, as the Broederbond had urged, to retain the initiative. But this would have been bad news for conservative white labour – and Botha knew it. His speech reveals his difficult position: because of the damage Soweto had done to South Africa's image abroad, the country had to be seen to acknowledge its problems and take bold steps to address them. At the same time, Botha had to downplay the NP's concerns and the potential consequences of reform in order to contain a possible backlash from strong conservative elements. His speech saw him oscillate between these two imperatives. Again using job reservation

---

[161] Hansard Vol. 68 Column 7478, 12 May 1977.
[162] Hansard Vol. 68 Column 7471, 7475–6, 7492–3, 12 May 1977.
[163] Hansard Vol. 68 Column 7495–6, 12 May 1977.
[164] Hansard Vol. 68 Column 7517–20, 12 May 1977.

as a pretext, he explained the necessity of an investigation given the changes in employment patterns that had occurred since the implementation of existing legislation: '[I]t has never been our point of departure, when we have a law, to preserve it in its existing form at all costs in the future.'[165] But this representation of the NP as pragmatic and flexible had to be balanced with its old image of a party steadfastly committed to white workers' protection. Hence Botha was quick to add that job reservation was a necessary and good measure, and that the investigation 'should not be seen as though we were now going to bring about a change of course in South Africa'. Aware that the PRP's praise of Wiehahn and his apparently reformist views could create an unwanted impression among NP conservatives, Botha chided Boraine to not misrepresent Wiehahn's words: 'Prof. Wiehahn has no intention, nor is he thinking on these lines either, of forcing South Africa onto a different course.'[166] After all, Botha added, this 'could create labour unrest in this country', again pointing to the industrial power of conservative white labour. For this reason, Botha insisted that organised labour would be consulted throughout the Wiehahn investigation.[167]

But such pronouncements had lost their gravity, not only because opposition parties had long ceased to make similar statements, but because the NP had clearly decided to chart a new course. Botha's ministerial tap-dance showed that the best the NP could do was to try to hold the centre for as long as possible by appealing to all elements of its broad and increasingly disparate support base. Hence the Minister, like his MP for Vanderbijlpark, paid tribute to both SACLA and TUCSA, with whom the Minister had conducted extensive deliberations in order to reach an understanding on fighting inflation. These good relations between government and organised labour, Botha insisted, proved that he was 'on the side of the employees of the country'. They distinguished South Africa from European countries where conflict between labour and the state had become insurmountable. Similar developments in South Africa needed to be avoided at all costs, Botha stressed. Hence, 'legislation has to be adjusted, and we must ensure that in South Africa we never build such a conflict into the relations between employer and employee that they cannot accommodate one another. If that happens, *it is all over with us.*'[168] This statement of survival may have been directed at white workers, but it was no longer about them. Conservative white

---

[165] Hansard Vol. 68 Column 7521–2, 12 May 1977.
[166] Hansard Vol. 68 Column 7522, 7520, 12 May 1977.
[167] Hansard Vol. 68 Column 7590–2, 13 May 1977.
[168] Hansard Vol. 68 Column 7531, 12 May 1977 (my emphasis).

workers' demand for the apartheid labour dispensation to remain in place now carried less weight in the face of a powerful and incensed black workforce.

Two months later, Prime Minister Vorster officially appointed the Commission of Inquiry into Labour Legislation. Three of its 14 members – Attie Nieuwoudt, Nic Hechter, and, of course, Nic Wiehahn – were drawn from the Broederbond's labour committee. The Commission was charged with investigating, reporting on, and making recommendations in connection with all existing labour legislation.[169] Soon after, Vorster appointed a second inquiry, the Riekert Commission, to deal with aspects surrounding the utilisation of labour omitted from the Wiehahn Commission's remit.[170] The announcement of the two commissions reflected the shifted balance of forces in South Africa's labour arena.

The Broederbond committee archive for this period is sparse, with minutes from only two meetings surviving. Yet they make instructive reading in terms of foreshadowing things to come. In September 1977, shortly after the appointment of the Wiehahn Commission, the Broeders discussed how their organisation could be mobilised to support the inquiry, while also noting that the Commission should 'not have the image of decisions already taken'.[171] The October 1978 minutes show that, a year later, the committee was discussing compulsory registration for black unions and the removal of job reservation – both policies would be mirrored in the Commission's recommendations the following year.[172]

White workers' response to such changes remained a topic of discussion. In a departure from previous styles, the October 1978 minutes attribute certain statements to specific members of the committee. They show Nieuwoudt stressing that white labour would reject the recognition of black unions through registration – white workers demanded protection from the political party which they 'sustained' and should not be alienated, he warned. But Wiehahn retorted that 'rational thought and argument with white trade union leaders is

---

[169] Department of Labour and of Mines, *Report of the Commission of Inquiry into Labour Legislation Part 1 (Key Issues)* (Pretoria: Government Printer, RP49/1979), p. v.

[170] Professor P. J. Riekert, Vorster's economic adviser, was the sole member. His inquiry focused on the role of the state in regulating labour markets, including in relation to issues of African urbanisation and influx control.

[171] Erfenisstigting, AB 10/7, 10/7/3, 'Verslag van 'n samespreking van die komitee i.v.m. arbeidsaangeleenthede', 9 September 1977.

[172] Erfenisstigting, AB 10/7, 10/7/3, 'Verslag van 'n gesprek i.v.m. arbeidsaangeleenthede', 4 October 1978.

impossible'. The meeting closed with the committee noting that the registration of black unions should be undertaken in such a way that 'guard[s] against unions governing the country'.[173] The archival record runs dry here, but the discussion is indicative of conservative white labour's loss of its central position in shaping labour debates and policy. In the early 1970s their opinions had been highly regarded, backed by their perceived political and industrial power; by the end of the decade, Wiehahn could dismiss them as irrational to the SACLA president's face. In a phrase strongly reminiscent of the politics of labour in Britain during the same period, the South African political elite's concerns were now with the danger of black workers 'governing the country'.

This was made clear in early 1979. On 5 March, MWU members at the O'Okiep copper mine in the Northern Cape downed tools in objection to the appointment of three coloured artisans in positions reserved for whites. The strikers were dismissed, setting a lightning sympathy strike in motion across the mining industry. On the eve of the Wiehahn recommendations, the strike was seen first and foremost as a warning to government not to tamper with job reservation in the mining industry.[174] This was the white industrial action of which MPs had long warned, the economic 'disaster ... which would make you shudder' that Viljoen had presaged. At its height, over 80 per cent of the MWU's 18,000 members in the gold and coal mines downed tools.[175] It was suggested that the timing of the strike in early March was intended to symbolically mirror the most extremist phase of the 1922 Rand Revolt.[176]

While the MWU leadership claimed that the strike had been spontaneous, the Chamber of Mines viewed it as illegal and dismissed the strikers en masse. Paulus appealed to the Ministry of Labour to intervene in the dispute, but Minister Botha refused, dismissing the matter – as the NP had the Durban strikes – as being between the mineworkers and their employers. Paulus's attempts to secure an audience with the Prime Minister also failed.[177] Unlike the five-day working week, there was now no government intervention in favour of the mineworkers – the miners' concerns, it seems, no longer corresponded with the 'national interest'. In the midst of the strike, the UP reproached the government for its aloofness, branding the MWU a Frankenstein monster 'created by

---

[173] Erfenisstigting, AB 10/7, 10/7/3, 'Verslag van 'n gesprek i.v.m. arbeidsaangeleenthede', 4 October 1978.
[174] Visser, 'From MWU to Solidarity', p. 23; C. Cooper, 'The mineworkers' strike', *South African Labour Bulletin* 5, no. 3 (1979), p. 4, 10.
[175] Friedman, *Building Tomorrow Today*, p. 164.
[176] Visser, *Van MWU tot Solidariteit*, p. 239.
[177] Cooper, 'The mineworkers' strike', pp. 9–14.

the NP, and those Frankensteins have now turned against their creators and their masters'. Fearing the economic impact of the strike, the UP castigated the government for washing its hands of 'that creature which has supported it through the years'.[178]

But given white miners' ever diminishing involvement in the actual production process, the stoppage had little impact on mining production. Conservative white labour had done its worst, and lost. By 13 March the strike had all but collapsed as most miners applied for reinstatement in their jobs.[179] Rather than the 1922-style bang that had been predicted, the 1979 confrontation ended with a whimper. Shortly afterwards, on 1 May 1979, the Wiehahn Commission released its first recommendations, advising government to abolish job reservation and recognise black unions, subject to registration.[180]

Conclusion

This chapter has shown how a focus on labour policy and debate provides insight into how the political imaginary of the apartheid state was evolving within Pretoria's corridors of power. The opening years of the 1970s saw the NP maintain its historical commitment to white working-class protection and privilege in the labour arena, even if this came at the cost of economic growth. Nationalist politicians pandered to the interests of white workers, particularly those organised in the conservative SACLA and its Co-ordinating Council, the NP's sweethearts since the 1940s. In the face of international labour turmoil, both the government and the Opposition displayed a wariness of white working-class power on the shop floor and at the ballot box – so much so that it seemed as if white workers held the power to determine the nature and pace of any changes in labour patterns or legislation.

This balance of power changed over the course of the 1970s, with initial shifts following the Durban strikes and Soweto prompting decisive change in the political elite's regard of the white working class. The government was now confronted with the potency of African labour discontent, the burden of international demands for reform, and the urgent need for economic growth. Addressing these pressures in such a way as to safeguard white rule now became the main priority. The appointment of the Wiehahn Commission signalled the political

---

[178] Hansard Vol. 79 Column 2956, 8 March 1979.
[179] Visser, *Van MWU tot Solidariteit*, pp. 235–48; Friedman, *Building Tomorrow Today*, pp. 164–5.
[180] Department of Labour and of Mines, *Report Part 1*.

Conclusion 115

establishment's willingness to reconsider the traditional apartheid labour pattern – a crucial aspect of the racial state underpinning the Afrikaner social alliance. More than simply the changing nature of the NP's support base and priorities, this move towards reform marked a greater reality mirroring the global shifts in the relations between states, labour, and capital in this period. In South Africa, this took the form of the abandonment of understandings of the survival of white identity and power as contingent on the protection and upliftment of white labour. Indeed, amid an escalating crisis of capital accumulation and political legitimacy, white labour's insistence on the maintenance of the status quo became a liability. Conservative white workers' interests needed to be made subservient to the national interest – much like black labour, white workers needed to be brought under control.

A focus on white labour at this historical juncture therefore expands our understanding of the shift towards reform during the late apartheid period. Some scholars have pointed out that the NP's move to implement labour and economic reforms from the late 1970s mirrored neo-liberal trends across the Western world; indeed, in subsequent years the NP moved towards the privatisation of state enterprises, the deregulation and liberalisation of terms of trade, and the removal of subsidies.[181] The evidence presented here broadens this picture to demonstrate that, as much as this decade was about efforts to placate a rising black worker movement, it was also about taming a powerful white worker movement of the NP's own creation. The MWU's confrontational stance on the eve of Wiehahn's recommendations and the cold shoulder with which the government responded were a taste of things to come as the 'disturbed seventies' gave way to the 'traumatic eighties'[182] – business interests would enjoy increasing priority, particularly under P. W. Botha's rule. But this outcome was not inevitable. First, these competing interests would come to a head before the Commission itself.

---

[181] Reynolds, *One World Divisible*, p. 455, 404–7; Terreblanche, *Lost in Transformation?*, pp. 20–3; Feinstein, *An Economic History of South Africa*, pp. 211–30, 243–4.
[182] Hobsbawm, *Age of Extremes*, p. 257.

3 Race and rights at the rock face of change
White organised labour and the Wiehahn reforms

Introduction

'Now I don't know, I don't know if it is wise.' The otherwise articulate chairman was suddenly tongue-tied, struggling to broach the next topic on his agenda. Then he rambled ahead:

I wonder if, apart from the chairman's name at the top, if we can't have the rest of the names alphabetically. Don't you think so, I think this is what we should do, because there is a bit of an element of snobbishness here, I think we should rather have things alphabetically – except for the chairman's name which unfortunately has to appear at the top, but the rest of the names I think we should rather arrange alphabetically, do you agree?[1]

The verbatim minutes do not record where he stuttered or paused, but Nic Wiehahn was clearly uncomfortable. On that Tuesday in September 1978, he was speaking about the list of names appearing in the State President's official appointment of South Africa's Commission of Inquiry into Labour Legislation – the Wiehahn Commission. The commissioners were gathered in the boardroom of the Department of Labour's headquarters for their first deliberation meeting after completing their gathering of evidence earlier that year. It was the apartheid state's arrangement of the 14 commissioners' names which Wiehahn found so discomfiting, and he was eager to remedy the situation.

While we cannot know what exactly Wiehahn meant by 'snobbish', scrutiny of the list suggests the grounds for his embarrassment. Most obviously, the list ordered the commissioners according to race, with the 11 white commissioners listed first before the Indian commissioner, followed by the coloured commissioner and ending with the African commissioner. The historian of apartheid South Africa is hardly surprised at the appearance of this racialised social scale. Yet perhaps not as immediately evident is another hierarchical logic governing the

---

[1] Steenkamp Archive/Wiehahn Documentation (SA/WD), Deliberation Meeting 43, Pretoria, 5 September 1978, p. 7260.

Introduction 117

list – one that ordered the names of the white commissioners according to social status, education, and employment. Those with academic titles headed the list, followed by those working in business, and then those from blue-collar backgrounds or employed in the civil service.[2]

Ann Stoler famously posited that commissions are 'stories states tell themselves'. Reflecting on the production of colonial archives as acts of governance, she warns that categories and distinctions created by states should not be treated as 'innocuous or benign', but that we should be alert to their consequences, including the power relations and social epistemologies they reflect.[3] Existing scholarly assessments have perhaps been too quick to take the Wiehahn Commission at face value, focusing on its recommendations for the abolition of race-based job reservation and the legalisation of African trade unions, and the 'story' these were seen to tell, without paying due attention to the process itself and the contestations it may reveal. This may be ascribed, at least in part, to the fact that existing analyses of the Commission rely solely on its published reports and do not engage with the voluminous records generated by the Commission in the course of its investigation.

This is not to say that historians have not taken a critical approach to Wiehahn. While the Commission's recommendations were celebrated – not least internationally – as major reforms, local labour observers and scholars were quick to point to underlying political objectives. Centrally, the reforms sought to forestall the radical politicisation of the African labour force. In order to gain legal recognition and participate in the industrial conciliation system, African unions were required to register with the newly created Department of Manpower Utilisation and subject their activities and finances to its scrutiny. In this way, the white-run state sought to gain control over these unions, prohibiting direct association with political movements, barring donations from foreign anti-apartheid organisations or liberation movements in exile, and restricting labour mobilisation to the workplace so that workers would not unite with other groups to challenge white rule. This, it was hoped, would divorce labour issues from political demands. Moreover, the state initially sought to grant labour rights only to Africans permanently residing in the cities,[4] while continuing to exclude the bulk of the black labour force, who were

---

[2] Department of Labour and of Mines, *Report Part 1*, pp. iv–v.
[3] A. L. Stoler, 'Colonial archives and the arts of governance', *Archival Science* 2 (2002), p. 103, 95. See also A. L. Stoler, *Along the Archival Grain: epistemic anxieties and colonial common sense* (Princeton NJ: Princeton University Press, 2009).
[4] Section 10 of the 1952 Urban Areas Act determined that Africans who could prove that they had been born in the city, had lived there for over 15 years, or had been employed by the same employer for ten years qualified for exemption to stay in the urban areas and not

seen as migrant workers from the so-called black homelands. This new politics of inclusion and exclusion, it was hoped, would give 'urban' Africans a stake in the system, secure their allegiance to the state that granted them industrial citizenship, and consequently see them relinquish any further claims to full citizenship.[5] The recommendations of the Riekert Commission reflected a similar strategy to regulate black access to employment and housing in a manner that would draw urban Africans into alliance with the apartheid state, while more firmly excluding rural Africans.[6] In this sense, these labour-related reforms foreshadowed later constitutional changes, which sought, in turn, to co-opt South Africa's coloured and Indian minorities by granting them the political power to elect their own representatives and preside over certain circumscribed community affairs. This aimed to imbue the system with some much-needed legitimacy while still leaving overall white political dominance in place.[7] At the same time, it would serve to stimulate economic growth by bringing South Africa more in line with a free market system by rolling back state intervention in the labour market.[8]

According to Adam Ashforth, commissions are political tools that emerge 'when new alignments in the structure of power within the state [are] forming' and social reality needs to be redefined according to the interests of the ruling orders. Thus, Ashforth posits, in a prefiguration of Stoler's later claim, that commissions represent 'the state speaking the "truth" about itself'.[9] In his analysis of the Wiehahn inquiry, Ashforth argues that reform constituted a redefinition or reimagining of the status of urban Africans, redefining them primarily not as black but as workers. This served to neutralise the political nature of their demands by focusing on labour rights. From the point of view of the ruling orders, this shift or redefinition served to foreclose the necessity of authentic political representation, thus facilitating the continued denial of full citizenship to Africans.[10]

---

be forced to relocate to the 'homeland' to which they were deemed to belong. Beinart, *Twentieth-century South Africa*, p. 158.

[5] On the concept of industrial citizenship, see Barchiesi, *Precarious Liberation*, p. 51; Lichtenstein, 'A measure of democracy', pp. 113–38.

[6] Ashforth, *The Politics of Official Discourse*, p. 196, 200–1, 211–13.

[7] Friedman, *Building Tomorrow Today*, pp. 156–8; Lodge, 'Resistance and reform', p. 425, 437, 443–4; Giliomee, *The Last Afrikaner Leaders*, p. 147; S. Greenberg, *Legitimating the Illegitimate: state, markets, and resistance in South Africa* (Berkeley CA: University of California Press, 1987).

[8] Ashforth, *The Politics of Official Discourse*, p. 216, 221.

[9] Ashforth, *The Politics of Official Discourse*, p. 2, 6.

[10] Ashforth, *The Politics of Official Discourse*, pp. 195–246.

Introduction

The late apartheid state's strategies in this regard were hardly novel. There is a larger literature outside South Africa on labour struggles and the redefinition of citizenship in the period leading up to decolonisation and majority rule. From the mid-1930s, French and British colonial regimes in Africa were confronted with increasingly forceful strike action and political movements among indigenous workers. Consequently, colonial bureaucrats were forced to reimagine African labour and implement reforms in order to pre-empt labour crises with the potential to spill over into other spheres. Frederick Cooper explains how both 'British and French governments, in quite different ways, were trying to construct some kind of junior citizenship through which colonized people could partake of some, but not all, of the qualities of a metropolitan citizen'.[11] These new conceptions would provide new legitimacy for colonial governments by incorporating labour into the post-war colonial system, while at the same time serving to regain control over African workers and to separate them from other groups with whom they might unite to challenge colonial rule. Ultimately, this project of reimagining African labour in such a way as to serve colonial interests failed, as African labour organisations seized upon late-colonial discourses and redefinitions to claim rights and entitlements.[12]

In South Africa, not only the apartheid state but capital too stood to benefit from labour reform. While the conditions created by racial oppression had long suited capitalist interests, the economic slowdown of the 1970s saw the constraints of racial capitalism shift to outweigh its benefits: not only did racial discrimination in the labour market obstruct the effective utilisation of labour, the exploitation of the majority black population also inhibited the development of wider domestic markets and was increasingly leading to labour unrest. Awareness of the political and economic hazards created by racial capitalism came unevenly to South African capital, but by the time Wiehahn was appointed, the business community had become a major advocate of reform.[13] From this point of view, the Commission's recommendation to scrap race-based job reservation would finally remove statutory obstructions to the reorganisation of labour, while industrial citizenship would deliver an acquiescent and more productive black labour force – and hence get the economy back on track.

---

[11] F. Cooper, *Decolonization and African Society: the labor question in French and British Africa* (Cambridge: Cambridge University Press, 1996), p. 266.
[12] Cooper, *Decolonization and African Society*.
[13] J. S. Saul and P. Bond, *South Africa – The Present as History: from Mrs Ples to Mandela and Marikana* (Auckland Park: Jacana, 2014), p. 112.

Scholars have since labelled these reforms 'neo-apartheid' attempts to 'remodel thoroughly the foundations of white supremacy';[14] a 'scheme' to 'share power without losing control';[15] and a new politics of inclusion and exclusion, reformulating the terms on which certain 'non-whites' participated in the state in order to bolster the legitimacy of the apartheid regime and gain control over the elements challenging it.[16] The literature typically creates the impression that such a 'scheme' – in as far as it sought to preserve white supremacy and capital accumulation in South Africa – was in the interests of and supported by all whites. Thus, the historiography of reform-era South Africa continues to be understood in terms of a racial balance of power, with a white capitalist state seeking to gain control over black resistance from below.

But Nic Wiehahn's discomfort at the apartheid state's 'snobbish' logic reveals the class tensions and interests that intersected with race at this point. It is this convergence which this chapter seeks to probe. In what follows, I examine white organised labour's response to and role in the Wiehahn process. Darcy du Toit and Christi van der Westhuizen have both recognised the class-based implications of reform (with Du Toit calling the reforms a shift from a 'traditional policy of racial domination to ... a policy of undisguised class domination'). Yet both authors only gesture towards the liability that this shift potentially presented for those whites not included in this elite project.[17] Steven Friedman and Hermann Giliomee have both paid more prolonged attention to the Wiehahn process and do take some account of contestations within the white community, especially white labour, around the envisioned reforms.[18] Yet none of these scholars utilised the exhaustive records and notes generated by the Commission to probe the role of white workers in the process.[19]

This chapter is the first investigation to utilise the Commission's extensive archive, supplemented by oral sources,[20] to understand how

---

[14] Dubow, *Apartheid*, p. 297.   [15] Giliomee, *The Last Afrikaner Leaders*, p. 139, 147.

[16] D. Posel, 'Language, legitimation and control: the South African state after 1978', *Social Dynamics: A Journal of African Studies* 10, no. 1 (1984), pp. 1–16.

[17] Du Toit, *Capital and Labour*, pp. 363–4; Van der Westhuizen, *White Power*, p. 111.

[18] Friedman, *Building Tomorrow Today*; Giliomee, *The Last Afrikaner Leaders*.

[19] For a discussion of the Wiehahn records, see D. van Zyl-Hermann, 'White workers in the late apartheid period: a report on the Wiehahn Commission and Mineworkers' Union archival collections', *History in Africa* 43 (2016), pp. 229–58.

[20] The Commission's archive is housed at the South African National Archives, Pretoria. Naas Steenkamp – who was the last surviving Wiehahn commissioner at the time of writing – retained a comprehensive private archive in Somerset West. This chapter draws on both collections. I interviewed Steenkamp in 2011 and 2013 at his home in Somerset West, and Piet Nieuwenhuizen, economic adviser to the Vorster and Botha governments, in 2012 in Bellville. In the late 2000s, Steenkamp with historian

white workers sought to influence the 'story' of South Africa's labour system on which the Commission's recommendations, and hence the state's response to the escalating crisis in the 1970s, would be based. White workers were intimately involved in the Wiehahn process, with unions submitting written evidence to the Commission and appearing before it to offer oral testimony, and white labour leaders serving as Wiehahn commissioners, involved in formulating the official report to government. In what follows, I discuss the composition and work of the Wiehahn Commission and the context in which this occurred. The body of the analysis then reconstructs and analyses the debates, strategies, and cleavages that characterised organised labour during the Wiehahn process. The focus falls on three confederate bodies in which white workers were represented, and what their testimonies reveal about their interests, perceptions of change, and efforts to negotiate transformation in the industrial arena and the dismantling of the system once set up for their protection. This brings into focus white workers' response to efforts to placate black political demands and the shifting needs of capital by reimagining black workers' status. Finally, this chapter offers the first consideration of the Wiehahn reforms' effects on white labour, discussing the outcome and aftermath of the Wiehahn process for this section of the white population. In this way, the chapter not only reassesses prevailing scholarly understandings of the late apartheid reform 'scheme', but also provides new insights into issues of race, labour, and citizenship in the late apartheid state.

Commission appointed

On 8 July 1977, Prime Minister Vorster appointed 14 commissioners to the Commission of Inquiry into Labour Legislation under the chairmanship of Nic Wiehahn, Professor of Industrial Relations in the UNISA School of Business Leadership. Wiehahn's biography embodied the story of upward social mobility and embourgeoisement that historians see as shaping the fortunes of large parts of the white working class during the twentieth century. He was born in 1929, on the eve of the Great Depression, his father a conductor on the Kimberley railways. The eldest child in a family of eight, young Nic repeatedly had to leave school to

---

Hermann Giliomee interviewed a number of Wiehahn commissioners and other key players who were deceased by the time I started my investigation. They generously granted me access to this material. Deborah Posel kindly shared an interview she conducted with Nic Wiehahn in 1984, while Adam Ashforth helpfully answered questions about his 1981 interview with Wiehahn (deposited at the Historical Papers Research Archive, University of the Witwatersrand) via email.

work as a steam-engine cleaner, one of the lowest occupations on the railways, in order to help the family make ends meet. At age 21 he finally completed secondary school and found work in Bloemfontein as a clerk. In the evenings, he studied law. After graduating, Wiehahn first lectured at the so-called Indian College in Durban before being appointed as a senior lecturer at the University of Port Elizabeth. In 1970 he became a member of the Broederbond[21] and was promoted to professor of law in the same year. As professor, and later government adviser and eventually Commission chair, Wiehahn became known for his signature bow tie and silk handkerchiefs. In 2006, Wiehahn's obituary noted that he had had no eminent background or social connections to rely on, but had earned his success through 'sheer hard work, intelligence, determination and his widely recognised bonhomie'.[22]

In an effort to maximise legitimacy and consensus, the Commission included representatives from across the spectrum of recognised stakeholders in the labour arena. Several were prominent trade union leaders: Arthur Grobbelaar was general secretary of TUCSA; Chris Botes was a unionist from a coloured TUCSA-affiliated union; Gopi Munsook was a unionist from an Indian TUCSA-affiliated union in Natal and also served on the government's South African Indian Council; Wally Grobler was general secretary of the railways' Artisans Staff Association, an unaffiliated white union; Tommie Neethling was general secretary of the white Amalgamated Engineering Union (AEU), which had disaffiliated from TUCSA in 1966; and Attie Nieuwoudt was president of the whites-only SACLA. A number of commissioners occupied prominent positions in business and management circles: Errol Drummond was director of the Steel and Engineering Industries Federation of South Africa; Chris du Toit was chairman of the South African Employers' Consultative Committee on Labour Affairs; Naas Steenkamp was personnel and industrial relations manager for the Afrikaner-controlled mining house Gencor; and Dick Sutton was chairman of the Associated Chambers of Commerce's Labour Affairs Committee. Nic Hechter, the only civil servant on the Commission, was a senior legal draftsman in the Department of Labour. In addition to Wiehahn, two further academics – Piet van der Merwe of the University of Pretoria, and Ben Mokoatle, an African lecturer in Wiehahn's UNISA institute – completed the Commission.[23]

---

[21] Wilkins and Strydom, *The Super-Afrikaners*, p. A138.
[22] J. Botha, 'Obituary: N. E. Wiehahn (1929–2006)', *South African Journal of Economics* 74, no. 2 (2006), p. 361.
[23] Giliomee, *The Last Afrikaner Leaders*, pp. 150–1; Friedman, *Building Tomorrow Today*, p. 74, 170–1; Ashforth, *The Politics of Official Discourse*, pp. 217–18; Naas Steenkamp, interviewed 6 December 2011.

Figure 3.1 The Wiehahn Commission. Front, left to right: C. A. Botes, Dr E. P. Drummond, A. I. Nieuwoudt, Professor N. E. Wiehahn (chairman), B. N. Mokoatle, C. W. H. du Toit. Back, left to right: R. V. Sutton, G. Munsook, Professor P. J. van der Merwe, J. A. Grobbelaar, D. van der Walt (secretary), C. P. Grobler, T. S. Neethling, N. J. Hechter, T. I. Steenkamp.
Source: Department of Labour and of Mines, *Report of the Commission of Inquiry into Labour Legislation Part 1 (Key Issues)* (Pretoria: Government Printer, RP49/1979)

As Chapter 2 showed, three of these Wiehahn commissioners served on the Broederbond's committee for labour matters, founded in 1975 (as did Commissioner Steenkamp's boss, Wim de Villiers). With three black members, the Wiehahn Commission was South Africa's first multiracial official inquiry. Yet none of these commissioners could be seen as speaking for African workers; indeed, only organised labour was represented on the Commission.[24] There were also no women on the Commission. The voices of the African majority therefore continued to be excluded from official processes. In terms of its white members, the Commission included both English- and Afrikaans-speakers, and it conducted its work in both languages as the situation dictated.

The Commission was charged with investigating, reporting on, and making recommendations in connection with all existing labour

---

[24] S. Coupe, 'Labour relations by authoritarian regimes since 1945: South Africa in international perspective', Wits History Workshop, 13–15 July 1994, p. 13, http://wiredspace.wits.ac.za/bitstream/handle/10539/7760/HWS-72.pdf?sequence=1 (accessed 29 January 2013).

legislation, most notably the 1956 Industrial Conciliation Act, and was ordered to submit interim reports 'in view of the urgency of the matter'.[25] By way of notice in the Government Gazette, the Commission invited written representations. It received 255 submissions from a variety of respondents, including employers' organisations, labour organisations, industrial councils, state departments, institutes, and individuals. The Commission convened sessions in South Africa's major industrial centres at which 184 institutions, organisations, and individuals gave oral testimony.[26] The Commission also visited a number of factories, training centres, and mines, while several commissioners travelled abroad to examine current labour trends and conduct research for the inquiry. In contrast to the piecemeal legislative adjustments that had characterised the NP's initial reaction to the crisis, the appointment of the Commission seemed to signal that a fundamental overhaul of the country's labour dispensation was on the cards.

White labour and the Wiehahn Commission

In the early 1950s, as the newly elected NP government was preparing to overhaul existing industrial relations legislation, we saw how the organised labour movement realised the importance and implications of the changes that were coming, and sought to form a united labour front. Almost 30 years later, the appointment of the Wiehahn Commission elicited a similar response. Realising that the inquiry represented a potential game change for labour, TUCSA general secretary Grobbelaar initiated discussions between South Africa's main labour factions on the prospect of submitting joint written evidence to the Commission. In September 1977, the multiracial TUCSA and the all-white SACLA, as well as the Confederation of Metal and Building Unions, the Federal Consultative Council of Railway and Harbours Staff Associations, the Federation of Salaried Staff Associations, and the South African Co-ordinating Council of the International Metal Workers' Federation, met in order to discuss and gain consensus on a range of key issues. A number of unregistered unions were also in attendance. At the meeting, the Joint Committee Representing All Organised Labour in the Republic of South Africa (the Joint Committee) was formed and set about drafting a memorandum for submission to the Commission.[27]

---

[25] Department of Labour and of Mines, *Report Part 1*, p. v.
[26] Department of Manpower Utilisation, *Report Part 6*, p. v, 30–5.
[27] SAIRR, *A Survey of Race Relations in South Africa 1977*, p. 287, 304; SA/WD, Testimony Meeting 29, 1 March 1978, p. 4608.

But the Wiehahn documentation shows that SACLA objected to the wording of the memorandum and, after consulting with its members, elected to withdraw from the Joint Committee.[28] Evidence suggests that SACLA president Nieuwoudt may have come under pressure from right-wing unions to withdraw. Arrie Paulus condemned Nieuwoudt's attendance of the meeting and his apparent willingness to participate in a multiracial forum. Paulus argued that SACLA should submit its own evidence and not compromise its views on job reservation and the protection of white workers.[29] Despite SACLA's exit, the Joint Committee still represented over a hundred unions with over 328,000 white, coloured, and Indian members[30] – but the attempt to unify organised labour on the eve of a major review of the country's labour legislation had failed. As will be shown, trade union rights for Africans and race-based job reservation persisted as the main points of contention within organised labour. The historical divisions that had characterised the labour movement since the 1920s and had been exacerbated in the 1950s continued to shape the late 1970s.

The South African Confederation of Labour

Chapter 2 showed how the rapidly changing political and economic conditions of the 1970s eroded SACLA's established position as the NP's sweetheart labour confederation. In the course of the decade, SACLA grew increasingly concerned about the implications of escalating challenges to South Africa's racialised labour dispensation for white workers' interests. During his presidential address at SACLA's annual congress in June 1976, Nieuwoudt stated that white workers feared an 'onslaught' on their positions amid efforts to facilitate African advancement.[31] The newly appointed Minister of Labour Fanie Botha, guest speaker at the congress, responded with the assurance that white workers would not lose their privileged position. Botha conceded that some labour reforms were being planned, yet he assured the Confederation's members that job reservation would be retained and he reaffirmed the partnership between the NP and conservative white labour: 'Any developments in the future will be something we plan

---

[28] SA/WD, Testimony Meeting 29, 1 March 1978, p. 4611.
[29] SAIRR, *A Survey of Race Relations in South Africa 1977*, p. 287.
[30] National Archives of South Africa, Pretoria (NA), SAB (National Archives Repository – Public Records of Government since 1910), K364, Vol. 33, AK 6/3/1/1/4 Vol. II, Documentation accompanying letter from Industrial Registrar to The Secretary, Commission of Inquiry into Labour Legislation, 10 July 1978, p. 3.
[31] SAIRR, *A Survey of Race Relations in South Africa 1977*, p. 316.

together,'[32] he said. He reiterated this assurance in Parliament less than a year later, while announcing the appointment of the Wiehahn Commission.[33]

But the 200,000 conservative white workers represented by SACLA may have been forgiven for detecting a hollow ring to such promises. In 1977, even before the Wiehahn inquiry was under way, Minister Botha accepted recommendations from the Industrial Tribunal to cancel 18 and suspend two of the existing 25 job reservation determinations. Only five reservations remained in force – apparently where strong whites-only unions had been able to exert pressure for their retention.[34] Amid escalating local and international pressure for apartheid to be abandoned, these developments created a climate of expectancy and uncertainty, and as the Commission started its work, it was perceived as a juncture at which the future shape of South Africa's labour dispensation was at stake.[35]

SACLA's deputation to the Wiehahn Commission was led by the Confederation's general secretary, Wessel Bornman of the South African Iron, Steel and Allied Industries Union (typically shortened to Iron and Steel). In addition to Bornman, the deputation included workers' representatives from the railways, public service, and mining industry. A number of the unions represented would also testify individually. In both written and oral testimony, these workers consistently based their opposition to labour reform on the policy of separate development and its objective of creating independent black nations distinct from 'white South Africa'. SACLA workers drew a distinction between themselves, as citizens entitled to state protection and privilege, and Africans as '*gasarbeiders*' – guest workers or foreign labour temporarily employed in the Republic without any claim to rights or residence.[36] '[T]his is the ultimate goal in white South Africa, that no Bantu will have any right in South Africa,'[37] insisted Paulus during the MWU's testimony. Hence, the SACLA deputation testified that job reservation and the exclusion of Africans from trade union rights were both matters of 'the principle of the protection of interests'[38] and the 'self-preservation of the white worker in his own country'.[39] When asked how it proposed

---

[32] Quoted in SAIRR, *A Survey of Race Relations in South Africa 1976*, p. 314.
[33] See Chapter 2.   [34] SAIRR, *A Survey of Race Relations in South Africa 1977*, pp. 226–7.
[35] Friedman, *Building Tomorrow Today*, p. 151.
[36] SA/WD, Testimony Meeting 8, Pretoria, 6 December 1977, pp. 913–14, 919–20.
[37] SA/WD, Testimony Meeting 24, Johannesburg, 22 February 1978, p. 3699.
[38] SA/WD, Testimony Meeting 8, Pretoria, 6 December 1977, p. 908.
[39] Letter from SACLA to the Wiehahn Commission, dated 12 May 1978, quoted in SA/WD, Deliberation Meeting 43, Pretoria, 5 September 1978, p. 7240.

Figure 3.2 Attie Nieuwoudt (left) with Prime Minister John Vorster (centre) and Minister of Labour Fanie Botha (right) at a meeting of labour representatives in Pretoria, 1977.
Source: *Die Transvaler*, 22 June 1977

to deal with the reality of a growing African labour movement, the deputation responded that African unionism should be restricted to African 'homelands' and banned in the 'white' Republic.[40] For SACLA, labour rights were thus inextricably linked to political rights and citizenship.[41]

Given the convergence of race and rights underlying separate development's politics of inclusion and exclusion, these white workers felt entitled to labour legislation and state action that protected their interests as white citizen workers.[42] According to the SACLA deputation, job reservation offered workers protection from 'exploitation'[43] by 'the capitalist businessman and his pursuit of maximum profit at minimum cost [which] will always seek out the cheapest labour' in the form of

---

[40] SA/WD, Testimony Meeting 8, Pretoria, 6 December 1977, p. 913, 924–5; NA, SAB, K364, Vol. 33 AK 6/3/1/1/4 Vol. II, Memorandum van die Suid-Afrikaanse Konfederasie van Arbeid aan Die Sekretaris, Kommissie van Ondersoek na Arbeidswetgewing, 21 November 1977 (Memorandum Dokument no. 00164), p. 2.

[41] See also SA/WD, Testimony Meeting 8, Pretoria, 6 December 1977, p. 925.

[42] For more on the concept of the 'white citizen worker' and its relation to SACLA's position, see D. van Zyl-Hermann, 'White workers and the unravelling of racial citizenship in late apartheid South Africa' in D. Money and D. van Zyl-Hermann (eds), *Rethinking White Societies in Southern Africa, 1930s–1990s* (Abingdon: Routledge, 2020), pp. 194–14. For a comparative perspective, see scholarship on white working-class investment in racial citizenship in the USA: for instance, Roediger, *The Wages of Whiteness*; D. Montgomery, *Citizen Worker: the experience of workers in the United States with democracy and the free market during the nineteenth century* (Cambridge: Cambridge University Press, 1993); Meeks, 'Protecting the "white citizen worker"', pp. 91–113.

[43] SA/WD, Testimony Meeting 8, Pretoria, 6 December 1977, p. 909.

'some other races' with 'lower living standards'.[44] During his own metalworkers' union's testimony, Bornman stated the mandate received from his union to unequivocally oppose the granting of union rights to Africans, support the retention of job reservation, and argue for the prioritisation of white employment.[45] The deputation defended job reservation particularly on behalf of lesser-skilled economically vulnerable white workers: job reservation protected 'specifically those people who do not have a trade that are rooted in these industries and who, should they leave, would be completely incapable of finding a similar income off [sic] their own accord anywhere else in the job market'.[46] This statement was reminiscent of the 'civilised labour' policy that offered higher compensation and insulation from competition to white workers with relatively few skills. Indeed, Bornman's union historically represented unskilled and semi-skilled white workers, many of whom were employed as production workers and operatives in the parastatal steel company Iscor, established by the Pact government. By 1976, Iron and Steel represented some 38,000 workers across the industry.[47] Nieuwoudt also displayed concern with the economic vulnerability of some of the workers he represented, as well as awareness of their dependence on legislative protection. This was tellingly demonstrated during a discussion of a draft of the Commission's report when Nieuwoudt objected to references to poor whiteism in the report's historical overview of South Africa's labour legislation:

NIEUWOUDT: Mr Chairman, down here we refer to the poor white question, is it really necessary to mention this?
WIEHAHN: But this poor white question was part of our history, Mr Nieuwoudt.
NIEUWOUDT: It can become part of [our] history again.
WIEHAHN: Sure, it can always become part of history and then other commissions in a hundred years can refer to it again.
NIEUWOUDT: Mr Chairman, it might be within ten months.
WIEHAHN: It is but history, Mr Nieuwoudt, simply a factual statement in historical interest.[48]

---

[44] NA, SAB, K364, Vol. 33 AK 6/3/1/1/4 Vol. II: SA Confederation of Labour (Memorandum Dokument no. 00164), p. 1; also SA/WD, Testimony Meeting 8, Pretoria, 6 December 1977, p. 909. Similar arguments were offered by the MWU: NA, SAB, K364, Vol. 33 AK 6/3/1/1/4 Vol. II: '[MWU] Memorandum in verband met Arbeidswetgewing' (Memorandum Dokument no. 00182), p. 2; also SA/WD, Testimony Meeting 24, Johannesburg, 22 February 1978, pp. 3716–17.
[45] SA/WD, Testimony Meeting 9, Pretoria, 7 December 1977, p. 1003.
[46] SA/WD, Testimony Meeting 9, Pretoria, 7 December 1977, p. 1004.
[47] Lewis, *Industrialisation and Trade Union Organisation*, pp. 78–83.
[48] SA/WD, Deliberation Meeting 52, Pretoria, 27 November 1978, pp. 8771–2.

The SACLA president knew that within the fold of his organisation, white poverty featured prominently in the historical consciousness of some white workers – particularly in older industries such as mining or the railways, which had absorbed large numbers of unskilled and impoverished whites and bolstered their position through civilised labour policies. Indeed, Nieuwoudt's words show that the spectre of white poverty was perceived as a *present* reality. For SACLA workers, the prospect of labour reform suggested that an order in which they enjoyed protection from job insecurity, the degradation of white poverty, and the exploitation of capitalist employers on account of their racial citizenship could be reversed. But Wiehahn dismissed Nieuwoudt's objection as a matter of historical semantics and seemed not to notice the much more fundamental, long-lived anxieties born of the formation of the white working class that it revealed.

The archive shows that Nieuwoudt remained in close contact with his constituency and under pressure from its members. In September 1978 (that is, while the Commission was still deliberating), the media reported statements by Minister Botha that the Commission would recommend the abrogation of job reservation. This elicited an outcry from sections of organised labour. Nieuwoudt reported that he had to deal with 'difficult people' who had the impression that the Commission's findings were being directed by the Minister. 'Someone told me again yesterday,' an exasperated Nieuwoudt related, 'the Minister and Professor Wiehahn have already decided, you are wasting your time on the Commission.'[49] Reiterating the white working-class's time-honoured threat, Nieuwoudt warned the Commission that unwanted changes to protective legislation could see white workers resort to 'the greatest industrial unrest that this Republic has ever seen'.[50] He repeatedly stressed that labour policies could not be divorced from the greater constitutional reality that excluded blacks from citizenship in the Republic. This insistence that white supremacy in the industrial sphere could not be separated from white supremacy in the political sphere saw SACLA workers not only resist any efforts to depoliticise the matter of labour reform but also insist on the fact that any changes to labour legislation were bound to have political ramifications. Hence, Nieuwoudt warned his fellow

---

[49] SA/WD, Deliberation Meeting 46, Pretoria, 8 September 1978, pp. 7775–6. This idea was raised during and after the inquiry from the right and left, and Friedman and Giliomee both suggest the existence of a government-level 'plan' underlaying the Wiehahn process. Friedman, *Building Tomorrow Today*, pp. 149–79; Giliomee, *The Last Afrikaner Leaders*, pp. 152–9.

[50] SA/WD, Deliberation Meeting 45, Pretoria, 7 September 1978, pp. 7711–12.

commissioners that 'we are busy deciding about the future of South Africa here, because the labour force will determine our direction, and politics will just have to follow suit',[51] imploring them to consider 'where are we going with this fatherland of ours?'[52]

For white workers in the SACLA fold, there was clearly much at stake in the reform process. The documentation offers evidence of real concerns about economic vulnerability and of continued dependence on the racial state's protectionist policies. Upward social mobility had not come to all whites in equal measure in the preceding decades of NP rule, and there were limits to white upward mobility in a context of labour fragmentation and changes in the racial division of labour.[53] But SACLA workers' testimonies also reveal a broader concern that labour reform would not only have an impact on its members' immediate material position, but would undermine racially privileged citizenship – first for white workers in the industrial arena, but inevitably for all whites in the Republic. Bornman pointed to such broader implications when, asked whether unions would be able to protect minorities should protective legislation such as job reservation be abrogated, he answered with a resounding 'No'.[54]

The Joint Committee

On the morning of 1 March 1978 – just a few months after the establishment of the Joint Committee Representing All Organised Labour in the Republic of South Africa, and SACLA's withdrawal from it – five labour leaders representing the Committee's member unions reported to Johannesburg's brutalist-style civic centre to present their testimony. The deputation was headed by Ben Nicholson of the South African Electrical Workers' Association, an all-white union affiliated to the 83,000-strong multiracial Confederation of Metal and Building Unions.[55] He was joined by Richard Beech of the Amalgamated Union of Building Trade Workers, an unaffiliated, multiracial union,[56] and by Morris Kagan, Abel van der Watt, and Alfieri Elisio, who between them

---

[51] SA/WD, Deliberation Meeting 54, Pretoria, 11 December 1978, p. 8987.
[52] SA/WD, Deliberation Meeting 47, Pretoria, 26 September 1978, p. 8028.
[53] Crankshaw, *Race, Class and the Changing Division of Labour*, pp. 98–9.
[54] SA/WD, Testimony Meeting 8, Pretoria, 6 December 1977, p. 923.
[55] NA, SAB, K364, Vol. 33, AK 6/3/1/1/4 Vol. II, Letter from W. Bornman to B. Nicholson, 6 December 1977; NA, SAB, K364, Vol. 33, AK 6/3/1/1/4 Vol. II, Documentation accompanying letter from Industrial Registrar to The Secretary, Commission of Inquiry into Labour Legislation, 10 July 1978, pp. 3–4.
[56] SA/WD, Testimony Meeting 29, Johannesburg, 1 March 1978, p. 4621.

represented TUCSA, the South African Co-ordinating Council of International Metal Workers Federation, and the African National Union of Clothing Workers.[57] As the latter two bodies were unregistered, its members were not included in the 328,000 legally organised workers noted as represented by the Joint Committee. Of these, approximately 45 per cent were white and 55 per cent coloured or Indian.[58]

Clearly a broad church of organised labour, the Joint Committee's testimony hearing was often characterised by different and even contrasting views. On the matter of job reservation, Nicholson declared the Committee 'in favour of the deletion of Section 77, the job reservation clause, but only provided that adequate protection can be built into legislation to provide for the protection of each minority group'. When Kagan expressed the view that discrimination should in fact be criminalised, Beech responded that his union wanted Section 77 to be retained. A discussion ensued and it was eventually concluded that the Committee could not reach a consensus.[59] Nicholson continued to explain that there were fears within the Committee's fold that the removal of protective legislation would see 'existing artisans' being 'swamped by numbers' or undercut by employers appointing cheaper African workers with 'inferior training'.[60] This, it was claimed, was already occurring in some industries where racial minorities were being 'unfairly excluded because of the dominance of numbers of another [racial] group'.[61]

Among the craft unions party to the Joint Committee was the 22,367-strong Artisans Staff Association and 28,648-strong AEU.[62] The general secretaries of these all-white unions – Wally Grobler and Tommie Neethling respectively – both served as Wiehahn commissioners and echoed calls for minority protection. Neethling in particular was unequivocal, insisting on several occasions that he would not support any labour reforms before knowing exactly what safeguards would be built into the system:

I cannot and will not commit myself to anything, not before I am positive, convinced, that my people will be secured, the people that I represent. I could

---

[57] NA, SAB, K364, Vol. 33, AK 6/3/1/1/4 Vol. II, Letter from D. van der Walt to Industrial Registrar, 27 June 1978.
[58] NA, SAB, K364, Vol. 33, AK 6/3/1/1/4 Vol. II, Letter and accompanying documentation from Industrial Registrar to The Secretary, Commission of Inquiry into Labour Legislation, 10 July 1978.
[59] SA/WD, Testimony Meeting 29, Johannesburg, 1 March 1978, pp. 4621–2, 4634–5.
[60] SA/WD, Testimony Meeting 29, Johannesburg, 1 March 1978, pp. 4661–2.
[61] SA/WD, Testimony Meeting 29, Johannesburg, 1 March 1978, pp. 4616–17.
[62] NA, SAB, K364, Vol. 33, AK 6/3/1/1/4 Vol. II, Documentation accompanying letter from Industrial Registrar to The Secretary, Commission of Inquiry into Labour Legislation, 10 July 1978, p. 3.

never be party to sit here and agree to things knowing very well ... that the future of my people will be jeopardised.[63]

This insistence on minority protection extended beyond job reservation to discussions on the possible legalisation of African trade unions and their participation in conciliatory mechanisms. 'I believe there are some things [that] should be put in place, so that we may know what direction we will be taking [on the industrial councils], before I am asked whether I will agree to the registration of black unions,' Neethling stated resolutely.[64] To give credence to his hard bargaining, Neethling provided examples demonstrating his – and white labour's – willingness to accept minority protection measures as an alternative to statutory protection. On several occasions he recounted his involvement in the removal of job reservation in the metal industry, stressing that this process had been successful because it had offered white workers a sense of security by devising an alternative to Section 77.[65] Both commissioners were adamant that legislative changes must be formulated and implemented in a way that would be acceptable to white workers. Grobler cautioned more than once that failing to do this would create 'enormous problems'.[66] Neethling went further, warning the Commission that 'emotions are running very high on this issue'[67] and issuing a chilling variant of the familiar threat: that reforms could result in a 'bloodbath ... if we can't give [white workers] their security and assure them that they are not in danger'.[68] It was no coincidence that Neethling made the latter statement in September 1978, when media reports created the impression that the Commission was being directed to remove job reservation. '[T]his is what I was told last night by people who are very militant in the organisations that we represent,' a tense Neethling explained to his fellow commissioners:

They are very militant and they say to me that: you are there as a puppet, the Minister has already given you instructions ... a lot of people phoned me last night, and they said to me: 'Why the hell don't you withdraw' – sorry for the word – but: why don't you withdraw from this Commission, the Minister has already issued instructions.[69]

---

[63] SA/WD, Deliberation Meeting 45, Pretoria, 7 September 1978, pp. 7612–14.
[64] SA/WD, Deliberation Meeting 45, Pretoria, 7 September 1978, pp. 7714–15.
[65] SA/WD, Deliberation Meeting 47, Pretoria, 26 September 1978, pp. 7982–3.
[66] SA/WD, Deliberation Meeting 45, Pretoria, 7 September 1978, pp. 7721–2; also SA/WD, Deliberation Meeting 51, Pretoria, 25 October 1978, p. 8681.
[67] SA/WD, Deliberation Meeting 50, Pretoria, 24 October 1978, p. 8413.
[68] SA/WD, Deliberation Meeting 45, Pretoria, 7 September 1978, pp. 7621–2.
[69] SA/WD, Deliberation Meeting 46, Pretoria, 8 September 1978, pp. 7773–5.

Figure 3.3 Minister Fanie Botha and his secretary Jaap Cilliers (both centre) attend a meeting of the Wiehahn Commission, 1977. Dennis van der Walt and Nic Wiehahn consult in the background, with Chris du Toit and Errol Drummond attending in the foreground.
Source: Die Erfenisstigting, Pretoria

When Commissioner Drummond tried to deflate the situation by suggesting that it was just a matter of a few 'rank and file people' making 'uncomfortable phone calls', Neethling immediately retorted that the outcry had not come from people who were simply 'emotionally a bit upset', but from 'responsible trade union leaders'. 'I wanted this on record,' he continued angrily, 'because these people, I think, have got the right to come and make queries after reading statements like that.'[70]

This evidence of anxiety and indignation among white artisans provides important insights into how white workers outside the SACLA fold perceived the climate of reform. Neethling's and Grobler's white artisans clearly shared concerns similar to those of the supervisory and semi-skilled white workers represented by Nieuwoudt. Moreover, these concerns were clearly not restricted to white workers. Beech's Amalgamated Union of Building Trade Workers represented 3,000 white and 5,000 coloured workers in the construction industry. As a representative of the Joint Committee, he explained to the Wiehahn Commission that

---

[70] SA/WD, Deliberation Meeting 46, Pretoria, 8 September 1978, pp. 7778–80.

'my Coloured members have asked for [the retention of Section 77]. Because they see the danger [in removing job reservation] more than [whites] see it.'[71] Insistence on minority protection thus often denoted the concerns shared by white, coloured, and Indian workers in the face of an African majority labour force.

Of those who testified before the Wiehahn Commission, Joint Committee representatives and unions advocated the idea of minority protection most clearly. But the archive suggests that it was already on the commissioners' minds. Even before the Joint Committee appeared before the Commission to appeal for the replacement of statutory discrimination with minority protection measures, Wiehahn himself had urged his fellow commissioners to engage seriously with the issue of minority protection, as 'it would appear that the criticism against job reservation and other discriminatory measures revolve around this one main theme namely, how do you protect minority groups in a heterogeneous society'.[72] This was not just a question for the labour arena. In the wake of the Soweto uprising, the government had appointed a Cabinet Committee (under the chairmanship of P. W. Botha, then Minister of Defence) to investigate 'possible and desirable adjustments to the existing constitutional order'.[73] Faced with a crisis of legitimacy, the government sought to formulate constitutional reforms that would remove the most offensive elements of white supremacy and draw other population groups into the system, thus shoring up the regime's legitimacy. Coloured and Indian South Africans, as minority groups alongside whites, were the central objects of these considerations, which revolved around a model of constitutional power sharing and the reimagination of South Africa as a multiracial state.[74] In the same breath as he appealed to his commissioners to consider minority protection measures in the labour arena, Wiehahn told them to bear in mind that the government was busy 'forming a new constitutional dispensation with regards to the Coloureds and the Asians',[75] referencing the reformist ideas and new rhetoric of pluralism circulating beyond the industrial arena at the time. While SACLA's Nieuwoudt claimed that changes in the industrial dispensation would direct the country's political future, Wiehahn seemed to suggest that labour reformers should take their cue from the political

---

[71] SA/WD, Testimony Meeting 23, Johannesburg, 21 February 1978, p. 3501.
[72] SA/WD, Testimony Meeting 24, Johannesburg, 22 February 1978, p. 3562.
[73] SAIRR, *A Survey of Race Relations in South Africa 1977*, p. 7.
[74] Giliomee, *The Last Afrikaner Leaders*, pp. 167–8; Giliomee, 'Broedertwis', pp. 353–4, 363; Greenberg, *Legitimating the Illegitimate*, p. xv; Lodge, 'Resistance and reform', p. 482.
[75] SA/WD, Testimony Meeting 24, Johannesburg, 22 February 1978, p. 3564.

agenda. The government's constitutional considerations would eventually lead to the 1983 Constitution Act, which replaced the exclusively white legislature with a tricameral parliament in which coloured and Indian people were granted limited political representation. Reforms of local government arrangements saw Africans receive new powers and responsibilities at community level, but they continued to be excluded from political citizenship.[76] Giliomee notes that, to more *verligte* white voters, government presented these reforms as 'a step in the right direction' towards 'normalising race relations' in South Africa,[77] while to more conservative voters, it was offered as 'an effective way of shoring up white power'.[78] The Joint Committee's suggestions for labour reform therefore resonated with emerging reformist political strategies of the time. Its emphasis on minority protection sought the institution of new measures which would continue to provide protection for white workers and would simultaneously appeal to workers from other minority racial groups who felt threatened by African advancement.

The Trade Union Council of South Africa

Since its formation in 1954, TUCSA had oscillated between including and excluding unregistered African unions in its fold.[79] After the Durban strikes, the Council decided once more to open its doors to unregistered African unions. In February 1976, the National Union of Clothing Workers (NUCW), an African trade union boasting some 23,000 members, rejoined TUCSA after having resigned its membership in 1967.[80] TUCSA general secretary Grobbelaar was defiant in the face of threats that the government might deregister TUCSA on account of its African members, stating that 'the Government might find it more difficult to do without TUCSA than TUCSA would to do without the Government'.[81] TUCSA condemned the government's efforts to appease striking workers by offering them negotiating powers on shop-floor committees, and called on the government to recognise African unions. But not all TUCSA members agreed with the Council's decision to support African workers. In September 1976, the 16,500-member Boilermakers' Society disaffiliated from TUCSA due to the Council's support for African advancement into skilled jobs. The Society's general secretary stated that 'our policy differs from TUCSA's. We have

---

[76] Lodge, 'Resistance and reform', p. 409, 437; Dubow, *Apartheid*, p. 205.
[77] Dubow, *Apartheid*, p. 204.   [78] Giliomee, *The Last Afrikaner Leaders*, p. 168.
[79] Greenberg, *Race and State*, pp. 298–9.   [80] Horrell, *South Africa's Workers*, p. 33.
[81] SAIRR, *A Survey of Race Relations in South Africa 1976*, p. 315.

thousands of Coloured and Asian [Indian] members whose jobs we have to protect. We can't do this at the same time as putting Africans into their union as proposed by TUCSA. We cannot allow African workers to move into their jobs.'[82] A month later, the National Union of Furniture and Allied Workers also disaffiliated from TUCSA, stating similar reasons for the protection of their approximately 10,000 coloured and Indian members. At the same time, the National Union of Motor Assembly and Rubber Workers of South Africa (NUMARWOSA), with some 4,000 coloured and Indian members, left TUCSA on the grounds that the Council was not doing enough to further the interests of African workers. Clearly, disparate forces were at play within TUCSA.[83]

At TUCSA's annual conference in September 1977, it elected a coloured president for the first time in its 23-year history. Ronnie Webb, general secretary of the Motor Industry Combined Workers' Union, had already been serving as TUCSA vice-president. Webb 'commented that his election gave full expression to TUCSA's declared policy of equal opportunity for all in South Africa'.[84] The conference passed a resolution appealing to the Prime Minister to end racial discrimination and accelerate 'meaningful and tangible' change.[85] In the same month, Grobbelaar initiated talks with other bodies in organised labour on the possibility of submitting joint evidence to the Commission. But despite being party to the subsequent formation of the Joint Committee, TUCSA still elected to bring independent testimony before the Wiehahn Commission.

The TUCSA deputation appearing before the Commission in February 1978 in Johannesburg was led by Webb. TUCSA's written submission from October 1977 noted its affiliated membership as 60 trade unions with a total of 223,652 workers, of whom 17,182 were Africans belonging to seven unregistered unions.[86] According to the Industrial Registrar's records, about 27 per cent of TUCSA's non-African members were white.[87] It is unclear what the skills level of

---

[82] Quoted in SAIRR, *A Survey of Race Relations in South Africa 1976*, p. 316.
[83] SAIRR, *A Survey of Race Relations in South Africa 1976*, p. 316; Du Toit, *Capital and Labour*, p. 330; Friedman, *Building Tomorrow Today*, pp. 180–1.
[84] SAIRR, *A Survey of Race Relations in South Africa 1977*, p. 286.
[85] SAIRR, *A Survey of Race Relations in South Africa 1977*, p. 287.
[86] NA, SAB, K364, Vol. 33 AK 6/3/1/1/4 Vol. II: 'Memorandum concerning a sound labour relations system, submitted by the Trade Union Council of South Africa to the Commission of Inquiry into Labour Legislation, October 1977' (Memorandum Dokument no. 00147), p. 1.
[87] NA, SAB, K364, Vol. 33, AK 6/3/1/1/4 Vol. II, Documentation accompanying letter from Industrial Registrar to The Secretary, Commission of Inquiry into Labour Legislation, 10 July 1978, pp. 1–3.

TUCSA's membership was – its written submission noted simply that the majority of its affiliates represented 'both "White" and "Blue" collar occupations', employed predominantly in the industrial and commercial sectors.[88]

TUCSA's testimony departed markedly from the cautious and conditional reformist attitude of the Joint Committee. The TUCSA deputation testified that it supported freedom of association and the complete elimination of racial discrimination.[89] In response to questioning by Commissioner Steenkamp, Webb affirmed that TUCSA wished to see 'non-statutory discrimination outlawed' as well as the introduction of measures 'akin to the American affirmative action programme in order to redress evils of the past'.[90] TUCSA argued that a 'new industrial relations system must ... conform to the accepted norms of the free Western World, in an effort to prevent the introduction of economic boycotts and sanctions'.[91] 'And I think here one can't confine yourself to just industrial legislation,' Webb added cautiously, 'I think [normalising change] has to run the whole course of all our legislation.'[92] For an organisation presenting itself as favouring democratising reform, Webb was very tentative when pointing to possible political change.

In a significant difference of opinion with the Joint Committee, TUCSA testified that it saw no need for minority protection measures: '[I]t is our considered opinion that if the concept of equal pay for equal work [or 'rate for the job'] is written into legislation, that will take care of the situation.'[93] TUCSA argued for the irrelevance of Section 77 and was

---

[88] NA, SAB, K364, Vol. 33 AK 6/3/1/1/4 Vol. II: 'Memorandum concerning a sound labour relations system, submitted by the Trade Union Council of South Africa to the Commission of Inquiry into Labour Legislation, October 1977' (Memorandum Dokument no. 00147), p. 1; SA/WD, Testimony Meeting 22, Johannesburg, 20 February 1978, p. 3223.
[89] SA/WD, Testimony Meeting 22, Johannesburg, 20 February 1978, pp. 3218–19. See also NA, SAB, K364, Vol. 33, AK 6/3/1/1/4 Vol. II: 'Memorandum concerning a sound labour relations system, submitted by the Trade Union Council of South Africa to the Commission of Inquiry into Labour Legislation, October 1977' (Memorandum Dokument no. 00147).
[90] SA/WD, Testimony Meeting 22, Johannesburg, 20 February 1978, p. 3220.
[91] NA, SAB, K364, Vol. 33 AK 6/3/1/1/4 Vol. II: 'Memorandum concerning a sound labour relations system, submitted by the Trade Union Council of South Africa to the Commission of Inquiry into Labour Legislation, October 1977' (Memorandum Dokument no. 00147), p. 3.
[92] SA/WD, Testimony Meeting 22, Johannesburg, 20 February 1978, p. 3231.
[93] SA/WD, Testimony Meeting 22, Johannesburg, 20 February 1978, p. 3268. Although at the time the principle was also interpreted as a form of white protection, as 'no employer will employ Blacks at the same wage when Whites are available'. M. A. du Toit, *South African Trade Unions: history, legislation, policy* (Johannesburg: McGraw-Hill Book Company, 1976), pp. 133–4.

adamant that in the new labour dispensation there would be no restrictions on the upward mobility of any workers, and therefore no need for protection.[94] TUCSA's general secretary, Arthur Grobbelaar, who also served on the Wiehahn Commission, stated before the Commission that protective legislation, specifically job reservation, was simply an 'emotional issue ... I don't believe it is any other sort of issue.'[95]

TUCSA argued for unqualified freedom of association meeting the standards advocated by the International Labour Organization (ILO). The only caveat the deputation proposed was that, in contrast to the ILO's convention, unions should not be forced to accept non-racialism but should be allowed to decide their own preferred racial composition and retain their group identities, if they so desired. Given this possibility, TUCSA argued that new labour laws should make provision for the registration of various types of coordinating bodies 'such as TUCSA' which would be able to embrace all ethnic or racial groups as members for the sake of cooperation between all workers.[96] It was adamant, however, that all trade unions should be required to register with the government, or not be allowed to operate.[97]

In the Wiehahn documentation, TUCSA's testimony comes across as progressive and democratising in its intent. But when the Commission came to formulating its recommendations, Grobbelaar wavered in his support for freedom of association. At the pivotal moment in 1978, when the Commission had to vote on this point, it was split. Commissioners Van der Merwe, Drummond, Hechter, Neethling, and Grobler (labelled 'the reformists' by Giliomee) favoured a recommendation that would restrict African eligibility for trade union membership to 'urban blacks', thus excluding the vast majority of the African labour force who were officially commuters and migrants from the 'homelands' or neighbouring countries. On the other side, commissioners Steenkamp, Du Toit, Sutton, Munsook, Botes, and Mokoatle ('the progressives') advocated complete freedom of association, thus incorporating all African workers

---

[94] SA/WD, Testimony Meeting 22, Johannesburg, 20 February 1978, p. 3271, 3282–4.
[95] SA/WD, Testimony Meeting 8, Pretoria, 6 December 1977, p. 878. A similar statement was made during Testimony Meeting 10, Pretoria, 8 December 1977, p. 1130.
[96] NA, SAB, K364, Vol. 33 AK 6/3/1/1/4 Vol. II: 'Memorandum concerning a sound labour relations system, submitted by the Trade Union Council of South Africa to the Commission of Inquiry into Labour Legislation, October 1977' (Memorandum Dokument no. 00147), p. 5, 8.
[97] SA/WD, Testimony Meeting 22, Johannesburg, 20 February 1978, p. 3248, 3260–1. See also NA, SAB, K364, Vol. 33 AK 6/3/1/1/4 Vol. II: 'Memorandum concerning a sound labour relations system, submitted by the Trade Union Council of South Africa to the Commission of Inquiry into Labour Legislation, October 1977' (Memorandum Dokument no. 00147), pp. 7–8.

within the labour movement. Nieuwoudt had already indicated his intention to submit a minority report opposing any form of African unionism within the Republic, while Wiehahn was attempting to the last to remain impartial in his position as chair (although Giliomee notes that Wiehahn tacitly supported the 'reformists'). Grobbelaar was thus in the decisive position: should he side with the 'reformists', the Commission would be tied without a clear majority recommendation. Should he side with the 'progressives', on the other hand, it would be a clear victory for freedom of association.[98] Given TUCSA's testimony, it would seem obvious where Grobbelaar's loyalties would lie. But Grobbelaar apparently hovered between these two camps. Many years later Steenkamp recalled how hard he had to work to convince Grobbelaar to support complete freedom of association, spending much time with him discussing the prospect and frequenting his home at weekends to bring one proposal after the other before the TUCSA leader. It was on a Sunday afternoon, the day before the Commission's final vote on the matter, that Steenkamp finally wheedled Grobbelaar into joining the 'progressives' by personally guaranteeing Grobbelaar a position on the soon-to-be-established National Manpower Commission (NMC) – an industrial watchdog to be set up under the Wiehahn recommendations, which would monitor and regulate the implementation of reforms.[99]

Why was Grobbelaar torn on this seemingly straightforward issue for TUCSA? We have seen that throughout its history, TUCSA had struggled with the issue of whether African workers should be included in the labour movement, and that its constant changing of position highlighted concomitant divisions and shifts within organised labour. In interviews, Commission insiders pointed to the difficult position in which Grobbelaar found himself. On the one hand, he faced opposition, particularly from coloured and Indian workers within the TUCSA fold, to the recognition of African unions. Grobbelaar admitted to Dennis van der Walt, the Commission's secretary, that he was having serious problems getting his members – especially coloured workers in the motor vehicle industry – on board with the envisioned changes and was afraid of losing their support. The tension was so great that, early in 1978, Grobbelaar called a special closed TUCSA conference to discuss impending changes. On that occasion, he illegally divulged information

---

[98] Naas Steenkamp, interviewed 6 December 2011. Also related in Giliomee, *The Last Afrikaner Leaders*, pp. 152–4.
[99] Naas Steenkamp, interviewed 6 December 2011; Dennis van der Walt interviewed by Naas Steenkamp, 7 October 2008; Department of Labour and of Mines, *Report Part 1*, p. 30, see also p. 11.

regarding the Commission's investigation, its likely recommendations, and resultant changes in the legislation. Steenkamp explained that Grobbelaar 'had a fragmented support base which he had to hold together, and that is why he spoke out at the apparently closed TUCSA meeting – he said that he simply had to do so in order to get his members on board'.[100] But the information was leaked and published in the media – leading to the chastisement of Grobbelaar before the Commission.[101] On the other hand, Grobbelaar was worried about TUCSA's (and his own) reputation with the ILO. According to Van der Walt, Grobbelaar was 'the only unionist worried about the international aspect, and he was truly afraid of being excluded in the future'.[102] In the most recent evaluation of the Wiehahn Commission, Giliomee explained Grobbelaar's hesitation as follows: 'He had to move cautiously because his federation included unions that favoured the recognition of black unions in the hope of controlling them, while others wanted to squash them.'[103] TUCSA's testimony before the Commission does not contain evidence of the latter intention – but Giliomee's assessment concurs with that of other labour observers. Du Toit, Friedman, and Lichtenstein have all pointed to TUCSA's opening of its ranks to unregistered African unions earlier in the decade as an opportunistic strategy to have its registered unions gain control over African workers under the pretence of guardianship and organisational support.[104] Hence, the NUCW's affiliation to TUCSA in 1976 was a coup for TUCSA rather than an advantage for the NUCW: 'not only major influence in the African trade-union movement but also financial advantage could be gained from controlling this union,' remarks Du Toit, proceeding to suggest that the NUCW was little more than a subservient TUCSA handmaiden.[105] With regard to TUCSA's call for 'equal pay for equal work', Friedman argues that 'registered unions could only enforce the "rate for the job" if they controlled African wage bargaining – if they alone represented African workers'.[106] In an interview, Steenkamp offered a related opinion, suggesting that in arguing for freedom of

---

[100] Naas Steenkamp, interviewed 23 August 2013.
[101] See SA/WD, Testimony Meeting 35, Pretoria, 1 May 1978.
[102] Dennis van der Walt interviewed by Naas Steenkamp, 7 October 2008.
[103] Giliomee, *The Last Afrikaner Leaders*, p. 154.
[104] Friedman, *Building Tomorrow Today*, p. 9, 69–81; Du Toit, *Capital and Labour*, pp. 232–3, 387–93; Lichtenstein, 'A measure of democracy', p. 125; A. Lichtenstein, '"The hope for white and black"? Race, labour and the state in South Africa and the United States, 1924–1956', *Journal of Southern African Studies* 30, no. 1 (2004), p. 151.
[105] Du Toit, *Capital and Labour*, p. 391.
[106] Friedman, *Building Tomorrow Today*, p. 75.

association before the Wiehahn Commission, TUCSA was hoping to capitalise on incorporating newly registered African unions into its membership, thus significantly bolstering its industrial muscle and position as a trade union federation in South Africa's post-reform labour dispensation.[107] This may well be what lay behind TUCSA's emphasis on the rights of unions to retain their group identities, provided provision was made for a greater coordinating body – such as itself.

What is clear is that TUCSA did not wish to see labour relations used as a platform for advancing political change, which is what emerging African trade unions wanted. Although Webb cautiously voiced the opinion that all South African legislation needed 'normalisation', TUCSA's testimony did not engage with the broader political context of labour reform. Indeed, during a debate on whether all African workers or only 'urban blacks' with residence rights in the Republic should be granted labour rights, Grobbelaar objected to squabbling over citizenship and appealed to the commissioners to focus on labour relations only:

> I don't care what happens in regard to political developments in South Africa in the years to come, I am not a politician so that is not my problem. I don't care what sort of political developments take place, all I know is one thing, that somewhere along the line you have got to take into account the determining of conditions of employment between the employers and their workers, irrespective of any sort of political development. And I submit, Mr Chairman, that this is the task of this Commission.[108]

This position certainly stood in stark contrast to that of SACLA, and the depoliticising tendency adopted by Grobbelaar may well have made TUCSA an attractive labour partner for the NP government – taking up the role once played by SACLA. As Chapter 2 showed, Labour Minister Fanie Botha was much more positively disposed towards TUCSA than his predecessor Marias Viljoen. Indeed, speaking in front of the Wiehahn Commission, Ronnie Webb testified that for many years the Department of Labour had treated TUCSA as 'step-children', with its unions coming up against 'undue opposition and pettiness' on the side of the Department, but that this had 'improved considerably in recent years'.[109]

Wiehahn's report and aftermath

On Labour Day 1979, the first and most important part of the Commission's report was tabled in Parliament. In what has been labelled

---

[107] Naas Steenkamp, interviewed 6 December 2011.
[108] SA/WD, Deliberation Meeting 54, Pretoria, 11 December 1978, p. 8991.
[109] SA/WD, Testimony Meeting 22, Johannesburg, 20 February 1978, pp. 3216–17.

a historical concession, the Commission recommended the principle of 'freedom of association', thereby extending trade union rights to Africans, and the recognition of African and multiracial unions. This proposal envisioned, for the first time in the country's history, an integrated system of labour relations that included Africans as 'employees'.[110] The near-miss composition of this majority recommendation has been described above. With regard to job reservation, 13 of the 14 commissioners supported the recommendation that Section 77 of the 1956 Act be repealed, the principle of statutory work reservation abolished, and that employers and established unions in industries where the last determinations were still active consult on phasing out these practices. The report did acknowledge that, due to the 'multidimensional characteristics' of South Africa's labour force, the interests of some workers in some contexts might need safeguarding.[111] It recommended a number of protective measures through which this could be achieved, including the principle of consultation between employers and employees before implementing changes in established practices; recourse to an Industrial Court for any aggrieved party; the requirement that industrial councils must reach consensus concerning proposed changes; and the strict enforcement of the principle of 'equal pay for equal work'.[112] Commissioner Nieuwoudt submitted minority reports on all major recommendations.

The Commission's recommendations were favourably received by local industry, multinationals, and foreign governments – they were even celebrated as the most significant concessions ever adopted by the apartheid state.[113] But if 'commissions are stories states tell themselves', then the recommendations did not offer the story the state wished to hear. In the subsequent White Paper, the government rejected the Commission's majority recommendation of freedom of association. Instead, it accepted the minority recommendation for restricting African eligibility for trade union membership to those with legal permission to reside in the Republic, thus continuing to exclude the majority of '*gasarbeiders*' from the homelands. This conformed to the strategy, also evident in the Riekert Commission's recommendations released the previous year, to divide the African population more firmly between urban insiders and

---

[110] Coupe, 'Labour relations by authoritarian regimes', p. 14.
[111] Department of Labour and of Mines, *Report Part 1*, p. 41.
[112] Department of Labour and of Mines, *Report Part 1*, p. 46. For a summary and critique of Part 1 of the Wiehahn report, see *South African Labour Bulletin* 5, no. 2 (1979).
[113] Mixed reactions came from the labour arena: 'Some initial reactions to Wiehahn', *South African Labour Bulletin* 5, no. 2 (1979), pp. 80–99.

Figure 3.4 Minister Fanie Botha and chairman Nic Wiehahn present Part 1 of the Commission's report to Prime Minister P. W. Botha (centre) in his office, 19 February 1979.
Source: Die Erfenisstigting, Pretoria

outsiders relegated to Bantustan citizenship.[114] While the government accepted most of Wiehahn's proposed controls (such as registration conditions) and minority protection measures, it continued to deny the registration of multiracial unions.[115] Reflecting the government's depoliticising goals, the White Paper emphasised that 'industrial relations solely concerns the relationship between the parties in the work context, and politics has no place there'.[116] Giliomee explains that this move allowed government to 'placate the fears of white workers and their conservative supporters. Andries Treurnicht and Ferdi Hartzenberg, leaders of the NP's right wing, congratulated Wiehahn on his report when he attended Parliament during the discussion of the labour bill.'[117] Giliomee's statement is misleading: the white workers represented by SACLA had unequivocally opposed trade union rights for all Africans.

[114] Feinstein, *An Economic History of South Africa*, pp. 241–2; Dubow, *Apartheid*, p. 198; Ashforth, *The Politics of Official Discourse*, pp. 195–246.
[115] Friedman, *Building Tomorrow Today*, pp. 158–9.
[116] Quoted in Ashforth, *The Politics of Official Discourse*, p. 229.
[117] Giliomee, *The Last Afrikaner Leaders*, p. 157.

Rather, it was the 'story' of limitations on the eligibility of trade union membership advanced by the multiracial members of the Joint Committee and proposed by the 'reformist' group of commissioners in their minority report that echoed reformist political thinking at the time, which the government accepted. Giliomee also makes no mention of the coloured and Indian workers who supported this position, and who may well have been 'placated' by the bill.

According to Friedman, the White Paper 'shattered the [Wiehahn] plan's reformist image, forced African unions into open opposition and lost the authorities most of their foreign goodwill' which the Commission's recommendations had initially raised. Most emerging African unions rejected the government's offer of registration, unwilling to abandon the majority of their members who did not have permanent residence in 'white' South Africa.[118] Even those unions that chose to register under the state's regulations ignored restrictions on signing up commuters and migrants as union members. Meanwhile, in the workplace, African unions circumvented the industrial council system whereby only registered unions could participate and established unions could potentially use the 'consensus' requirement to veto changes; instead, they bargained with employers at plant level.[119] It soon became apparent that the government's 'scheme' to 'share power without losing control' was failing. By recognising unions for 'urban blacks', it had hoped to gain control of emerging unions while dismissing the demands of the remainder of the African workforce under the auspices of separate development. Instead, its recognition of some emerging unions opened up avenues for the organisation of the entire African labour force. Increasingly, African workers were forcing employers to negotiate with them on a large scale, asserting what the government had sought to continue to deny: that broad-based African unions were a permanent force to be reckoned with.[120] And, where the state had hoped its concessions would appease international critics by demonstrating the NP's willingness to reform apartheid, these limited reforms served only to highlight the continued denial of labour rights to the majority of South Africa's workforce.

Hence, in Commissioner Van der Merwe's words, the situation 'changed dramatically' in the 18 months following the publication of Part 1 of the Commission's report: not only did the labour situation get

---

[118] Friedman, *Building Tomorrow Today*, p. 158, 160.
[119] Giliomee, *The Last Afrikaner Leaders*, pp. 158–9.
[120] J. Maree, 'The emergence, struggles and achievements of black trade unions in South Africa from 1973 to 1984', *Labour, Capital and Society* 18, no. 2 (1985), pp. 278–303.

increasingly out of hand, but 'the external climate got worse and the sanctions threat became much more real'.[121] When the Commission released Part 5 of its report in 1981, it recommended the principle of freedom of association with a much clearer majority than two years earlier.[122] This time, government heeded the Commission's recommendation, extending union rights to migrants and commuters, and legalising multiracial unions. The state still attempted to control the unions through tight registration regulations, including efforts to depoliticise the labour movement by prohibiting unions from direct association with political movements. But, as before, such regulations were ignored. Even as the government sought to gain control over African labour, it was overwhelmed by the reform process it had set in motion as African workers 'remade the labour environment despite government intentions'.[123] The government's 'scheme' had the unintended consequences of affording African unions a voice and space for legal struggles, resulting in significant growth and forays into the political arena. From 100,000 workers in 1979, the membership of the new African unions increased rapidly, reaching 750,000 by 1986 and 2 million on the eve of democracy in 1993.[124] 'By the mid-1980s,' writes Giliomee, 'it was clear that the attempt to prevent trade unions from becoming agents for political transformation in South Africa had failed.'[125] The growth of the African labour movement 'had significantly altered the balance of power between government and opposition'.[126]

What happened to white, coloured, and Indian workers in this process? There has been no attempt to track the effectiveness of the new minority protection measures in safeguarding non-African workers from displacement. While measures such as 'rate for the job' and compulsory consultation have been portrayed as euphemisms for continued discriminatory practices, Friedman notes that such mechanisms were 'designed more to soothe white workers than to slow African job advancement and the government would only use [these measures] when white unions forced

---

[121] Piet van der Merwe interviewed by Hermann Giliomee, 18 March 2009, as quoted in Giliomee, *The Last Afrikaner Leaders*, p. 159.
[122] Drummond, Hechter, Neethling and Nieuwoudt still opposed freedom of association. Department of Manpower Utilisation, *Report of the Commission of Inquiry into Labour Legislation Part 5 (Industrial Relations)* (Pretoria: Government Printer, RP27/1981), pp. 25–6.
[123] Greenberg, *Legitimating the Illegitimate*, p. 194.
[124] Giliomee, *The Last Afrikaner Leaders*, p. 158, 161; O'Meara, *Forty Lost Years*, p. 273; Greenberg, *Legitimating the Illegitimate*, p. 194.
[125] Giliomee, *The Last Afrikaner Leaders*, p. 161.
[126] Lodge, 'Resistance and reform', p. 409.

it to'.[127] In an interview, Steenkamp concurred that minority protection was primarily a way of co-opting white workers into the reform process so as to neutralise resistance on their part.[128] Already during the Wiehahn process, members of the Commission had expressed reservations about the effectiveness of some of the proposed regulatory and protection mechanisms such as compulsory consultation[129] or the NMC.[130] Moreover, unlike statutory job reservation, the proposed minority protection measures moved protection out of the ambit of the state and into a more informal and decentralised sphere of authority. In line with global trends towards the retreat of the state and local efforts to depoliticise labour relations, 'the state took itself out of direct involvement in labour conflicts, leaving it to capital and labour to negotiate their differences'.[131] According to Friedman, ultimately 'few of the promised [minority] "safeguards" found their way into the law and none was used to keep Africans out of skilled work'.[132]

Owen Crankshaw's study on the changing racial division of labour under apartheid provides some rare structural insights to place alongside these observations. He shows how the proportion of African artisans increased from 2 per cent in 1965 to 19 per cent in 1989, while African employment in front-line management jobs (such as chargehand, supervisor, or foreman) rose from 13 per cent to 30 per cent over the same period.[133] In contrast to claims by revisionist historians that African advancement during apartheid amounted to the 'mere "blurring" of the racial hierarchy at lower skills levels', Crankshaw argues that 'the trends in formal urban employment suggest that the erosion of the racial division of labour has proceeded much further, at least in some occupational categories, than was generally anticipated'.[134] In the wake of the Wiehahn process, therefore, there was a clear – although not

---

[127] Friedman, *Building Tomorrow Today*, p. 156.
[128] Naas Steenkamp, interviewed 23 August 2013.
[129] See Commissioner Neethling's objection in SA/WD, Deliberation Meeting 48, Pretoria, 28 September 1978, p. 8147. A similar point is made in Friedman, *Building Tomorrow Today*, p. 167.
[130] See the following objections: SA/WD, Deliberation Meeting 50, Pretoria, 24 October 1978, p. 8443 (Steenkamp); Deliberation Meeting 56, Pretoria, 29 January 1979, p. 9286 (Steenkamp); Deliberation Meeting 50, Pretoria, 24 October 1978, p. 8527 (Neethling); Deliberation Meeting 51, Pretoria, 25 October 1978, p. 8563 (Nieuwoudt); Deliberation Meeting 52, Pretoria, 27 November 1978, pp. 8721–2 (Van der Merwe).
[131] O'Meara, *Forty Lost Years*, p. 273. [132] Friedman, *Building Tomorrow Today*, p. 173.
[133] Crankshaw, *Race, Class and the Changing Division of Labour*, p. 17, 115. These figures reflect averages across different industries – trends would vary between specific industries.
[134] Crankshaw, *Race, Class and the Changing Division of Labour*, p. 18.

overwhelming – advance of African workers into supervisory, routine white-collar, and artisanal jobs, and, conversely, a decline of whites in these occupations from 1979. While Crankshaw ascribes some of this to white upward mobility, he notes that this 'only proceeded up to a certain point': whites in 'semi-skilled and skilled work could be re-trained and promoted only into the skilled trades, supervisory positions and, at a stretch, into certain technical jobs'.[135] It is precisely these categories to which many of the white workers testifying before the Wiehahn Commission would have belonged. Writing as the Commission was completing its inquiry, Greenberg noted ominously that 'the [artisanal] citadels of electricians and iron moulders will not automatically fall before the rush of organised semiskilled and unskilled African workers. But African trade unionism almost certainly threatens the position of the European [white] mailman, truck driver, foundry worker, or miner whose position depends on organisation at the work place and access to the state.'[136] It is likely, therefore, that in the wake of the Wiehahn process, the rate of African advancement in these lesser-skilled jobs would have been even more pronounced.

Additionally, post-Wiehahn minority protection measures represented a much softer and more flexible form of protection than statutory job reservation or the denial of African labour rights had offered in the pre-Wiehahn period. This meant that non-African workers had to rely on their skills, rather than their privileged position in the racial hierarchy, to secure material privilege, or needed to 'force' government to provide them with protection, in Friedman's words. And Friedman suggests that most of these workers were not able to prevent changes: 'only on the mines did white workers successfully resist job changes after Wiehahn'.[137]

Indeed, while the mining industry offers an example of how white workers resisted state efforts to remove discriminatory legislation, it also offers an exceptional example of government's disregard for minority protection measures. Part 6 of the Wiehahn report, dealing specifically with industrial relations in the mining industry, recommended the reservation of blasting certificates for whites be phased out as soon as possible and through a process of consultation between the parties involved. In this way, the responsibility for dealing with this particularly thorny issue was passed from the state to employers and workers. The MWU obstinately opposed negotiations with the Chamber of Mines on the removal of what amounted to its members' privileged position, and in this way

---

[135] Crankshaw, *Race, Class and the Changing Division of Labour*, pp. 98–9, also p. 30.
[136] Greenberg, *Race and State*, p. 322.
[137] Friedman, *Building Tomorrow Today*, p. 156. See also Chapter 4.

managed to keep the blasting certificate reservation in place (see Chapter 4). Van der Merwe recalled the enormous pressure throughout the 1980s to remove the reservation as the last piece of discriminatory legislation still on the law books. But even after receiving a six-month ultimatum, the Chamber and the MWU still could not reach an agreement. Desperate, Minister Botha approached Van der Merwe for advice. The latter recounted:

> I told him: Uncle Fanie ... let's place a notice in Friday's Government Gazette in which we retract the regulation concerning the blasting certificate, but don't say a word and we tell the media nothing. And you know what happened? Three weeks later, a reporter phoned me and asked: when are you repealing [the blasting certificate]? And it was already done. And no one could do anything about it. The critical moment had already passed.[138]

Thus the reservation of the blasting certificate, as the first job reservation measure introduced in South Africa in 1893, was the last to be scrapped in 1987. In the face of direct opposition from white workers, Minister Botha reneged on his commitment to consultation as a way of safeguarding the interests of labour minorities.

Figure 3.5 Clamorous mineworkers disrupting a public meeting in Welkom, at which Minister Fanie Botha spoke, following the release of the Wiehahn report in 1979.
Source: Volksblad, 26 October 1979

---

[138] Piet van der Merwe interviewed by Hermann Giliomee, 18 March 2009.

Moreover, established unions' loss of strength – first through the removal of their formal race-based power and protection, and then when more flexible protective measures proved to be weak – was compounded by the growth of African unions. Friedman notes that most state efforts to control the registration of African unions had collapsed by the end of 1982. African unions had gained a strong foothold in the factories and were starting to mobilise on the national level.[139] This new balance of power in labour relations inevitably had an impact on the position of established labour confederations. Steenkamp explained that employers turned their backs on established unions, eager instead to bargain with black unions representing much larger sections of the workforce.[140] In the years immediately following the Wiehahn process, many of SACLA's members elected to or were forced to open their doors to workers of other races, and many unions left the Confederation. The overall membership of white-only unions declined from 240,000 in 1980 to under 100,000 in 1989.[141] Already by the mid-1980s, says Friedman, SACLA 'was a little noticed oddity'.[142] Meanwhile, any hopes TUCSA may have had of becoming the foremost coordinating voice of labour were soon dashed. In the context of a new labour dispensation, TUCSA could no longer claim to represent the majority of organised labour or to be at the forefront of pushing for workplace change. As African unions gained access to industrial councils in the 1980s, while also benefiting from factory-based negotiations with employers, it became clear that neither the government nor employers needed TUCSA to mediate between them and the newly organised African labour force. Internationally, too, ILO support switched from TUCSA to independent African unions.[143] TUCSA disbanded in 1986, just a year after a number of black unions and labour federations formed the 650,000-strong Congress of South African Trade Unions.[144]

These developments suggest that, like the NP government, the established labour movement was overwhelmed by the rise of the emerging unions. But there was a crucial difference: while NP politicians were certainly shaken by the force of African trade unionism and the unintended consequences their reforms unleashed, they retained their positions of power, held in place by the continuation of white political

---

[139] Friedman, *Building Tomorrow Today*, p. 277. See also A. Lichtenstein, '"We feel that our strength is on the factory floor": dualism, shop-floor power, and labor law in late apartheid South Africa', *Labor History* 60, no. 6 (2019), pp. 606–25.

[140] Naas Steenkamp, interviewed 23 August 2013.   [141] Van Rooyen, *Hard Right*, p. 31.

[142] Friedman, *Building Tomorrow Today*, p. 166.

[143] *South African Labour Bulletin* 5, no. 2 (1979), p. 9.

[144] Giliomee, *The Last Afrikaner Leaders*, pp. 162–3.

supremacy. White workers were in a very different position: while they retained race-based political rights they (and other non-African workers[145]) found themselves in an industrial system working to dismantle racial privilege in order to preserve white supremacy in other spheres. For many white workers, Wiehahn had 'turned' their world 'on its head'.[146]

Conclusion

The list of names appearing in the State President's official appointment of the Wiehahn Commission reflected the racial hierarchy governing South African society – and expected to govern the Commission – which arranged white as superior and black as inferior. It revealed a state wishing to appear committed to reform and democratisation by including blacks in an official inquiry for the first time, while in fact continuing colonial-era practices in which white men determined the fate of a black majority population.

But as this chapter has shown, close examination of the Wiehahn process can take us beyond race-focused analyses to reveal other tensions and forces animating the reform process. It reveals that, as a 'scheme' to shore up white power, the labour reforms initiated in the late 1970s were not in the interests of all whites. A significant section of white labour, represented by the conservative SACLA, vociferously opposed reform – and several other sections also expressed opposition. Particularly lesser-skilled and historically more vulnerable white workers recognised that labour reform endangered their positions. As Friedman notes:

[Many] owed their privilege – sometimes their very jobs – to direct government intervention. [SACLA] was strongest either on the railways and in state owned steel plants, which were created partially to offer whites protected jobs, or on the mines where white workers relied on job bars in the law to bolster their privilege. Its members had no skilled trade to protect them.[147]

If reform constituted a redefinition or reimagining of the status of urban Africans, as Ashforth argues, it follows that this would also entail the redefinition of the status of white workers, whose very position relied on the exclusion of Africans from the privileges of industrial citizenship, and

---

[145] Friedman has paid some attention to the role of coloured and Indian workers and their unions in relation to the independent trade union movement in the 1970s and 1980s, but their strategies and perspectives deserve further investigation. Friedman, *Building Tomorrow Today*, pp. 180–96.
[146] Giliomee, *The Last Afrikaner Leaders*, p. 164.
[147] Friedman, *Building Tomorrow Today*, p. 76.

whose identity was intimately bound up with the rightlessness of blacks. Indeed, conferring some rights and recognition on (sections of) the black population in the industrial arena inevitably meant that white workers would have to forfeit some of their privileges and power. Thus, if we continue to follow Stoler, and Ashforth, in seeing commissions as revealing state rationale and power politics, the class hierarchy inherent in the list of commissioners' names suggests a state that now placed the interests of the white elite above those of white labour. As Wiehahn told Ashforth some years after the event, 'You must read more in a report than just the words.'[148] The escalating economic and political crises of the 1970s evoked a change in the priorities of capital and the state which saw them move away from the post-war social contract that had brought the NP to power and the importance this afforded white working-class interests. Giving a bit more legal, economic, and social space to blacks, hitherto largely confined to the lower rungs of society, made little difference to the lives of white elites – at least initially, before the process's unintended consequences started to gain momentum. It was blue-collar whites on the shop floor who would bear the brunt of a shift in the terms of white supremacy, their position and identity as citizens of the racial state threatened by the new politics of inclusion and exclusion. The Wiehahn reforms and its withdrawal of state support for working-class whiteness marked the end of the post-war Afrikaner social alliance and moral economy.

SACLA workers' unified opposition to reform stood in stark contrast to the lack of consensus within the Joint Committee and the divaricating dynamics within TUCSA. Indeed, the Wiehahn archive confirms the longevity of divisions in South Africa's organised labour movement. This demonstrates the complexity of labour positions and politics at the time, showing that these were never clear-cut along racial lines but informed by historical fissures, as well as by the skills, shifting industrial and political fortunes, and ambitions of different sections of organised labour. In contrast to Stoler, who portrays commissions as state instruments apparently homogeneous in their composition and intent, the analysis offered here clearly shows that diverse and often opposing dynamics were at work not only within the Commission at large, but specifically among organised labour and white workers. This highlights

---

[148] Nic Wiehahn interviewed by Adam Ashforth, 10 October 1981, quoted in Ashforth, *The Politics of Official Discourse*, epigraph. See also Interview: Prof. Nic Wiehahn, AG2738-152, Institute for Advanced Social Research Collection, Historical Papers Research Archive, University of the Witwatersrand, Johannesburg.

the limitations of the existing literature's homogenising view of white labour.

As a 'scheme' to 'share power without losing control', late apartheid reforms clearly failed in the long run. As in parts of British and French colonial Africa earlier in the century, labour and constitutional reform served only to highlight Africans' continued political disenfranchisement and exclusion from full citizenship. Like their counterparts elsewhere on the continent, South Africa's black workers seized upon the new, albeit restricted, opportunities accorded by the legalisation of their labour organisations to mobilise resistance to white domination and claim full political rights. COSATU took up a central role in the liberation struggle, uniting over half a million black workers around the 'inseparability of shop-floor struggles and the broader political struggle'[149] alongside the ANC. Ultimately, this would see the achievement of majority rule in 1994.

In this sense, SACLA's testimony to the Wiehahn Commission was clairvoyant. 'The labour force will determine our direction, and politics will just have to follow suit,' Nieuwoudt had warned his fellow commissioners. In an interview in 1984, Wiehahn freely discussed his efforts to depoliticise the process of labour reform and roll back state intervention in the labour market by deliberately couching the Commission's reports in technical terms. 'You can't speak about freedom, so you call it labour mobility … that's a technical term … When you tell the man in the street about horizontal labour mobility, he won't react.' This example demonstrated what Wiehahn claimed was his motto in compiling the report: 'If you can't convince them, confuse them.' If he had not adopted this strategy, he concluded, his Commission's report 'would have been shelved'.[150] Wiehahn's version of events seems somewhat simplistic, particularly given the evidence this chapter has offered of the divisions characterising the Commission. This is quite apart from the fact that he was not the sole author of the reports; we have seen that the wording of the reports, from references to white poverty to the order of commissioners' names, was discussed among the members. It seems highly unlikely that someone such as Nieuwoudt or Tommie Neethling would have supported a 'if you can't convince them, confuse them' approach, or would themselves have been hoodwinked by such efforts.

Rather, the historical entanglement of labour and racial politics in South Africa meant that these workers' testimonies highlighted the fallacy inherent in the reform scheme: that black workers could somehow be granted industrial but not political citizenship. As Iron and Steel's

---

[149] Lodge, 'Resistance and reform', p. 454.
[150] Nic Wiehahn interviewed by Deborah Posel, 1 August 1984.

Bornman stated bitterly in response to the government's acceptance of the Commission's recommendations, trade union rights for black workers represented a 'step towards one-man-one-vote'.[151] Arrie Paulus of the MWU similarly warned that 'with the acceptance of the Wiehahn report, there will in future be no distinction between Blacks and Whites'.[152] Many years later, commissioners Steenkamp and Van der Merwe agreed in an interview that white workers were much more attuned to the possible political ramifications of labour reform than commissioners drawn from other circles.[153] It is unsurprising that white workers would have been most sensitive in this regard. The granting of industrial rights to Africans called the established convergence between race and rights into question, reversing the full citizenship white workers had demanded from capital and the state in 1922 and had secured in 1924.

Existing scholarship has examined the evolution of ideas of citizenship and national identity in South Africa, how the country's black population was stripped of its citizen rights, and blacks' protracted struggle to be recognised as full citizens, as well as the challenges facing the realisation of common, democratic citizenship in contemporary South Africa.[154] But already before 1994, the dismantling of racially privileged citizenship commenced with reforms in the labour arena. Prior to the reform period, South Africans were a 'white nation' and South Africa a 'white country' in which racially privileged citizenship allowed a minority to assume majority status by excluding 'non-whites' from full citizenship. In the 1970s, labour became the terrain on which this order was first contested – and white workers were the first to be confronted with democratising change. Industrial reforms had little impact on the position of the many whites in middle-class and professional positions. But for blue-collar whites working alongside Africans in the mineshafts and on the factory floors, this was a long transition: long before 1994, the redesign of labour relations constituted the renegotiation of their own status and the unravelling of their privileged position – both in the workplace and in their relationship to the state and the white body politic. The next chapter examines how the MWU negotiated white workers' fall from grace.

---

[151] *South African Labour Bulletin* 5, no. 2 (1979), p. 83.
[152] *South African Labour Bulletin* 5, no. 2 (1979), p. 80.
[153] Piet van der Merwe interviewed by Naas Steenkamp, 7 October 2008. Also see Piet van der Merwe interviewed by Hermann Giliomee, 18 March 2009.
[154] See, for instance, D. Conway, 'Struggles for citizenship in South Africa' in E. F. Isin and P. Nyers (eds), *Routledge Handbook of Global Citizenship Studies* (New York NY: Routledge, 2014), pp. 240–8; S. Dubow, 'South Africa and South Africans: nationality, belonging, citizenship' in Ross et al., *The Cambridge History of South Africa*, pp. 17–65; M. Ramphele, 'Citizenship challenges for South Africa's young democracy', *Daedalus* 130, no. 1 (2001), pp. 1–17.

Part II

White workers and civil society mobilisation

4 From trade union to social movement
The Mineworkers' Union/Solidarity's formation of a post-apartheid social alliance

Introduction

'Greatest act of treason against white workers!' Thus ran the damning headline on the front page of the MWU's official mouthpiece, *The Mineworker*, just days after the National Party accepted the Wiehahn Commission's recommendations for the removal of statutory job reservation and the legalisation of African trade unions. Perhaps still smarting from the union's failed strike two months earlier, the article's vitriolic author, general secretary Arrie Paulus, likened the government's decision to the state's violent suppression of the 1922 Rand Revolt, 'when hundreds of miners were shot because they rebelled against the Chamber of Mines' efforts to force them to share their work with blacks'.[1] The reference to the slain miners of the early twentieth century resonated powerfully with the union's warnings about the threat that labour reform posed to white workers' survival in the present.

But despite the failure of the MWU's anti-reform strike in March 1979, this was not 'the dinosaur's last stand', as labour analyst Steven Friedman put it.[2] As Chapter 3 showed, the Wiehahn reforms marked the advent of a new politics of inclusion and exclusion which saw the state withdraw its patronage of the white working class. Together with the subsequent rise of the black labour movement, this led to a reconfiguration of the labour arena in which the likes of SACLA and TUCSA shrunk and faded over the course of the 1980s. Yet, in sharp contrast, the same period saw a dramatic expansion in the MWU's membership. From some 18,000 members in 1979, it grew to 44,000 in 1992 on the eve of South Africa's first democratic elections.[3] In 2002, the union

---

[1] P. J. Paulus, 'Grootste verraad teenoor blanke werkers!', *The Mineworker*, 16 May 1979, p. 1. Others also felt this way. Wessel Bornman, general secretary of the South African Iron and Steel Union, called the Wiehahn report an 'embarrassment and slap in the face' for white workers. *South African Labour Bulletin* 5, no. 2 (1979), p. 82.
[2] Friedman, *Building Tomorrow Today*, p. 163.
[3] Finansiële bundels (Rekenmeester), MWU Archive, Solidarity Headquarters, Pretoria.

celebrated its centenary, boasting a 120,000-strong membership and an estimated annual income of over R50 million.[4] In the same year, it was re-established as Solidarity, a social movement union performing not only its traditional trade union functions but also providing financial services and involved in training, job creation, and charity work.[5]

The Introduction noted Wessel Visser's biography of the MWU – which covers the period from 1902 to 2002 – as one of only a handful of studies of white workers looking beyond 1948, and indeed the only work on white labour to span the apartheid and post-apartheid periods.[6] The book includes an analysis of the organisational changes occurring within the union in the decades following Wiehahn, which Visser deftly contextualises within the rapidly changing political and economic landscape of this period. The arguments offered below build on and challenge existing understandings of the MWU/Solidarity. This chapter takes the organisational shifts and political context Visser addresses as the backdrop for a discursive analysis of the MWU's articulation of its members' interests and experiences. Centrally, I track the shifting intersection of race, class, and ethnicity within the organisation during this period. This provides new insight into how white workers experienced and negotiated the dismantling of the racial state and the establishment of black majority rule under the ANC. This analytical focus opens up new questions that remain unanswered by Visser's analysis, which is focused squarely on organisational and political developments. It allows us to ask how white workers' experiences of this period related to the responses identified in the existing literature as characterising whites' and Afrikaners' reactions to majority rule. Put differently: if the long transition perspective reveals that white workers were confronted with democratising change more than a decade before the end of apartheid, what happened when these experiences met with broader white experiences of 'dislocation' and 'identity crisis' in the years following 1994? Visser does not bring his historical narrative into conversation with this scholarship on post-apartheid white and Afrikaner experiences – despite the fact that the MWU, in its 'reinvented' guise of Solidarity, claimed to speak on behalf of these very communities. I will argue that the MWU's 'reinvention' in fact reflects an effort to merge white workers' experiences with those of

---

[4] Giliomee, *The Afrikaners*, p. 661; Visser, 'From MWU to Solidarity', p. 34.
[5] F. Buys, 'MWU-Solidariteit se plan: Selfbemagtiging is die antwoord!', *Solidarity* 5 (2001), pp. 2–3.
[6] Visser, *Van MWU tot Solidariteit*. An updated and abridged version has since appeared in English: W. Visser, *A History of the South African Mine Workers' Union, 1902–2014* (Lewiston NY: Edwin Mellen Press, 2016). This chapter draws primarily on the in-depth Afrikaans book.

Introduction

the broader white population, particularly white Afrikaans-speakers, in order to build a more general Afrikaner social alliance in post-apartheid South Africa. These developments, I will further contend, need to be understood within the global context of this period.

Drawing largely on Visser, the first section of this chapter opens with a synopsis of the MWU's organisational 'reinvention' as it relates to the political changes marking South Africa's transition to majority rule. It then moves to focus on the articulations of post-apartheid white and Afrikaner 'dislocation' identified in existing social science literature, to ask how this intersects with the MWU/Solidarity's post-1994 claims and what it may reveal about the relative importance of class in white experiences of the transition. I also outline international developments relating to the weakening of organised labour, the rise of social movements, and the ascendance of identity politics in the post-Cold War world during this period. The second section of the chapter seeks to answer these questions by tracking the discursive shifts within the union that underlay organisational changes, from the appointment of the Wiehahn Commission to the union's centenary in 2002. These shifts, I argue, reflected and facilitated the merger of cross-class Afrikaner experiences, as articulated by the MWU/Solidarity, in terms of cultural identity. In the wake of the demise of the racial state and the National Party as the patron of Afrikaners, this marked the genesis of a new, post-apartheid Afrikaner social alliance in the form of a movement mobilised on the basis of cultural identity.

The chapter is primarily based on an analysis of the union's newspaper – the most complete and continuous historical record available in the union's archive – supplemented with archival documentation such as the minutes of MWU Executive Council meetings, correspondence, and membership records.[7] Newspaper content reflects and inflects its readership, articulating the opinions, views, and experiences of its readers and writers, while at the same time shaping those very views and experiences.[8] Rory Pilossof has argued that the periodicals produced by organisations, interest groups, or specific communities have largely been neglected in studies of Africa's past, and that they may be put to productive use for writing nuanced social and cultural histories.[9] The MWU's newspaper is an exceptionally rich historical source. Not only

---

[7] On the MWU archive, see Van Zyl-Hermann, 'White workers in the late apartheid period', pp. 229–58.
[8] R. Darnton, *The Kiss of Lamourette: reflections in cultural history* (New York NY and London: W. W. Norton & Company, 1990), pp. 60–93.
[9] R. Pilosoff, 'For farmers, by farmers', *Media History* 19, no. 1 (2013), pp. 32–44.

does it offer insight into the issues that concerned this section of white mining labour, their workplaces, and, to some extent, the communities in which they lived, but it also provides access to the discourses and representations employed to talk about and understand these issues. The newspaper was first published on 30 July 1934 as *Die Mynwerker/The Mineworker*.[10] Until 1991, it was published in newspaper format, appearing approximately every two weeks. In 1991 it was renamed *MWU-Nuus/MWU-News* and was still published in newspaper form, but it now appeared on a monthly basis. Finally, it was revamped in 2001, taking its current magazine format and appearing every two months as *Solidariteit/Solidarity*. As we will see, the publication's evolution followed the changes occurring in the organisation during this period.

Despite these shifts in format, a number of features remained more or less constant throughout the period under investigation here. These were the lead front-page article (which up until 1991 formed the main body of the often very slim newspaper), a separate editorial feature (from 1991), the speeches delivered by the general secretary and the president to the annual MWU congress (which were typically printed in full following the meeting), and end-of-year reflections and messages to the readers penned by the general secretary and other union officials. My analysis focuses on these elements of the publication. The newspaper was primarily a mouthpiece – an organ of communication with the main purpose of speaking to and for the workers of the MWU. It typically centred around a main article by the general secretary, who until 1991 fulfilled the role of editor. This conveyed the union's views on current issues facing this section of the white mining community. It carried both Afrikaans and English articles,[11] and, until the late 1990s, it was the union's main channel for communicating with its members about union and workplace matters – informing them on everything from union elections, wage negotiations, and strike ballots to safety regulations, legislative changes, and production figures. *The Mineworker* was typically distributed directly in workplaces and change houses,[12] free of charge. At the same time, the newspaper was clearly intended as a means

---

[10] See the plate of the first edition of *Die Mynwerker/The Mineworker* in Visser, *Van MWU tot Solidariteit*.

[11] Until the mid-1980s, articles were typically published in both Afrikaans and English, and in the 18 December 1985 edition, Christmas messages also appeared in French, Portuguese, and Polish. From the late 1980s, the balance shifted more decisively towards Afrikaans. By the 2000s, *Solidarity* magazine was overwhelmingly Afrikaans.

[12] A change house is the building where miners change in and out of their work clothes before and after a shift.

of communicating on behalf of MWU members, acting as their voice to other interested parties in the mining sector. Especially until the early 1990s, Paulus and his successor Peet Ungerer used the paper to respond to accusations in the press, challenge other union leaders, or confront employers or the government, and there is evidence that the MWU newspaper was indeed read by these parties.[13] In 1991, Flip Buys took up the editorship, the role shifting away from the general secretary for the first time. Nevertheless, a contribution by the general secretary remained an important part of the publication throughout the period under investigation here. As the union adapted to technological advances from the late 1990s, it switched to electronic communication as the main means of relaying important (often industry- or workplace-specific) information to its growing membership. Consequently, *Solidarity* magazine appeared less frequently and was distributed via post. Unlike its predecessor newspaper, the magazine was not a platform for communicating with employers or the state: Solidarity issued press statements or petitions. Nevertheless, it remained an important means for the union's leadership to communicate with its broad membership collectively, and it continued as an instrument for conveying the union's views and informing members of developments within different industries and the Solidarity Movement.[14]

The MWU's 'reinvention' and its broader context

Following the MWU's failure to block labour reform, the union adopted a new strategy. In order to resist the implementation of reform from a wider power base, it set out to consolidate the ranks of white labour by opening up its membership to white blue-collar workers beyond mining. This appealed particularly to white workers in the steel, chemical, and distribution industries, where white unions were desegregating in the context of the new labour dispensation – indeed, Chapter 3 has shown the extent of resistance to labour reform existing beyond the MWU among white blue-collar workers and artisans. Affirming the dissolution of the historical alliance between white labour and the NP, the MWU

---

[13] For instance, the archive of Marais Viljoen, Minister of Labour from 1966 to 1976, contains an extensive collection of cuttings from *The Mineworker*. Archive for Contemporary Affairs, University of the Free State, Bloemfontein, PV14: Marais Viljoen.

[14] Circulation figures were published for a short period between 1993 and 2001 in each issue, along with the details of the editorial staff. These were noted as 41,000 in February 1993, rising to 42,000 in August 1994 and remaining constant until they stopped being listed in 2001.

also aligned itself with right-wing political parties, notably the Herstigte Nasionale Party.[15] Unashamedly Afrikaner nationalist and anti-capitalist, the HNP advocated a return to strict Verwoerdian apartheid. By-elections in 1979 and the 1981 general election recorded a strong anti-NP protest vote in white working-class constituencies and were the only elections in which the HNP drew substantial – albeit still minority – white support. In the 1979 by-elections, MWU president Cor de Jager ran in his home mining constituency of Rustenburg as an HNP candidate. Yet, overall, the NP remained comfortably in power.[16] A more serious challenge to the Nationalists' hegemony emerged in 1982 when 15 MPs broke away from the NP in objection to the government's plans to expand reform beyond labour to the Constitution, establishing the multiracial tricameral parliament. The breakaway MPs formed the Conservative Party, advocating a return to pre-reform separate development.[17] That same year also saw the formation of the National Union of Mineworkers (NUM), marking the revitalisation of African unionism in mining. By the end of 1982, the Chamber of Mines announced that it would bargain with the NUM, raising serious concerns for the MWU.[18] Thus, the MWU threw its weight behind the CP, which was also rapidly gaining broader white support amid the government's dismantling of social apartheid. In 1987, the CP became the official Opposition, and Paulus was elected to Parliament as MP for his home mineworking constituency of Carletonville.

Peet Ungerer replaced Paulus as general secretary in 1987. In the same year, Minister of Labour Botha unilaterally scrapped the racial reservation of blasting certificates in the mining industry. In February 1990, NP leader and State President F. W. de Klerk announced the unbanning of African liberation organisations, the release of political prisoners, and the start of negotiations for the transition to a democratic constitution – a move endorsed in a whites-only referendum two years later.[19] In response to the accelerating pace of change, Ungerer intensified the MWU's recruitment drive in an effort to build a 'super white union' to fortify the white labour movement. The union also increasingly looked beyond the labour arena to the 'political, economic and cultural needs of the Afrikaner working class',[20] articulating growing concerns about the desegregation of working-class neighbourhoods and public facilities, and

---

[15] See Chapter 2.
[16] O'Meara, *Forty Lost Years*, pp. 310–11; Visser, 'From MWU to Solidarity', p. 8.
[17] O'Meara, *Forty Lost Years*, pp. 307–8, 311–12; Hyslop, 'Why was the white right unable to stop South Africa's democratic transition?', p. 148.
[18] Friedman, *Building Tomorrow Today*, p. 355.   [19] O'Meara, *Forty Lost Years*, p. 410.
[20] Visser, 'From MWU to Solidarity', p. 10.

The MWU's 'reinvention' and its broader context 163

Figure 4.1 MWU organisers lead a Volksfront rally at Vanderbijlpark, 22 May 1993.
Source: *MWU-News*, June 1993.

the possible future implementation of race-based affirmative action. These concerns also reflected the company kept by the MWU. In May 1993, along with a coalition of right-wing organisations including the CP, the paramilitary Afrikaner Weerstandsbeweging (Afrikaner Resistance Movement or AWB), the Transvaal Agricultural Union, and the South African Iron, Steel and Allied Industries Union, the MWU formed the Afrikaner Volksfront (Afrikaner People's Front). Led by former Chief of the South African Defence Force, General Constand Viljoen, the Volksfront's goal was to resist the transition to democracy and press for the formation of an independent Afrikaner *volkstaat* (people's state).[21]

But ideological tensions plagued the Volksfront. In 1994, Viljoen broke away to participate in the first democratic elections under the banner of his own political party, the Freedom Front (FF), with the goal of attaining an independent Afrikaner republic. A *volkstaat* would 'ensure language rights ... mother tongue education, the right to autonomy in matters affecting cultural identity ... the right to separate organisations and associations, and the right to territorial autonomy in negotiated areas where majority occupation by Afrikaners could be

---

[21] Hyslop, 'Why was the white right unable to stop South Africa's democratic transition?', pp. 145–65.

established'.²² In the 1994 elections, the FF won 2.2 per cent of the national vote.²³ Visser's lengthy discussion of Ungerer's fallout with Viljoen over electoral participation suggests that the MWU remained on the side of the apartheid restorationists,²⁴ but the inauguration of black majority government under the ANC in 1994 rendered the MWU an anachronism from a bygone racist era. According to Visser, the union struggled to respond to the new political and economic landscape and 'stagnated' from 1994, suffering from an extremely negative and stereotyped public image.²⁵

Ungerer retired in 1997 and was replaced by Flip Buys, the first MWU general secretary who was not himself a miner. As a politics and communication student at Potchefstroom in the late 1980s, Buys had been chairman of the CP student division. Buys first joined the MWU in 1991 and acted as general secretary while Ungerer was on sick leave in 1994. In July 1995, he left the union to work for the FF.²⁶ According to Visser, Buys' appointment as MWU general secretary 'imbued the organisation with a new vitality' and 'expounded a new vision in terms of strategic thinking'.²⁷ Buys set out to expand the MWU's membership beyond blue-collar workers and to modernise the union. Training and development initiatives, research capacities, infrastructure and technology upgrades, communication and marketing, and financial services were developed within the organisation, and new academically trained personnel appointed accordingly. Buys' inspiration for this restructuring was the Israeli labour federation, the Histadrut.²⁸ In response to the introduction of affirmative action policies – understood by Buys as unfair discrimination against whites – the union shifted its strategy to appealing to the principles of non-racialism and anti-discrimination inscribed in the new South African Constitution. It asked the Human Rights Commission to investigate affirmative action as a policy of 'neo-racism' and 'ethnic purification' in the workplace, and embarked on a number of legal actions related to employment policies as well as the diminishing

---

²² A. Norval, 'Reinventing the politics of cultural recognition: the Freedom Front and the demand for a *volkstaat*' in D. Howarth and A. Norval (eds), *South Africa in Transition* (New York NY: St Martin's Press, 1998), p. 96.
²³ Giliomee, *The Afrikaners*, pp. 645–7; Hyslop, 'Why was the white right unable to stop South Africa's democratic transition?'
²⁴ Visser, *Van MWU tot Solidariteit*, pp. 306–9.
²⁵ Visser, 'From MWU to Solidarity', p. 11. See also G. Mantashe, 'The decline of the mining industry and the response of the mining unions' (MA research report, University of the Witwatersrand, 2008), p. 80.
²⁶ Visser, *Van MWU tot Solidariteit*, p. 311; 'Buys sê tot siens; maar nie vaarwel', *MWU-News*, June 1995, p. 2.
²⁷ Visser, 'From MWU to Solidarity', p. 12.   ²⁸ See Chapter 5.

use of Afrikaans in the workplace, achieving several high-profile legal successes against state- and private-sector employers.[29] In a first for South African trade unionism, the MWU established a division for individual members desiring labour protection, especially in response to trends towards outsourcing and subcontracting. Within two years, 8,000 unorganised individuals had joined the MWU, benefiting especially from its legal services and new call centre.

In 2001, the MWU absorbed four other trade unions – including Iron and Steel – bringing its membership to 93,000. This, it claimed, made it South Africa's largest independent trade union and an effective counterweight to the ANC-aligned COSATU. It identified its goal as protecting Afrikaner workers' interests in a discriminatory environment. But beyond labour, too, it would seek to defend the Afrikaans minority against the power of the black majority and would cater to Afrikaner cultural needs.[30] The following year marked the union's centenary, upon which the MWU was renamed Solidarity. Once an industry-based trade union representing white mineworkers, by 2002 many white-collar workers and professionals had joined the union's ranks.[31] It now represented some 120,000 workers who were predominantly, but no longer exclusively, white. By 2003, 10 per cent of its membership was coloured; by 2005, 6 per cent was female.[32] Solidarity increasingly commanded a significant public presence, both in the labour arena and in a civil society capacity, and seemed to find wide resonance among the public. Indeed, by 2000 it was the largest Afrikaans-membership organisation in South Africa.[33] Its new image was reflected in the positive media coverage it enjoyed, especially from the Afrikaans press: *Volksblad* reported in 2002 that the union had been transformed 'from a dying, hard right white club of disgruntled ranters to a dynamic, growing and inclusive Afrikaans trade union' that 'commands respect'.[34]

The Introduction noted the substantial sociological literature observing the sense of dislocation among whites in post-apartheid South Africa. For them, the end of minority rule is said to have been 'nothing less than traumatic',[35] their loss of political power and their struggle to come to

---

[29] Visser, 'From MWU to Solidarity', p. 17.
[30] Visser, 'From MWU to Solidarity', p. 18.
[31] D. Hermann, 'Propvol 2002', *Solidarity* 7 (2002), p. 17.
[32] Visser, 'From MWU to Solidarity', pp. 19–20.
[33] Giliomee, *The Afrikaners*, p. 661; Visser, *Van MWU tot Solidariteit*, pp. 311–23; Visser, 'From MWU to Solidarity', pp. 33-5; Mantashe, 'The decline of the mining industry', p. 74, 79–81.
[34] 'Praat só met ANC', *Volksblad*, 26 July 2002, p. 10 (my translation).
[35] W. Visser, 'Post-hegemonic Afrikanerdom and diaspora: redefining Afrikaner identity in post-apartheid South Africa', *New Contree* 54 (2007), p. 1.

terms with their 'new' minority status[36] magnified by an assertive Africanism in national politics and the public service, racial redress policies, and strains produced by high levels of unemployment and crime in a deeply unequal society. For Afrikaners in particular, the overhaul of national symbols and narratives by discourses of multiculturalism and nation building, as well as revelations of state brutality emerging from the work of the Truth and Reconciliation Commission, undermined once unquestioned understandings of Afrikaner history, identity, and morality.[37] This 'identity crisis'[38] seemed to be mirrored on an institutional level. Efforts by the NP to reinvent itself came to naught and it disbanded in 2005. Meanwhile, established Afrikaner institutions such as churches and universities struggled to redefine their own role and position in the young democracy.[39] Many who continued to identify as Afrikaners experienced this loss of political and social dominance as the 'implosion' of the world as they knew it, and they felt that they no longer had a voice in their land of birth.[40] Myriad reactions followed. Small-scale efforts at Afrikaner autonomy in self-constructed enclaves were constitutionally controversial and practically problematic, given the territorial dispersal of white Afrikaans-speakers throughout the Republic. Overall, such efforts attracted too little support to be politically significant.[41] Much more widespread was the tendency to withdraw from political engagement and public life into private 'comfort zones'[42] and

---

[36] Y. Alsheh and F. Elliker, 'The art of becoming a minority: Afrikaner re-politicisation and Afrikaans political ethnicity', *African Studies* 74, no. 3 (2015), pp. 429–48.

[37] Vestergaard, 'Who's got the map?', pp. 19–44; P. E. Louw, *The Rise, Fall and Legacy of Apartheid* (Westport CT: Praeger, 2004), pp. 176–89; P. E. Louw, 'Political power, national identity, and language: the case of Afrikaans', *International Journal of the Sociology of Language* 170 (2004), pp. 43–58; N. Southern, 'The Freedom Front Plus: an analysis of Afrikaner politics and ethnic identity in the new South Africa', *Contemporary Politics* 14, no. 4 (2008), pp. 463–78; J. D. Jansen, *Knowledge in the Blood: confronting race and the apartheid past* (Stanford CA: Stanford University Press, 2009), p. 13, 45, 284, 290.

[38] Steyn, *'Whiteness Just Isn't What It Used to Be'*; Visser, 'Post-hegemonic Afrikanerdom'; T. M. Blaser and C. van der Westhuizen, 'Introduction: the paradox of post-apartheid "Afrikaner" identity: deployments of ethnicity and neo-liberalism', *African Studies* 71, no. 3 (2012), pp. 380–90; M. Verwey and C. Quayle, 'Whiteness, racism and Afrikaner identity in post-apartheid South Africa', *African Affairs* 111, no. 445 (2012), pp. 551–75.

[39] Giliomee, *The Afrikaners*, pp. 658–61, 694–703.

[40] Steyn, 'Rehabilitating a whiteness disgraced', p. 143.

[41] F. C. de Beer, 'Exercise in futility or dawn of Afrikaner self-determination: an exploratory ethno-historical investigation of Orania', *Anthropology Southern Africa* 29, nos 3–4 (2006), pp. 105–14; Southern, 'The Freedom Front Plus'; J. S. van Wyk, 'Buying into Kleinfontein: the financial implications of Afrikaner self-determination' (MSocSci thesis, University of Pretoria, 2015).

[42] Ballard, 'Assimilation, emigration, semigration, and integration', pp. 51–66.

homogeneous cultural circles, adopting a defensive and exclusivist ethnic identity through discourses of post-apartheid victimhood and second-class citizenship.[43] According to Rebecca Davies, some middle-class and elite Afrikaners jettisoned ethnic identity altogether, embracing instead the individualism and consumerism of the neoliberal economy.[44] Many chose to emigrate.[45] For those who remained behind, feelings of marginalisation and victimhood seemed to permeate much of their experience in post-apartheid South Africa.

I have critiqued this literature for its overemphasis on 1994 and its lack of attention to issues of class. In this regard, Visser's history of the MWU clearly represents an important intervention. Yet Visser does not bring his historical narrative into conversation with the scholarship on post-apartheid white and Afrikaner experiences – despite the fact that the MWU, in its 'reinvented' guise of Solidarity, claimed to speak on behalf of precisely these communities. I argue that this overlooks a critical historical intersection and an opportunity to investigate the shifting significance of class within the white population during this period.

Moreover, we need to look beyond local intersections to international developments in order to fully understand the MWU's 'reinvention' – and its consequences in the present, to which Chapter 5 attends. The MWU's 'transformation', including its massive membership growth, seemingly ran counter to the decline of trade unionism occurring across much of the globe during the same period. As states gripped by economic depression prioritised fighting high inflation and achieving economic competitiveness in increasingly globalised markets, rising unemployment and the switch to post-Fordist production saw union membership decline. In some contexts, such as Margaret Thatcher's Britain and the USA under Ronald Reagan, neoliberal governments and businesses hostile to worker demands used policies of deregulation and privatisation and high unemployment to discipline labour movements. In contrast to the last years of the Golden Age, the period from the late 1970s to the 1990s witnessed a sharp decline in strike action, and unions regularly conceded on wages and benefits. This resulted in diminishing political power for labour, reinforced by a general weakening of socialist politics in the wake of the fall of communism in the Soviet Union and Eastern

---

[43] Steyn, *'Whiteness Just Isn't What It Used to Be'*; Van der Waal and Robins, '"De La Rey" and the revival of "Boer heritage"', pp. 763–79; Verwey and Quayle, 'Whiteness, racism and Afrikaner identity'.
[44] Davies, *Afrikaners in the New South Africa*; Blaser and Van der Westhuizen, 'Introduction'.
[45] Ballard, 'Assimilation, emigration, semigration, and integration'.

Europe.[46] As Cold War antagonisms dissolved, Hobsbawm noted, they were replaced by new political forces, 'ranging from the xenophobic and racist on the right, via secessionist parties (mainly, but not only ethnic/nationalist) to the various "Green" parties and other "new social movements" which claimed a place on the Left'. Many of these pursued an exclusionary politics of identity.[47] Indeed, globally, the focus of popular struggles seemed to shift from class-based 'issues of *redistribution* ... to identity politics and questions of cultural *recognition*'.[48] In the newer industrialising contexts of postcolonial Africa, Asia, and Latin America, the decline of organised labour did not proceed in precisely the same manner – but the 1970s' global recession, the ensuing debt crisis in the Global South, and the subsequent imposition of structural adjustment programmes saw comparable trajectories of economic liberalisation and state retreat result in growing unemployment, inequality, and informalisation.[49]

Capitalism entered a 'new post-union era'[50] – except, it seemed, in South Africa, where, as Chapter 3 noted, mass trade unionism was revived in the late 1970s and early 1980s as African workers gained industrial citizenship. The Wiehahn reforms created space for black workers to legally organise, and their shop-floor struggles and organisational experience functioned as a springboard for broader political mobilisation. Thus, while other societies experienced a decline in labour power and prominence, South Africa's black workers were at the forefront of the country's political struggle. The 1990s saw trade unions, in the form of COSATU's partnership with the ANC and the SACP in the Tripartite Alliance, involved in negotiation and policy formulation for South Africa's future government and economic development. From 1994, labour representatives entered Parliament under the auspices of the ANC. While, in 1995, the largest labour body in the USA, the American Federation of Labor and Congress of Industrial Organizations (AFL-CIO), met to confront 'the spectre of its own demise',[51] South Africa's new Government of National Unity

---

[46] G. Friedman, 'Is labor dead?', *International Labor and Working-class History* 75 (2009), pp. 126–44; Clawson and Clawson, 'What has happened to the US labor movement?', pp. 97–101.

[47] Hobsbawm, *Age of Extremes*, p. 417 (also the quote in the previous sentence).

[48] S. Robins, 'Introduction' in S. Robins (ed.), *Limits to Liberation after Apartheid: citizenship, governance and culture* (Oxford: James Currey, 2005), p. 8 (emphasis in original).

[49] G. Curless, 'Introduction: trade unions in the Global South from imperialism to the present day', *Labor History* 57, no. 1 (2016), pp. 1–19.

[50] Friedman, 'Is labor dead?', p. 126.

[51] Clawson and Clawson, 'What has happened to the US labor movement?', p. 96.

promulgated a labour relations act providing all workers with a range of rights and supportive institutions. It also started implementing its Reconstruction and Development Programme, which prioritised the interests of working-class communities by extending access to housing, water provision, and electrification.[52]

Yet South Africa and its workers did not escape the global neoliberal turn. Although the Wiehahn Commission was appointed by Prime Minister Vorster, it was his successor, P. W. Botha, who implemented reforms in response to the crises of the 1970s and 1980s. Botha regarded the restoration of economic growth as essential if South Africa was to triumph over what he saw as a communist onslaught on white minority rule. Hence Botha's policies marked a shift towards free market enterprise and the retraction of state intervention in the economy.[53] This 'coalesced very well with transnational percolating neoliberalised discourse'[54] in a context in which conservative Western governments saw white South Africa as an anti-communist ally. Under Botha, parastatal enterprises such as Iscor were privatised, as was public transport and housing in black townships. The Wiehahn reforms saw the state retreat from its role in the labour market, and subsidisation and regulation of the agricultural sector were rolled back.[55] A 1987 government White Paper on privatisation noted that 'services, production and consumption can be regulated more efficiently by the market and price mechanisms'.[56]

The restructuring, rationalisation, and outsourcing accompanying privatisation led to massive job losses. Mondli Hlatshwayo argues that the privatisation of Iscor in the late 1980s was a major setback for the labour movement in the steel industry, with the position of the newly established black National Union of Metalworkers of South Africa (NUMSA) significantly weakened by the ensuing reduction of the labour force. Moreover, the loss of such an important state-run enterprise to the private sector meant that it was no longer available as a tool for implementing the post-apartheid development goals championed by the labour movement. This was no accident. The neoliberal policies adopted by the Botha regime from the 1980s were not only geared towards

---

[52] Buhlungu, *A Paradox of Victory*, pp. 59–77.
[53] Dubow, *Apartheid*, p. 201; O'Meara, *Forty Lost Years*, pp. 294–5.
[54] G. Super, *Governing through Crime in South Africa: the politics of race and class in neoliberalizing regimes* (Burlington VT: Ashgate, 2013), p. 9.
[55] Beinart, *Twentieth-century South Africa*, p. 245; Feinstein, *An Economic History of South Africa*, pp. 243–4.
[56] *White Paper on Privatisation and Deregulation in the Republic of South Africa* (Pretoria: Government Printer, 1987), p. 8, quoted in S. Narsiah, 'Neoliberalism and privatisation in South Africa', *GeoJournal* 57, nos 1–2 (2002), p. 33.

strengthening South Africa's economic position as the country suffered the sting of international sanctions in the context of a globalising world economy. They were also intended to undermine labour unity and power – as per the Wiehahn reforms – and secure future conditions for capital accumulation in South Africa.[57]

The ANC, with its close ties to the SACP, had long articulated a socialist vision for a democratic South Africa.[58] Yet amid the global hegemony of neoliberalism, the ANC in power abandoned many of its social democratic goals. In 1996, it replaced the RDP with the market-led development strategy GEAR. Thus, even as COSATU representatives were entering the corridors of formal political power, workers' interests such as job creation and security and improvements in wages and living standards were being sidelined in favour of labour market flexibility, deregulation, and fiscal austerity. The tactical privatisation that started under the NP became systematic under the ANC.[59] And while COSATU protested against the implementation of GEAR and called regular general strikes against privatisation and job losses, it did not break with the ANC. Sakhela Buhlungu laments how, under GEAR, workplace restructuring and retrenchment saw trade unions experience a 'massive membership haemorrhage'.[60] This undermined the effectiveness of the industrial union model and worker solidarity.

South African workers of all colours were exposed to the consequences of rationalisation and privatisation. Hlatshwayo notes how at Iscor's privatised incarnation, ArcelorMittal South Africa, the move towards 'lean production' amid declining steel prices saw restructuring in the 1990s initially target older, lesser-skilled workers before moving on to also affect those in white-collar jobs such as administrators, human resources personnel, and managers. Some 50,000 jobs were lost between 1989 and 2012. Many of the retrenched workers were white.[61] Across the globe, the end of the Golden Age had seen insecurity return to the lives of blue-collar workers; by the 1990s, many in the white-collar labour force and professional classes also increasingly felt as though their jobs and futures were no longer safe. 'These were times when people, their old ways of life already undermined and crumbling in any case, were likely to lose their bearings.'[62]

---

[57] Hlatshwayo, 'Neo-liberal restructuring and the fate of South Africa's labour unions', pp. 116–23, 134.
[58] S. Ellis, 'The ANC in exile', *African Affairs* 90, no. 360 (1991), pp. 439–47.
[59] Narsiah, 'Neoliberalism and privatisation in South Africa', p. 33.
[60] Buhlungu, *A Paradox of Victory*, quote on p. 89, see more broadly pp. 77–98.
[61] Hlatshwayo, 'Neo-liberal restructuring and the fate of South Africa's labour unions', pp. 123–4.
[62] Hobsbawm, *Age of Extremes*, p. 416.

In this context of insecurity and state retreat, many communities – particularly the poor and marginalised struggling for access to land, housing, and public services – increasingly mobilised in various forms of social movement-based action.[63] This reflected global trends. Since the 1990s, there had been a surge in social justice campaigns across the world as processes of democratisation and economic globalisation and the rise of a human rights regime opened up spaces of contestation. This saw broad, often diverse coalitions of citizens and civil society actors mobilise against neoliberal globalisation and its consequences. These included a wide variety of issues, from basic survival rights, to social entitlement, to post-material concerns.[64] Movements also arose around the politics of ethnic or nationalist identity, as indigenous or 'first people' movements demanded rights from their nation states and the international community.[65] Increasingly, ordinary people were mobilising to challenge and appeal to governments, state institutions, and global organisations.

In what follows, I offer an analysis of the MWU/Solidarity's shifting discourse from the late 1970s to 2002, reflecting its response to the evolving political, economic, and social context. I show how working-class experiences of loss and dislocation, dating from period of late-apartheid reform, merged with those of the more general white, Afrikaans-speaking population after 1994. My analysis demonstrates the manner in which the MWU/Solidarity articulated and harnessed this intersection, particularly after Buys assumed the leadership in 1997, revealing important continuities throughout the long transition. Moreover, I suggest that the MWU's 'reinvention' as Solidarity reflected global trends in the shift towards identity politics and rise of social movement-based mobilisation characterising the late twentieth and early twenty-first century.

Bread, butter, and the racial order: claims as white citizen workers

The appointment of the Wiehahn Commission came within a broader context of falling living standards for white labour in the 1970s.[66] Throughout the late 1970s, the MWU expressed concerns about high

---

[63] R. Ballard, A. Habib, and I. Valodia (eds), *Voices of Protest: social movements in post-apartheid South Africa* (Durban: University of KwaZulu-Natal Press, 2006); Robins, *From Revolution to Rights in South Africa*. See also Chapter 5.
[64] D. Della Porta and M. Diani (eds), *The Oxford Handbook of Social Movements* (Oxford: Oxford University Press, 2015), pp. vii–viii.
[65] See, for instance, D. Muro, 'Ethnicity, nationalism, and social movements' in Della Porta and Diani, *The Oxford Handbook of Social Movements*, pp. 185–99.
[66] Du Toit, *Capital and Labour*, p. 222.

inflation, meagre mining pensions, and inadequate wages – problems it perceived as plaguing the working class in particular, and which it expected the government to solve. 'We're starting to get the impression that this is no longer a government for the workers, but a capitalist or rich man's government,'[67] smouldered Paulus in *The Mineworker* amidst wage negotiations with the Chamber of Mines. The Chamber was hiding behind government calls for wage controls and pocketing the cash, he claimed, adding that this 'could lead to a poor white working class'.[68] 'We, the workers, are getting restless. The government is not offering us sufficient protection from exploitation.'[69]

As the Wiehahn investigation got under way, the strain of the recession and the possibility of reform merged in the MWU's discourse as dual threats to the survival of white workers in material and racial terms. The union responded to this by emphasising its members' entitlement to protection and privilege as white citizen workers: 'We will not allow the bread to be snatched from our members' mouths by reforms. In ... the homeland of the whites, we have the primary right to all the occupations available.'[70] In a statement reminiscent of older arguments surrounding 'civilised labour', Paulus warned that white miners' living standards would soon sink to the same level as those of Africans, and 'then the replacement of the white man will be easy'.[71] Like other white working-class organisations testifying before the Wiehahn Commission, the MWU regarded displacement in the workplace as a political matter akin to the withdrawal of citizenship rights. Hence, in a rousing speech at the 1979 congress, MWU president Cor de Jager warned that white workers were at risk of becoming *gasarbeiders* (immigrant workers) 'in our own country'. 'Nowadays everyone seems concerned with the advancement of the black worker, but no one pays the white worker any attention,' he added bitterly.[72]

Thus, at the same congress, Paulus announced the MWU General Council's decision to open union membership to 'all white workers who feel that their survival as workers is being threatened'. According to

---

[67] P. J. Paulus, 'Mynvakbonde verklaar dispuut oor die 1977-verhogings', *The Mineworker*, 27 April 1977, p. 4.
[68] Paulus, 'Mynvakbonde verklaar dispuut'; also 'Wit werkers boer nou agteruit: iewers groot fout met pryse, winste', *The Mineworker*, 22 June 1977, p. 1.
[69] 'Wit werkers boer nou agteruit'.
[70] 'Paulus on future of whites in mining industry', *The Mineworker*, 27 September 1978, p. 1.
[71] 'Vakbondraad verklaar dispuut met KvM: Myne pleit bankrotskap', *The Mineworker*, 26 April 1978, p. 1.
[72] 'Cor de Jager praat kaalkop oor inflasie en gooi MWU se deure wyd-oop', *The Mineworker*, 7 February 1979, pp. 3–4.

Figure 4.2 Cor de Jager and Arrie Paulus emerge from a meeting with Minister Fanie Botha, 1976.
Source: *Beeld*, 17 July 1976

Paulus, workers in the steel and electricity industries had already approached the MWU for protection – it was time to form 'a white force which can fight for survival'.[73] This unity was imagined in both racial and class terms, mirroring 1922's meshing of class concerns with racist politics. But while workers in 1922 had fought for the *establishment* of a social order in which they too enjoyed inclusion in the racially privileged citizenry, Paulus's generation of white workers were now fighting for its *retention*. 'The MWU will never allow labour equality in the mining industry ... even if this means that the 1922 strike must be repeated, that brother must fight against brother,'[74] Paulus stated defiantly amidst rumours that new legislation was already being prepared in advance of the Wiehahn reports. It is significant that, at this stage, the antagonisms expressed by the union were clearly directed against employers and the white government, rather than black workers and their emerging unions.

Paulus's use of the 1922 trope signalled the threat of white working-class militancy in the present. Indeed, these statements came on the eve of the MWU's 1979 general strike – and its subsequent miscarriage. *The Mineworker* reported positively on the strike, calling it a 'battle of principle' for South Africa's 'racial policy',[75] but the writing was on the wall. Soon afterwards, the government accepted Wiehahn's

---

[73] P. J. Paulus, 'Alle blanke werkers moet lid van een vakbond wees', *The Mineworker*, 7 February 1979, p. 1.
[74] 'MWU sal nooit brood uit wit monde laat neem', *The Mineworker*, 7 March 1979, p. 1.
[75] P. J. Paulus, 'Die Werkstilstand', *The Mineworker*, 21 March 1979, p. 1.

recommendations. An outraged Paulus lambasted the NP: '[I]n accepting the Wiehahn report, the government has committed the greatest act of treason against the white workers of South Africa since 1922, when hundreds of miners were shot because they rebelled against the Chamber of Mines' efforts to force them to share their work with blacks.'[76] *The Mineworker* printed the entire Wiehahn report for its members to scrutinise and subsequent editions reported white miners' 'overwhelming rejection' of the recommendations, printing letters from members and union representatives bewailing the government's decision, quoting an opinion poll taken by the union of its members, and later pointing to by-election results where the NP lost support.[77] Paulus was unimpressed when the government restricted labour rights to Africans with permanent residence in the Republic – the '"Wiehahn arsenic" has simply been temporarily sugar-coated', he scoffed.[78] In his Christmas message, Paulus lamented 1979 as the year in which 'the authorities abandoned the white worker in the industrial sphere'.[79]

Following the release of the Wiehahn recommendations, the blasting certificate became the focus of the MWU's opposition to reform. The government had accepted the Commission's recommendation for the removal of all forms of job reservation, and required the MWU to negotiate with the Chamber of Mines for the opening of this certification to all races. Addressing the MWU General Council, De Jager was adamant that 'the Nationalist government of 1981 is no longer the same NP that we helped bring to power in 1948. Then they listened to the important voice of the white miner ... But, regrettably, times have changed and the current Minister of Manpower [Labour] apparently only has ears for capitalists and unions that want to advance blacks at all costs.'[80] The MWU resolutely resisted the elimination of job reservation long after similar arrangements had been removed in other industries. Paulus warned that if 'a black worker obtains a blasting certificate,

---

[76] Paulus, 'Grootste verraad teenoor blanke werkers!'

[77] P. Ungerer, 'Toekoms van die blanke werker op die spel!', *The Mineworker*, 30 May 1979, p. 4; 'Randfontein openbaar sterk protesstem teen Wiehahn-verslag', *The Mineworker*, 13 June 1979, p. 1; 'Swart vakbond in mynbedryf sal meer as 200 000 lede kan hê!', *The Mineworker*, 17 October 1979, p. 1.

[78] P. J. Paulus, '"Wiehahn-arseenpil" slegs tydelik 'n bietjie versuiker', *The Mineworker*, 11 July 1979, p. 1.

[79] P. J. Paulus, 'Kersvreugde, maar 'n sombere toekoms wag in 1980', *The Mineworker*, 26 December 1979, p. 1.

[80] '"Toegewings sal die swartes nie tevrede stel nie" – Cor de Jager', *The Mineworker*, 28 January 1981, pp. 2–5. See also P. J. Paulus, 'Byna elke NP-beleidspunt van 1948 is nou oorboord', *The Mineworker*, 20 August 1980, p. 3; 'Een minuut voor twaalf – sê Mnr Cor de Jager: Boodskap aan Kongres', *The Mineworker*, 27 January 1982, p. 3; '"Ons is reg vir praat", sê Arrie Paulus aan dr Treurnicht', *The Mineworker*, 1 July 1981, p. 1.

he could also ... become a shift boss, mining captain or mine manager. If this recommendation would be accepted, this inevitably implies that sooner or later white miners would work under blacks.'[81] Moreover, the MWU increasingly expressed this threat to the racial order as no longer confined to the workplace. Africans 'desire political dominance and nothing less',[82] De Jager claimed, while Paulus warned that workplace integration would lead to 'full-fledged integration and inevitable miscegenation!'[83] State investment in public facilities, which was intended to attract urban Africans' support for reformed apartheid, also drew white working-class ire. The MWU denounced government spending on black schools and housing, while 'no relief was being offered to whites living below the poverty line' and 'the high rate of inflation' left pensioned miners 'in perilous circumstances'. 'The white worker is concerned about his survival as the breadwinner of his household,'[84] worried De Jager. Such fears about racial mixing, creeping poverty, unemployment, and threats especially to traditional male identity, status, and working-class dignity had long been mainstays of white working-class anxieties. In this context, said De Jager, the white mineworker felt 'wronged, incensed, humiliated and very concerned'.[85] Indeed, African advancement not only threatened to undercut white workers' material conditions but was also perceived as destabilising the social hierarchy in which white working men formed part of the white, racially dominant power bloc. Racial and class concerns were deeply entangled.[86] Hence, in anticipation of the 1981 general election, De Jager stated that mineworkers would not 'content themselves with the crumbs from rich men's tables';[87] rather, 'the white worker will increasingly rebel [against the government] ... in order to protect his rights'.[88]

[81] P. J. Paulus, 'Verslag No. 6 – Gee ons die feite vóór 29 April!', *The Mineworker*, 25 March 1981, p. 1.
[82] 'Toegewings sal die swartes nie tevrede stel nie'.
[83] 'Spoorweg-drywers knorrig oor aanvaarding van Wiehahn-verslag', *The Mineworker*, 12 November 1980, p. 3. See also 'Yskor-dokument verwys glad nie na kleur nie', *The Mineworker*, 29 July 1978, p. 1; P. J. Paulus, 'Amptenare gooi die handdoek in die kryt', *The Mineworker*, 15 February 1978, p. 1.
[84] 'Alg Raad: MWU-President praat reguit; Min Fanie Botha loop deur!', *The Mineworker*, 6 February 1980, p. 1.
[85] 'Cor de Jager se beroep op Regering', *The Mineworker*, 2 February 1983, p. 2.
[86] 'Een minuut voor twaalf'; 'Cor de Jager se beroep'; P. J. Paulus, 'Stop integrasie! Sit mynhuise op hul plek', *The Mineworker*, 16 February 1983, p. 1; P. J. Paulus, ''n Uitdaging wat Prog Doc nie kan ignoreer', *The Mineworker*, 2 March 1983, p. 1; P. J. Paulus, 'MWU wen in stryd teen integrasie', *The Mineworker*, 27 April 1983, p. 1.
[87] 'Toegewings sal die swartes nie tevrede stel nie'.
[88] 'Tradisionele arbeidsvrede kry 'n verdiende knou: Arbeidsonrus neem toe', *The Mineworker*, 6 August 1980, p. 1.

For the economically vulnerable white mineworkers who formed the majority of the MWU's 18,588 members, South Africa must have seemed like a rapidly changing place.[89] Only a few years earlier, they had been firmly established in their superior positions – in the workplace, the industrial relations system, and society at large. By the early 1980s, theirs was one of the last remaining protected jobs in industry and they were being forced into negotiations for phasing out job reservation. Social apartheid was being dismantled and the NP was moving ahead with its plans for establishing the multiracial tricameral parliament. The 'white homeland' on which the MWU depended was rapidly slipping away. Hence, the union now presented itself as a 'refuge'[90] for whites in the mining industry and beyond. *The Mineworker* regularly reported on its membership expansion among white workers in other industries,[91] telling readers that the union felt that it was 'called to secure the white worker's future'[92] and 'rightful place'[93] in South Africa. Speaking at the MWU's 1982 congress, De Jager reaffirmed the MWU's commitment to maintain white domination ('*baasskap*'; literally, 'boss-ship'), ensuring that 'the underling does not become king of the castle'.[94] This anxiety about the inversion of the racial order reflected the threat black unions' recognition was seen to pose to white supremacy in the labour arena and beyond. Jeremy Krikler has noted how, with master–servant relations so 'ubiquitously shap[ing] the relations between the races' in minority-ruled South Africa, the appearance of black people outside their familiar position of 'servant' or 'underling' caused whites great distress and drove them to seek to control or exclude blacks socially.[95] Krikler notes that:

---

[89] Membership as at 31 December 1981, Finansiële bundels (Rekenmeester), MWU Archive.

[90] See, for instance, 'Mynwerkersunie 'n toevlugsoord vir blanke werkers', *The Mineworker*, 6 July 1983, p. 1.

[91] P. J. Paulus, 'Bekommerde werkers soek hulp by MWU', *The Mineworker*, 15 July 1981, p. 1; 'Paulus se verslag aan die Kongres van MWU', *The Mineworker*, 2 February 1983, p. 1; 'MWU growth in Vaal Triangle', *The Mineworker*, 30 March 1983, p. 1; 'MWU se mooi groei in Vaaldriehoek', *The Mineworker*, 11 May 1983, p. 2; 'Mynwerkersunie 'n toevlugsoord'; 'MWU vra oral uitbreiding van bestek', *The Mineworker*, 31 August 1983, p. 2; 'MWU se groei laat ander vakbonde koorsagtig word', *The Mineworker*, 28 September 1983, p. 1; 'Ons praat met ons lede by Yskor en Modderfontein', *The Mineworker*, 12 October 1983, p. 1.

[92] 'MWU se groei laat ander vakbonde koorsagtig word'.

[93] '"Laat ons ons staal vir die geroottaak [sic] wat op die MWU wag" – Arrie Paulus', *The Mineworker*, 21 December 1983, p. 1.

[94] This was expressed in the unmistakably rural Afrikaans idiom '*nie toelaat dat die jong baas van die plaas word nie*'. 'Een minuut voor twaalf'.

[95] Krikler, 'Re-thinking race and class', p. 136, 139.

Bread, butter, and the racial order 177

for much of the twentieth century, black people generally addressed white men ... as *Baas* (master) ... *Baas* was so inescapably a term denoting a member of a master class *and* race that no white worker could possibly use it.[96]

But in the pages of *The Mineworker*, white workers' anxieties about reform led to a jarring development in workers' discourse. Amidst wage negotiations in January 1984, De Jager warned employers not to attempt a return to the mining relations of the early twentieth century, when mine owners were '*baas*' and miners were '*wit Klaas*', with the latter worked like slaves. De Jager was invoking the Afrikaans expression *baas en Klaas* ('master and servant' or 'boss and Jim'), with all the racial and class connotations Krikler identifies. But the MWU president used the expression to refer to the relationship between white employers and white workers, casting master–servant relations in mainly class rather than racial terms. Notice that De Jager deemed it necessary to qualify *Klaas* with 'white' ('*wit*'), indicating the distortion of the idiom.[97] This powerfully captured the threat that reform posed to economically vulnerable white miners' racial identity and social position: in their eyes, employers were forcing them into the inferior position of *Klaas* – a position of competition and equality with rightless blacks that was simultaneously a position of inferiority vis-à-vis other whites. The reference to the early twentieth century reveals an enduring consciousness of white miners' precarious position earlier in the century, from which they had risen to partnership in the Nationalist social alliance. 'We have stated before,' Paulus fumed on another occasion, 'that the employer in the mining industry should not act as though he is boss and the employee is "*Klaas*". It is both psychologically foolish to treat employees in this manner, and also humiliating for union members'.[98] White workers would not be dictated to, Paulus was saying; they would not be treated in the same way as 'servants' or rightless blacks by other whites. As the MWU and employers continued to struggle over the removal of job reservation in the mining industry, Paulus reproached the 'liberalist Chamber of Mines and Government' for trying to 'rob the white mineworker of his identity, namely the blasting certificate'.[99]

In the 1987 and 1989 elections, the MWU supported the CP. *The Mineworker* argued that a vote against the NP was a vote against the

---

[96] Krikler, 'Re-thinking race and class', p. 137.
[97] 'Cor de Jager lewer staatsmansrede voor Kongres van die MWU', *The Mineworker*, 8 February 1984, p. 5.
[98] P. J. Paulus, 'Arrogante en eensydige optrede gelaak', *The Mineworker*, 6 November 1985, p. 1.
[99] F. Bond, 'Vakbond bied sekuriteit', *The Mineworker*, 24 December 1986, p. 7.

'disregard, impoverishment and denial of justice of the white worker'.[100] Indeed, for some time the union had been warming to the Opposition. While in the 1970s NP politicians or representatives from the Chamber of Mines had regularly featured as guest speakers at MWU congresses, the 1980s saw them replaced by CP MPs. But there is evidence that the CP and the MWU were not speaking the same language. The speech by Louis Stofberg, CP MP for Sasolburg, to the MWU's 1986 congress centred on the 'Afrikaner people' and their enemy, the black majority. The speech wallowed in nationalist rhetoric and Stofberg concluded with a clumsy nod to his audience's class position as 'Afrikaner-whiteman-workers'.[101] In 1987, the CP founding member Connie Mulder opened the congress with an arguably more apposite speech, talking about the 'battle' to protect white mineworkers from undercutting by unskilled black labour.[102] Yet, despite the class- and industry-specific terms in which Mulder endeavoured to speak, he, like Stofberg, highlighted racial antagonisms and represented African advancement as the main threat to white working-class interests. This did not correspond to the union's understanding of its situation. While both organisations spoke in terms of a 'battle' being waged in South Africa and saw blacks as foreigners in the 'white Republic', the MWU saw the reformist white government and white business as its main enemies. Despite becoming a CP MP, Paulus seems to have sensed this disconnect, aware that the CP was not focused on working-class interests. 'Without any doubt in my mind, I am the only person in the [all-white] House of Assembly that knows the white mineworker and can talk on his behalf,' he said in an interview. 'Most other MPs are doctors and lawyers.' He stridently opposed government moves towards deregulation and the privatisation of state industries that had long provided employment for poor and working-class whites.[103]

Workers as a white minority: working-class unity and the volk

Under Peet Ungerer, the MWU continued its scathing criticism of the NP government. Addressing readers for the first time as general secretary, Ungerer continued Paulus's line that the MWU was 'locked in a fierce battle against not only the employer, but also his former ally, the government, who abolished job reservation in the mines in order to

[100] P. Ungerer, 'Dag van beslissing vir blanke werker', *The Mineworker*, August 1989, p. 1.
[101] 'Witman het steeds die mag in die hand', *The Mineworker*, 5 February 1986, p. 3.
[102] 'Blanke word jaar na jaar armer', *The Mineworker*, 4 February 1987, p. 1.
[103] Leach, *The Afrikaners*, pp. 86–7.

please the mine magnates and the international community'.[104] Just days before Ungerer's appointment, the racial reservation of blasting certificates was repealed, marking the final failure of the union's resistance to labour reform. The MWU slammed the unilateral legislative amendment for removing the protection 'offered ... to the white minority in mining'[105] and accused the government of having 'sold out and betrayed' its 'own blood'.[106] In a press statement, Ungerer declared that 'those who are concerned about racial discrimination should note that whites are increasingly being discriminated against'.[107]

This was the first time the union referred to its members as a minority. Moreover, drawing on black struggles and prevailing anti-apartheid discourse, the idea of white workers being treated in a manner unfitting their racial position by their own white government and employers was now cast as discrimination. In one instance, *The Mineworker* reported with indignation on the institution of 1 May as a public holiday in the Republic. It reproached the NP for bowing to 'threats from black unions' and 'communist agitation', and labelled the 'red' Labour Day a 'defeat' for white workers. As a way for white workers to 'regain their self-respect', the MWU argued for the institution of a 'white workers' public holiday' commemorating the 1922 Rand Revolt. Should the proposal be rejected, Ungerer said, this would only serve to emphasise the discrimination white workers were now suffering.[108] While previously the MWU had invoked 1922 as a plebeian revolt, it was now portrayed as a 'peaceful protest' that cast white workers as the victims of a gross injustice.[109] This resonated powerfully with experiences of 'humiliation' and 'defeat' in the present, as white workers were sidelined by the white political and business establishment, their one-time partners in racial citizenship, in the wake of the Wiehahn reforms. This left white workers at the mercy of '[i]mpoverishment, discrimination ... unfair labour practices, inflation, unemployment, expensive housing, poor medical insurance, and competing with poorly qualified, unproductive and even impudent blacks on the factory floor'.[110] In his 1988 Christmas message, Ungerer summed up white workers' experiences of the withdrawal of state support for working-class whiteness: 'moneyed interests' and 'the current

[104] 'Mnr Peet Ungerer se boodskap', *The Mineworker*, September 1987, 1.
[105] P. Ungerer, 'Skietsertifikaat: Stryd duur voort', *The Mineworker*, October 1987, p. 1.
[106] P. Ungerer, 'Die finale verraad', *The Mineworker*, August 1988, p. 1.
[107] P. Ungerer, 'Persverklaring', *The Mineworker*, November 1988, p. 1.
[108] 'Onthou die mynstaking van 1922', *The Mineworker*, November 1988, p. 1.
[109] See also 'Cor de Jager se presidentsrede: Blanke se stryd duur voort', *The Mineworker*, January 1990, p. 2.
[110] 'Onthou die mynstaking van 1922'.

government' were 'doing [their] utmost to deny the white worker, not only in the mines but across the labour front, his birthright to his own place and a fair wage in his own country. To step by step push him into equality with blacks in employment, to destroy his identity and his right to living out a whiteman's existence.'[111]

Ungerer was no longer speaking only to white mineworkers or simply about workplace concerns. In 1988, he had called for unity among all white workers,[112] arguing that 'the white worker's economic, cultural, political and even physical survival' was dependent on unification in a 'super union'[113] that could fight to 'liberate [him] from organised money power and its allies' strategy of dividing and ruling over the white worker'.[114] Ungerer's calls for workers' unity reflected anxieties about the accelerating pace of change. The CP failed to block the NP's reform programme in the 1989 general election. Soon after, De Klerk unbanned black liberation leaders and organisations and entered into negotiations with those previously regarded as terrorists. Working-class desperation may be detected in *The Mineworker*'s claims that employers were treating white workers as 'spare tyres': they were given some 'recognition and appreciation' during black strikes when business was dependent on their labour, but once the strikes ended, white workers were discarded and employers returned to catering to the needs of their black employees only.[115] 'Has the white worker now become completely dispensable?'[116] the paper agonised.

Ungerer's call for the establishment of a 'super white trade union' seemingly found wide resonance among white workers, and the MWU's membership grew steadily. In 1991, Flip Buys was appointed to 'develop the super white union ideal'. This was explained in a short article in *The Mineworker* which introduced Buys to readers under the heading 'Eskom-man joins MWU team'.[117] Indeed, Buys had previously

---

[111] P. Ungerer, 'Eenheidsoproep aan alle Blanke Vakbonde', *The Mineworker*, Christmas and New Year edition 1988, p. 1.
[112] Ungerer, 'Eenheidsoproep'.
[113] P. Ungerer, 'Een wit vakbond', *The Mineworker*, September 1990, p. 1.
[114] P. Ungerer, 'Volstoom na een, wit vakbond', *The Mineworker*, November/December 1990, p. 1. Also 'Eenheidsfront ideaal vir '90', *The Mineworker*, November/December 1989, p. 1.
[115] 'Een wit vakbond!', *The Mineworker*, July 1990, p. 1; 'Hoofartikel', *MWU-News*, July 1992, p. 4. See also P. Ungerer, 'Alles styg: Die Kamer van Mynwese swyg', *The Mineworker*, May 1989, p. 1.
[116] C. de Jager, 'Blanke werker die slagoffer van verbreekte beloftes', *The Mineworker*, November/December 1989, p. 1.
[117] 'Eskom-man word deel van MWU-span', *The Mineworker*, April 1991, p. 4.

Figure 4.3 Andries Treurnicht, leader of the Conservative Party, with Cor de Jager (left) and Peet Ungerer (right) at the MWU's 1993 annual congress.
Source: *MWU-News*, February 1993

been employed as Head of Labour Relations and Communication at one of the public utility's major power stations. Although Buys was academically trained, his description as an 'Eskom-man' may be read as an appeal to the newspaper's blue-collar readership. The article appeared in the first edition for which Buys was responsible, and he probably authored it himself. His responsibilities included the editorship of the union newspaper. Over the next few years, until he briefly left the MWU in 1995, Buys' editorial staff included a number of veteran MWU officials such as Krappie Cronje and Fred Bond. The first edition for which Buys was responsible heralded a significant departure from previous editions, with a much more formal appearance and content that aspired to the standards of a professional newspaper.[118] Under Buys' direction, important changes also occurred in the newspaper's name and tagline. It changed from *The Mineworker: Official organ of the MWU* to *The Mineworker: The newspaper for **all** white workers* in April 1991, then to *MWU-News: The newspaper for **all** white workers* just one month later, and finally to *MWU-News: The voice of the white worker* in July 1991. It is likely that these changes sought to reflect the union's expanding membership beyond its traditional mining nucleus. Thus, the goal of a 'super white union' saw the MWU's attention expand from white mineworkers to representing 'white workers across the entire labour front'.[119] By 1992, its membership had risen to 44,000.[120]

At the same time, the union's resistance to democratising change saw it throw its weight against efforts to desegregate amenities, neighbourhoods, and services. Indeed, Paulus had often warned his readers that workplace integration would lead to social integration, and the MWU regularly expressed its opposition to the effects of desegregation and transformation on the white workers' world beyond the workplace. But this also stretched beyond just working-class issues and areas, and the newspaper increasingly reported on perceived threats to whites' cultural and racial survival. Moreover, race and class concerns now joined with ethnic elements. In the early 1990s, for instance, the *MWU-News* expressed the union's opposition to pressures by mining houses to instate a seven-day working week. Utilising the *baas–Klaas* trope, the MWU condemned these suggestions as 'slave-working weeks'[121] and urged all white workers to join the MWU in order to halt the 'total onslaught on the white Afrikaner man'.[122] Although the issue at stake pertained specifically to the blue-collar mining industry and sought to resist the perceived exploitation of white miners, it was represented as resonating with a wider 'onslaught' in ethnic and racial terms. It remains unclear to which elements of its members' identity the union was appealing. The fact that the mine owners were also white, and perhaps even Afrikaners, did not seem to be particularly problematic to the article's argument.

---

[118] The masthead, layout, and presentation of the newspaper changed markedly, creating a much more ordered impression, incorporating elements standard in mainstream news publications such as the names and contact details of the editor and staff members, an editorial piece and political cartoon, and readers' letters.
[119] P. Ungerer, 'Blanke werker keelvol vir "bending backwards"-beleid', *The Mineworker*, February 1989, p. 4.
[120] Finansiële bundels (Rekenmeester), MWU Archive; Visser, 'From MWU to Solidarity', p. 27.
[121] 'Verwerp slaweweke, sê Ungerer', *MWU-News*, March 1993, p. 2.
[122] P. H. du Plooy, 'Gebruik jou mag, of sterf as slaaf', *MWU-News*, October 1994, p. 14.

Figure 4.4 MWU members from Evander on the East Rand protest against Eskom's decision to allow the desegregation of residential areas under its control, 1991.
Source: *MWU-News*, July 1991

Following the 1992 white referendum in favour of a negotiated transition, the union became increasingly concerned with 'the interests of our people' ('*volksbelange*')[123] and more frequently used the terms 'whites' and 'white workers' interchangeably. The early 1990s saw the union 'supporting the farmers' in their grievances against change, and at the MWU's 1992 annual congress, the president of the Transvaal Agricultural Union (also a CP MP) delivered the opening speech.[124] This pointed to a developing conservative, ethnic solidarity beyond a specific industrial or blue-collar work identity. In his February 1992 editorial, Buys returned to the Rand Revolt, taking up the discourse of white victimisation and unjust treatment that it had come to symbolise. The strike saw mineworkers protest against 'poor treatment ... by the capitalists, the danger of foreign workers and the unsympathetic stance of the then government'. Extending the trope to apply beyond just the MWU's members in mining, he stated that 'seventy years later, the white worker faces the same situation' of discrimination, the denial of rights, 'reasonable requests' falling on deaf ears, and demonisation.[125] No specific grievances, either in the workplace or socially, were mentioned, but 1922 signalled a general experience of oppression, discrimination, and victimhood. In the September 1992 edition, these same notions were raised – this time communicated via the imagery of the South African

---

[123] 'Ekonomiese imperialiste moet hand en tand beveg word', *MWU-News*, December 1992, p. 4.
[124] 'Blanke Vakbonde moet groter rol speel, sê Bruwer', *MWU-News*, February 1992, p. 1.
[125] 'Weer terug in 1922?', *MWU-News*, February 1992, p. 4.

184   From trade union to social movement

Figure 4.5 Peet Ungerer (second from left) and Cor de Jager (right) flank General Constand Viljoen at the founding meeting of the Afrikaner Volksfront, 1993.
Source: *MWU-News*, May 1993

War. The paper ran an image of an emaciated child, apparently an Afrikaner interned exactly 90 years earlier in a concentration camp. 'We cannot allow their sacrifices to have been in vain,'[126] the caption urged ominously. Whereas the union's invocation of sacrifice and victimhood had previously recalled the oppressive power of the state and employers, this instance saw these ideas remoulded to resonate with the Boer battle for political freedom, casting sacrifice and struggle in ethnic rather than class terms. These ideas were arguably reflected in the MWU's political alignment at the time. In May 1993, it was party to the formation of the right-wing Afrikaner Volksfront. The union therefore seemed to be joining the battle against political democratisation and majority rule that conservative politicians had addressed at the union's congresses in the late 1980s.

As we have seen, disunity in Volksfront ranks saw it split immediately prior to the 1994 election. Writing in the first edition of *MWU-News* following the ANC's electoral victory, Ungerer argued that the MWU

[126] *MWU-News*, September 1992, p. 5.

was now 'the only organisation which can protect our members', as there were no other channels left through which whites could advance their interests.[127] In the face of the formal loss of white political power, the MWU's mouthpiece increasingly extended its established expression of white working-class humiliation, indignation, and subordination to encompass the experience of all whites: the NP had once betrayed white miners by abolishing job reservation, but now it had abandoned all whites by capitulating to a black majority government, while big business eagerly adopted race-based affirmative action policies in order to please the new powers that be.

The union was defiant in the face of black majority government, stating that it was 'not concerned ... After all, we have years of experience with a government which is unsympathetic towards the rights of white workers.'[128] This statement equated the new regime with the 1922 Smuts government and the reformist NP. Indeed, the MWU's hostility transferred seamlessly from the white NP government to the black ANC government. It reproached the ANC both for its 'unreasonable' employment equity policy, which 'hurts, humiliates and tramples the rights of white workers',[129] and for its 'discrimination' against Afrikaners, whose language was being 'denied' in public.[130] The MWU's talk of humiliation and a denial of rights often hovered ambiguously between issues of class, race, and ethnicity. At the 1996 annual congress, Ungerer told union representatives that 'the poor white problem of sixty years ago is fast re-emerging' due to affirmative action and discrimination.[131] De Jager followed, arguing that the union could no longer confine itself to jobs and wages, but also had to see to training opportunities for MWU members and their children.[132] The editorial in the *MWU-News* went even further, claiming that the MWU was 'one of the few surviving power bases of the Afrikaner': 'merely protecting' members' jobs and incomes was 'futile' when their 'language, religion, social circumstances, living space, security, right to self-determination, and the education of ... children are under attack'.[133] These statements strikingly demonstrate the fluidity of workplace and social issues in the

---

[127] 'MWU is reg vir toekoms', *MWU-News*, May 1994, p. 1.
[128] 'Nuwe tye bied nuwe geleenthede', *MWU-News*, September 1994, p. 4.
[129] P. Ungerer, 'Staak!', *MWU-News*, October 1994, p. 1.
[130] F. Buys, 'Miskenning van Afrikaans: Maatskappye is ook skuldig', *MWU-News*, May 1995, p. 15; P. Möller, 'Afrikaans asseblief', *MWU-News*, November/December 1995, p. 13.
[131] 'MWU remains white and fighting', *MWU-News*, February 1996, p. 1.
[132] 'MWU-president: Só gaan 1996 lyk', *MWU-News*, February 1996, p. 2.
[133] 'Kongres wys nuwe uidagings uit', *MWU-News*, February 1996, p. 4.

MWU during this period, as well as the ever growing emphasis on race and ethnicity. This saw old concerns reframed and linked to new ones. The spectre of white poverty, for instance, had long haunted vulnerable white workers facing rising inflation and labour reform. The MWU of Arrie Paulus understood white poverty as a threat faced by white miners due to their structural position. While it is unlikely that this understanding was completely effaced in the wake of the political transition, white impoverishment now became tied to the policies of a black majority government understood in racial and ethnic terms. Hence, white poverty could function discursively alongside perceived infringements on language and religion, and the need for training for MWU members could be placed alongside fears for the future of white children in South Africa. This reflected not only the new political dispensation, but also the expansion of the MWU's membership base to deal with the impact of economic changes and policies on white blue-collar workers across South Africa. As in the late 1970s, the paper's discourse remained characterised by resistance to change, but the issues discussed – education, the public use of Afrikaans, crime, corruption, and affirmative action – were now framed in anti-white, or specifically anti-Afrikaner, terms, rather than in terms of the exploitation of workers by employers, insufficient protection by government, or exclusion from racial citizenship. Critiques of the public education system, affirmative action policies, and the public demise of Afrikaans dominated the paper's content. It explicitly called the government 'the enemy' of 'our people', and whites, specifically Afrikaners, were consistently portrayed as victims. Of course, we have seen that race was always deeply implicated in the class identity of the MWU – whether in 1922 or in the late 1970s. The crescendo in the union's assertion of an Afrikaner identity seems more novel. Even though the MWU had long been a predominantly Afrikaner organisation, the union under Paulus, as well as during the early years of Ungerer's leadership, rarely pushed its ethnic identity to the fore[134] – perhaps it had felt no need to do so in the context of Afrikaner political dominance. However, it seems clear that, until the late 1980s, the union's identity as mineworkers and as a racialised working class had been central. By the mid-1990s, this had clearly changed.

[134] The handful of instances where this was done include Arrie Paulus's reproach of the mining house Gencor as a company under 'Afrikaans-speaking control' for its disregard for white miners' interests (see P. J. Paulus, 'Gencor-brief getuig van harteloosheid', *The Mineworker*, 19 September 1984, p. 1; P. J. Paulus, 'MWU en Gencor beraadslaag oor foutiewe sirkulêre', *The Mineworker*, 31 October 1984, p. 1) and Peet Ungerer's defence of mineworkers' day off on 16 December, celebrating the Day of the Covenant (P. Ungerer, 'Geloftedag', *The Mineworker*, October 1988, p. 1).

Visser's verdict that, 'between 1994 and 1997, the MWU stagnated'[135] is not reflected in the sources. Visser himself notes the union's rapid growth in membership to become the largest white trade union in South Africa by 1992.[136] By 1995, it sported some 54,000 members.[137] In October 1996, the newspaper ran a cartoon visually representing the MWU as a mighty fortress with great streams of 'members of other [white] unions' pouring through its gates. A banner proclaimed 'MWU: home of the white worker', and the caption read 'MWU fort is now finished'.[138] Rather than a stagnant and disgraced organisation, the MWU portrayed itself as triumphant: it had accomplished its goal of becoming a 'super white union' and claimed to be the only white union left in South Africa.[139] Indeed, its rapid membership growth suggests that those white workers rushing to join its ranks shared the view that the MWU was one of the few remaining bastions of white Afrikaner power.

Figure 4.6 Flip Buys (left) acts as MWU signatory of the union's recognition agreement with Telkom, marking another significant expansion of the union, 1993.
Source: *MWU-News*, November 1993

---

[135] Visser, 'From MWU to Solidarity', p. 11.
[136] Visser, 'From MWU to Solidarity', p. 27.
[137] 'Report: MWU is the biggest and growing!', *MWU-News*, March 1995, pp. 1–2; 'Bont vakbonde se lede stroom uit', *MWU-News*, March 1996, pp. 1–2.
[138] *MWU-News*, October 1996, p. 4.
[139] 'Boeke afgesluit', *MWU-News*, November/December 1995, p. 4.

Majority rule and new leadership: race as culture

When Peet Ungerer retired in 1997, Flip Buys was the only applicant for his post and was unanimously elected by the executive management.[140] Soon after his appointment, Buys reassumed the role of *MWU-News* editor. While big business was still condemned in the MWU's rhetoric up to 1996, this was no longer the case under Buys' leadership. Rather, racial hostility and ethnic victimhood dominated the union's representation of the plight of its members and the country under black majority rule. In a February 1998 article, Dirk Hermann – a Potchefstroom industrial sociology graduate appointed by Buys – offered an overview of Afrikaner history and the role of the MWU in it. Historical overviews were popular within the union – Paulus and De Jager had often reminded MWU members of the union's history and historical battle against exploitation and 'hostile governments'. But Hermann now cast this history in ethnic terms, as part of 'the Afrikaner's fight for freedom' in the twentieth century: Afrikaners lost their freedom following the 'Second War of Independence' (as he labelled the South African War), regained it in the 1948 general election, only to lose it again in 1994. Hermann seemed at pains to cast this political narrative in labour terms, explaining how during their 'period of power' following 1948, Afrikaners 'abdicated' their labour power by letting 'others' do their manual labour. The article initially referred to 'foreigners' (*volksvreemdes*), then reverted to the term 'non-whites' and eventually 'blacks'. As a result of the foothold given to them by Afrikaners, blacks were able to build their labour power and use it to agitate for political rights, so that the Afrikaner 'again lost his freedom by being swamped by foreign labour numbers' in 1994.[141] While previously employers had been accused of treating workers like white servants, the newspaper now focused on the ostensible loss of political freedom at the hands of blacks. The 1922 trope was incorporated into this narrative, but it was no longer recounted as a militant plebeian revolt or even as a peaceful protest. Instead, 1922 was invoked as an example of the MWU's centrality in and commitment to 'Afrikaner work-interests': the union's efforts to defend the rights of members made it the 'primary target' of the Smuts government's violent repression during the 1922 strike, Hermann claimed. Similarly, it was 'specifically the MWU' that had contributed to the NP winning the 1948 election and Afrikaners' freedom with it. This representation

---

[140] Visser, *Van MWU tot Solidariteit*, p. 311; Flip Buys, interviewed 19 September 2011.
[141] D. Herman [sic], 'Deur arbeid het ons ons vryheid verloor – deur arbeid moet ons ons vryheid herwin', *MWU-News*, February 1998, p. 5.

corresponded closely to Paulus's portrayals of the MWU as a 'refuge' for white workers – but, in 1998, Hermann did not reproach 'moneyed interests' nor did he appeal to 'white workers'. Rather, he sought to present the MWU as the legitimate voice of Afrikaner interests and a vehicle of Afrikaner power, offering a solution to the volk's perceived servitude:

> The MWU led the Afrikaner to victory in 1948. Fifty years later the MWU is again faced with the challenge of attending to Afrikaner work-interests by offering a strategic labour plan for a volk that has lost its freedom ... Through labour we lost our freedom and through labour we will regain our freedom.[142]

Despite Hermann's talk of 'labour power', his framing was firmly set in terms of ethnicity. Previously, the MWU had presented its members specifically as white workers being denied their rightful position in the racial state, left behind by the reformist government and its capitalist supporters. Now, it pointed to the position of white Afrikaans-speakers, irrespective of class, portraying them as relegated to a subordinate and disempowered position vis-à-vis the black majority. Race had previously been articulated in class terms, now it was reformulated as culture. This effectively claimed a homogeneous experience of political disempowerment and marginalisation for Afrikaners on the basis of their ethnic identity, allowing the MWU to appeal to broader white and Afrikaner sentiments in the post-1994 context, thus bolstering its membership expansion beyond blue-collar industries and collective representation.

This reformulation formed part of Buys' vision for the union. At the 1998 annual congress, he identified 'the feeling amongst whites that they no longer have effective say in government decisions that affect them and that government policy discriminates against them'. In response, the MWU would expand its traditional role as a trade union to support its 'members and their children' by 'creating jobs, helping with private education, private health services and welfare'.[143] It was for this purpose that Buys initiated the *Wenplan 2002*, his five-year strategy for reorganising, modernising, and expanding the MWU. Throughout, Buys appointed young university-educated graduates to drive this transformation.[144]

This strategy may be read as the union's latest response in the long transition, as white workers sought new ways to secure their interests in the wake of the withdrawal of state support for working-class whiteness after Wiehahn. Resisting reform in the labour arena had failed, and

---

[142] Herman [sic], 'Deur arbeid het ons ons vryheid verloor'.
[143] 'MWU moet Arbeidsbeweging word', *MWU-News*, January 1998, p. 1.
[144] Visser, *Van MWU tot Solidariteit*, p. 315.

supporting the CP had come to naught. But with the end of the racial state and the establishment of non-racial democracy, white working-class experiences were joined by those of other sections of white society, perhaps notably conservative Afrikaners disillusioned with the promise of an Afrikaner *volkstaat* held out by the FF. Buys himself had spent time working for the FF before returning to the MWU. Now, it seemed, the MWU itself was being put forward as the vehicle for Afrikaner survival in the new South Africa. This vehicle, however, was no longer defined in its original working-class terms. Buys was repositioning the MWU as a civil society organisation bargaining for the rights of minorities in general and Afrikaans-speaking whites in particular. Indeed, by the turn of the millennium, the MWU's discourse had not only muted explicit class references but was sufficiently ambiguous to speak to whites in general and Afrikaners in particular in the new political context. While the emphasis had previously been on how white workers were sidelined in the labour arena, their interests as white citizen workers ignored by the racial state, the *MWU-News* now condemned the ANC government, claiming that it 'marginalises us and our interests, retrenches our people from their jobs, disadvantages our language, changes the names of towns left, right and centre, without seeming to care that our friends and families and some of the best brainpower is rushing to leave the country'.[145] On several occasions, affirmative action policies were provocatively likened to 'ethnic cleansing'.[146] This framing intensified the union's existing discourse of threat and survival by adding the notion of violence directed at a minority group by a hostile majority. Indeed, this kind of reasoning was also present in the 'neo-racism hearings' the union held throughout the country in 2001 where victims of affirmative action could tell their stories – a parallel to the post-apartheid Truth and Reconciliation Commission.[147]

In contrast to the anti-capitalist sentiments and hostility towards employers displayed by the MWU in previous decades, Buys started to make overtures towards partnerships with employers. Big businesses such as Telkom, Eskom, Iscor, and the Chamber of Mines were invited

---

[145] 'Kongres 2002: Flip Buys praat oor Solidariteit en die regering', *Solidarity* 2 (2002), pp. 14–15.
[146] 'Regering preek een ding en doen 'n ander', *MWU-News*, September 1999, p. 5; 'Die balanskant van "regstellende aksie"', *MWU-News*, February 2000, p. 1; 'MWU oefen druk uit om wet "reg te stel"', *MWU-News*, August 2000, p. 3; D. Hermann, 'Institutional racism in the workplace', *MWU-News*, September 2000, p. 3; F. Buys, 'SA en Zimbabwe: Soek die verskil!', *Solidarity* 3 (2001), p. 3.
[147] 'MWU-Solidariteit gaan landswye veldtog loods teen neo-rassisme', *Solidarity* 3 (2001), pp. 4–5; '"Regstellende aksie" slaan geniepsig en onverdiend, getuig wit werkers', *Solidarity* 5 (2001), pp. 8–10.

to make submissions to the MWU concerning existing labour relations, and Buys stressed the 'importance of partnerships between employers and employees' in addressing the 'crisis' of unemployment in South Africa.[148] In June 1999, the *MWU-News* pointed to the shared interests of its members and their employers:

> As responsible workers, the MWU and its members realise that our own welfare is tied to the success of employers. Damage to equipment, loss of labour hours due to accidents and loss of production due to illness have a negative impact on the profitability of the company and thus on the share which is the workers' due. Therefore, and also due to basic civilised loyalty, MWU members protect the interests of the employer by for instance promoting health and safety in the workplace.[149]

Such statements contrasted sharply with the MWU's strident anti-employer rhetoric under Arrie Paulus. This does not mean that the MWU never criticised employers, but the union's hostility was ultimately aimed at the black majority government. In 2000, for instance, the MWU charged a number of companies before the Pan-South African Language Board (PANSAB) with exclusively using English in company communications. This amounted to 'unfair language discrimination', claimed the MWU. PANSAB ruled in the union's favour. Despite the fact that the MWU's legal action was directed against employers, it ultimately claimed that the state was the biggest violator of the Constitution, as it tolerated this kind of discrimination.[150] Similarly, in an affirmative action case against Eskom, the MWU's main reproach was against the Constitution and legislation which, it claimed, facilitated 'discrimination' against whites.[151]

The MWU's sympathy towards employers did not mean it never resorted to strike action. However, the union insisted that this was done within the framework of 'responsible forcefulness', causing as little public disruption as possible.[152] It was on this basis that it appealed to potential members: when announcing that its membership was being opened to individuals, the MWU explained that individuals not employed in large companies 'desire membership with a strong, yet responsible trade union in order to ensure their job security'.[153] 'Times have changed,' warned

---

[148] 'Doen iets: dit help beslis!', *MWU-News*, October 1998, p. 4. Also 'Die MWU maak geskiedenis', *MWU-News*, January 1998, p. 5.
[149] 'Veiligheid eerste', *MWU-News*, June 1999, p. 4.
[150] 'Eskom skuldig!', *MWU-News*, May 2000, p. 1.
[151] 'Eskom uitspraak skrei teen billikheid', *MWU-News*, August 2000, p. 4.
[152] 'Bennie Blignaut en Eskom', *Solidarity* 5 (2001), pp. 18–19.
[153] 'Individuals can now join the MWU', *MWU-News*, May/June 1998, p. 1; also 'Ope brief aan alle Telkom-werkers wat nie aan 'n vakbond behoort nie', *MWU-News*, September 1998, p. 15.

192 From trade union to social movement

Figure 4.7 Flip Buys (centre) leads a media conference following the MWU's Labour Court victory against affirmative action policies at Eskom in 1997. Among the MWU legal and union representatives is Dirk Hermann (far left). Note the MWU slogan 'Times have changed ... you need the MWU now!'
Source: *MWU-News*, September 1997

the union during its 2000 recruitment drive among professionals, and even white employees in management positions 'need a responsible trade union like the MWU!'[154] In 2001, the union boasted that on several occasions its members had shown that they were able to act 'forcefully but responsibly' during negotiations and strikes,[155] thus distinguishing them from black mass action, which it associated with large-scale service disruption, violence, and vandalism. Yet, the MWU/Solidarity was willing to oppose management in partnership with black unions when it served its interests. In 2001, the union and its old nemesis the NUM protested together against the exclusion of workers from the distribution of company shares by De Beers Mining Company. *Solidarity* magazine reported on the action in terms of 'workers' condemning 'management' for the latter's 'gross discrimination'.[156] In another protest, white and black workers united in protest against Iscor's paying of bonuses to

---

[154] See picture (p. 1) and political cartoon (p. 4) in *MWU-News*, February 2000.
[155] F. Buys, '2001: die einde van die begin', *Solidariteit* 8 (2001), p. 2.
[156] 'Werkers klap Premiermyn se bestuur oor growwe diskriminasie', *Solidariteit* 5 (2001), p. 6.

management amidst large-scale labour redundancies.[157] When explaining its reasons for cooperating with unions such as the NUM, however, the union was at pains to maintain its distinctiveness. Emphasising the 'strong differences' between itself and the COSATU unions, about which 'we will continue to clash in future', it stated that there were also certain issues of 'common interests', in which case 'strategic partnerships' could serve to 'improve the position of our members'.[158]

In 2001, when the MWU merged with four other unions, it consisted of a labour wing providing traditional trade union services, an economic wing offering financial services and job creation through the mobilisation of capital, and a development wing involved in charity activities and training.[159] While many of these new services and initiatives – from retraining opportunities to legal support and medical insurance – were developed in response to changing economic trends, they were presented in politicised and ethnicised terms as efforts to resist 'unfair discrimination'. The union adopted the slogan 'We protect our people'. The following year marked the MWU's centenary, and the completion of the five-year *Wenplan*. Inspired by the Polish union Solidarność, the union was renamed Solidarity. Although the MWU/Solidarity had no links to its Polish namesake, it saw Solidarność as an example of a labour movement that had formed a power bloc opposing the unpopular communist regime in Poland.[160] This mirrored how the MWU/Solidarity sought to represent its own role in majority-ruled South Africa.

The MWU had once been an industry-based trade union representing white miners. By 2002, many white-collar workers and professionals had joined Solidarity.[161] Rather than the 'home of the white worker', it now identified as 'an organisation for people ... disadvantaged by the negative consequences of affirmative action'[162] and focused on the 'protection of our members as a minority'.[163] It boasted 120,000 members who were predominantly white, but no longer exclusively so. Nevertheless, Buys stated that the organisation's goal was to 'send out the message that whites also have a future in this country' and to 'allow us to live out our collective identity'.[164] Earlier statements about the 'humiliation' suffered by white workers in the face of African advancement in the labour arena and the need for workers to 'regain their self-respect' amid the indifference of employers and the NP government echoed in Buys'

---

[157] 'Vanderbijl nou mededingend met armstes in die wêreld', *Solidarity* 8 (2001), pp. 8–9.
[158] 'Bennie Blignaut en Eskom'. [159] Buys, 'MWU-Solidariteit se plan'.
[160] Visser, 'From MWU to Solidarity', p. 34. [161] Hermann, 'Propvol 2002'.
[162] F. Buys, 'Oorsig oor 2002', *Solidarity* 7 (2002), p. 5.
[163] F. Buys, 'Hoofsekretaris kyk na 2002', *Solidarity* 1 (2002), pp. 6–7.
[164] Buys, 'Hoofsekretaris kyk na 2002'.

declarations that 'our people must take back their self-respect and self-confidence ... We must learn that we are allowed to be on our own side without feeling ashamed or guilty.'[165] But it was clear that 'our people' no longer referred specifically to the working-class constituencies who had elected Arrie Paulus to Parliament in the wake of the Wiehahn reforms. Class designations had been replaced by an emphasis on ethnicity, and race was expressed in cultural terms. Hence, Buys articulated the union's goal of creating opportunities and mechanisms to 'empower our members'[166] in the distinct nationalist idiom of the Afrikaner economic movement of the 1930s: *''n Volk red homself!*'[167]

Conclusion

By 2002, the MWU/Solidarity was expressing many of the same discourses of white victimhood and defensive ethnic identity that various scholars have identified within the white population after 1994. Indeed, Steyn, in her landmark study, quotes Buys as an example of 'white talk' representing Afrikaners as disadvantaged: deposed from their 'normal place as first-class citizens' and relegated to 'second-class citizenship' in the new South Africa.[168]

This chapter has revealed the merging of white working-class responses to the dismantling of the racial state with the post-1994 'identity struggles' of the white, specifically Afrikaner, minority. Expressions of entitlement and rights centred on citizenship, coupled with experiences of loss, humiliation, anxiety, and contempt for a lack of recognition, had been present within the MWU for many decades. Under Arrie Paulus, race-based entitlement was refracted through MWU members' class position. Yet, as the political situation shifted and the MWU drew nearer to right-wing Afrikaner elements, ethnic articulations came more strongly to the fore. Finally, after Flip Buys assumed the leadership in 1997, class-based claims were completely effaced in favour of race-based entitlement expressed in cultural terms. These discursive shifts both reflected and facilitated the MWU/Solidarity's repositioning from a trade union to a civil society organisation catering to the needs of the Afrikaner minority. Arguably, this saw the organisation consolidate the fragmented expressions of post-1994

[165] F. Buys, 'Kom ons wees aan ons eie kant', *Solidarity* 4 (2002), p. 7.
[166] F. Buys, ''n Selfdoenkultuur is probleme se moses!', *Solidarity* 1 (2002), p. 3.
[167] 'A people rescues itself!' (see Chapter 2). F. Buys, ''n Volk red homself', *Solidarity* 6 (2002), p. 5. Also 'Wat beplan die MWU vir 2000?', *MWU-News*, February 2000, p. 2.
[168] Quoted in Steyn, 'Rehabilitating a whiteness disgraced', p. 158.

Conclusion 195

Afrikaner 'identity crisis' and 'disgraced' whiteness identified by scholars, giving them coherence and focus within the post-apartheid context. This is explored in further depth in Chapter 5.

For Visser, the MWU's 'reinvention' under Buys constituted a significant break in the organisation's history, thanks to Buys' 'visionary' and 'strategic' leadership. Important changes certainly did occur after Buys took over in 1997, both in organisational and discursive terms – and, as Chapter 5 will show, these were consolidated and expanded in subsequent years. However, there are limits to the extent to which these constituted a 'reinvention' of the union. The MWU/Solidarity resisted democratising and deracialising change throughout the period under investigation here, even though the terms in which this resistance was imagined and articulated shifted over time. Under Paulus, the intersection of MWU members' class position vis-à-vis other whites and their racial position vis-à-vis blacks saw the expression of white working-class consciousness and interests in opposition to big business and the white government. As apartheid was dismantled and majority rule established, expressions of class identity gave way to more overtly racial and increasingly ethnic articulations. This was demonstrated, for instance, in the changing ways in which the resentment and humiliation born of the loss of power and status were framed. This is not to say that class-based interests and concerns disappeared completely from the organisation's agenda. However, these were either reformulated in racial terms or subsumed by ethnic interests in the new political context of majority rule.

In addition to the continuities visible in the organisation's resistant stance, we should also recall the 'super white union' ideal of the 1980s. To be sure, by 2002 Solidarity was no longer exclusively white. But its membership was overwhelmingly white and Afrikaans-speaking, and it presented its *raison d'être* in exactly these terms. Under Paulus and Ungerer, the union expanded beyond its originally narrow mineworking membership to incorporate blue-collar workers across industries. It also increasingly engaged in reactionary race-based political mobilisation. Under Buys, and in the context of a transformed political landscape, this process of broadening the organisation's functional and political appeal continued. Membership was opened to individuals, the organisation jettisoned its traditional trade union identity through its rebranding and reframing as a social movement involved in labour and civil rights issues, and it engaged more overtly in cultural politics. This saw the organisation's membership expand as middle-class elements joined the established blue-collar fold.

Indeed, in 1977, when the Wiehahn Commission started its work, the MWU represented mainly semi-skilled white production workers in the mining industry. By 2002, the union had expanded across all industries of the South African economy and represented a wide diversity of workers, including individuals and professionals outside traditional areas of collective bargaining. Throughout my period of engagement with Solidarity, I was unable to gain access to membership statistics other than those appearing in the sources examined here. Apart from basic membership figures kept by the union's accountant during the 1980s, no membership records for the MWU are available prior to about 2000 – a fact attributed to the union's lack of technological capacity and the decentralised administrative system before Buys' leadership. Moreover, since 2000, members have apparently not been required to provide details of their occupation when joining the union, which now relies on an external company to manage membership administration with employers and to collect membership fees. In 2011, Solidarity's leadership variously estimated that its membership profile was between 60 per cent and 80 per cent blue-collar.[169] This dearth of employment and income data makes it impossible to track the changing social base of the MWU/Solidarity's membership in a quantitative manner over the course of the long transition.

However, the discursive analysis offered here clearly suggests the intersection of articulations of the experiences of the union's traditional blue-collar membership and its newer middle-class members as the latter joined the organisation. In this way, the MWU/Solidarity may be understood as representing a new post-apartheid social alliance in the civil society sphere, now led by middle-class figures such as Buys and Hermann, but based on a working-class foundation in terms of organisational framework and membership. This alliance comprised those sections of the white, predominantly Afrikaner working and middle classes for whom the demise of the racial state was accompanied and compounded by a changing labour market, which, 'for the majority of people, even those traditionally included within the middle class, [was] becoming more "precarious"'.[170] This group stood in contrast to those middle-class and elite whites analysed by Rebecca Davies – members of the cultural intelligentsia, media, and business communities for whom post-transition neoliberal policies and the country's reintegration into the global economy offered new opportunities for material prosperity and

---

[169] Dirk Hermann, interviewed 17 October 2011; Dawid Durie (Head of Member Administration, Solidarity), personal communication, 10 August 2011.

[170] R. Southall, *The New Black Middle Class in South Africa* (Auckland Park: Jacana, 2016), p. 17.

identification.[171] Shifting the emphasis of the organisation's internal discourse from the politics of class to the politics of culture, the MWU/Solidarity's new leaders effectively appealed to a wide spectrum of the post-apartheid white population, drawing legitimacy from the global shift towards identity politics and civil society-based action.

These findings bring South Africa's long transition since the 1970s into focus – a perspective that otherwise remains invisible in the established literature's emphasis on 1994 as a critical turning point. In the 1980s, South Africa's black labour movement – and COSATU in particular – was considered the epitome of social movement unionism, mobilising beyond the workplace and forming coalitions with other working-class or community-based organisations to further political goals. Yet, by the late 1990s, COSATU's alliance with the ANC increasingly undermined its ability to find common cause with social movements and effectively represent workers' interests.[172] This chapter has shown how, in an inverse development, by the new millennium the MWU had significantly expanded its social appeal along the same racial lines as its historical membership. The Wiehahn reforms had prompted the disintegration of the half-century-old Nationalist social alliance and the dismantling of the racial state, leading white workers to search for a new patron to protect their interests. By the 2000s, it seemed that this was being realised within their own organisation. The MWU/Solidarity represented a new Afrikaner social alliance, now organised in the civil society sphere. And, rather than being the apogee of its post-apartheid rise, the realisation of Buys' *Wenplan* by the union's centenary in 2002 was merely the springboard for the MWU/Solidarity's ambitions. Chapter 5 brings this story into the present through an investigation of the contemporary strategies of this ambitious and increasingly assertive social movement.

---

[171] R. Davies, *Afrikaners in the New South Africa: identity politics in a globalised economy* (London: Tauris Academic Studies, 2009).
[172] Buhlungu, *A Paradox of Victory*, pp. 97–8.

5 An 'alternative government'
The Solidarity Movement's contemporary strategies

Introduction

In many respects, the Solidarity of the 2010s bore little resemblance to the old Mineworkers' Union. For decades, the MWU's headquarters had been located in Johannesburg's inner-city district of Braamfontein, just a few blocks from the offices of its traditional nemesis, the Chamber of Mines. It is unsurprising that these two organisations, representing the organised power and interests of the main opposing groups in the mining industry, would have settled in the very lap of Egoli, the City of Gold, not far from where the first mine shafts of the Witwatersrand were sunk, and in one of the neighbourhoods where workers and state forces clashed during the 1922 Rand Revolt.

But in 2001 the MWU left its old mining stomping grounds when it relocated to rented office space in Centurion, a hub of white middle-class suburbia fast unfolding halfway between Johannesburg and Pretoria. Wessel Visser describes the move as 'symbolic of the metamorphosis' that the MWU/Solidarity had undergone from a mining-specific to a cross-industry, more highly skilled trade union.[1] True, the move northwards took the union closer to the headquarters of a number of companies where it had recently acquired recognition rights.[2] But it also formed part of a wave of white flight from inner-city Johannesburg since the late 1980s following the onset of racial desegregation and associated with urban decay and rising crime levels.[3]

Four years later, Solidarity again relocated its headquarters – this time, more resolutely towards the capital city – after acquiring its current

---

[1] Visser, *Van MWU tot Solidariteit*, p. 322.
[2] This included telecommunications company Telkom, Kumba Iron Ore, the South African Nuclear Energy Corporation, and a number of universities. Visser, *Van MWU tot Solidariteit*, p. 323.
[3] O. Crankshaw and C. White, 'Racial desegregation and inner city decay in Johannesburg', *International Journal of Urban and Regional Research* 19, no. 4 (1995), p. 622. Visser cites the 'social decay' befalling Braamfontein as contributing to the decision to quit the old headquarters. Visser, *Van MWU tot Solidariteit*, p. 322.

Introduction

corporate-style office site in Kloofsig, just outside Pretoria. The consolidation of the organisation's move northwards seemed to confirm its evolution from a trade union to a broad-based social movement representing white, predominantly Afrikaner, minority interests in post-apartheid South Africa. Pretoria – in contrast to Johannesburg, or even to other major cities such as Cape Town or Durban – was a historical Afrikaner 'heartland', the executive seat of power where Afrikaners had long 'called the shots'.[4]

Yet the move to Pretoria was more than simply a reflection of the organisational transformation the MWU had undergone since the days of Arrie Paulus, or an expression of its shift towards mobilising around Afrikaner identity rather than working-class issues. Solidarity's relocation from South Africa's financial to its political capital – settling on the doorstep of executive government – marked the new playing field on which this increasingly powerful social movement sought to assert itself. By 2011, when I conducted an extended period of research at the organisation, Solidarity not only claimed to be the legitimate representative of Afrikaners in post-apartheid South Africa but also presented itself as a key extra-parliamentary opponent to the ruling ANC.

At the time, this positioning was dramatically demonstrated in the legal action and accusation of hate speech that AfriForum, the Movement's civil rights organisation, was waging in the South African High Court against the ANC Youth League president of the time, Julius Malema. Of course, social movements – particularly in African contexts – are regarded as instrumental in holding political elites accountable to the citizenry, and such movements and states are seen as 'natural' adversaries in much the same way as the old MWU and the mine magnates had once been.[5] But, as this chapter will show, Solidarity's power claims went much further, as the Movement sought to assert a form of political parity with the ruling party. By 2015, these assertions were augmented when Solidarity stepped forward to overtly position itself as an 'alternative government' or 'state' for Afrikaners amid ANC-led majority rule.

This astounding announcement came in the face of mounting public concern over the political and economic trajectory along which South Africa was heading. The crescendo of corruption allegations surrounding President Jacob Zuma, alongside slowing economic growth, deepening

---

[4] Sharp and Van Wyk, 'Beyond the market', p. 120.
[5] However, social movements may also utilise state institutions or enter into partnership with the state in order to attain their goals. S. Ellis and I. van Kessel, 'Introduction: African social movements or social movements in Africa?' in S. Ellis and I. van Kessel (eds), *Movers and Shakers: social movements in Africa* (Leiden: Brill, 2009), p. 3, 9–12; Muro, 'Ethnicity, nationalism, and social movements', p. 193.

inequality, and rising unemployment, fuelled public frustration and community-based protests. State failure and poor governance compounded already existing struggles in the national economy at a time of international competition and neoliberal pressures. These conditions, notes Roger Southall, saw workers 'beset by multiple forms of insecurity, subject to temporary, short-term, often part-time, employment contracts; to the erosion of their benefits if in employment; and vulnerability to loss of income, rendered more acute by the reduction of state benefits'.[6]

It was in this context that Solidarity stepped forward to offer itself as an 'alternative government' for Afrikaners. But it was proposing neither conventional electoral political mobilisation nor territorial separatism.

Examining white workers' responses to the dismantling of the racial state and the establishment of majority rule, Chapter 4 tracked the MWU's 'transformation' from the late 1970s to become the broad-based social movement union Solidarity by 2002. This chapter brings the analysis of the MWU/Solidarity into the present, investigating the discursive and organisational strategies that underlie the Movement's contemporary campaigns and assertions in the 2010s. While Solidarity presented them as responses to the failings of ANC rule, these strategies represented ongoing efforts by a section of the white population to negotiate the demise of the racial state and the accompanying changing political economy. This chapter reveals how these efforts reflected and inflected opportunities offered by neoliberal policies, rationalities, and discourse amid the local specifics of majority rule. In this way, it contributes to broader global debates on the political and cultural consequences of neoliberal globalisation for precarious workers. Specifically, Solidarity's discursive and organisational strategies offer new insight into the opportunities for extra-parliamentary political mobilisation in the context of constitutional democracy and late capitalism, and how race is refashioned in the neoliberal epoch. As will be shown, these insights also invite a reconsideration of the existing scholarship's core assumptions regarding the progressive, anti-hegemonic nature of social movements.

Discursive strategies

In considering the Solidarity Movement's discursive strategies, I examine the interpretative framing Solidarity employs to 'mobilise

---

[6] Southall, *The New Black Middle Class in South Africa*, p. 16.

potential adherents and constituents'.[7] 'Framing' describes the process whereby activists may offer a master narrative that identifies social problems and assigns blame, suggests solutions, and offers a course of action for achieving their desired outcome. A social movement's interpretative framework shapes the way in which issues and events are understood – both within the movement and beyond – and hence how they are responded to. Investigating discursive strategies or framing thus offers insight into the ways in which a movement justifies its strategies and goals, and the basis on which it makes claims to power.[8]

A selective historical narrative

Solidarity's post-1997 leadership advanced a particular historical narrative that interwove the history of the union with that of Afrikaners' political and economic struggles in South Africa. This historical narrative eulogised the century-old union, placing it at the centre of an emotive story which drew parallels between Afrikaners' plight in the early twentieth century and in the post-apartheid present. In this way, the union's past and present, and its vision for the future, were imbued with a sense of coherence and purpose tied closely to the fortunes of the 'Afrikaner people'.

By 2011, when I started my fieldwork at Solidarity's headquarters, this narrative was ubiquitous throughout all sections of the Movement. It was continually communicated to members and employees by way of the in-house magazine, newsletters, electronic communications, and meetings, and also transmitted to the wider public through promotional material, press statements, and the Movement's websites, publications, and films.

Depending on the forum where it was presented, the content of the historical narrative was more developed, the meaning-making embroidered and extended to form a powerful interpretative framing of the Movement, of Afrikaners, and of post-apartheid South Africa. An online video introducing the Solidarity Movement to the public presented this narrative in broad strokes. It placed the 1902 establishment of Solidarity – then the MWU – in the aftermath of the 'Anglo-Boer War', a time of hardship and struggle for the 'young volk' as they lost the political independence of their Boer republics and, with it, their freedom. The destruction and misery wrought by the war forced thousands of

---

[7] F. Polletta and J. M. Jasper, 'Collective identity and social movements', *Annual Review of Sociology* 27 (2001), p. 291.
[8] C. J. Stewart, C. A. Smith, and R. E. Denton, *Persuasion and Social Movements* (Long Grove IL: Waveland Press, 2012), p. 150.

Afrikaners off the countryside and into the mines to eke out a living as strangers in the new urban economy. Foregrounding the political events of this period and the cultural-political identity of its members as Afrikaners, the video explained that it was in these 'challenging circumstances' that the MWU was founded to 'protect the rights' of this community.[9]

From the sepia-coloured stills representing these early years, the video then switched to lively images of Solidarity's contemporary leaders and rallies. 'A century later,' a male voice-over boomed, 'we are Solidarity, the oldest civil rights organisation in South Africa, still marching forward to defend and promote its members' interests.' This was followed by a rapid succession of images depicting South Africa's political transition, the dawn of the new millennium, and technological advances, thus signalling a modern, rapidly changing world. In an implied parallel with the early twentieth century, the emphasis again fell on the political consequences of these developments: in this 'new reality', 'our people experience extreme pressure, unlawful affirmative action, and policies which eschew human rights', a concerned female voice now narrated. Meanwhile, headlines announcing soaring crime levels, rampant corruption, and failing service delivery moved across the screen. In the face of this latest struggle, Solidarity continued to work to secure a 'safe, free, and prosperous' future for 'our people'.[10]

This historical narrative was presented in more detail in communications directed at the Movement's members. In a claim clearly intended to rival black South Africans' battle for freedom and rights, the early years of the MWU's existence were said to amount to Afrikaners' – and the union's – own struggle history. Throughout this 'struggle', the MWU is said to have consistently demonstrated its commitment to its members, who were portrayed as marginalised and socially disadvantaged. Thus, the union was at the forefront of the 1922 strike, an event represented as reflecting a disempowered people's rejection of a hostile government as much as fear surrounding the loss of white jobs.[11] The MWU also claimed close involvement in community efforts during the 1930s and 1940s to uplift the Afrikaner poor.[12] The nature of the union's involvement in establishing Afrikaner charities, financial institutions, and

---

[9] 'Ontmoet die Solidariteit Beweging' [video], https://solidariteit.co.za/solidariteit-beweging/ (accessed 18 July 2016).
[10] 'Ontmoet die Solidariteit Beweging'.
[11] *Solidariteitskunde*, 13 September 2011; Dirk Hermann, interviewed 17 October 2011, Kloofsig; I. Nieuwoudt, 'Aangrypende Randse Staking: 90 jaar later', *Solidarity* 2 (2012), p. 18.
[12] D. Hermann, 'Die Solidariteit Beweging: 110 jaar jonk', *Solidarity* 2 (2012), p. 12.

cultural and welfare organisations during this period was not specified. What was consistently highlighted, however, was the community-based character of these efforts to 'empower' the volk – independently from the state, Afrikaners 'pulled themselves up by their bootstraps'.[13]

The Movement's past was thus remoulded to present it as being rooted in Afrikaner struggle and distinguished by a record of resisting injustice, defending the vulnerable, and defying hostile political forces. Its trade union roots were downplayed, instead presenting the Movement as South Africa's 'oldest civil rights organisation' with a strong emphasis on political community and ethnicity. This claim to a historical role of defending and assisting 'its people' resonated neatly with the role the Movement claimed for itself in the present, as the representative of Afrikaners. Indeed, statements legitimising the Solidarity Movement's claims to Afrikaner leadership abounded during the MWU's one hundred and tenth anniversary in 2012. In a revealing statement in the present tense, Flip Buys declared that the 'union's historical fate runs hand in hand with that of white South Africans'.[14] Meanwhile, equating Afrikaners' political defeat in 1902 with the transition to majority rule in 1994, Dirk Hermann explained that Solidarity was 'making it possible for our people to live within these changes – that was what we were originally founded for, [and] one hundred years later, we are again facing this challenge'.[15]

The ostensible historical continuities foregrounded by this framing meant that the intervening period – the apartheid era, marked by Afrikaner political power and privilege under the racial state – was obscured in favour of an emotive representation of Afrikaners as disadvantaged and marginalised. Buys declared in his regular *Solidarity* magazine column: 'The ANC also doesn't want to be reminded that the Afrikaner himself was the victim of colonialism for some 200 years, and that his present success is no more than a generation deep!'[16] Indeed, Solidarity's claims constructed Afrikaner history and identity as characterised by victimhood and resilience in the face of hostile forces. Representing Afrikaners as a precarious minority in majority-ruled

---

[13] *Solidariteitkunde*, 13 September 2011; see also D. Langner, 'Reddingsdaadkongres: Kongres van hoop', *Solidarity* 6 (2009), p. 53; C. van der Walt, 'Elke tree daar deur trotse geskiedenis', *Solidarity* 2 (2012), pp. 14–15; F. Buys, 'SpreekBuys: Helpmekaarkrag vir die volgende geslag', *Solidarity* 2 (2014), pp. 8–9.
[14] F. Buys, 'SpreekBuys: Om 'n toekoms vir volgende geslag te skep', *Solidarity* 3 (2012), p. 8. Similar statements were made during *Solidariteitkunde*, 13 September 2011; also Hermann, 'Die Solidariteit Beweging'; Van der Walt, 'Elke tree'.
[15] *Solidariteitkunde*, 13 September 2011.
[16] F. Buys, 'Saai vir toekoms, ploeg nie in verlede', *Solidarity* 4 (2007), p. 8.

South Africa legitimised Solidarity's emergence as their defender – their 'saviour' organisation. This framing was not new – Christian Nationalism and its proponents had long mobilised a 'mythology of bitter grievances and solemn heroics'.[17] Solidarity's frequent invocation of 'the people' and its presentation of itself as their redeemer clearly echoed the populist tone of earlier cultural nationalist discourse.[18]

Perhaps the most elaborate version of this historical narrative was presented during *Solidariteitkunde*, a compulsory seminar that introduced newly appointed staff members to the Movement.[19] I attended the seminar in September 2011, while conducting research at the trade union headquarters. To my mind, *Solidariteitkunde* provided the clearest example of the Movement's highly selective, even intentionally misleading, discursive strategies. It also revealed the power of ethnic identification in supporting meaning-making and mobilisation within Solidarity.

The seminar was presented by Dirk Hermann, who by 2011 had risen to the position of Deputy Chief Executive of the Solidarity Movement. Hermann was a natural storyteller who, through his easy-going and jovial nature, engendered familiarity. He opened the session with introductions around the table, identifying which institution within the Movement each new employee had been appointed to and welcoming them to the 'Solidarity family'. That morning, everyone was in high spirits: the previous day, High Court Judge Colin Lamont had ruled that Julius Malema's singing of the liberation song '*Dubula iBhunu*' ('Shoot the Boer/farmer') constituted hate speech. AfriForum had won its case.[20] The victory animated the atmosphere in the room and galvanised already existing identification among the participants – all white and Afrikaans-speaking, more than half of them women and several under 30 years of age. This sense of implied solidarity, of ostensibly common convictions and interests, was consistently appealed to over the course of the next few hours as Hermann instructed the group through stories[21] – stories familiar from

---

[17] L. M. Thompson, 'Afrikaner nationalist historiography and the policy of apartheid', *Journal of African History* 3, no. 1 (1962) p. 141.
[18] For closer analysis of Solidarity's populism, see D. van Zyl-Hermann, 'Make Afrikaners great again! National populism, democracy and the new white minority politics in post-apartheid South Africa', *Ethnic and Racial Studies* 41, no. 15 (2017), pp. 2673–92.
[19] *Solidariteitkunde* literally means 'the study of Solidarity'. I was told that trade union representatives also present the seminar to union members in the workplace.
[20] '"Shoot the Boer": it's hate speech, says judge', *Mail and Guardian*, 12 September 2011; 'ANC Julius Malema's shoot the Boer ruled "hate speech"', BBC News Africa, 12 September 2011, www.bbc.co.uk/news/world-africa-14878102 (accessed 2 August 2014).
[21] Storytelling is an important tool employed by social movements. The concept suggests elements of drama, imagination, and emotional appeal, and is useful for highlighting the

the participants' shared Afrikaans educational backgrounds, stories that nudged certain deeply ingrained cultural understandings, tugged at collective heartstrings, and stirred memories, real or imagined.[22] As the morning passed, my recording of the session registered the unspoken understanding in the room: the participants all belonged to the same camp and were all listening and thinking from the same position. The murmurs of agreement, the jokes that elicited bursts of laughter, and the topics that provoked consternation all overwhelmingly testified to this apparently shared *Afrikaner* perspective.

Hermann offered an enthralling narrative presenting the history of Solidarity and of Afrikaners as inextricably intertwined. From political defeat and economic destitution at the beginning of the century, he plotted the triumphant 'self-help' rise of the volk to independence and political power. The MWU was described as 'a golden thread [running] through this early development of the Afrikaner' and it was 'thanks to the [support of] mining districts, where the MWU played a central role', that the NP came to power in 1948, by implication restoring the rights and freedoms Afrikaners had lost at the beginning of the century.[23] No mention was made of the policies of the NP, which the MWU so eagerly 'helped' vote into power, or the majority at whose expense they came. Yet, wary that his listeners might take the MWU's support for the NP in 1948 as support for apartheid, Hermann was quick to note the union's apparently problematic relationship with the NP over the next few decades:

Then, for a time, we were on and off with the National Party; often there was great tension [between the MWU and the NP], there were even frequent efforts to take over [the union], but to a large degree we were always successful in maintaining our independence.[24]

This statement revealed how Solidarity's historical narrative often relied on ambiguity and omission, or even downright distortion of the past. Certainly, Hermann was correct in pointing to nationalist efforts to infiltrate the MWU – but these had taken place *prior* to 1948.

---

affective dimensions of framing and narrative that are often particularly salient where collective identity is constructed as the basis for mobilisation. See Stewart, Smith, and Denton, *Persuasion and Social Movements*, pp. 150–1; F. Polletta and B. G. Gardner, 'Narrative and social movements' in Della Porta and Diani, *The Oxford Handbook of Social Movements*, pp. 534–48.

[22] On the pervasive influence of Christian National Education on generations of Afrikaners and the dissemination of nationalist mythology through the apartheid school system, see Van Rooyen, *Hard Right*, pp. 39–40; L. Thompson, *The Political Mythology of Apartheid* (New Haven CT: Yale University Press, 1985), pp. 46–62, 231–3, 237.

[23] *Solidariteitkunde*, 13 September 2011.   [24] *Solidariteitkunde*, 13 September 2011.

Moreover, while in the case of many unions infiltration did indeed fail, the Nationalist putsch in the MWU succeeded, and the MWU is regarded as one of the trade unions decisively captured for the Nationalist movement.[25]

During interviews, I sought to probe the intentionality of such misrepresentations. Both Hermann and Buys maintained this version of history, albeit with some qualifications. 'Look, in the case of Solidarity during apartheid, we were only part of the government framework for a reasonably short time,' Hermann told me. 'Actually, throughout our entire history we were almost always against the government ... [This resistance] of course reached a climax with the appointment of the Wiehahn Commission.'[26] Buys, too, offered this story, although he admitted that the MWU's 'opposition' to the NP was reactionary rather than progressive in nature: 'We were never party to the previous government – the MWU was in the opposition, even though it was from the right, but they never depended on the government.'[27] The fact that Hermann pointed to the Wiehahn Commission as the 'climax' of the MWU's opposition to the NP showed that he was quite aware that the MWU had opposed efforts to modify apartheid, rather than the system itself. Yet the false chronology and ambiguity of his statements during *Solidariteitkunde* left this fact opaque. The leadership seemed bent on portraying Solidarity as having a history of political opposition, independence, and being critical of the government of the day. Meanwhile, this hazy treatment of the MWU's relationship with the NP allowed the narrative to unproblematically bypass the apartheid period and the racial injustices of the past.[28] Indeed, my recordings of the *Solidariteitkunde* seminar show that, in the course of the three-hour seminar, Hermann spent only 59 seconds talking about the period following the 1948 election before leaping ahead to 1994. When I later asked him about this obvious omission, he explained:

[P]eople are only getting apartheid contexts as though apartheid is the sum total of the pre-history of the Afrikaner. And I like to explain to people that there was a time before apartheid ... because the subjectivity with which they are now being

---

[25] As discussed in Chapter 1.
[26] Dirk Hermann, interviewed 17 October 2011, Kloofsig.
[27] Flip Buys, interviewed 25 October 2011, Kloofsig.
[28] For similar treatment of the union's past in its magazine, see 'Solidariteit, 1902–2008', *Solidarity* 2 (2008), pp. 36–7; Hermann, 'Die Solidariteit Beweging'; Van der Walt, 'Elke tree'; Buys, 'SpreekBuys: Om 'n toekoms'; F. Buys, 'SpreekBuys: Arbeid – omskep die probleem in die oplossing vir SA', *Solidarity* 3 (2014), pp. 8–9.

bombarded about apartheid, as though our history is 100 per cent evil, is simply not correct. So ... I just want to give them another perspective.[29]

As Chapter 4 showed, this understanding of Afrikaner history as criminalised, and of Afrikaner identity, status, and belonging in South Africa as threatened or denied, was a familiar one in the post-apartheid context. In response, Solidarity's discursive framing repositioned Afrikaners at the centre of South African history and concentrated on their victimhood and resilience, rather than their complicity in apartheid and privilege in a racial state.[30]

This selective history and efforts to decriminalise the Afrikaner past also found expression in the Movement's products. Earlier in 2011, for instance, the Movement's publishing house produced Dirk Hermann's book *Basta! Ons voetspore is in Afrika (Basta! Our footprints are in Africa)*.[31] Written as a letter to Hermann's daughters, this glossy publication tracks the family history from the moment a German ancestor first 'turned his face from Europe and towards Africa'[32] in 1658. In a vocabulary clearly echoing Solidarity's historical narrative, Hermann chronicles the stories of individuals in the family tree who conveniently passed by the main landmarks of Afrikaner nationalist history – the settlement from Europe, the Great Trek, the wars of independence – and were part of the volk who 'stood up' in the early twentieth century. Afrikaners' success – a notion that remained unclarified but presumably referred to their political and economic power from 1948 – thus came by the sweat of their brow. Indeed, *Basta!* characterised the twentieth century in terms of 'inner strength – not affirmative action',[33] stating that Afrikaners' success was the result of 'the discipline of extreme frugality and hard work ... rather than the external system of apartheid'.[34] The period of Afrikaner nationalism's mobilisation was therefore portrayed in terms of the resourcefulness and apparently spontaneous organisation of ordinary people. Rather

---

[29] Dirk Hermann, interviewed 17 October 2011, Kloofsig.
[30] On selective representations of the past in the broader African context, see S. Dorman, D. Hammett, and P. Nugent (eds), *Making Nations, Creating Strangers: states and citizenship in Africa* (Leiden: Brill, 2007), pp. 13–14; F. Cooper, 'Possibility and constraint: African independence in historical perspective', *Journal of African History* 49, no. 2 (2008), p. 195.
[31] D. Hermann, *Basta! Ons voetspore is in Afrika* (Pretoria: Kraal Uitgewers, 2011). Other examples of products that reflect the Movement's selective reading of the past include the book *Gebroke Land* on white poverty, and the film *Tainted Heroes* on the ANC and the liberation struggle. D. Langner (ed.), *Gebroke Land: armoede in die Afrikaanse gemeenskap sedert 1902* (Centurion: Kraal Uitgewers, 2009); *Tainted Heroes* (Forum Films, 2015). Forum Films is a subsidiary of AfriForum, and the film was produced by AfriForum Deputy CEO Ernst Roets.
[32] Hermann, *Basta!*, p. 11.   [33] Hermann, *Basta!*, p. 51.   [34] Hermann, *Basta!*, p. 76.

than a racial state and the mass exploitation of African labour, Afrikaners' 'standing up' seemed entirely rooted in their own efforts and initiatives.[35] This representation implied that the period of Afrikaner political control and white-only citizenship somehow reflected a 'rightful', just state of affairs – and that this was being infringed upon in the post-apartheid period. Thus, the book explicitly sought to decriminalise the past. Addressing his children, Hermann wrote:

[N]o one really knows what the truth is any more ... Your family story is free of loaded representations of history, which are nothing other than political instruments ... I want to free you from the myth that, because of privilege and exploitation, we carry 350 years' worth of guilt. I want to free you from the tyranny of the majority-led representation of the past. Daddy is writing this letter because you are my children of Africa; you are free Afrikaners. Live this freedom.[36]

Despite being cloaked in the story of an individual family, Hermann's narrative made a powerful populist claim to Afrikaner universality, his personal history representing the destiny of the entire volk much as the *Solidariteitkunde* narrative portrayed the MWU/Solidarity as a 'golden thread' running through Afrikaner – or white – history. By defiantly declaring that 'our footprints are in Africa', he lay collective claim, on behalf of all Afrikaners, to African autochthony and to a right to belong, with political implications for their entitlement to rights and citizenship.[37] Meanwhile, Hermann cast himself as the liberator-redeemer of his daughters' history, mirroring the way in which Solidarity was represented as Afrikaners' 'saviour' organisation.

Solidarity's historical narrative – whether in simpler or more elaborate form – stood in stark contrast to prevailing national accounts celebrating the end of apartheid and the birth of the rainbow nation. Rather, democratisation was represented in distinctly negative terms – a 'total change in the political order' that rendered 'our people' an 'increasingly alienated' 'minority in a majority setting'.[38] In a mix of sarcasm and

---

[35] Narratives that emphasise 'sweat-of-our-brow' hard work while negating structural privilege are not unique to South African whites. See R. Pilossof, 'The unbearable whiteness of being: land, race and belonging in the memoirs of white Zimbabweans', *South African Historical Journal* 61, no. 3 (2009), pp. 631–28; B. A. Rutherford, *Working on the Margins: black workers, white farmers in postcolonial Zimbabwe* (London: Zed Books, 2001), pp. 82–95.
[36] Hermann, *Basta!*, pp. 8–9.
[37] See P. Geschiere, *The Perils of Belonging: autochthony, citizenship, and exclusion in Africa and Europe* (Chicago IL: University of Chicago Press, 2009).
[38] *Solidariteitkunde*, 13 September 2011.

scaremongering, Hermann illustrated this view in his preferred storytelling mode:

> A lamb and two wolves were walking down the road. Soon it was lunchtime and all three grew hungry. So they decided to vote about what to have for lunch – democracy is the right thing, after all. And so the two wolves voted to eat the lamb – and they did.[39]

'That's the problem with a normal democracy,' Hermann concluded drily. 'That's why we need extra protection.'[40] This representation served to undermine democratic equality and claim special privileges and protection for Afrikaners, or whites, by representing them as victimised on account of their racial identity. Indeed, such statements demonstrated the ambiguity of the Movement's discursive framing – appealing to Afrikaners one moment while speaking in broader racial terms the next. Buys, too, represented government policy and legislation as leaving whites 'excluded', 'feeling vulnerable' and often 'targeted'.[41] In this hostile political environment, Solidarity saw it as its 'express task' to protect whites and make sure that they were not, as Hermann's parable suggested, devoured by the majority.

Social movements often seek to intercede on behalf of society's vulnerable and marginalised – in Africa, often in a context of 'deprivation, rights denial and injustice'. Social movement scholarship typically regards such activism and mobilisation as counter-hegemonic and progressive.[42] Solidarity's discursive strategies sought to represent its *raison d'être* in precisely this way: defending vulnerable whites in an unjust context. But its focus was not on material deprivation relating to land, housing, or healthcare, or the denial of rights for the resourceless – indeed, as Buys' statement about Afrikaners' 'colonial victimhood' betrayed, they were generally recognised as enjoying material 'success'. Rather, when Solidarity spoke of a community relegated to 'second-class citizenship',[43] this was framed in terms of ethnic and racial politics, with marginalisation more social than structural. Indeed, Solidarity's discursive strategy consistently emphasised political developments and their

---

[39] *Solidariteitkunde*, 13 September 2011. The same motif appears in F. Buys, 'SpreekBuys: democratic labour dispensation: important for democracy and economy', *Solidarity* 5 (2010), pp. 8–9.
[40] *Solidariteitkunde*, 13 September 2011.   [41] Buys, 'Saai vir toekoms'.
[42] A. Habib and P. Opoku-Mensah, 'Speaking to global debates through a national and continental lens: South African and African social movements in comparative perspective' in Ellis and Van Kessel, *Movers and Shakers*, p. 55.
[43] F. Buys, 'Krisisberaad: Raamwerk vir 'n toekomsplan van hoop', Crisis Summit speech, Maroela Media, 5 May 2015, http://maroelamedia.co.za/debat/meningsvormers/krisisberaad-raamwerk-vir-n-toekomsplan-van-hoop/ (accessed 6 May 2016).

consequences, while only peripherally acknowledging the role of economic developments shaping the nature of post-apartheid society. Black majority government under the ANC was blamed for all Afrikaners' woes, while structural and economic factors were negated.

Responsibilisation and recasting difference

The historical narrative's negative portrayals of majority rule were reinforced by powerful ideological distinctions. Solidarity identified itself as being rooted in the Christian tradition of trade unionism, similar to European trade unions in Belgium, Germany, and the Netherlands. This was juxtaposed with COSATU and its predominantly black affiliates, who were identified as socialist – 'the other main tradition of trade unionism' – and thus drew on Marxist convictions.[44] This representation effortlessly established a set of mutually exclusive 'us and them' divisions with clear racial undertones. To Solidarity's predominantly Afrikaner audience, these designations resonated with apartheid-era notions of the threats of African nationalism and of communism, and recalled black liberation movements' links to communist states.[45] Meanwhile, Solidarity was positioned as part of a global Western community. Indeed, in my conversations with Buys, it became clear how readily 'Christian' could slip from a trade union label to a cultural, racial, or even moral marker. When I asked whether South Africans outside the Afrikaner community joined Solidarity, Buys affirmed that the Movement also had white English-speaking members. After all, he explained, Afrikaans- and English-speaking whites were fundamentally 'Westerners', sharing an 'intellectual ... Christian heritage'. Hence, English-speakers felt 'much more at home' with Solidarity than in the Africanised new South Africa.[46] Buys again recast race as culture when, on another occasion, he questioned whether President Jacob Zuma – someone with a 'traditionalist' value system – was able to run South Africa's 'modern, sophisticated market economy'. This 'clash of values', Buys argued, made 'the people' distrust the ANC government.[47]

---

[44] *Solidariteitkunde*, 13 September 2011; also Buys, 'Saai vir toekoms'.
[45] The notions of the *swart gevaar* ('black peril') and the *rooi gevaar* ('red menace') were a staple of NP propaganda as early as the 1930s. Signalling the threats of black swamping and of communism respectively, they were often fused together in efforts to demonise and suppress opposition. H. Giliomee, *The Afrikaners: biography of a people* (London: Hurst & Co., 2003), p. 499.
[46] Flip Buys, interviewed 25 October 2011, Kloofsig. He identified the importance of the individual, the constitutional state, capitalism, civil society, and checks on the powers of government as key Western values. See also Buys, 'SpreekBuys: Om 'n toekoms'.
[47] Flip Buys, interviewed 19 September 2011, Kloofsig.

The interactive setting of the *Solidariteitkunde* seminar again demonstrated the extent to which the Movement's discursive strategies could rely on existing discourses and prejudices among its audience to reproduce its racialised and moralised framing. During the seminar, Hermann identified equality as the 'core value' of socialist trade unionism. This, he explained, was why socialist unions were eager to stick closely to the ruling party, so that those who hold centralised power 'can realise their socialist goals' of redistribution. 'But you have to line your own pockets first!' one participant interjected jokingly – a comment that was greeted with chuckles from those present. This remark, and the reaction it elicited, demonstrated the instinctive intelligibility of the 'us and them' divisions and their moral implications – so much so that the participants were ready to add their own embellishments. And Hermann knew exactly how to capitalise on this: 'Yes, look, that's unfortunately the dishonesty of that tradition,' he affirmed, 'because it is used for self-aggrandisement, it is absolutely prone to corruption.' But he was eager to make a crucial, different point: 'The problem [with the socialist tradition],' he continued, 'is, of course, that it makes you *dependent* ... because the *state* will provide.' He pointed to South Africa's system of social welfare grants as an example of socialist tendencies manifesting under ANC rule. This dependence on the state meant that socialists were loath to take on personal responsibility, he claimed, which resulted in 'a strong culture of blame: that is, it's someone else's fault – the government, apartheid, colonialism, everyone, because it is not your responsibility'. Socialists also emphasised collective action over individual identity, Hermann claimed, which explained their propensity for striking. 'That collective's behaviour can sometimes be so inexplicable,' he continued in animated fashion. 'You won't believe it! That same NUMSA guy with whom you have such a good relationship will go and, you'll see on television, he actually goes and breaks a car window. Can't believe it. Because he *becomes* the collective.'[48] Hermann's apparently benevolent attitude to his black fellow trade unionists as individuals allowed him to pathologise socialism and condemn its loathsome symptoms without openly demonising African workers. Nevertheless, he presented *Solidariteitkunde* participants with an interpretative framework that associated blacks with rampant mob behaviour and demonstrated that they were not to be trusted, evoking enduring colonial-era understandings of 'dangerous natives'.

---

[48] All quotations *Solidariteitkunde*, 13 September 2011 (his emphasis).

Hermann contrasted socialist unions' dependence on a strong interventionist state with Solidarity's 'self-help' values. Whereas 'equality' was the central value of socialist unionism, the concept of a 'calling' was presented as the core tenet of the Christian tradition of trade unionism in which Solidarity stood.[49] This represented a resourceful reinvention of a central mobilising idea in Christian Nationalism and the Afrikaner nationalist movement of the 1930s and 1940s – the very years that Solidarity eulogised as a time of Afrikaners' spontaneous 'standing up'.[50] The parallels with Solidarity's post-apartheid strategies were, therefore, both real and imagined; it was clear that this 'calling' did similar mobilising work in the hands of those who saw themselves as the contemporary leaders of the volk. Hermann defined 'calling' as 'receiving a specific task from God'. But it was the human rather than the divine that this discursive strategy emphasised: '[This means] *you* are responsible for living out that calling. You can't say it is the responsibility of the central power, because remember ... then you become dependent on it.' 'Calling' therefore represented a 'strong ideology of self-reliance, not dependence', Hermann explained, 'which means *we* have to put institutions in place to accomplish things, not the state.'[51]

Solidarity's discourse of 'self-help' presented a strong critique of state intervention while idealising individual responsibility and community action. As such, the Movement's discursive strategy seemed to promote a core feature of neoliberal discourse and policy: namely, the devolution of responsibility to local-level government, civil society, and individual citizens amid the retreat of the state.[52] As a political project, neoliberalism's belief in the inevitable failure of the state drives efforts to roll back forms of state intervention.[53] As state provision in areas such as healthcare, education, security, and social welfare is withdrawn, the market encroaches on these former state territories. The resulting 'freedom' from state intervention, David Goldberg observes, represents 'liberty ... so long as one can buy one's way in'.[54] For those unable to participate in this 'growing commodification of life', 'ideas of self-help, community

---

[49] *Solidariteitkunde*, 13 September 2011; https://solidariteit.co.za/wie-is-ons/ (accessed 10 March 2016).
[50] On the malleability of Christian Nationalist discourse, see S. Dubow, 'Afrikaner nationalism, apartheid and the conceptualization of "race"', *Journal of African History* 33 (1992), pp. 209–37.
[51] *Solidariteitkunde*, 13 September 2011 (his emphasis).
[52] Marais, *South Africa Pushed to the Limit*, p. 136.
[53] B. Jessop, 'Liberalism, neoliberalism and urban governance: a state-theoretical perspective', *Antipode* 34, no. 3 (2002), p. 454.
[54] D. T. Goldberg, *The Threat of Race: reflections on racial neoliberalism* (Oxford and Malden MA: Wiley-Blackwell, 2009), p. 312.

development, and decentralised capacity building' are offered as compensation.[55] Neoliberal responsibilisation thus renders vulnerable those without the means to access market provisions where the state has retreated or failed – a process that, in South Africa, is closely associated with the continued 'limits to liberation' for vast, impoverished sections of the black population. Community-based initiatives typically play a central role in these arrangements, acting as what Bob Jessop calls 'a flanking, compensatory mechanism for the inadequacies of the market mechanism'.[56] The idealisation of 'self-help' and responsibilisation thus has the effect of reinforcing neoliberal rationality even as it seeks to offset its failures.[57]

Discourses of community responsibility vis-à-vis the failure of state action were strikingly demonstrated in Solidarity's framing of events surrounding the Stilfontein mine closure. This was a well-rehearsed story within the Movement, often recounted to me in interviews and informal conversations as practical evidence of the fundamental differences between socialist and Christian trade unions. In 2005, the Stilfontein goldmine outside Klerksdorp was liquidated following earthquake damage, leaving some 6,500 workers unemployed. While assisting with retraining and alternative employment opportunities, Solidarity also started to provide food to its struggling members. Two days later, members of the COSATU-affiliated NUM occupied Solidarity's food distribution point. 'They were hungry, I understand that,'[58] said Hermann, striking a compassionate tone as he relayed the story during *Solidariteitkunde*. In response to the occupation, Flip Buys contacted then NUM general secretary Gwede Mantashe, suggesting that the two unions work together to raise emergency relief financing. Hermann's sympathy was replaced with a disapproving air as he continued the story:

And what did Gwede tell Flip? ... Gwede said, 'The government will take care of it, Flip, it's not our responsibility, government will do it.' Government did *not* take care of it, so what happened? *We* [Solidarity] went – because we are Christian, so we definitely won't say, 'You're black and you're from NUM so

---

[55] Barchiesi, *Precarious Liberation*, p. 17.
[56] Jessop, 'Liberalism, neoliberalism and urban governance', p. 455, see also p. 456.
[57] Marais, *South Africa Pushed to the Limit*, p. 136. On neoliberal governmentality in the South African context more broadly, see I. Chipkin, '"Functional" and "dysfunctional" communities: the making of national citizens', *Journal of Southern African Studies* 29, no. 1 (2003), pp. 63–82; D. James, 'Citizenship and land in South Africa: from rights to responsibilities, *Critique of Anthropology* 33, no. 1 (2013), pp. 26–46; A. von Schnitzler, 'Citizenship prepaid: water, calculability, and techno-politics in South Africa', *Journal of Southern African Studies* 34, no. 4 (2008), pp. 899–917.
[58] *Solidariteitkunde*, 13 September 2011.

you're not getting any food.' In the end, for several *months*, we fed three or four thousand miners, of which about 10 per cent were our members.⁵⁹

Hermann, rapidly ascending to the moral high ground, encouraged his listeners to join him: 'The logical thing is for us to offer help!' – grunts of agreement sounded around the table – 'You don't think twice about it, you know, it's *in* you!'⁶⁰ In one swift move, individual and community responsibilisation was naturalised, becoming an inherent Solidarity attribute. But the underlying racialisation was clear. Relating the same Stilfontein incident in an interview, Buys extended this attribute beyond Christian trade unionism to encompass a broader white, or Afrikaner, morality. Visibly agitated, he told me how even white farmers 'with their two-tone shirts and *vierkleur* stickers' contributed food to the struggling Stilfontein residents, while the NUM 'did nothing'. His intentional caricature of the white farming community as arch-conservative yet willing to help anyone in need was a strong moral condemnation of the African trade union. 'I can't imagine how these [NUM] guys sleep at night, I just can't understand it,' continued Buys, shaking his head.⁶¹ On another occasion, he similarly asserted that Solidarity members – or Afrikaners (he used these labels interchangeably) – possessed an inherent '*selfdoenkultuur*' (literally 'self-doing culture'), which meant that they naturally responded proactively to challenges. '[T]hat's the difference between us and COSATU, NUM. If there's a crisis, their people don't have a *selfdoenkultuur*; they are socialists who wait for the state,' stated Buys categorically. 'That's how they work. I don't like it, but I can't change it, it's in them. I have the impression they're programmed like that.'⁶²

The Stilfontein story demonstrated the convenient ambiguity the Movement's narratives sustained with regard to ethnicity and race. Despite its self-identification as an Afrikaner organisation, Solidarity's language was often supple and ambiguous, ready one moment to appeal to an explicit Afrikaner identity and the rich discursive repertoire of nationalist rhetoric and history it unlocked, while speaking in broader racial terms the next. This ambiguity was already identified in Chapter 4, emerging in the course of the MWU's 'reinvention' as Solidarity; indeed, it had been inherent in the apartheid project's definition of the nation.⁶³ By 2011, it formed a crucial part of the Movement's discursive

---

⁵⁹ *Solidariteitkunde*, 13 September 2011 (his emphasis).
⁶⁰ *Solidariteitkunde*, 13 September 2011.
⁶¹ Flip Buys, interviewed 19 September 2011, Kloofsig.
⁶² Flip Buys, interviewed 25 October 2011, Kloofsig.
⁶³ Posel, 'The apartheid project', p. 327.

Figure 5.1 Flip Buys and ANC general secretary Gwede Mantashe during a press briefing on the out-of-court settlement following the Malema hate speech case, 2012.
Source: *Pretoria News*, 1 November 2012/African News Agency (ANA)

framework. Sufficiently opaque in its framing of the 'unpopular minority' or 'Christian trade unionists' to leave space for other whites to identify with the Movement's campaigns and assertions, it incorporated powerful racial rather than ethnic binaries.

By presenting different trade union traditions as the basis for the social divisions it identified, the Solidarity Movement constructed a clear 'us and them' division between itself, Afrikaners, and whites on the one hand, and COSATU, the ANC, and Africans on the other. This populist polarisation represented a truly innovative discursive strategy on the part of Solidarity's contemporary leadership: by reframing primarily race-based social divisions in terms of different trade union traditions, they could claim an apparently objective basis for their divisive identity politics – even as their critical portrayal of socialist unionism and its ostensibly loathsome consequences appealed to cultural and biological differences and drew on existing understandings prevalent among their target audience. Deborah Posel has noted how Christian Nationalism was imbued with the logic of racial difference, its 'abiding imperative … to promote racial – and unequal – separate development'.[64] The

---

[64] Posel, 'The apartheid project', p. 325.

Solidarity Movement's utilisation and reformulation of such discourses facilitated the implicit demonisation of African workers and the black majority. By presenting a moral hierarchy in which whites – in the guise of Christian trade unionists – emerged as morally superior, this discursive strategy served to cast aspersions on black majority rule and subvert its audience's moral obligation to the state in favour of naturalised racial and ethnic solidarities. In this way, authority was transposed from the governing party to the Solidarity Movement as 'saviour' organisation, making it a contender for political power and legitimacy, albeit outside formal party politics.

A powerful interpretative framework comes full circle

Social movement scholarship alerts us to the ways in which the crafting of identities – of deserving claim makers and their rightful leaders; of victims and perpetrators; of friends, allies, and foes – is central to movements' efforts to establish legitimacy and mobilise support for their campaigns.[65] This may see activists 'rework the pieces of tradition into new stories to befit their ideologies', allowing them to claim a certain heritage and with it a historical mandate or moral mission.[66] In the conclusion to the *Solidariteitkunde* seminar, the linking of the Movement's historical and ideological meaning-making came full circle in a powerful mobilising framework with distinctly national populist echoes. Addressing the participants, Hermann connected the dots using a striking naturalising idiom:

> You'll start to see now that the ideas we are talking about here are very familiar in the Afrikaner's DNA. If you look back through our history, you'll recognise *exactly* the same DNA that was used to stand up after the war. It's exactly the DNA which was employed to stand up out of the 1930s. Those ideas – simple ideas – of calling, work, responsibility. These were powerful things that were used to let Afrikaners stand up out of difficult circumstances ... The fact that Solidarity is part of the Christian tradition of trade unionism is a powerful instrument for Afrikaners to also stand up after 1994, it is a powerful political answer to say that we will take responsibility, we want to be self-reliant, we won't be dependent on the government.[67]

The *Solidariteitkunde* participants, like the readers of *Solidarity* magazine or white Afrikaans-speakers visiting the Movement's website, were

---

[65] M. McDermott and F. L. Samson, 'White racial and ethnic identity in the United States', *Annual Review of Sociology* 31 (2005), pp. 252–3.
[66] Stewart, Smit, and Denton, *Persuasion and Social Movements*, p. 65, also p. 62.
[67] *Solidariteitkunde*, 13 September 2011 (his emphasis).

encouraged to see their own lives reflected unmistakeably in those of their early twentieth-century ancestors – not only in terms of historical parallels but in their shared 'Afrikaner DNA': they were fundamentally predisposed to desire independence, to take responsibility, and to act proactively in the interests of 'their people'. Just as their ancestors had yearned for their sovereignty to be restored after the loss of the Boer republics, this narrative held, so contemporary Afrikaners desired independence from the post-apartheid state. Similar ideas around Afrikaner autonomy had once centred on efforts to establish a *volkstaat*; over two decades later, Solidarity's discursive strategy showed that this sentiment of wanting to retain racial privilege and ethnic identity through separation endured and was emerging in a reformulated guise. Amid the reality of majority rule, the failings of the ANC-governed state, and the hegemony of neoliberalism, these ideas were being reinvented through discourses of responsibilisation and community-based initiatives.

Recent theorisation on race and neoliberalism has looked beyond the racialised consequences of neoliberal policy reforms to examine how the neoliberal project itself modifies the ways in which race is understood and experienced.[68] By championing meritocratic visions of individual ability and responsibility, argues Goldberg, neoliberalism suppresses race as a legitimate basis for politics and policy, replacing anti-racism with anti-racialism. This not only undermines race-based state efforts – such as affirmative action and social welfare policies – to address structural injustices, but also fosters social amnesia with regard to the structural injustices of the past. Non-racialism – when signalling the negation of racism, its effects, and efforts to remedy them – thus 'offers the perfect conceptual partner for a neoliberal politics bent on delimiting state power and empowering the interests of privately preferred partnerships and projects'.[69] This manifests culturally in meritocratic discourse and personalised responsibilisation that render race structurally irrelevant.[70] Thus, neoliberal practices use 'capitalism to hide racial (and other) inequalities by relocating racially coded economic disadvantage and reassigning identity-based biases to the private and personal spheres'.[71]

---

[68] D. J. Roberts and M. Mahtani, 'Neoliberalizing race, racing neoliberalism: placing "race" in neoliberal discourses', *Antipode* 42, no. 2 (2010), pp. 248–57.
[69] Goldberg, *The Threat of Race*, p. 318.
[70] On the cultural consequences of neoliberal globalisation more broadly, see Harvey, *The Condition of Postmodernity*; J. Comaroff and J. L. Comaroff (eds), *Millennial Capitalism and the Culture of Neoliberalism* (Durham NC: Duke University Press, 2001).
[71] D. Davis, 'Narrating the mute: racializing and racism in a neoliberal moment', *Souls* 9, no. 4 (2007), p. 349 quoted in Roberts and Mahtani, 'Neoliberalizing race, racing neoliberalism', pp. 252–3; also D. Enck-Wanzer, 'Barack Obama, the Tea Party, and

In this process, neoliberalism fosters a shift to less overt forms of racism. Racism therefore does not disappear, but is reinvented – 'born again' – in social discourse as 'racism without race, racism gone private, racism without the categories to name it as such'.[72] While this racialisation is not a new product of neoliberalism – in fact, it draws on older, established 'racist lexicons' – neoliberalism offers opportunities for the development of 'new discourses that reinforce this process'.[73]

Solidarity's discursive framing provides crucial insight into how neoliberalism modifies race and reproduces racist ideologies. The Movement's opposition to state-driven affirmative action and welfarist interventions was expressed in racialised and moralised terms even as it ostensibly promoted deracialised meritocracy. Its historical narrative of Afrikaners' 'self-help' past and its juxtaposition of Christian 'calling' with socialist equality similarly reformulated what were clearly racialised understandings in alternative, 'seemingly race-neutral' terms, while denying past structural injustice.[74] These findings contribute to understandings of neoliberalism as raced – here, in a white minority context.

Organisational strategies

The Movement's organisational strategies revealed the tactics through which it sought to 'protect our people', as the union's motto held, and to restore to Afrikaners the freedom they were ostensibly being denied. Hermann told the *Solidariteitkunde* participants that the Movement followed a two-pronged strategy to create 'spaces' or 'realities' for its members. First, it pursued legal action to create or defend '*de jure* spaces' for its members where their rights were being infringed upon. As an example, Hermann pointed to AfriForum's victory in the hate speech case as a landmark ruling that created legal space for minorities and confirmed their constitutional rights. Similarly, the Solidarity trade union embarked on hundreds of labour court cases annually to contest instances when unfair dismissal and affirmative action sought to 'restrict' their members' 'space'.[75]

---

the threat of race: on racial neoliberalism and born again racism', *Communication, Culture and Critique* 4 (2011), p. 26.
[72] Goldberg, *The Threat of Race*, p. 23; see also Roberts and Mahtani, 'Neoliberalizing race, racing neoliberalism', p. 254.
[73] Roberts and Mahtani, 'Neoliberalizing race, racing neoliberalism', pp. 251–2.
[74] Roberts and Mahtani, 'Neoliberalizing race, racing neoliberalism', p. 254.
[75] *Solidariteitkunde*, 13 September 2011.

Recourse to legal action and state organs such as the courts is a staple strategy of social movements, particularly in Africa.[76] The extent of the Solidarity Movement's activities in this regard – in 2011, Hermann claimed that at any given time the Movement was involved in some 1,400 court cases, including 400 labour court cases[77] – demonstrated the degree to which its organisational strategies involved operating within and utilising state structures. Legal recourse, however, represented more than just an avenue through which to hold the authorities to account or to defend established rights. As Stewart et al. note, social movements often employ strategies that, through the reaction they provoke from established institutions such as the courts, demonstrate the social order as illegitimate.[78] To be sure, AfriForum's hate speech case marked an important step in clarifying constitutional provisions. Yet the Movement's representation of the victory as a 'landmark ruling for minorities' offered an interpretation which – echoing its discursive strategies – portrayed the Afrikaner minority as the innocent victim of an immoral majority-ruled state that must be kept in check. Solidarity's most prominent legal cases were routinely marked by a similar politics of race, which negated past injustices and did not challenge present structural conditions but rather called the legitimacy of the state and of government policies into question.[79]

---

[76] Ellis and Van Kessel, 'Introduction', pp. 9–12; Robins, *From Revolution to Rights in South Africa*, pp. 3–4.
[77] *Solidariteitkunde*, 13 September 2011.
[78] Stewart, Smit, and Denton, *Persuasion and Social Movements*, pp. 69–70.
[79] The Movement's legal actions are usually fronted by its trade union or by AfriForum. The Solidarity union's cases typically contest the workplace implementations of affirmative action on behalf of minority or 'non-designated' groups by challenging government priorities around employment equity as a 'racial quota system'. See, for instance, O. V. Mooki, 'SAPS affirmative action policies under scrutiny', *Mail and Guardian*, 17 November 2009, http://mg.co.za/article/2009-11-17-saps-affirmative-action-policies-under-scrutiny (accessed 9 August 2016); 'Agtergrond oor Renate Barnard-saak' [Solidarity press release], 28 November 2013, https://solidariteit.co.za/agtergrond-oor-renate-barnard-saak/ (accessed 9 August 2016); SAPA, 'Renate Barnard resigns from SAPS over race discrimination', *Mail and Guardian*, 4 June 2014, http://mg.co.za/article/2014-06-04-renate-barnard-resigns-from-saps-over-race-discrimination (accessed 9 August 2016); E. Mabuza, 'Constitutional Court ruling a victory for minority groups: coloured DCS employees', TimesLIVE, 15 July 2016, www.timeslive.co.za/local/2016/07/15/Constitutional-Court-ruling-a-victory-for-minority-groups-coloured-DCS-employees (accessed 9 August 2016). AfriForum's cases typically revolve around identity politics, language, and minority rights. See N. Jordaan, 'UFS language policy court ruling a victory for Afrikaans: AfriForum', TimesLIVE, 21 July 2016, www.timeslive.co.za/local/2016/07/21/UFS-language-policy-court-ruling-a-victory-for-Afrikaans-Afriforum (accessed 9 August 2016); M. Batt, 'Konstitusionele Hof behou uitspraak voor in AfriForum-/Gshwane Metroraad-geding oor Pretoria-straatname', AfriForum News, 19 May 2016, www.afriforum.co.za/pretoria-straatnaamdebakel-

Figure 5.2 AfriForum legal spokesperson Willie Spies braves the crowd of Malema supporters outside the Johannesburg High Court during the hate speech case in 2011.
Source: Gallo Images

But recourse to state institutions was not the main focus of the Movement's organisational strategies. '[W]e are not naïve,' Hermann told *Solidariteitkunde* participants ominously, 'we know we can't just rely on the law. The courts won't remain independent for ever.' Thus the second, arguably more important, part of the Movement's organisational strategy involved operating outside state structures. Hermann explained that without a majority in Parliament, *de jure* realities could not be changed. But by establishing its 'own institutions', by 'physically creating realities on the ground', Solidarity could shape de facto reality through private initiatives. In this way, an animated Hermann explained, 'You take up the same authority as a majority party in Parliament. These initiatives make us stronger than the ANC.' The Movement's educational institutions were offered as examples of the 'de facto

ontbloot-anc-se-gebrek-aan-respek-vir-verskeidenheid-2/ (accessed 9 August 2016); F. Rabkin, 'AfriForum is selfish and use of Constitution's preamble is "ironic", Mogoeng says', BDLive, 21 July 2016, www.bdlive.co.za/national/2016/07/21/afriforum-is-selfish-and-use-of-constitutions-preamble-is-ironic-mogoeng-says (accessed 22 July 2016).

realities' it was establishing: the *de jure* reality, Hermann explained, was that 'white youth are screwed because of affirmative action'. Thus, Solidarity established SolTech, its technical training institute, and Akademia, its private university, both offering Afrikaans-medium education in order to equip students with skills in demand by employers and thus ensure their future employability. 'In this way, we are liberating our youth from affirmative action, one by one ... You see how liberated this makes you feel when you think about it in this sense,' Hermann continued excitedly. 'It's not true that the ANC simply dominates everything with no hope for any of us! ... *De jure* things are important, but it's de facto things that really make the difference.'[80]

'Our own institutions'

The strategy of creating 'de facto realities' by operating outside state structures underlay the Movement's continued expansion. As Chapter 4 demonstrated, upon the culmination of the *Wenplan 2002*, the MWU/Solidarity had already expanded to include financial, charity, and training sections in addition to its main trade union activities. A decade later, the trade union had become simply one among a number of distinct institutions comprising the Solidarity Movement.

In 2005, Solidarity's charity wing was registered as the independent non-profit organisation Helping Hand. As a community welfare institution, Helping Hand claimed to respond to the negative consequences that affirmative action and the racialisation of welfare spending had for the Afrikaner community. Promoting 'self-help' rather than dependence on state welfare, Helping Hand undertook a range of projects, including food relief schemes in white squatter camps, school feeding projects and material support for needy Afrikaner children, and assistance to the elderly. A central aspect of Helping Hand's work was its study fund, which provided bursaries to the children of Solidarity members and other prospective Afrikaans students, typically to pursue studies at either Akademia or SolTech.[81]

Maroela Media, the Movement's online media and news platform, was launched in 2011 in response to what Solidarity identified as 'the desire within the Afrikaner community for an independent, objective media house offering competition for existing Afrikaans media monopolies in

---

[80] All quotations *Solidariteitkunde*, 13 September 2011.
[81] See http://helpendehand.co.za/ (accessed 15 March 2016); W. Visser, 'Die vestiging van Solidariteit se Helpende Hand as 'n suksesvolle gemeenskapsgebaseerde welsynsorganisasie', *Tydskrif vir Geesteswetenskappe* 51, no. 1 (2011), pp. 21–35.

the print, digital and broadcasting industry'. Openly oriented towards the white, Afrikaans-speaking community, it promised 'free, objective news' alongside a 'nostalgic cultural experience'.[82] A much more important outlet of knowledge production than the Movement's publishing house, Maroela Media was Solidarity's premium channel of communication with the public. Indeed, Hermann explained that it was to be a *lekker kuierplek* ('nice place to hang out') for the Movement's supporters, one that would see them eventually become members.[83] The website gave extensive coverage to the Movement and reported on current affairs in a manner which suited the Movement's strategies and agenda. Maroela Media was also a marketplace: in addition to offering users access to news, opinions, and lifestyle pieces, it acted as a platform for selling 'authentically Afrikaans' products and services to a market of its own creation. This included everything from T-shirts printed with nostalgic images or Afrikaans idioms to short-term insurance products in Afrikaans. I return to this 'commodification of culture' later in the chapter.

In addition, the Movement had spawned a range of other institutions. The Solidarity Research Institute was a think tank that supported the development of the Movement's initiatives and produced publications and media statements on its behalf on matters of public interest. AfriForum Youth was founded as the official youth division of AfriForum and sought to mobilise Afrikaans students on university campuses across South Africa, often around language policies in higher education and the preservation of Afrikaner campus culture. It stated that it opposed affirmative action and state intervention in education.[84] The FAK, originally founded by the Broederbond in 1929, was incorporated into the Movement in 2014 and now identified as a community organisation supporting the 'positive promotion' of the Afrikaans language and Afrikaner history.[85]

This expansion of the Movement and its various subsidiaries resulted in the creation of a wide spectrum of employment opportunities – from specialised research, financial, and legal positions to more general jobs in

---

[82] See http://maroelamedia.co.za/oor-ons/ (accessed 15 March 2016).
[83] *Solidariteitkunde*, 13 September 2011.
[84] See http://afriforumjeug.co.za/oor-ons/ (accessed 29 October 2016).
[85] See https://solidariteit.co.za/solidariteit-beweging/ (accessed 26 July 2014); www.fak.org.za/welkom-by-fak/my-fak/ (accessed 29 October 2016); see also Chapter 1. The process by which the FAK was incorporated into the Solidarity Movement has not been investigated, but it is likely that this was motivated by financial difficulties on the FAK's part. The irony of this once-elitist Broederbond organisation being bailed out by the MWU's successor organisation will not be lost on readers.

management and administration. Solidarity's Kloofsig office park, which housed several of the Movement's institutions' headquarters, was populated by an army of call-centre operators, fundraisers, graphic designers, copy writers, and technicians. I found these positions to be uniformly filled with white Afrikaans-speakers – something that, despite South Africa's legislation on employment equity and representativity, Buys dismissed as 'natural' in an organisation catering for specific cultural interests.[86]

The Movement's expansion manifested not only at its office park but also in its rapidly growing membership. In 2011, it claimed a total of 165,000 members.[87] By May 2015, Buys announced that this had reached the 300,000 mark and support was 'growing by the day'. Indeed, by the end of the year, this figure had apparently climbed to 320,000.[88] On various occasions, Movement executives would almost casually extend this figure to claim that, if one included the households of official members, Solidarity represented one million Afrikaners – a powerful assertion in an overall national population of some 2.7 million.[89] The publicity and, often, the success surrounding Solidarity's legal endeavours certainly contributed to this growth – AfriForum had added 18,000 members to its ranks over the course of its hate speech case, leading some to joke that Julius Malema was the Movement's 'best recruiter'.[90]

Solidarity's de facto strategy of creating 'own institutions' was an expensive endeavour. Developing a campus for the planned expansion of the Movement's higher education institutions alone was set to cost R150 billion. Securing the necessary funds was represented as a community effort, coupled with clever business skills. Hermann identified two further entities within the Movement – the Solidarity Building Fund and the Solidarity Investment Company (SIC) – as its main sources of income. The Building Fund, which was not a separate legal entity but

---

[86] Flip Buys, interviewed 19 September and 25 October 2011, Kloofsig.
[87] *Solidariteitkunde*, 13 September 2011.
[88] This referred to the combined membership of Solidarity, AfriForum, Helpende Hand, and the FAK. Buys, 'Krisisberaad'; 'Beweging stel Helpmekaarplan van R3,5 miljard bekend', *Solidarity* 6 (2015), pp. 16–17. Membership of one of the Movement's institutions did not automatically entail membership of all the others – in practice, therefore, the same person could be a member of each of these institutions and counted separately in each case. See https://vrae.solidariteit.co.za/as-ek-by-die-een-instelling-n-lid-is-en-maandeliks-n-fooi-betaal-beteken-dit-ek-is-n-lid-van-die-ander-instellings-ook/ (accessed 28 October 2016).
[89] A total of 2.7 million South Africans could be classified as Afrikaners in 2011, if the intersection of race and mother language markers is followed. Statistics South Africa, *Census 2011: census in brief*, Report no. 03-01-41 (Pretoria: Statistics South Africa, 2012).
[90] *Solidariteitkunde*, 13 September 2011.

part of the Solidarity trade union, collected a percentage of all membership fees and also received 'some donations'. In this way, the Movement was assured of a steady income with which it could pursue new projects, financed by the faithful contributions of ordinary people.[91] Its other source of income was derived from the various businesses managed by the SIC. These included SolTech and Akademia, as well as the Solidarity Property Company, which managed the Movement's properties and new developments. The SIC also included Solidarity Financial Services, a registered financial services provider which was, in Hermann's words, 'our cash cow'. This company offered financial products – such as retirement annuities and short-term or life insurance – to the Movement's members as well as to the general public.[92]

In practice, therefore, establishing 'own institutions' was largely dependent on the ability of the various organisations to generate an income and channel this into funding future initiatives. Hermann explained, for instance, how initially the Solidarity trade union had assisted in establishing AfriForum, which, once it became financially sound, in turn supported the foundation of Kraal Publishers. AfriForum – like a number of the Movement's organisations – was registered as a non-profit organisation. In 2011, Hermann claimed that it earned a monthly income of some R1.4 million from its 30,000 members. Meanwhile, this practice of institutional cross-subsidisation was supplemented commercially through, for instance, the profits derived from selling financial products. In this way, the R50 million required for the establishment of the private Afrikaans university Akademia was provided jointly by the Solidarity Building Fund and by profits derived from Solidarity Financial Services' Virseker insurance products.[93]

The marketing of the Solidarity Movement's institutions, as well as its various products and services, resonates with the global emergence of what has been labelled the 'identity economy'. Jean and John Comaroff identify the contemporary 'commodification of culture' – involving both the marketing and the making of identity – as reflecting the 'transformative impact of neoliberalism' on ethnicity as well as the rise of the politics of identity, multiculturalism, citizenship, and rights in the post-Cold War

---

[91] *Solidariteitkunde*, 13 September 2011; https://solidariteit.co.za/ (accessed 28 October 2016).
[92] *Solidariteitkunde*, 13 September 2011; see also https://finansies.solidariteit.co.za/ (accessed 28 October 2016).
[93] *Solidariteitkunde*, 13 September 2011; www.virseker.co.za/dagboek/virseker-trust/die-virseker-trust-help-om-n-afrikaanse-universiteit-te-bou/; https://boufonds.solidariteit.co.za/ (accessed 29 October 2016).

world. Often, the Comaroffs observe, the commodification of culture is intimately bound up with issues of cultural survival, rendering the material and the political deeply entangled. The identity economy may take many different forms, from commercialising marginality and culture for consumption by the global tourist industry to selling consumer goods to a created local target market.[94] The latter captures well the strategy deployed by Solidarity. The Movement distinguished its products and services – whether short-term insurance, higher education, or a news service – as distinctively Afrikaans. This was as much about the language in which the product or service was offered as it was about the identity, values, and affect associated with it. Crucially, the accompanying imagery – from stock images to promotional material to staff profiles – revealed that this cultural identity was clearly racialised as white.[95] This was a key political move in a country in which more coloured than white people claimed Afrikaans as their first language.[96] The customer segment for which value was being created was therefore first and foremost Afrikaans *and* white: 'Afrikaners'. Under the neoliberal dominance of the market, there was much space for selling culture – and, in this context, Solidarity touted unapologetically and assertively Afrikaner organisations, products, and services. The interested reader may browse the websites of the Movement's various institutions and services to witness these and other visual cultural invocations mentioned in this chapter in action. This particular ethnic and racial focus reflected more than simply targeted marketing; it expressed the Movement's organisational and political identity and aspirations.

Solidarity's strategies in this regard clearly echoed those of the Afrikaner economic movement of the 1930s and 1940s. As described in Chapter 1, the ethnic mobilisation of this period utilised a nationalist language of struggle centred on the idea of a unified volk, calling it to economic self-reliance.[97] Afrikaner businesses were established in order to expand Afrikaners' share of the economy, often using capital mobilised through cultural organisations and initiatives. The volk was constantly encouraged to support these fledgling organisations, which, in turn, would create employment for the Afrikaner poor and spawn further

---

[94] J. L. Comaroff and J. Comaroff, *Ethnicity, Inc.* (Scottsville: University of KwaZulu-Natal Press, 2009).

[95] An exception in this regard was Virseker's television commercials, which made limited use of coloured Afrikaans-speakers. The Movement's approach towards the coloured population is examined in Chapter 7.

[96] In 2011, 3.4 million coloured South Africans indicated that Afrikaans was their first language. Statistics South Africa, *Census 2011*.

[97] O'Meara, *Volkskapitalisme*, p. 75, 86, 137, 150.

initiatives. Cultural, economic, and political mobilisation became fundamentally entangled.[98] Dan O'Meara, in his analysis of the particular class configurations comprising the economic movement, ascribes a key role to petty bourgeois actors: lawyers, teachers, church ministers, and the like – many of whom were Broederbond members. He identifies this group as perceiving a particular economic insecurity at this historical juncture. Afrikaner nationalism, bringing with it the potential for economic mobilisation, therefore held particular advantages for creating an economy in which their positions would be sustainable and their class aspirations could be fulfilled.[99] Arguably, the creation of the Solidarity Movement in its contemporary guise has similar economic advantages for those sections of the white Afrikaans-speaking population that it represents and is led by.

The Afrikaner nationalist mobilisation of the 1930s and 1940s bore economic and political fruit, with the Nationalists securing control of state power and resources for the volk in 1948. Solidarity's twenty-first-century form of 'ethnic entrepreneurship'[100] has also met with great success – the Movement is one of South Africa's wealthiest non-governmental organisations.[101] With the capital it commanded, it could afford to be highly aspirational. But while the Movement's leadership often invoked the community spirit and 'inherent *selfdoenkultuur*' of earlier Afrikaner generations, they identified the Zionist labour movement, the Histadrut, rather than the Afrikaner economic movement as the blueprint on which Solidarity and its private initiatives were modelled.[102] Founded in 1920 during the British Mandate for Palestine, the Histadrut was the product of efforts to organise all Jewish workers in a unified organisation. As the colonial government did not interfere with its activities, it enjoyed great social, political, and economic autonomy. As such, Zeev Sternhell explains, its position was 'unique' and 'unparalleled anywhere else in the free world', and it faced few of the challenges against which workers' movements elsewhere were struggling at the time.

---

[98] Giliomee, *The Afrikaners*, pp. 434–9.
[99] O'Meara, *Volkskapitalisme*, particularly p. 56, 65, 83, 84, 101, 115, 135, 163.
[100] Van der Westhuizen and Blaser use this term in reference to Solidarity, while Boersema opts for the term 'identity entrepreneurs'. None of these authors, however, actually refer to the Solidarity Movement's strategies for capital mobilisation; rather, they focus on the social and political profitability of creating and reinforcing group identities. Blaser and Van der Westhuizen, 'Introduction', p. 384; Boersema, 'Between recognition and resentment', p. 410, 423.
[101] M. du Preez, 'AfriForum "hijacking the Afrikaner mainstream"', News24, 26 July 2016, www.news24.com/Columnists/MaxduPreez/afriforum-hijacking-the-afrikaner-mainstream-20160726 (accessed 26 July 2016).
[102] *Solidariteitkunde*, 13 September 2011.

These favourable conditions, as well as charismatic leadership, saw the organisation's membership grow rapidly. 'In a short time,' Sternhell continues, 'the Histadrut became an economic giant, the largest employer in the country, the main supplier of health services, and the main purveyor of employment through its labour exchange.' Within the specific political context of the region, this workers' movement soon emerged at the forefront of 'the enterprise of national rebirth', and the Histadrut assumed a central state-building role. When the state of Israel was founded in 1948, the Histadrut represented close to 40 per cent of the adult Jewish population and controlled some 25 per cent of the economy.[103] To the *Solidariteitkunde* participants, Hermann described the Histadrut as a labour movement which became a 'state within a state. They created private realities in Israel ... by mobilising labour and labour's capital. They created kibbutzim, irrigation schemes, schools, colleges, hospitals, clinics, industries, even sports stadiums and a self-defence unit!' With his earlier hints about the failing of democracy and democratic institutions under the ANC government still echoing in the room, these statements dazzled Hermann's listeners with the implied parallel between the Histadrut's accomplishments and Solidarity's de facto goals.

An Afrikaner 'state'

The Solidarity Movement's aspirations to become a state within a state were made public in the course of 2015. In May, the Movement convened a *Krisisberaad* (Crisis Summit) at the Voortrekker monument in Pretoria to consider South Africa's 'imminent state collapse' and the 'growing danger that the government, despite paying lip service to the Constitution, is moving from majority rule to majority domination'[104] and 'governing against Afrikaners'.[105] The summit was presented as an opportunity for public input and consultation, with the goal of formulating solutions to these crises.

In his opening speech, Flip Buys pointed to dysfunctional state departments, hospitals, and schools, failures in municipal service delivery, the inability of the police service to deal with crime, the breakdown of the

---

[103] Z. Sternhell, *The Founding Myths of Israel: nationalism, socialism and the making of the Jewish state* (Princeton NJ: Princeton University Press, 1998), pp. 178–80.
[104] 'Solidariteit hou krisisberaad', Maroela Media, 27 April 2015, http://maroelamedia.co.za/nuus/sa-nuus/solidariteit-hou-krisisberaad/ (accessed 11 August 2016).
[105] 'Krisisberaad besin oor groeiende krisis in land', Maroela Media, 4 May 2015, http://maroelamedia.co.za/nuus/sa-nuus/krisisberaad-besin-oor-die-groeiende-krisis-in-land/ (accessed 11 August 2016).

country's electricity supply, and outbreaks of xenophobic violence as warning signs of partial or imminent state collapse. He claimed, moreover, that while the financial success of 'a handful of world-class Afrikaans businessmen' was being taken as evidence of Afrikaners' continued economic strength and privilege under the new dispensation, in practice Afrikaners were increasingly subject to majority domination. This was embodied in pressure for 'transformation' that made Afrikaans schools and universities political targets, forcing English unilingualism and racial representativity onto them in the name of equality and redress. Racial transformation had similarly landed most institutions under ANC or black political control, Buys continued, while constitutional institutions intended to safeguard these provisions were toothless, dysfunctional, or co-opted by the government. The time had come to 'stand up' and formulate solutions for the Afrikaner community, Buys declared, and the *Krisisberaad* represented the start of this process.[106] Buys was followed by a parade of other prominent Movement figures issuing similar galvanising calls. AfriForum CEO Kallie Kriel warned that the ANC could not be trusted with Afrikaners' future, and declared that Afrikaners 'want to decide for ourselves'.[107] Dirk Hermann, referencing the 'community responsibility' of earlier generations of Afrikaners, called for community-based action and urged the public to support Afrikaans products and services.[108] Finally, the FAK's managing director, Danie Langner, used his time on the podium to condemn the criminalisation of Afrikaner history. Directing his closing words at Jacob Zuma, he declared defiantly: 'Mr President, we will not be erased!'[109]

These speeches added nothing new to the Movement's established interpretative framing of Afrikaner history and the state of majority-ruled South Africa. This was the first time, however, that it was communicated from such a public platform with all of the Movement's constituent organisations coming together to share their message: South Africa was going to the dogs, and a solution was needed urgently.

---

[106] Buys, 'Krisisberaad'. A shortened version of the speech appeared as F. Buys, 'Kom ons werk saam aan oplossings', *Solidarity* 3 (2015), p. 9.

[107] K. Kriel, 'Krisisberaad: Ons wil self besluit', Crisis Summit speech, Maroela Media, 5 May 2015, http://maroelamedia.co.za/debat/meningsvormers/krisisberaad-ons-wil-self-besluit-2/ (accessed 6 May 2015).

[108] D. Hermann, 'Krisisberaad: Ek is 'n Afrikaner en ek wil hier bly', Crisis Summit speech, Maroela Media, 5 May 2015, http://maroelamedia.co.za/blog/debat/meningsvormers/krisisberaad-ek-is-n-afrikaner-en-ek-wil-hier-bly/ (accessed 6 May 2015).

[109] D. Langner, 'Krisisberaad: Meneer die President, ons sal ons nie laat uitvee nie', Crisis Summit speech, Maroela Media, 5 May 2015, http://maroelamedia.co.za/debat/meningsvormers/krisisberaad-meneer-die-president-ons-sal-ons-nie-laat-uitvee-nie/ (accessed 6 May 2015).

The 1,500 summit-goers, primarily Movement members,[110] were presented with a number of discussion points relating to various aspects of 'state collapse' and 'majority domination' as identified by the speakers. These included the leadership of President Zuma, concerns about growing state interference in the private sector, the intensification of race-based legislation, the criminalisation of Afrikaner history, and deteriorating community security and municipal services. A lone discussion point on labour downplayed the consequences of the changing nature of production under neoliberal globalisation and instead emphasised the ANC government's 'ideology of race representativity' and the economic uncertainty caused by its macro-economic and political policies as the main causes of workplace insecurity. Each issue was accompanied by a formal proposal for future action and was subsequently passed as a motion. These proposals consistently centred on the Solidarity Movement, instructing it to expand its existing activities and campaigns in order to – as Buys put it – 'rebuild a future in which we [Afrikaners] can enjoy lasting freedom, security and prosperity'.[111]

Effectively, the public nature of this event functioned as the extrapolitical equivalent of an election. Through its own engineering, the Solidarity Movement received a popular mandate to speak and act on behalf of Afrikaners, and to shape their future. This public effort to stage a mass event and thereby perform a mandate signalled that the Movement was seeking to step up in a capacity that went beyond its official membership. Indeed, in a motion entitled 'Afrikaner unity and cooperation', the Solidarity Movement was instructed to expand its efforts to unite and secure cooperation within the Afrikaner community at large, in order to form 'a power bloc with the will and ability to make and execute decisions in the community's interests, and where necessary engage constructively with the authorities on matters of interest'.[112] Yet this mandate did not involve the Movement entering politics – it would pursue its goals outside the formal political sphere.

Having defined the crisis and received its mandate in May, Solidarity returned to the public a few months later with a plan for securing

---

[110] A. Rademeyer, 'ANC kan nie met Afrikaner-erfernis of Afrikaanse onderrig vertrou word nie – AfriForum', Maroela Media, 5 May 2015, http://maroelamedia.co.za/nuus/sa-nuus/anc-kan-nie-met-afrikaner-erfenis-of-afrikaanse-onderrig-vertrou-word-nie-afriforum/ (accessed 11 August 2016).
[111] Buys, 'Krisisberaad'; 'Solidariteit Beweging: Krisisberaad 2015 Mosies', 5 May 2015, p. 6, http://krisisberaad.co.za/wp-content/uploads/2015/05/Mosies.pdf (accessed 6 May 2015).
[112] 'Solidariteit Beweging: Krisisberaad 2015 Mosies'.

Figure 5.3 Dirk Hermann (left) and Flip Buys (right) meet with President Jacob Zuma as part of an anticrime campaign initiated by the Solidarity trade union, 2010.
Source: Gallo Images

Afrikaners' future. As a follow-up to its Crisis Summit, the Movement mounted its *Toekomsberaad* (Future Summit) on 10 October 2015, in Centurion. The date was significant – in apartheid-era South Africa, 10 October was celebrated as Heroes' Day, commemorating the birth of Paul Kruger, father of the Transvaal Republic. The year 2015 marked the one hundred and ninetieth anniversary of Kruger's birth; indeed, 'Uncle Paul' was present at the summit in the shape of a cardboard cutout with which participants could have themselves photographed. Speakers also quoted Kruger, who, in the wake of the Boers' 1902 defeat, implored his volk to 'seek in the past all the good and beauty there is to discover, then form your ideal and endeavour for the future to realise this ideal'.[113] The organisation once personified by Arrie Paulus seemingly now preferred the bearded Boer patriarch as its figurehead.

To a backdrop of orange Solidarity Movement banners, Buys announced the launch of *Helpmekaar 2020* (Mutual Aid 2020) to some

---

[113] M. Thamm, 'Back to the future: Afrikaners unveil R3.5-billion plan to secure future autonomy', *Daily Maverick*, 12 October 2015, www.dailymaverick.co.za/article/2015-10-12-back-to-the-future-afrikaners-unveil-r3.5-billion-plan-to-secure-future-autonomy/#.VuZhRPmGPIU (accessed 14 March 2016).

Organisational strategies

2,700 Movement delegates and members of the public.[114] The plan's name was no coincidence. *Helpmekaar* invoked the Mutual Aid Association, set up in 1916 to provide financial support to poor Afrikaners facing fines and civil liability claims following their participation in the 1914–15 rebellion against South Africa's decision to participate in the First World War as a British ally. The Association's fundraising, which proceeded on the back of nationalist sentiment and Christian obligation, was enormously successful and revealed the capital potential of the Afrikaner population at a time when wheat and wine farming communities in particular were enjoying growing prosperity. After the Afrikaner rebels' debt had been settled, the Association shifted to financing the promotion of Afrikaner culture and education.[115]

At the *Toekomsberaad*, a number of speakers explicitly placed the 2020 plan in the same tradition as its early twentieth-century namesake, calling it a 'modern-day *Helpmekaar* movement'.[116] 'The plan's power lies in … us taking responsibility to create a future in South Africa,' Buys explained. 'We have long noticed that we cannot rely on the state to create a future for us.'[117] The Movement's institutions were central to the R3.5 billion plan and its goal of community self-reliance. The Solidarity trade union would be the vehicle for securing 'good work' for its members, particularly through developing new electronic training methods. The union had also earmarked millions to undertake legal action and international campaigns against race quotas. R1 billion would be invested in Afrikaans education and training. Helping Hand would scale up its scholarship fund for Afrikaans students, while Akademia would be developed into a comprehensive Afrikaans private university, and Sol-Tech expanded to train 1,500 Afrikaans-speaking technical workers annually. Over the course of the five-year plan, AfriForum would invest R735 million in communities by setting up security structures, stepping in where municipal service delivery was failing, and assisting schools and community projects. The plan would further support the Movement's cultural partners such as the FAK and Kraal

---

[114] E. M. Jansen, 'Toekomsberaad: 'n Toekoms wat vry, veilig en voorspoedig is', Maroela Media, 10 October 2015, http://maroelamedia.co.za/nuus/sa-nuus/toekomsberaad-n-toekoms-wat-vry-veilig-en-voorspoedig-is/ (accessed 12 August 2016).

[115] A. Ehlers, 'The Helpmekaar: rescuing the "volk" through reading, writing and arithmetic, c.1916–1965', *Historia* 60, no. 2 (2015), pp. 87–108; A. Ehlers, *Die Kaapse Helpmekaar, c.1916–c.2014: bemiddelaar in Afrikaner opheffing, selfrespek en respektabiliteit* (Stellenbosch: SUN Media, 2018).

[116] See 'Toekomsberaad: Hoe gaan die kapitaal gemobiliseer word?', Maroela Media, 10 October 2015, http://maroelamedia.co.za/nuus/sa-nuus/toekomsberaad-hoe-gaan-die-kapitaal-gemobiliseer-word/ (accessed 12 August 2016).

[117] 'Beweging stel Helpmekaarplan'.

Publishers to promote Afrikaans in all sectors of society, to establish a virtual Afrikaner museum, and to develop lecture plans for Afrikaner history to supplement school curriculums.[118]

The *Helpmekaar* plan offered the Solidarity Movement as the tailor-made solution to the crises it identified as facing the South African state, and Afrikaners in particular, under majority rule. The groundwork for this had been lain long before. Within the Movement's sphere of influence – one million Afrikaners, it was claimed – its interpretative framework was well established. Its institutions, now offered as part of a new 'plan' for Afrikaners, by and large were already up and running – although they were certainly set to expand. And its business model, centred on ethnicity and race, had already proved to be successful.

A week before the Future Summit, details of the *Helpmekaar* plan was released in the Afrikaans media. Headlines announced it as a 'Plan B' for Afrikaners which would see the Solidarity Movement 'establish a parallel government, to do the things the government is not doing for Afrikaners'.[119] South Africa's 'original plan' of a constitutional majority-ruled democracy, as negotiated in the early 1990s, had deteriorated into an ANC regime focused only on the interests of blacks, Buys told the press. Hence, the Movement would cater specifically for the Afrikaner community. While Buys added that Solidarity remained 'inclusive of other races', he mused that the plan might well inspire other movements, such as the Black Management Forum, to undertake similar initiatives 'in other communities'.[120] Despite its lip service to inclusion, the Movement clearly saw cultural communities and racial groups as the basis of societal organisation, with each being fundamentally responsible for its own 'future'.

Public reactions arguably mirrored the loci and extent of support for the Movement's strategies. The Crisis and Future Summits received extensive positive coverage on Maroela Media, where comment sections reflected its readers' enthusiasm for Solidarity's plans. The broader

---

[118] 'Beweging stel Helpmekaarplan'; 'Toekomsberaad: Hoe gaan die kapitaal gemobiliseer word?'

[119] S. Carstens and J. Eybers, '"Ons Plan B vir SA": "ANC focus op swart mense, ons sal fokus op Afrikaners"', Netwerk24, 4 October 2015, www.netwerk24.com/nuus/2015-10-04-ons-plan-b-vir-sa (accessed 9 October 2015). The article is based on an interview with Buys. It is unclear whether the 'parallel government' comment repeats his words or is the journalist's interpretation of the plan. The former is likely, however, given Buys' as well as Hermann's description of Solidarity's role to me in exactly those terms: Buys said that Afrikaners look to Solidarity to fulfil the functions of a state, while Hermann called the Movement 'Afrikaners' government'. Flip Buys, interviewed 19 September 2011, Kloofsig; Dirk Hermann interviewed 17 October 2011, Kloofsig.

[120] Carstens and Eybers, 'Ons Plan B vir SA'.

Afrikaans media carried a handful of reports on the summits, often displaying deep ambivalence about where Solidarity was headed. While acknowledging the positive impact of many of Solidarity's labour, charity, and community-based campaigns, former editor of the Afrikaans daily *Beeld* Adriaan Basson condemned the Movement's 'parallel government' plans as a 'cynical scheme to make money off Afrikaners fed up with corruption, poor service delivery and a dysfunctional government' that would worsen race relations. While commending Solidarity's proactive approach, he condemned the isolationist impulses of their proposals, pointing out that all South Africans – not just Afrikaners – were suffering the failures of ANC rule.[121] Theuns Eloff, chair of the F. W. de Klerk Foundation, pointed out that aspects of Plan B – such as AfriForum's proposals for repairing infrastructure or supporting community security – held advantages for all South Africans, in addition to those campaigns that were specifically geared towards the promotion of Afrikaner culture and heritage. Fundamentally, Plan B complied with the Constitution, he concluded, and hence could not be faulted.[122] Outside the Afrikaans media, the summits received little attention.[123] The ANC dismissed Solidarity's plans for advancing Afrikaner independence as a 'revival of the *volkstaat* mentality, which has no place in a democratic South Africa'.[124]

Chapter 4 noted the Afrikaner Volksfront and Freedom Front's goal of establishing an independent Afrikaner *volkstaat* where Afrikaners would enjoy autonomy regarding language, cultural identity, education, and association. Indeed, these were the very same goals pursued by the Solidarity Movement. The ANC's assessment of the Movement displaying a '*volkstaat* mentality' was therefore not off the mark. Political echoes of separate development sounded through Solidarity's plans. Yet when claiming to offer a 'state' or 'alternative government for Afrikaners', Solidarity clearly did not envision territorial self-determination. The Movement did not seek an independent Afrikaner homeland, self-sufficient and cut off from black-ruled South Africa as pursued in the

---

[121] A. Basson, '5 redes waarom Solidariteit se "Plan B" sleg is vir Suid-Afrika (en vir Afrikaners)', Netwerk24, 7 October 2015, www.netwerk24.com/Stemme/Menings/5-redes-waarom-Solidariteit-se-Plan-B-sleg-is-vir-Suid-Afrika-en-Afrikaners-20151008 (accessed 4 February 2016).
[122] T. Eloff, 'Plan B se kritici bly in kamma-land', F. W. de Klerk Foundation, 18 October 2015, www.fwdeklerk.org/index.php/afr/nuus/474-artikel-plan-b-se-kritici-bly-in-kamma-land (accessed 4 February 2016).
[123] The *Daily Maverick* reported on the Future Summit under the ironic headline 'Back to the future'. See note 113.
[124] L. Price, 'ANC kap Solidariteit', Netwerk24, 7 May 2015, www.netwerk24.com/Nuus/Politiek/ANC-kap-Solidariteit-20150507 (accessed 7 May 2015).

1990s and attempted in contemporary enclaves such as Orania or Kleinfontein.[125] Buys admitted that 'demographic realities' and Afrikaners' 'economic entanglement' with broader South African society meant that Afrikaner self-determination was 'currently not practically attainable'. Nevertheless, the Movement aspired to create 'spaces in which [minorities] function as majorities and can protect their own interests'. While *volkstaat* advocates sought formal political autonomy, Solidarity pursued its goals in the civil society sphere, and, instead of establishing a physical autonomous territory, the Movement created institutional, community, and even virtual spaces for 'self-determination'.

A privatised neo-racial state

By the 2010s, Solidarity's efforts to 'protect our people' thus emerged as a complex combination of state-like, political, and market-based aspirations. On the one hand, the Movement sought to perform state-like functions for its members, as well as for the wider Afrikaner population. In the arena of higher education, for instance, it set up the infrastructure for mother-tongue university and technical training. Movement members and their children enjoyed significant subsidies at Akademia and SolTech, while Helping Hand's study fund offered a number of full bursaries. Parents who themselves had no university education could not afford university fees for their children and needed assistance, Buys told me. For this reason, the Movement's training institutes were not built on a 'purely capitalist' business model focused on investor returns, but rather kept fees low by functioning according to a 'community model'.[126] The Solidarity trade union, meanwhile, took a cradle-to-grave approach with regard to the benefits and services it offered its members. In addition to collective representation and workplace support, it provided medical, maternity, and death benefits; legal services; financial and investment advice; health, career, and family advice, including access to life coaching and psychological support; study and schooling support;

---

[125] These separatist Afrikaner settlements infamously exist on the margins of South African society, and, while not politically independent, they nevertheless seek to function autonomously by eschewing 'foreign' (black) labour in favour of *volkseie arbeid* (people's own labour). De Beer, 'Exercise in futility or dawn of Afrikaner self-determination', pp. 105–14; L. Veracini, 'Afterword: Orania as settler self-transfer', *Settler Colonial Studies* 1, no. 2 (2011), pp. 190–6; J. Sharp. and S. van Wyk. 'The most intractable whites in South Africa? Ethnography of a 'Boere-Afrikaner' settlement'. Paper presented to the 5th ECAS Conference, Lisbon, 2013.

[126] Flip Buys, interviewed 19 September 2011, Kloofsig.

and leisure offers. This could all be accessed through the union's online platform, revealingly titled 'Solidarity World'.[127] Indeed, with the union accepting individual members in addition to traditional collective representation, any member of the public could access these benefits for a monthly fee. It has already been noted how the Movement's expansion in itself resulted in job creation in various fields, offering employment opportunities to its targeted constituency. AfriForum, in turn, increasingly focused on issues of security and service delivery, in addition to its civil rights initiatives and legal actions. The organisation's ambition was to set up a branch in every major South African town, and established branches were already involved in repairing local water infrastructure and maintaining public places such as parks and monuments. Especially in rural areas, branches had working relationships with agricultural unions to jointly mount patrols in order to improve community security.[128]

The manner in which the Movement sought to protect and advance the well-being of its members and target community evoked clear welfare state-like resonances – albeit in a privatised capacity for a circumscribed population. Indeed, Solidarity's efforts at 'self-determination' through 'own institutions' may be read as an exclusionary form of privatisation.[129] These state-like functions ran together with forms of commercial service provision. While members certainly enjoyed particular benefits and preferential access, many services and products offered by the Movement were available to the general consuming and paying public. This included all South Africans, even though the products and services targeted a particular constituency.

Solidarity's strategies thus reflected the opening of both markets and state-like spaces and their entanglement, under the hegemony of neoliberal policies and governmentality. Writing on developments in the USA and South Africa, the Comaroffs identify this 'dispersal of state sovereignty' as 'a function of the anti-etatism of our age'. This sees state authority appropriated by 'business firms, nongovernmental organisations, religious movements, ethnopolities, organised crime, civic associations of various sorts ... all of which seek to control semi-enclaved terrains, their micro- and moral economies, and the lives (and sometimes

---

[127] Solidarity World, https://solidariteit.co.za/ (accessed 10 March 2016); on trade union benefits, see https://solidariteit.co.za/vakbondvoordele/ (accessed 10 March 2016).
[128] Solidariteit Beweging, 'Helpmekaarplan', 10 October 2015, http://krisisberaad.co.za/wp-content/uploads/2015/10/verkorte-plan-uitleg.pdf (accessed 12 August 2016).
[129] Goldberg argues that exclusionary anti-immigrant sentiments in the USA represented 'emphatic privatization ... perfectly represent[ing] neoliberal state commitment'. Goldberg, *The Threat of Race*, p. 336.

deaths) of those who fall under their sway'. These appropriated 'lateral sovereignties' typically see the erection of state-like structures, and their performance through rhetoric and rituals.[130]

The expanded space for civil society action held distinct political advantages for Solidarity, allowing it to assert itself as a key political actor while operating outside state structures and formal political rules. By 2015, the breadth of the Movement's campaigns – and indeed the capital it commanded – gave it the confidence to publicly claim to be the voice and vehicle of Afrikaner minority interests in contemporary South Africa. As a social movement rather than a political party, Solidarity did not need to officially secure the support of the majority of Afrikaners to proceed with its plans, despite doing so in their name. The publicly staged mandate obtained during the Crisis Summit provided enough symbolic legitimacy for the Movement to proclaim itself as an 'alternative government' for Afrikaners which would manage their affairs, implement the policies set out in Plan B, and fashion Afrikaners' future accordingly. It even sought to perform this self-proclaimed political role internationally. In 2015, representatives from the Solidarity trade union and AfriForum led a deputation to the United Nations (UN) to lodge a complaint against the ANC government's affirmative action policies with the UN Committee on the Elimination of Racial Discrimination (CERD). The UN General Assembly had declared apartheid a crime against humanity in 1973,[131] and Solidarity's complaint was the first to be brought against the South African government since the end of white minority rule in 1994. It contended that the state's policies went beyond international allowances for affirmative action and amounted to neo-racism. Solidarity's delegates reportedly also visited the European Parliament in Strasbourg and met with foreign interest groups, UN officials, and the ILO to garner support for their campaign.[132]

As we have seen, the fragile social order and eroded social contract born of retreating states and aggressive markets are often compensated for by individual and community responsibilisation. The Solidarity

---

[130] J. Comaroff and J. L. Comaroff, *The Truth about Crime: sovereignty, knowledge, social order* (Chicago IL: University of Chicago Press, 2016), p. 28.
[131] Dubow, *Apartheid*, p. 278.
[132] This was reported in Solidarity's own communications. No closer details, or information on these institutions' responses, were given. 'Solidariteit maak VN-konsepverslag teen SA-regering bekend' [Solidarity press release], 7 May 2015, https://solidariteit.co.za/solidariteit-maak-vn-konsepklag-teen-sa-regering-bekend/ (accessed 11 January 2016); I. Strydom, 'Solidariteit vat regstellendeaksievergrype VN toe', *Solidarity* 4 (2015), p. 10; 'SA regering by VN aangekla oor raskwotas', *Solidarity* 6 (2015), pp. 12–13; J. van den Heever, 'VN hoor oor restellendeaksievergrype in SA', *Solidarity* 5 (2015), p. 10.

Movement represented its campaigns and ventures as the natural response of Afrikaners' 'self-doing culture' to the political realities of majority rule. Yet rather than 'Afrikaner DNA', the Movement's strategies arose from a selective mobilising framework based on ethnicity and race that utilised the discourses and opportunities available in the contemporary neoliberal context. Converging on *Helpmekaar 2020*, the Movement's discursive and organisational strategies championed responsibilisation, community self-reliance, suspicion of and freedom from state intervention, and the market as the answer to social needs. This not only reflected prevailing neoliberal rationalities but also served to entrench them. The practical strategies put in place by the Movement's various institutions – from the establishment of private educational opportunities to the repair of public infrastructure or taking responsibility for community security – acted as flanking mechanisms to compensate for the failings of the state.

Solidarity's discursive and organisational strategies therefore render visible how a social movement can utilise the spaces and opportunities characterising the neoliberal political economy to pursue its own interests. In the case of Solidarity, these interests converge on an ethnicity- and race-based politics that undermines the legitimacy and integrity of majority rule, non-racialism, and the authority of the nation state itself. These regressive political proclivities, as well as Solidarity's apparent embrace of neoliberal discourse and logic, reveal a gap in social movement literature that challenges the existing scholarly consensus. The burgeoning field of anthropological and sociological scholarship on neoliberalism typically sees social movements as contesting the uneven effects and inequalities produced by neoliberal globalisation on behalf of vulnerable communities. Particularly in contemporary Africa, where social movements are typically attributed a progressive, anti-capitalist, and pro-democratic role, this has led to a certain scholarly romanticism about social movements.

Yet such readings assume the existence of simple power configurations in which actors are either hegemonic or marginalised, and in which social movements unproblematically represent society's vulnerable and resist the consequences of neoliberal globalisation. Solidarity presents a more ambiguous case. While Solidarity did lay claim to citizenship and rights and utilised a vocabulary of marginalisation, its focus was not primarily on the material deprivation of society's most vulnerable. Moreover, rather than resisting neoliberal capitalism and its consequences, it actively utilised the opportunities offered by state withdrawal, the ascendency of the markets, and neoliberal rationales of freedom and responsibilisation. Ironically, given its labour roots, the Movement itself seemed to emerge as a neoliberal agent, enforcing neoliberal logics, flanking state failure, encroaching on state spaces, and eroding state legitimacy. Scant attention has been given to the ways in which social movements may themselves represent a response to the gaps left by the state and by the new markets opening up as a result of neoliberal hegemony. The case study of the Solidarity Movement reveals a movement driving a divisive and exclusionary politics of race that seeks to shore up race-based privilege. In contrast to the prevailing romanticism in social movement scholarship, Solidarity emerges as neither anti-hegemonic nor progressive.

Yet viewing the Solidarity Movement as a neoliberal agent in turn oversimplifies a much more ambiguous phenomenon, as the contradictions emerging from an analysis of the Movement's discursive and organisational strategies demonstrate. For instance, Solidarity's discourse of freedom and liberation – and, conversely, its condemnation of constraint, of space being limited – certainly had a strong neoliberal resonance. Dirk Hermann had explained that by establishing educational institutions and offering study bursaries (and, we might add, by creating jobs), Solidarity 'liberated' young white South Africans from the constraints of state-enforced affirmative action. Its institutions created spaces in which the minority could 'function as a majority', thereby restoring to whites their freedom. This idea of a 'restored' freedom – regaining something that was lost – echoed the Movement's apartheid denialism, negating the history of the racial state and of structures of white privilege built on the collective exploitation of blacks. Instead, whites' past 'success' was credited to the cultural, even biological, aptitude of their 'Afrikaner DNA'. Solidarity's discourse thus saw the liberation of personal choice, individualisation of success, and denial of structural factors that characterise neoliberal logic undergoing a communitarian distortion: the Movement's national populism portrayed the desire for freedom as a collective cultural attribute, just as the ingredients for success were not simply those of individualised meritocracy, but collective characteristics and values. A similar contradiction was evident in the Movement's discourse of 'self-help' and responsibilisation. Certainly, neoliberal rationale champions these very values. Yet Solidarity focused this logic on the community, portraying the individual's identity and destiny as lying with her own ethno-racial configuration and in clear opposition to the racial other. The Movement's organisational strategies, too, contradicted conventional neoliberal logic. Solidarity's opposition to state policies and interventions aimed at racial redress could be read as reflecting a key neoliberal tenet. However, the Movement's own efforts to offer welfare state-like support to its members contradict such readings. Despite utilising neoliberal discourses and rationalities challenging state sovereignty, the Movement was in favour of a centralised structure which 'takes care' of 'the people'. Solidarity did not oppose state intervention per se – but it did oppose state intervention on behalf of blacks. This is clear from its historical narrative, which patently lamented the passing of the racial state. Thus, its organisational strategies were themselves state-like, seeking to cater for the welfare and interests of a particular constituency. The Movement's push against state intervention and towards private initiative was less about a commitment to neoliberal ideology and more about an aversion to the nature and priorities of the majority-ruled state. This particular kind of state – one perceived as 'governing against Afrikaners' – needed to be driven back, or, indeed, replaced with an alternative that would 'do the things the government is not doing for Afrikaners'.

Conclusion

Like the Movement's interpretative framework, my arguments suggest a historical 'full circle'. In response to the demise of the racial state, Solidarity was pursuing its re-establishment, albeit in reformulated form. While many middle-class Afrikaners and white elites could 'capitalise on the liberation of the domestic economy' by virtue of their strong material position and access to global circuits of capital, movement, and identity,[133] these opportunities were not available to all whites: blue-collar, often more precarious whites, but also growing sections of the middle class – figures such as Buys and Hermann, and the growing army of white-collar administrators and skilled graduates working for and buying membership of the Solidarity Movement. The contemporary discursive and organisational strategies of the Movement represented an answer to the demise of the racial state from and for the social alliance representing this group of people. Under the populist motto 'We protect our people', and echoing the efforts of earlier cultural entrepreneurs, the Movement sought to create alternative avenues of material security and sustainability for this section of the white population. To be sure, the Movement's 'own institutions' strategy was often presented as a straightforward and legitimate effort to cater to the interests of a specific cultural group – particularly in terms of language preference. Yet in the context of the broader framing of the Movement (an 'alternative government' for Afrikaners) and of the ANC-ruled state ('majority dominance' from which Afrikaners and whites in general need to be 'liberated'), this

---

[133] Blaser and Van der Westhuizen, 'Introduction', p. 384.

strategy smacked of apartheid-style separate development – only now in privatised, extra-parliamentary, and interest-based form: not territorial in nature, but institutional, community-based, and even virtual.

This chapter has examined the meaning-making, mobilising, and money-spinning strategies by which the Movement sought to accomplish this. Solidarity's emergence as a saviour organisation – a 'neo-racial state' – was the outcome of efforts since the 1970s and throughout the long transition to negotiate the demise of the racial state. Rising membership numbers as well as the Movement's increasing assertiveness testified to the popularity and evident legitimacy it and its strategies enjoyed among its target constituency.

These arguments provide new direction to existing theorisation on neoliberalism and race. Critical scholars have argued that neoliberalism modifies the way in which race is understood in contemporary society, and, in so doing, advances elite class interests. Solidarity's strategies suggest that racial ideology and race-, ethnicity-, and class-based interests may in turn modify neoliberal logics and discourses, transforming the meaning, direction, and outcome of neoliberal rationales and policies. In the post-Cold War context, the dominance of cultural politics has seen economic precarity repackaged as a matter of ethnic or racial survival. In the process, neoliberal policies, rationalities, and practices may be utilised and reinvented by non-elites for race- and ethnicity-based politics.

Solidarity's contemporary strategies and self-presentation as Afrikaners' saviour organisation are thus revealed not only as a response to the local demise of the racial state, but also as inflections of broader global processes. Yet in the midst of the Movement's organisational framing – of Afrikaners as a homogeneous volk with a particular history, and Solidarity as the post-apartheid defender of this marginalised minority – I was aware of important sub- and counternarratives circulating within the Movement, among its executives and blue-collar members respectively. These contradicted key elements of Solidarity's discursive framing. Chapters 6 and 7 examine these narratives against the backdrop of the framing set out above. In different quarters of the Movement, they revealed underswells of class-based prejudices, tensions, and anxieties that continued to course through the social alliance.

6 Discursive labour and strategic contradiction
Managing the working-class roots of a declassed organisation

Introduction

Nearly ten years after the completion of Buys' *Wenplan 2002* and the MWU's reinvention as Solidarity, I started a period of fieldwork at the organisation's Kloofsig headquarters. August 2011 was an exciting time for the Movement – Maroela Media had just been successfully launched, AfriForum had just won its highly publicised hate speech case against Julius Malema, and the Movement was preparing to set up its distance-learning higher education institution, Akademia. By all measures, Solidarity was flourishing. With the boom in its membership since the Malema case commenced, AfriForum alone was earning a monthly income of R1.4 million.[1] 'We are going from strength to strength, where other Afrikaner organisations have failed,' Dirk Hermann declared confidently as he escorted me from the headquarters' polished entrance foyer up the stairs to his office on my first morning.

Hermann's words were my first introduction to the discursive framing which underlay the Movement's public positioning and campaigns. As Chapter 5 showed, Solidarity presented itself as a civil society actor focused on white Afrikaans-speakers; as the defender and legitimate representative of this culturally homogeneous nation in a social and political landscape in which Afrikaners formed an increasingly precarious minority; and as a dynamic organisation growing in stature, scope, support, and ambition. Recall that the organisation's historical narrative consistently sought to demonstrate continuity in the values, struggles, and aspirations of 'our people' and of the Movement itself throughout the twentieth century. The 'volk' was represented as united across generations by their 'Afrikaner DNA' – a virtuous, hardworking people who, in the face of discrimination and poverty, 'pulled themselves up by their bootstraps' and rightfully desired autonomy. The Movement, in turn, was the 'oldest civil rights organisation' in South Africa, with a century-long

---

[1] *Solidariteitkunde*, 13 September 2011.

track record of defending the vulnerable, resisting injustice, and empowering Afrikaners to realise the freedom they naturally desired. Solidarity presented the South African past and present as populated by distinct ethnic and racial groups, and the post-apartheid era as characterised by a 'clash of values' between the degenerative agendas of traditionalist and socialist African politicians such as Zuma, and the proactive impulses of white South Africans' Western, Christian heritage. Chapter 5 demonstrated the various platforms on which this interpretative framework was communicated – from the Movement's in-house magazine to its internet platform, webpages, and press statements.

However, in the months spent at Solidarity's headquarters, I encountered a subterranean story – more anecdotal in form, but equally suggestive in its meaning-making – running parallel to this official framing. Emanating from the leadership itself, this sub-narrative focused on the decades before Buys became general secretary. Instead of demonstrating continuity throughout the MWU/Solidarity's 100-year history, this sub-narrative highlighted stark contrasts between the Movement and its apartheid-era mother organisation. Similarly, representations of Afrikaners as a culturally homogeneous volk with a common past and future 'calling' were contradicted by emphasising irreconcilable class-based differences between the long-time union members and blue-collar leadership of old on the one hand, and the organisation's growing body of professional, high-skilled members and graduate staff on the other. Often, these contradictions surfaced in personal interviews, typically behind closed doors, or in semi-private settings and conversations. The *Solidariteitkunde* course was one such space. As Chapter 5 explained, attendance at this seminar was compulsory for newly appointed Solidarity staff, introducing them not only to the Movement's organisational structure, operation, and campaigns, but also to its official historical and ideological framing. However, the collegial atmosphere created by Hermann, who presented the seminar, and his penchant for anecdotes created a space in which he often strayed, perhaps unwittingly, or contradicted, often for effect, the institutional line. Similarly, during interviews with the Movement's chief executives, the closed nature of the conversations often saw Buys and Hermann share opinions, experiences, and understandings of Solidarity not expressed elsewhere. On a number of occasions, therefore, I observed the leadership contradict their own institutional narrative, disrupting the ideas of historical continuity, and of Afrikaners as a classless, ethnically united, and virtuous people.

This chapter examines the contradictions evident in this sub-narrative, including the tensions its reveals and the functions it fulfils in terms of the Solidarity Movement's contemporary positioning. As such, the analysis functions in counterpoint to Chapter 5's examination of Solidarity's official discursive framing. In terms of sources, here I extend the previous chapter's analysis of the *Solidariteitkunde* course and interviews with the Movement's two most senior executives. I also draw on interviews with blue-collar Solidarity members and evidence from the union newspaper. The analysis plots the contours of Buys and Hermann's sub-narrative, demonstrating how it reveals the presence of raw class-based stereotyping and moralism among the Movement's executives which directly contradicted the organisation's official framing by vilifying its blue-collar roots. I argue that the contradictions expressed by the leadership are reflective of the opportunities and challenges that resulted from appropriating a working-class organisation as the vehicle for a declassed, ethnicity-based agenda. This chapter therefore explores the discursive labour involved in managing the working-class roots of the Solidarity Movement.

Uncouth roughnecks and backward racists: vilifying Solidarity's working-class roots

An hour into the *Solidariteitkunde* course, Dirk Hermann set out to explain to his audience 'how the union got to where it is now'. This seemed like a superfluous point on the agenda – after all, Hermann had just completed the dramatic chronicle of the Movement's formation in the aftermath of the South African War as champion of Afrikaner interests, its persistent support of the volk as it struggled and triumphed in the face of discrimination and adversity, and its continued defence of minority rights in the contemporary context of a hostile government and majority domination. But he now changed tack. Switching to a more personal narrative, Hermann described how, when he first joined the MWU in 1997, the organisation was in dire straits. 'When I arrived here, there was no Akademia, no SolTech, no Research Institute, no Communications Department ...'[2] One by one, he erased the departments or institutions in which each of the seminar participants had recently been appointed, painting a picture of an organisation struggling to survive. '[It] was bankrupt on two levels,' he went on:

[I]n terms of ideas, we [the MWU] didn't know how to react to the post-1994 situation, Afrikaners in general [didn't know how to react]. In fact, all the Afrikaner institutions had collapsed ... And we were really part of that collapse, there was nothing left of us. So bankrupt in terms of ideas, but also physically

---

[2] *Solidariteitkunde*, 13 September 2011.

bankrupt – there wasn't any money either. Fleet vehicles were being sold off for cash flow, just to survive.[3]

In stark contrast to his hitherto heroic portrayal of the Movement – and to the elegant corporate environment in which he delivered these words – Hermann presented a lethargic and unpopular organisation with 'only about 33,000 members, which is 25 per cent of our membership today'. 'In the eyes of the public, no one even wanted to touch [this] old union with a barge pole,' he stated contemptuously. Hermann continued in storytelling mode:

> I was appointed in the Pretoria office. When I got there ... a child's Wendy house ... had been used to build an office cubicle ... I brought my *own* furniture to the office. But we also didn't have computers, only typewriters ... This wasn't because these were the 'old days', it was because we didn't have the stuff! ... They nicknamed me 'Lizard' – I had a hard time at the MWU, because I hadn't come through the ranks but from university ... Uncle Krappie Cronje was our office manager ... he could yell your head off. In fact, those days everybody yelled at each other and you really had to know how to curse to manage ... Uncle Krappie was also a general in the AWB. Now, I had to write my monthly report. I brought my computer and my printer to work ... I typed my report ... I was expecting Uncle Krappie to phone me and tell me 'Good job!' I had gone to so much trouble to have everything ... perfect ... So Uncle Krappie phones: 'Mr Hermann, can you please submit your report in the right format!' I was flabbergasted. I said, 'Mr Cronje, what is the right format?' He replied, 'Typed on a fucking typewriter!'

Hermann gave an animated performance of this exchange between himself, the upright newcomer, and the foul-mouthed 'Uncle Krappie', taking care to dip his voice when he reached the expletive – but without sacrificing the punchline. Laughter erupted from the *Solidariteitkunde* participants. The humour demonstrated the intelligibility of the distinctions Hermann was drawing: the MWU he joined in 1997 was a languishing organisation, incompetent due to its conservatism, unwilling to adapt, and ridiculous to the point of being laughable. More importantly, its politics and morals were dubious – Hermann's colleagues were coarse right-wing militants straight from the mineshaft and the shop floor. This working-class caricature contrasted sharply with the way in which Hermann represented himself: a fresh-faced industrial sociology graduate who entered the regional office with a personal computer and sense of respectability.

Like the events surrounding the Stilfontein mine closure,[4] aspects of this sub-narrative – especially regarding the technological backwardness

---

[3] *Solidariteitkunde*, 13 September 2011.   [4] See Chapter 5.

of the MWU and its opposition to 'modernisation' – were often repeated to me during informal conversations with staff members at Solidarity's headquarters, with either Hermann or Buys featuring as the tales' protagonist. Notably, my interlocutors in this regard were typically themselves white-collar administrators or university graduates who had joined the organisation after Buys took over the reins. The stories seemed well rehearsed and readily available when conversations drifted to the recent history of Solidarity.

During an interview, I asked Buys what the union was like when he joined in 1991. He immediately replied: '[I]t was terrible. I was the first graduate to survive.'[5] Indeed, both Buys and Hermann instinctively highlighted their university education as the feature that marked them as outsiders when they joined the MWU. They also identified socio-economic status as a distinguishing factor, but did not emphasise this nearly as much as education. Hermann explained that he was raised in an 'elite home', his father having been the managing director of a large dairy company. Buys' mother was a teacher and his father owned 'a small farm' – he mentioned that his father had left school at 14 and that they were 'terribly poor', but also emphasised that many of his father's friends were professors who regularly visited the Buys family at home, and that he was not working class because he had attended university.[6]

Buys attributed the difficulties he encountered as a new MWU employee to a 'clash of values' – the union was arch-conservative, in terms of not only its politics but also its management style. Buys related how, after joining the organisation in 1991, he revised the union's remuneration system, leading to better salaries for employees, acquired computers and new furniture for the offices, and made provision for a health plan for employees. Nevertheless, the blue-collar officials and members remained 'not just conservative, even reactionary'.[7] Buys recounted:

It was *terrible*, the guys opposed everything [improvements Buys sought to introduce]. This one guy, Fred Bond, told me one day: 'Flip, I know your plans work, but I am against it all; there is too much change going on.' Remember, these guys really struggled with the country's changes, and they saw the union as something that should never change ... Somewhere they could feel safe. Somewhere everything was still like the good old days.[8]

---

[5] Flip Buys, interviewed 25 October 2011, Kloofsig.
[6] Dirk Hermann, interviewed 16 September 2011, Kloofsig; Flip Buys, interviewed 19 September 2011, Kloofsig; Flip Buys, interviewed 25 October 2011, Kloofsig.
[7] Flip Buys, interviewed 19 September 2011, Kloofsig.
[8] Flip Buys, interviewed 25 October 2011, Kloofsig.

246   Discursive labour and strategic contradiction

These words presented the blue-collar MWU as desperately struggling to come to terms with the changing context in which it found itself in the early 1990s. As Chapter 4 indicated, Fred Bond and Krappie Cronje were both members of Buys' editorial staff when he assumed the editorship of the union newspaper in 1991. But Buys was quick to move on from any sympathy that this anxiety might engender for the old MWU leadership, and his narrative, like Hermann's during *Solidariteitkunde*, focused on representing the MWU as politically and morally distasteful. Relating another personal experience, Buys described how general secretary Peet Ungerer had sought to prepare his staff for Buys' arrival in 1991, warning them that 'we're getting a guy with a degree and he's a *Dopper* [member of the Reformed Church]; he doesn't like swearing and drinking, so you fellows, you're not to take him along [drinking], or swear'. Buys chuckled. 'So he gave them that description of how he saw me, my culture.'[9] In an interview, Hermann drew similar lines of difference, extending the negative behaviour and morals thus far attributed to the MWU's leadership to its members. He described how, at the first regional union meeting he attended as a new organiser, 'the members turned up drunk at the meeting, they swore the socks off the previous organiser, [so] that I wondered what I was even doing there ... a young guy, graduated, busy with his masters studies'.[10] Not that Hermann thought that the previous organiser deserved much sympathy. 'Before me, the organiser was old Jan Deacon,' Hermann told me a few minutes later. 'Jan Deacon didn't have any qualifications that I knew of. Now Jan Deacon drank like a fish – he later drank himself to death. And old Jan Deacon had' – he paused to highlight the coming euphemism – '*relationships* with almost all, well, the few female members that we had.' Hermann gave an embarrassed smile at the thought. 'But Jan Deacon and I were ...'[11] His voice trailed off as he made a gesture indicating that they were worlds apart.

On some occasions, this classist sub-narrative about the apparent recalcitrant attitudes and moral failings of the MWU old guard moved from innuendo to outright ridicule. During one interview, as I was questioning Buys about his work as editor of *The Mineworker* and *MWU-News*, he drew my attention to the annual Christmas messages published in the newspaper. Every year, most of the final edition was dedicated to the union management's and regional representatives'

---

[9] Flip Buys, interviewed 25 October 2011, Kloofsig.
[10] Dirk Hermann, interviewed 16 September 2011, Kloofsig.
[11] Dirk Hermann, interviewed 16 September 2011, Kloofsig (his emphasis).

holiday wishes to their members. 'Those Christmas messages drove me up the wall!' Buys cried. 'Because the guys would write these saccharine [messages] – you would have this brandy-tippler writing about the sweet baby Jesus lying in the manger, you know. Jeez! For me, I couldn't stand that mawkish stuff, but the guys wanted it in [the newspaper].' 'So I should not read the Christmas messages as reflecting religious beliefs and a genuine spirituality in the union?' I asked. 'Not at all. No, not at all,' Buys dismissed the idea immediately. 'I used to mock them about it ... and everyone would laugh their heads off.' The certainty with which Buys ridiculed these messages and asserted that their authors' beliefs were spurious seemed particularly jarring in the context of Solidarity, a consciously self-identified Christian organisation that invoked the notion of a 'calling' as a mobilising tool.

Buys framed the ostensible differences between contemporary Solidarity and the old MWU in terms of conflicting sets of 'values' or 'cultures'. As Chapter 5 demonstrated, these notions were employed within the Movement's official narrative to draw racialised 'us and them' distinctions between Solidarity and its overwhelmingly white, Christian, and Western-oriented membership on the one hand, and COSATU, the ANC-ruled state, and the black majority on the other. Within the executives' sub-narrative, however, 'culture' was transposed to describe intraracial differences. In an interview, I asked Buys to explain the basis of this 'value clash'. In response, he pointed specifically to the union's roots in the mining industry and its racist politics. The classed nature of this 'clash' was clearly demonstrated in an aside by Buys: 'Just for interest's sake, the only guy [within the MWU] who had a permanent headache was the accountant, who came from a different culture.'[12] It was perfectly clear that Buys did not mean that MWU members were linguistically, ethnically, or racially distinct from the accountant or Buys himself, and thus displayed different social behaviour or customs. Indeed, there was never any doubt that the MWU members and leaders described by Buys and Hermann were Afrikaners like themselves. The difference was, in Hermann's words, that the old MWU was 'Afrikaner, but *blue-collar* Afrikaner'.[13]

Only one person's cultural credentials were called into question – those of Arrie Paulus, MWU general secretary from 1967 to 1987. Paulus was a Syrian immigrant who adopted an Afrikaner identity in

---

[12] Flip Buys, interviewed 25 October 2011, Kloofsig.
[13] Dirk Hermann, interviewed 16 September 2011, Kloofsig (his emphasis).

the mines, Buys told me on more than one occasion.[14] To Buys, Paulus personified the old MWU. And, while Buys claimed never to have actually met Paulus, he nevertheless attributed what he regarded as the MWU's conservative organisational culture and racist politics to Paulus as an individual. He told me that Paulus 'appointed terrible racists, Arrie, you know, because that worked for him', and that he 'picked the wrong fights'.[15] '[H]e was a very emotional guy, he had a typical Syrian temperament, people say he would get angry' – Buys snapped his fingers – 'just like that ... At the drop of a hat he would say "You're going on strike!" and pound on the table.'[16]

Solidarity's executives thus drew fundamentally classed divisions between themselves and their predecessors in terms of education, respectability, and political attitudes. This effectively saw the leadership contradict its own official framing. Rather than the 'oldest civil society organisation' with a long-standing commitment to protecting the vulnerable and fighting discrimination, the leadership's anecdotes depicted a backward-looking organisation run by racist and disreputable people with little capacity or inclination to 'protect the people'. Whereas the Movement's historical-ideological framing emphasised the continuities between Solidarity and the MWU, this classed sub-narrative sought to distance the organisation in its contemporary guise from its predecessor.

This discursive move held important value for the Movement's executives as a way of legitimising their leadership. To be sure, this sub-narrative effectively demonstrated – as Hermann had set out to do during *Solidariteitkunde* – 'how the union got to where it is now'. Despite the official narrative of a century-old saviour organisation, this sub-narrative illustrated how the MWU had been transformed from a flailing and unpopular trade union to an ever expanding multimillion-rand social movement since people like himself and Flip Buys had taken over the reins. 'We simply had to start turning the situation around,' Hermann insisted. 'And today,' he continued, brightening, 'the organisation has changed *dramatically*.'[17]

Buys' negative portrayal of Arrie Paulus offers an effective illustration of the legitimising function of these sub-narratives. The rumour about Paulus's ostensibly foreign roots allowed Buys to attribute the racist politics and organisational culture that had characterised the MWU in

---

[14] Both Naas Steenkamp and Piet Nieuwenhuizen repeated a similar story to me, while Fanie Botha made similar comments in an interview with Wessel Visser. See Van Zyl-Hermann, 'Race, rumour and the politics of class', pp. 509–30.
[15] Flip Buys, interviewed 19 September 2011, Kloofsig.
[16] Flip Buys, interviewed 25 October 2011, Kloofsig.
[17] *Solidariteitkunde*, 13 September 2011.

the past to an external, foreign source. Thus, Buys claimed that, '[b]efore Arrie Paulus ... there was an Afrikaner cultural identity and worker [identity in the MWU]. The guys thought of themselves as ... *Afrikaner* workers. Then with Arrie, because he wasn't himself an Afrikaner, it changed to race; we are the *white* workers.'[18] Thus Paulus, the outsider, was held responsible for the MWU's turn to racist politics, and the union and its members were whitewashed of their right-wing past. Moreover, the story allowed Buys to present himself as the antithesis of Paulus: a reasonable, intellectual, and strategic leader – and a real Afrikaner. This positively distinguished him from his predecessor in the same way in which the overall sub-narrative set Solidarity apart from the racist politics of the apartheid-era MWU. Indeed, Buys explained how he was moving the organisation away from a focus on race and 'back' towards a focus on its apparently natural or inherent 'cultural identity'. This seemed to imply that any form of class identity or hostility between Afrikaners was also artificial or foreign. In fact, Buys said in a casual moment of further self-contradiction, 'class has never really been an Afrikaner thing'.[19]

By emphasising difference rather than continuity, the executives engaged in strategic contradiction, their sub-narrative allowing them to manage their organisation's working-class roots to their advantage. They formulated a version of the past that saw the union 'turned around' by the influx of men – always men – such as Buys and Hermann, and the departure of men like Arrie Paulus, Krappie Cronje, Fred Bond, and Jan Deacon. On the surface, this narrative was one of practical improvement and organisational progress: monthly reports typed on computers, membership growth, improved salaries, and better office furniture. Visser's biography of the MWU reports this apparently objective 'reinvention' of the organisation under Buys' leadership as the 'modernisation' of the union and the shedding of its racist image. But Visser does not draw out the classed dimensions and moralised implications that underlie this narrative: under Buys' leadership, the swearing, drinking, and sexual impropriety, the resistant conservatism and racist politics – indeed, the classed 'culture' identified as making the MWU a distinctly mineworkers' or blue-collar organisation – were banished or abated. Indeed, Buys claimed to have made a point of dismissing people with 'different values'. '[W]hen you have a guy who doesn't share your values, then you have to fire him even if he's a good worker,'[20] he told me – a truly astounding

---

[18] Flip Buys, interviewed 25 October 2011, Kloofsig (his emphasis).
[19] Flip Buys, interviewed 19 September 2011, Kloofsig.
[20] Flip Buys, interviewed 19 September 2011, Kloofsig.

statement from someone with experience in the fields of labour relations and human resources. Due to changes in the labour market, Buys continued, there was also a change in the union's membership base, so that Solidarity today, unlike the MWU of old, represented hardly any 'manual workers' but mostly people in 'higher-class work'.[21] Members with tertiary qualifications, Hermann pointed out, were 'on another level of Maslow's hierarchy of needs'.[22] This sub-narrative therefore claimed that, under the stewardship of *non*-working-class men like Buys and Hermann, the union had not only improved practically, but had also become respectable and sophisticated – leading to the 'reinvention' of the organisation and the 'elevation' of its membership. The union seemed to emerge from this process not simply as a declassed and culturally focused organisation, but perhaps more accurately as a middle-classed organisation. As Solidarity's polished entrance foyer where I had met Hermann on my first morning testified, this was no longer a coarse mineworkers' union, but a refined and sophisticated corporate organisation.

This classed sub-narrative therefore allowed the Movement's leadership to manage the working-class roots of their organisation to their advantage. By claiming to have reinvented the racist and backward MWU, the sub-narrative lent legitimacy to their own leadership, absolved the Movement of its racist past, and legitimised the manner in which, under the new middle-class leadership, working-class interests within the MWU/Solidarity had been eschewed in favour of declassed cultural and racial agendas.

It is crucial, at this point, to recall that I encountered this sub-narrative only in personal interviews with the leadership and in the semi-private setting of *Solidariteitkunde*, and not in the Movement's more public communications. It was, after all, *within* the Movement that affirming the legitimacy of the current leadership and its vision for the organisation was most important. The contradictions expressed by the leadership therefore enjoyed only limited circulation and thus did not threaten to undermine the overall official framing articulated throughout the Movement and on more public platforms. It is in this sense that I characterise this classed discourse as a *sub*-narrative, rather than a *counter*-narrative: despite involving stark contradictions, its overall effect was not to challenge the official narrative but to lend legitimacy to Solidarity in its contemporary guise.

---

[21] Flip Buys, interviewed 25 October 2011, Kloofsig.
[22] Dirk Hermann, interviewed 17 October 2011, Kloofsig.

People with a 'special character': appeasing Solidarity's working-class membership

Yet, although the leadership's sub-narrative did not contradict the overall official institutional framing, the classist moralism it expressed did involve certain risks. In 2011, many Solidarity members were blue-collar, technically trained workers such as those derided by Buys and Hermann. Many had joined the MWU long before the new leadership had appeared on the scene. As Chapter 7 will show, I interviewed a number of men who had joined the MWU during the 1970s and 1980s and continued to be active in the union during the period under study here. In addition to these extensive personal interviews, I also conducted shorter telephone interviews with a further cohort of long-time trade union members, all of whom had joined the MWU/Solidarity between 1963 and 1985 – the period coinciding with Arrie Paulus's headship. The bulk of my interviewees did not hold senior school certificates, most had left school at around 16 years of age, and some had subsequently completed an apprenticeship or technical training. In contrast to Buys' claim that Solidarity no longer represented the same 'manual workers' who had formed the bulk of its predecessor's membership base, many long-time members still belonged to the organisation and even served in prominent positions.

Perhaps the most visible, if symbolic, example of this was Cor de Jager, the MWU's longest-serving president (from 1967 until his retirement in 1995) and the one-time right-hand man of Paulus. De Jager had joined the MWU in 1951 as a young developer in the Rustenburg platinum mines and became active as shaft steward in the 1960s.[23] He was a member of the intractable MWU deputation testifying before the Wiehahn Commission on the union's opposition to labour reform. It is also likely that he was the 'ultra-conservative trade union leader by the name of De Jager' identified as a leading figure in the 1993 storming of the Kempton Park World Trade Centre, when multiparty negotiations for the ending of apartheid were disrupted by the right-wing forces of the AWB and Afrikaner Volksfront.[24] Indeed, a number of the men with whom I conducted personal interviews admitted to having once belonged to or sympathised with the AWB.[25] In 2011, De Jager, then a kindly

---

[23] Cor de Jager, telephone interview, 9 September 2011; 'Solidariteit-veterane word gevier!', *Solidarity* 4 (2014), https://tydskrif.solidariteit.co.za/solidariteit-veterane-word-gevier/ (accessed 28 September 2018).
[24] J. Heunis, *The Inner Circle: reflections on the last days of white rule* (Johannesburg: Jonathan Ball, 2007), p. 185.
[25] This, as well as the incident at the World Trade Centre, is discussed in detail in Chapter 7.

octogenarian, held a position on the executive as representative of the union's retried members. He still lived in Carletonville – Paulus's one-time CP constituency – but regularly travelled the length of the West Rand up to Pretoria to attend meetings. Although I did not have access to membership statistics, it is clear, therefore, that the educational – and, to an extent, political – profile of a significant section of the Solidarity union's membership coincided with the 'culture' that Buys and Hermann represented as 'clashing' with their own respectable middle-class subjectivities and values. Nevertheless, in 2011, Solidarity continued to incorporate and employ members of the old guard and rely on the structural basis lain by the MWU. Indeed, Wessel Visser notes in his biography of the MWU that the expansion of union membership beyond mining and the resulting reorganisation of union structures that had been initiated by Arrie Paulus in response to the Wiehahn reforms in fact 'lay the foundations for Solidarity's success by the end of the twentieth century'.[26]

The contemporary leadership therefore had to be circumspect in the articulation of their classist sub-narrative. In interviews, both Buys and Hermann displayed awareness of the problematic nature of their emphasis on class-based differences among Afrikaners, and of the forceful moral judgements they expressed in this regard. Not only did these disrupt the Movement's carefully crafted public representation of Afrikaners as a homogeneous, culturally united people and of Solidarity as their legitimate champion and defender, but these views also threatened to alienate or antagonise the many blue-collar members and employees on whom the Movement depended for support. As a result, Buys and Hermann would often rapidly shift their stance or resort to self-contradiction in an effort to resolve these dissonances and merge back into the official framing. Despite efforts to distance themselves from the old MWU and its members on the basis of class, they would also abnegate the validity of classed divisions between Afrikaners and reverse the sub-narrative of their own making by shifting their positionality and the social categories that they emphasised.

Recall, for instance, that during *Solidariteitkunde* Hermann recounted that he had been nicknamed 'Lizard' by his MWU colleagues because he 'hadn't come through the ranks but from university'. During an interview, I enquired, 'Why "lizard"?' 'I never actually asked,' he mused. 'I suspect it was "Learned Lizard", you know.[27] Look, initially it [the appointment of a graduate] was peculiar and there was some gossiping,

---

[26] Visser, *Van MWU tot Solidariteit*, p. 266.
[27] He used the term '*Akademie Akkedis*' in Afrikaans.

but then it actually became quite a bit easier after a while.'[28] In a self-contradictory move, Hermann now downplayed the apparently stark education-related differences he had previously emphasised in such a colourful manner. Certainly, a reptilian nickname evoked a myriad of potential associations – a slippery, perhaps untrustworthy or disagreeable character – but none necessarily related to education. I tried to corroborate the 'Lizard' nickname with a number of the old hands I interviewed. This kind of treatment of graduate appointments to the union did not ring a bell with them, and although they did not rule out the possibility that some teasing might have occurred, they dismissed the idea that any real animosity or suspicion underlay it.[29] In fact, many testified that changing the union's name from the MWU to Solidarity in 2002, thus shifting its emphasis from the mining industry towards wider industrial representation, had seen much more concerted opposition than the appointment of graduates, and that Buys and others were easily incorporated despite not having come through the ranks.[30] Hermann told me that, with time, he and other graduates gained the trust of union members and employees: '[T]hey started to realise we *really* believe in the union's cause, and I think people simply started to trust us.' Moreover, Hermann continued, graduate members of the leadership were accepted because 'we *became* them, you see. And I think even today, it's not a matter of an us and a them ... I think those tensions have fallen away.'[31] 'At this stage,' he commented in another interview, 'I have such a good relationship with the blue-collar guys, it's really ... I've become one of them.'[32] These seem like extraordinary statements if we recall Hermann's damning representation and caricature of the MWU's blue-collar membership during *Solidariteitkunde*, and the manner in which both he and Buys in other instances drew clear 'us and them' distinctions in class terms.

Such self-contradictions were not the product of a change in setting – they would occur in the same breath. In an interview, I asked Hermann to describe the workers he represented as a union organiser in 1997. After characterising them as 'Afrikaner, but blue-collar Afrikaner', he

---

[28] Dirk Hermann, interviewed 17 October 2011, Kloofsig.
[29] For instance, Louis, interviewed 18 October 2011; Paul, interviewed 20 October 2011; group interview, 14 September 2011. All interviews in Kloofsig.
[30] For instance, Wouter, interviewed 20 September 2011; Schalk, interviewed 28 October 2011; Frans, interviewed 22 September 2011; group interview, 14 September 2011; Louis, interviewed 18 October 2011; Frik, interviewed 8 September 2011; Anton, interviewed 28 October 2011; Paul, interviewed 20 October 2011. All interviews in Kloofsig.
[31] Dirk Hermann, interviewed 17 October 2011, Kloofsig (his emphasis).
[32] Dirk Hermann, interviewed 16 September 2011, Kloofsig.

continued: 'And probably the majority would have seen themselves as Christians – although if you looked at them, you sometimes had to wonder!' He chuckled, then caught himself abruptly and turned serious again: 'But *good* people, really good people.' Hermann was thus careful not to undermine the respectability of his organisation's past or present membership. This self-contradiction saw him merge back into line with the Movement's official framing of Afrikaners as a virtuous, 'self-help' people. Indeed, he went on to speak about the 'special character' of these 'working-class Afrikaners', and in particular their propensity for 'hard work ... a unique work ethic'.[33] Buys similarly muddied the distinctions he otherwise drew so clearly between himself and the MWU old guard. Like Hermann, he claimed that the initial tension caused by his appointment as the union's first graduate employee diffused once he established a rapport with his blue-collar colleagues. This was because he was able to 'understand *their* language ... I had a good connection with *them*' – although he was quick to remind me that he 'had a different lifeworld to them, [because] I went to university'. Nevertheless, Buys insisted that 'the people were never simply workers; the fact is they always had an Afrikaner, a cultural identity also'.[34] Thus Buys, too, reverted to the declassed interpretative framework, claiming that the 'Afrikaner values' of freedom, responsibility, and hard work had always been part of the organisation's 'historical value system'.[35]

The discursive to and fro performed by Hermann and Buys made for deeply contradictory statements about themselves, their organisation, and its members. They claimed a class identity for their blue-collar members and colleagues, only to efface class divisions a moment later; they stigmatised blue-collar workers as racist and immoral, while commending them as virtuous, 'hard-working' people in the very next breath. This attests to the discursive labour the leadership had to perform in order to manage the working-class roots of their organisation.

Indeed, there is evidence that Buys in particular had long been careful to retain the support of the old guard. The *MWU-News* shows how, in 1997, in his first message to MWU members as the new general secretary, he stated that he was 'taking over the MWU in a very good condition', that 'no drastic changes are required' to the organisation. Acknowledging the work of his predecessors, he emphasised his intention 'to build upon the strong foundation which has already been laid in our

---

[33] Dirk Hermann, interviewed 16 September 2011, Kloofsig.
[34] Flip Buys, interviewed 25 October 2011, Kloofsig.
[35] Flip Buys, interviewed 25 October 2011, Kloofsig.

members' interests'.³⁶ This apparent appreciation for the union's achievements stood in stark contrast to the damning assessment of its condition that he voiced to me in interviews years later. It is unclear whether Buys' 1997 message reflected his true assessment of the state of the organisation, or whether he, as the first general secretary from outside mineworking ranks, was seeking to win trust by adopting a mollifying approach. Certainly, his caution was illustrated in the way in which he tackled the amendment of the MWU's constitution in the late 1990s. Throughout most of its history, MWU membership – by virtue of the closed shop agreement in the mining industry – had been restricted to white mining production workers. Under Arrie Paulus and Peet Ungerer, the union had opened its membership to white blue-collar workers across the mining, steel, and distribution industries, and amended its constitution accordingly. After 1994, new legislation was passed prohibiting organisations from restricting their membership in terms of race. The MWU thus risked being deregistered with the Department of Labour. Writing in the *MWU-News*, Buys explained that the MWU would seek to comply with the new law by reformulating its membership criteria: first in linguistic and cultural terms, and second to include people who were being collectively disadvantaged by 'unreasonable discrimination'. 'The MWU is, however, not expecting any change in the composition of its membership, because these two determinations simply underwrite its current membership,' he wrote.[37] Approximately a year later, the *MWU-News* reported that the union had finally been registered under the new legislation. In an article entitled 'Changes in the MWU constitution in perspective', Buys reiterated that, 'in order to survive', the MWU had to adhere to the new legislation. He explained that a special committee had been appointed to consult on how the union might comply with the new legislation while 'keeping the character and identity of the union intact'. Buys' explanation clearly indicated that this was a matter of race:

[The committee's suggestions] were not aimed at changing [the union's] membership composition, but at finding a way of legally maintaining our character without putting it in racial terms. It must be made clear that the omission of the word 'white' from the draft suggestion does not mean that the word will be replaced by 'multiracial'. Rather, it means that the union will have to maintain its character in other ways.[38]

[36] F. Buys, 'Waarheen nou?', *MWU-News*, June/July 1997, p. 2.
[37] Buys, 'Waarheen nou?'
[38] F. Buys, 'Die veranderinge van die MWU se Grondwet in perspektief', *MWU-News*, May/June 1998, p. 6.

This framing of the union's constitutional changes was saturated with a discourse of preservation and retention. Buys' kid-glove handling of the issue may be taken as proof of his wariness of a backlash from MWU old hands, who – as Buys claimed during an interview – 'saw the union as something that should never change'.[39] Perhaps this was what Buys was addressing when he assured readers that the MWU would not become multiracial. At the same time, Buys' approach may be read as fitting his own plans for the organisation. After all, he had himself joined the MWU in 1991 to 'develop the super white union ideal'.[40] Writing in the *MWU-News*, Buys concluded that 'the MWU's new constitution means that we are standing by our principles, [and] preserving our character while complying with the legislation. We stand by our current policy of being an interests-based union and are not interested in becoming a union that's only interested in expanding its numbers.'[41] Like long-time MWU members, Buys had no interest in deracialising the union – yet the reformulation of its membership terms did create the opportunity to expand beyond blue-collar job brackets and to reformulate the organisational identity in cultural rather than class terms. This was reflected, many years later, in Hermann's statement during an interview that Solidarity's blue-collar and professional members were in fact united because 'they are all in the same dilemma, and at the moment, that is that there is no hope for us in the political environment, and that the government is actually hostile, or perhaps rather apathetic, towards Afrikaners.'[42] Buys concurred: the Solidarity member was 'under threat because he is white, not because he is a worker'.[43] Thus, while the contemporary leadership vilified the old MWU and its members in order to legitimate their own authority and agenda, it was simultaneously vital that they engage in self-contradiction, downplaying class difference and claiming ethnic unity in order to utilise the union as a vehicle for promoting racial and ethnic interests.

A contradictory founding myth: appropriating working-class struggle

Using Solidarity with its specific working-class history and membership as a vehicle for advancing declassed Afrikaner interests therefore

---

[39] Flip Buys, interviewed 25 October 2011, Kloofsig.
[40] 'Eskom-man word deel van MWU-span', *The Mineworker*, April 1991, p. 4.
[41] Buys, 'Die veranderinge van die MWU se Grondwet'.
[42] Dirk Hermann, interviewed 17 October 2011, Kloofsig.
[43] Flip Buys, interviewed 25 October 2011, Kloofsig.

presented the Movement's executives with both opportunities and challenges. Although managing the resulting contradictions and tensions saw Hermann and Buys resort to awkward discursive contortions, the leadership was clearly willing to tolerate this because of the advantages that their appropriation of an originally working-class organisation offered.

That these advantages reached beyond the discursive labour performed in relation to the leadership's classist sub-narrative was demonstrated in the Movement's employment of the 1922 Rand Revolt. At the union's headquarters, the first-floor landing leading to the executive wing was prominently occupied by a photo exhibition on the strike. Visitors were greeted by images of early twentieth-century Johannesburg, its streets filled with masses of protesting workers, mounted troops struggling to secure order, burnt-out buildings, and armed civilians. In the bottom corner of one photograph, the banner reading 'Workers of the world unite and fight for a white South Africa' was just visible. To be sure, Chapter 4 showed that the MWU under Arrie Paulus and Peet Ungerer attached great importance to the events of 1922. During their leadership and in the context of the struggles they articulated, 1922 remained an important orientation point. But, in 2011, it was surprising to encounter images of working-class struggle so prominently displayed in the headquarters of an organisation projecting itself as focused primarily on cultural and civil society issues. Indeed, I perceived a strange dissonance between the grainy black-and-white photographs of striking wage workers and the smart corporate setting in which they were exhibited. Like Buys' and Hermann's classist sub-narrative, therefore, the apparent commemoration of 1922 presented a further institutional contradiction: an organisation that self-identified in ethno-cultural and Western terms choosing to commemorate a working-class, communist-inspired strike, and a Movement with aspirations to a high public profile and habitual claims to the moral high ground highlighting an event involving what Jeremy Krikler termed 'racial killing'.[44]

During the *Solidariteitkunde* seminar, the leadership's contemporary use of the strike – and its management of these contradictions – became clear. As Chapter 5 showed, the events of 1922 were embedded within the leadership's framing of the MWU's history as a civil society organisation committed to protecting the interests of socially marginalised and disadvantaged Afrikaners. Through vague references to the loss of the Boer republics, 1922 was portrayed as a politically motivated uprising of a disempowered people against a hostile government, rather than a strike

[44] Krikler, *The Rand Revolt.*

by aggrieved workers. Hermann's narration made no mention of the strike's actual catalyst: namely, efforts by the Chamber of Mines to undermine the practice of race-based job reservation. Nor was there any acknowledgement of the cultural and ideological heterogeneity of the strikers. Rather, Hermann portrayed the strike as a 'blow for Afrikaners' during which '254 of our members were killed'. Moreover, he connected the violent suppression of the strike with the election of the labour-friendly Pact government in 1924, thus presenting it as a political event in which the Afrikaner volk lost the battle but won the war. The events of 1922 were therefore represented as a moment of political defiance, their racial, structural, and anti-capitalist dimensions obscured. Clearly, portraying the strike as an incidence of public, anti-government protest resonated powerfully with the Solidarity Movement's representation of Afrikaners, South Africa, and its own role in the post-apartheid present. The tropes of victimhood and suppression offered a convenient parallel to the 'politically and economically hostile environment' Afrikaners had purportedly been facing since 1994, while the depiction of the strikers as a homogeneous volk challenging and eventually triumphing over its political adversaries held powerful galvanising appeal in the present.

This representation made the 1922 strike – what seemed to be an irrelevant and out-of-place historical event in 2011 – an ideal founding myth for the Movement. As we have seen, the Movement's executives were aware of the MWU's historical support for the racist policies of the National Party, the union's defence of the retention of race-based legislation when the NP started to move towards reform, and its endorsement of conservative and reactionary political movements on the eve of South Africa's transition to majority rule. For this reason, as Chapter 5 showed, Hermann and Buys glossed over, even misrepresented, this part of their organisation's past – apparently, as Hermann claimed, in an effort to demonstrate that apartheid was not 'the sum total of the pre-history of the Afrikaner ... as though our history is 100 per cent evil'.[45] The 1922 strike offered Solidarity a pre-1948 founding myth untainted by an association with apartheid. This meant that it could legitimately be commemorated without fear of accusations that the organisation was harking back to apartheid and a racist, Afrikaner nationalist regime.

Of course, the events of 1922 were hardly free from racist animosity and violence. But, in South Africa, the strike was a relatively unknown historical event. It was never associated with the nationalist

---

[45] Dirk Hermann, interviewed 17 October 2011, Kloofsig.

memorialisation practised by the apartheid state nor included in Christian Nationalist history curricula, perhaps precisely because of the socialist elements involved in the uprising and the intra-white tensions it lay bare. In 2011, therefore, it was unlikely that the average South African was even aware of what had transpired in 1922. If anyone was likely to be familiar with the Rand Revolt, it would have been the traditional mineworking members of the MWU for whom the strike had long carried positive connotations as an example of working-class mobilisation and power. During *Solidariteitkunde*, it was clear that none of the participants were familiar with the strike, its context, or its aftermath. This was demonstrated in the lack of response to a parenthetical remark by Hermann during the seminar. Having just recounted the events of 1922, Hermann paused the historical narrative for a moment, drawing his audience's attention back to the present and the photo exhibition down the hall. He encouraged his listeners to have a look at the exhibition during the coffee break:

You'll notice a photo ... [of] some people holding a banner. It's a bit unclear [on the photo] what the banner says. Now, interestingly the 1922 strike was jointly driven by the Mineworkers' Union and the South African Communist Party ... And the slogan of the SACP – try to get the picture, right, Blade Nzimande is currently general secretary, Gwede Mantashe is chairman, now you've got the picture of who the communists are. Now, their banner at that strike read 'Workers of the world unite for a white South Africa'. The SACP.[46]

Hermann paused for a moment, letting his words sink in. The participants stared at him in befuddled silence, waiting for him to explain the deeply confusing scenario he had just sketched – of black communists marching for a white South Africa, trying to square this with Hermann's earlier racialised portrayal of socialist and Christian trade unions. 'Why is it important to understand this?' Hermann finally offered. 'Because [it shows that] one must never judge history outside the context of its time, because if you attempt to explain history from today's perspective, you wouldn't be able to understand it at all.' At that, Hermann plunged back into the historical narrative, now picking up in the 1930s, still leaving the participants to work out their own explanations. In my eyes, this incident was a vivid portrayal of how ignorance about the past could be exploited to serve contemporary agendas, with Hermann's platitude acting as a blanket exoneration of any dubious past action on the organisation's part. The 1922 strike thus offered Solidarity's leadership an event in their organisation's past which, due to its relative obscurity, could be (re)

---

[46] *Solidariteitkunde*, 13 September 2011.

inscribed to serve the interests of the leadership in the present. When I questioned Hermann on the Movement's commemoration of 1922 almost a century later, his answer was highly revealing of the advantages that the contemporary leadership's appropriation of an originally working-class organisation offered in the present:

> Look, we want people to have a historical consciousness about Solidarity. We had a choice: we could also have decided to break with the MWU, [to] found a new institution ... breaking with this historical baggage, all this bothersome history and positioning of the old MWU. But we intentionally decided to keep the historical link ... And with 1922 as probably the central moment to commemorate, one places the entire Solidarity in a historical context which shows that we've come a long way and been around for a long time, we have survived everything ... we've been doing it for a hundred years, so the expectation is probably that we'll be able to do it for another century.[47]

Thus, the MWU's century-long history – reinscribed in declassed terms – could be utilised to lend gravitas and legitimacy to the Solidarity Movement in the present. The manner in which the leadership deployed the events of 1922 demonstrated the tensions that had to be overcome and the realities that needed to be obscured in order to successfully appropriate the working-class past in this way. After all, commemorating a strike which involved strong socialist and communist elements as its founding myth did not sit comfortably with Solidarity's ideological position. The union's constitution clearly outlined that it 'promotes an economic system of free enterprise',[48] and during *Solidariteitkunde*, Hermann had vilified 'the socialist tradition of trade unionism' he associated with COSATU and the SACP. In fact, striking itself was portrayed as distasteful to the organisation and those it represented. Buys told me that 'our members' as Afrikaners 'do not believe in striking; [they believe] a person works – your Calvinist work ethic, you know. They don't like striking.'[49] Eschewing class divisions in favour of cultural solidarity, he sought to illustrate this conviction:

> The [Solidarity member] feels closer to his manager, who has the same culture as he does – the guy [member] understands the cultural values, or the free-market system which forms part of his value system, he understands that. He [the member] would tell the COSATU guy next to him, who wants to strike, 'No, we shouldn't harm the company.'[50]

---

[47] Dirk Hermann, interviewed 17 October 2011, Kloofsig.
[48] Solidarity constitution as approved by the National Council on 26 March 2009, courtesy of Hennie de Wet (10 August 2011), p. 3.
[49] Flip Buys, interviewed 19 September 2011, Kloofsig.
[50] Flip Buys, interviewed 19 September 2011, Kloofsig.

Buys' statement stood in sharp contrast to the anti-employer and anti-capitalist sentiments identified in *The Mineworker* under Arrie Paulus's leadership. Under Buys' leadership, Solidarity did in fact occasionally engage in strike action, but the leadership was at pains to emphasise that industrial action was a last resort and was conducted in an orderly manner with the least possible disruption to the South African public. In *Solidarity* magazine, Buys stated categorically that 'Solidarity does not favour strikes and less than 1% of our negotiations result in industrial action'. He explained:

> [W]e regard [industrial action] as the very last resort when no other options remain. We reject strikes that are accompanied by violence or misconduct. Strikers who overturn rubbish bins achieve nothing except to bedevil their own cause. Strikes are the final economic 'weapon' available to trade unions to register their objections to management decisions … There are instances, therefore, when soft words and negotiations fail and where our members feel that they have no other choice than a form of industrial action, like a short and legal strike.[51]

Buys seemed convinced that Solidarity members were inherently opposed to strike action and needed persuading that this was occasionally justified. Moreover, he was at pains to differentiate Solidarity's actions from the menacing mob-like behaviour which, as Chapter 5 showed, the Movement ascribed to black workers and COSATU unions. These representations allowed Solidarity to utilise labour power in the interests of its members and simultaneously claim the moral high ground in the eyes of the public. Interestingly, Buys did not invoke the 1922 strike – the organisation's founding myth – as an example of the necessity of industrial action, confirming that 1922 was principally deployed as a political event that fit the Movement's anti-socialist and anti-government orientation.

Conclusion

In 1997, the MWU's management passed from the blue-collar control in which it had been rooted for almost a century to the stewardship of an academically trained middle-class executive. As Chapter 4 showed, this was a voluntary move: the old guard of men such as Krappie Cronje, Jan Deacon, and Fred Bond unanimously elected Flip Buys – albeit the only applicant for the job[52] – to take over the reins from Peet Ungerer. In terms of white workers' response to the dismantling of the racial state

---

[51] F. Buys, 'Why do we strike?', *Solidarity* 5 (2005), pp. 24–5.
[52] Visser, *Van MWU tot Solidariteit*, p. 311.

throughout the long transition, the establishment of majority rule seemed to have impelled these men to place the future of their organisation, and of themselves, in the hands of a non-miner for the first time. It is doubtful that they would have foreseen how their organisation would be transformed as a result of this move. By 2011, the MWU had become the Solidarity Movement, a broad-based civil society organisation of which trade union activity was just one component, of declining importance. Most importantly, Solidarity now mobilised around a declassed agenda of Afrikaner, minority interests. As Chapter 5 showed, the Movement's public framing effaced much of the working-class character of its past in favour of a historical and ideological narrative emphasising Afrikaner unity and the politics of culture and race. Hence Buys' claim, during interviews, that the precarity of Solidarity's members was due to their racial and ethnic identity, not their class position.

Yet this chapter has exposed the profoundly classist attitudes, stereotypes, and judgement harboured by the very same men who claimed that 'class has never really been an Afrikaner thing'. The distinctions Buys and Hermann drew between themselves and their predecessors in terms of education, respectability, and morality attest to the actuality of deep class-based prejudice among the Movement's most senior leadership, despite their public claims to the contrary. Indeed, the apparent self-evidence with which these men articulated such classed distinctions during interviews, their easy intelligibility to Solidarity employees during *Solidariteitkunde*, and the manner in which anecdotes around the MWU's ostensibly class-based conservatism and backwardness were effortlessly assimilated and repeated by other recent appointees in the organisation demonstrate the broader currency of these views within this section of society.

Beyond the persistence of strong class-based prejudice within Solidarity and broader white society, these findings reveal the discursive labour, tensions, and opportunities resulting from the process of appropriating a working-class organisation as the vehicle for a declassed, ethnicity-based agenda. This demanded careful management. While Buys' and Hermann's sub-narrative vilifying the MWU's blue-collar character lent legitimacy to the leadership and its agenda for the organisation in the present, it also necessitated various instances of strategic contradiction so as not to alienate Solidarity's substantial blue-collar membership. Despite presenting itself as an organisation with a predominantly cultural rather than class identity, these working-class roots remained instrumental to Solidarity, and were actively utilised by its leadership, as the example of the reformulation and commemoration of the 1922 Rand Revolt demonstrated.

While incorporated into the Movement, white workers' class-specific voices no longer sounded explicitly in their organisation. Despite its 'reinvention' and the reformulation of their concerns in cultural terms, this in no way signalled a resolution of the precarious position that they had been seeking to insulate since the time of the Wiehahn reforms. The final chapter returns to their voices.

7 'Guys like us are left to our own mercy'
Counternarratives, ambivalence, and the pressures of racial gatekeeping among Solidarity's blue-collar members

Introduction

Over the course of September and October 2011, I interviewed a number of trade union veterans who had joined the MWU during the heady days of Arrie Paulus, the Wiehahn reforms, and the MWU's 'super white union' ideal. As technical or production workers in the mining, metal, and electrical industries across South Africa, many had entered work in the 1970s under the race-based labour regime of the 1956 Industrial Conciliation Act. All had been confronted with the rise of the black labour movement on the shop floors and in the mineshafts, and lived and toiled through the dismantling of race-based industrial citizenship long before the political transition touched other sections of white society. In the course – and in the face – of these developments, these men had become shop stewards and later full-time union representatives. While processes of privatisation and deindustrialisation in the 1980s and 1990s hit large swathes of the industrial white working class with redundancy and unemployment,[1] these men managed to hold on to their jobs and remain active in trade unionism, with some rising through the ranks to become appointed trade union employees in the late 1990s and 2000s. Decades after first joining the MWU, their political reality and organisation now radically changed, they remained intimately involved in their specific industries, working closely with union members in the workplace.

These men spent many hours telling me about their workplaces, their union, and the changes sweeping South Africa over the course of their working lives. These conversations took place in 2011, in the first years of Jacob Zuma's presidency. Internationally, the fallout from the 2008 financial crisis was starting to come into focus and debates around precarity were gaining ground with analysts commenting on widening inequality and contemplating its possible political ramifications. There

---

[1] Sharp, 'Market, race and nation', pp. 82–105.

was growing disquiet, but no one could yet imagine the dramatic developments of 2016, when Brexit and Trumpism would come to encapsulate the rise of anti-globalisation, anti-multiculturalism, and right-wing populism now associated with the 2010s. In Europe and the USA, this would see the spotlight of popular and scholarly attention refocus on the white working class with new interest and urgency. Scholarship appearing in the midst of these developments – often based, like my own work, on research started before white workers became 'the explanation for everything' – thematised the feelings of resentment, humiliation, and loss fermenting among white working-class communities variously viewed as 'the left behind' by sympathisers and 'a basket of deplorables' by critics.[2]

Back in South Africa, the late apartheid past rather than the precarious present was foremost in my mind as I listened to the stories of Solidarity's trade union representatives. In hindsight, it is clear that there are remarkable touchpoints between the sentiments they articulated and, for instance, the resentment expressed by Tea Party supporters in Louisiana's petrochemical belt, or the distress caused by perceptions of a loss of national identity and social values among the inhabitants of Lyon's impoverished eighth *arrondissement*.[3] The loss of past certainties, perceptions of social decline and community breakdown, anxiety about the future and the family, wounded masculinity, and defensive racism echo across these very different contexts. Certainly, it is interesting to consider how these expressions and experiences may be connected, and what they reveal about the current historical juncture. I will return to this in the Conclusion. Here, however, I do not wish to overstate the connections between these experiences – not least because the international literature often proceeded from very different analytical questions to my own, with most seeking to explain the shift to the right and the attraction of nationalist populism by 'traveling to the heart of the right', as Arlie Hochschild put it. While the men quoted in this chapter clearly all supported the Solidarity Movement, their narratives defy simple classification as 'conservative' or 'Afrikaner nationalist', and I do not believe that a sincere and critical effort to understand how they experienced the dismantling of the racial state and have sought to negotiate the transition to majority rule necessitates the deployment of such labels. This is evident from their own testimonies, which reveal nostalgia, deeply felt ambivalences and anxieties not easily captured by clear-cut populist

---

[2] See Introduction.
[3] See Hochschild, *Strangers in their Own Land*; Open Society Foundations, *Europe's White Working Class Communities*.

catchphrases of 'us and them' or 'then and now'. As this chapter will show, it is precisely the blue-collar subjectivities and workplace experiences of these men that produced positionalities and experiences resisting simple explanation.

During individual as well as group-based interviews, I invited my interlocutors to approach my questions through their individual narratives. My interest in their personal experiences and how they made sense of these was met with sincerity and a willingness to engage with what were often uncomfortable, controversial, or emotive issues. At the same time, I was profoundly aware that information was being entrusted to me on account of the similarities my interviewees perceived between us. As with the unspoken assumption of a shared Afrikaner perspective that had governed the atmosphere of the *Solidariteitkunde* seminar and facilitated my smooth integration at the Movement's headquarters, my interviewees presumed that I would attach the same meanings and importance to our 'shared' racial and cultural identities. Such assumptions shaped the interviews as well as the ethnography informing this chapter. I have discussed my acceptance as an 'insider' in the Introduction, outlining how this offered revealing insights into categories, attitudes, and ideologies within the organisation, and the views that it assumed were universal to 'Afrikaners'. Yet, interestingly, there were moments during my conversations with trade union representatives when this rapport and ease of communication broke down. This occurred when the men became aware of or sought to express and explain something about the *differences* they perceived between themselves and me – differences consistently pertaining to class-based experiences, identity, and perspectives. When class interfered, it became clear that our 'shared' Afrikaner perspective took us only so far.

The specificity of my interviewees' blue-collar perspectives and experiences as working-class whites is at the centre of the analysis offered here.[4] Previous chapters set out the Solidarity Movement's official historical and ideological framing, while also tracing how, within the organisation and in private conversations, the Movement's leadership contradicted the official narrative in ways that revealed a deeply rooted classism. Throughout, I have shown how Solidarity's working-class past was reformulated in declassed, race- and ethnicity-centred terms in order to suit the Movement's contemporary agenda.

---

[4] On black workers' attitudes, anxieties, and subjectivities in the post-apartheid period, see S. Buhlungu (ed.), *Trade Unions and Democracy: Cosatu workers' political attitudes in South Africa* (Cape Town: HSRC Press, 2006); Barchiesi, *Precarious Liberation*.

This chapter functions in counterpoint to these findings. By foregrounding working-class voices, it reveals a further set of contradictions circulating within Solidarity. To be sure, my discussions with workers also revealed similarities to the institutional interpretative framework and instances of its acceptance. Yet their workplace experiences since the late 1970s had engendered alternative ways of meaning-making and they often expressed understandings that contradicted the interpretations propagated by the Movement's leadership.

The oral evidence presented here reveals the experience and impact of the long transition and the dismantling of the racial state on white working-class lives in workers' own words. The first section follows the men's narration of joining Arrie Paulus's MWU and of the changes wrought in their workplaces and union by the Wiehahn reforms. Their testimony demonstrates the persistence of working-class identification within this section of the white population, a reality that sits uneasily with Solidarity's efforts to declass its history and cast Afrikaners as a homogeneous volk. Section two shifts from the men's reminiscences to their anxieties in the present. Speaking about the post-apartheid workplace and society, they mourn the loss of past certainties and express a deep sense of disquiet in the face of developments following the dismantling of the racial state. Yet in contrast to the Movement's institutional framing, their concerns do not map onto simplistic tropes of a marginalised minority and a hostile majority. Rather, speaking from their workplace experiences and blue-collar communities, they express a profound ambivalence regarding whiteness itself. The final section follows my interviewees' experience of the pressures which the Movement places on its trade union representatives on the ground. Even as Solidarity claims to offer an 'alternative government' for Afrikaners, this idyll demands its grassroots representatives and employees put themselves at risk in the post-apartheid workplace. I argue that, in this way, the reinvented racial state promises to take care of 'the people' but in fact renders its blue-collar representatives all the more precarious.

The good old days: blue-collar counternarratives about Solidarity's past

I opened each interview by asking my interlocutor where they started their career and when they had joined the MWU. 'I belonged to the MWU before it was even possible,' boasted Anton, a large smiling man whose sentences came in enthusiastic bursts, during one such conversation. He had worked as a craftsman in the mining industry since he entered employment in 1979. He joined the MWU during the early days of Paulus's efforts to have closed shop agreements removed in order to expand the union's membership beyond mining production workers. The union to which Anton initially belonged was one of the first to deracialise its membership criteria.[5]

> Before I was with the old Metal and Boilermakers' Union ... Those days they still said you can't [join the MWU], you had to belong to your union, in the 1980s. Then things opened up to join the union of your choice, and I immediately moved to the MWU, and that same year I was elected representative ... I think the MWU was a kind of passion; I grew up with ... the union at home through my dad. He was a miner, a shift boss, with the MWU.[6]

In a group interview, I spoke with Jake, Werner, Bertus, and Neels – like Anton, all four were old hands from the mining industry. The men had been working as miners or craftsmen on the coalfields of Mpumalanga since the first Sasol collieries were established there in 1978. 'Those days the MWU was already very strong in all the gold mines across South Africa,' explained Bertus, a bullish man with a rough voice. In the early 1980s, in the wake of the government's acceptance of the Wiehahn recommendations, he had started recruiting in the collieries 'along with the late Fred Bond ... So people started joining, and we grew, and got a foot in the door, so the MWU got in [gained recognition].'[7] Before moving to the new eastern Transvaal collieries, Jake had been a miner on the Natal coalfields – so he, like many Sasol employees, 'came from other mines' and was 'used to trade unionism', he answered in response to my questions.[8]

Workers from other industries similarly spoke of the MWU's strength and its anti-reform stance as making it attractive as a union. Louis had worked underground as a mining electrician for ten years before moving to a job with Eskom in 1983. '[T]hat was just as the political events were starting, so things were tense. So when I started with Eskom ... I immediately started talking with people and recruiting for the MWU.' Louis remembered the MWU's growth in the context of labour reform and the desegregation of amenities: 'that was when the guys had to start showering and dressing and undressing with the others [blacks], and the guys wouldn't have it. [So] immediately [the union] had a great impact and drew very strong support. This had a ripple effect throughout Eskom, and before long MWU membership on all the [power] stations

---

[5] Visser, *Van MWU tot Solidariteit*, pp. 249–53.
[6] Anton, interviewed 28 October 2011, Kloofsig.
[7] Group interview, 14 September 2011, Kloofsig.
[8] Group interview, 14 September 2011, Kloofsig.

The good old days 269

Figure 7.1 MWU members at a protest meeting against Eskom's decision to desegregate its residential areas, 1991.
Source: *MWU-News*, July 1991

was expanding rapidly.'[9] Eddie, a fitter and turner with Eskom, joined the MWU in this context:

The change came from about 1985 ... There was lots of pressure from the ANC ... And that's how I got involved with the union and with politics, hand in hand, because blacks were getting the upper hand, so obviously the whites had to stick together ... 1985, 1986 [the MWU] didn't have recognition yet, but our membership was growing so rapidly – we were really riding the political tide because there were no other institutions looking out for whites.[10]

On the other side of the country, workers were also joining the MWU. Frans was working at Eskom's Koeberg power station outside Cape Town. 'I was a union rep for the Iron and Steel Union, but I wasn't happy with them ... Those days I was also involved in a bit of politics, with the CP. I got to know Arrie Paulus ... So that's how I heard about the MWU.'[11] Meanwhile, the MWU was also stirring in the steel industry. 'The Witbank and Vaal Triangle districts became mighty MWU outposts in the steel industry, there was an enormous surge in membership,'[12] recounted Hugo, who worked in wire manufacturing at Iscor's Vanderbijlpark plant. Paul, a millwright at the same plant since the 1980s, explained this growth in membership:

One year, Iscor reached an agreement for a 3 per cent increase with the unions ... In Iscor there was the Iron and Steel Union, the Traders, Stokers and

[9] Louis, interviewed 18 October 2011, Kloofsig.
[10] Eddie, interviewed 18 August 2011, Kloofsig.
[11] Frans, interviewed 22 September 2011, Bellville.
[12] Hugo, interviewed 18 August 2011, Kloofsig.

Figure 7.2 Peet Ungerer and Flip Buys (front centre) with other MWU representatives after presenting Eskom officials with a petition against the company's decision to desegregate its residential areas, 1991.
Source: *MWU-News*, July 1991

Boilermakers' Union, and the Amalgamated Engineering Union. The workers weren't happy with this agreement. But unions weren't militant in those days; employers called the shots ... I went to see the local MWU organiser and said we have to get the MWU on board, because they were the most militant union at that stage – they struck and you regularly saw them in the media; Arrie Paulus was a very prominent figure.[13]

Paul rapidly recruited members for the MWU and established an MWU branch at Vanderbijlpark. Wouter, a production foreman at a Witbank steel works during the mid-1980s, similarly testified that the MWU consistently attracted members because it was seen to act when other unions did not and because it refused to open its membership to black workers following the Wiehahn reforms:

[W]e were expanding because other unions were doing nothing. Remember, if you were a [racially] mixed union, it's your [black] members who suddenly want to start using the white guys' bathroom, so your hands are tied, you've got to keep quiet. And because [the MWU] made a bit of noise and because we resisted, I would argue that we were in fact attracting members because of what we were doing for them.[14]

Recalling the MWU they joined in the late 1970s and early 1980s, the men all spoke of a strong and rapidly growing union whose resistant political stance made it attractive to white workers dissatisfied with their

---

[13] Paul, interviewed 20 October 2011, Kloofsig.
[14] Wouter, interviewed 20 September 2011, Kloofsig.

The good old days 271

Figure 7.3 Some 2,500 MWU members protest against affirmative action policies at Iscor's Vanderbijlpark works on 15 March 1995.
Source: *MWU-News*, March 1995

own unions and anxious about labour reform.[15] These recollections stood in stark contrast to the image of the MWU as a weak, failing, and offensive organisation put forward in the leadership's sub-narrative. When in an interview I asked Buys about membership growth in the MWU, he was adamant: 'None before 1991. Not at all, no, not a chance.'[16] In contrast, all the workers I interviewed had been involved in membership recruitment in the late apartheid period and clearly remembered the MWU as rapidly amassing new members throughout the 1980s and early 1990s.

Moreover, while Solidarity's leadership vilified the MWU for its apparently rough institutional culture and portrayed its conservative and racist politics as a reason for the union's decline, my interviewees often celebrated the brinkmanship and abrasiveness for which the MWU had been notorious. 'When Arrie was still around,' Bertus explained with a grin during the group interview, 'a member would call and say he hadn't received the week's pay, then Arrie would drive to the mine and walk into the mine manager's office and say "If that guy doesn't get his pay on

---

[15] Paul and Frans both described their dissatisfaction with the South African Iron, Steel and Allied Industries Union (Iron and Steel) to which they belonged. This union, which Chapter 2 introduced as a SACLA member and defender of race-based job reservation, attempted after 1994 to reinvent itself in a non-racial guise. These efforts failed and, along with three other unions, Iron and Steel was incorporated by the MWU in 2001, when it was re-established as MWU/Solidarity. See Chapter 4; Visser, 'From MWU to Solidarity', p. 33.
[16] Flip Buys, interviewed 19 September 2011, Kloofsig.

Friday, I'll shut this mine down."' 'And could he do it?' I asked. 'Oh yes, he could!' the men roared back. Bertus continued: 'What I mean is, with negotiations, that was the way of doing things, that's how times have changed. Back then it was just the thing, that's what they did back when you could still give it to them straight; today you can't do that any more ...'[17] His voice was lost in a chorus of agreement, laughter about the good old days, and remarks about how things had changed. In another interview, Gert also reminisced about the old MWU's tactics:

[A]t that stage, if a manager did a bit too much talking, then you turned over his desk on him. That was the MWU of those days, those were hard miners who didn't listen twice before tackling you ... [T]hese guys turned over tables and swore your socks off ... Remember, those days management called the shots – it wasn't like today where you can sit down with him and talk about a matter and find a solution that's beneficial for both parties; he would tell you in straight Afrikaans to get lost. That's precisely where [the MWU's tactics] originated from, because you couldn't get through otherwise.[18]

This roughhouse behaviour was not only reserved for employers, but also characterised the internal workings of the MWU under Paulus and Peet Ungerer. Schalk relished the memory of working alongside Ungerer:

I was privileged to be elected to the Head Council ... The first five years were with Mr Peet Ungerer. He was a rogue! Can I put it to you nicely? He was a bastard! ... Everything was done absolutely 100 per cent his way; people lived in fear of him. He would pummel them; he would let them have it! That man had a memory like an elephant ... so I have eternal respect for him. But that was a tough era, boy! That was a wild era.[19]

My blue-collar interviewees consistently offered this portrayal of the MWU – a tough world with tough men, a rough union culture in which one had to hold one's own. This was not dissimilar to the picture painted by Solidarity's management, in distinctly negative terms, of the old MWU before Buys and other more respectable middle-class men assumed leadership. But in contrast to the current executive, the workers spoke about the swearing, the hard-handed negotiation tactics, and the political intractability with obvious glee and nostalgia. They also continued to identify with this hard union culture, communicating a distinct sense of continuity between the past and the present. During the group interview, Jake, grinning, made a comment that resonated with Schalk's: 'Remember, for a guy to be a union representative, it's usually a

---

[17] Group interview, 14 September 2011, Kloofsig.
[18] Gert, interviewed 27 October 2011, Kloofsig.
[19] Schalk, interviewed 28 October 2011, Kloofsig.

guy – and now let me speak a bit of mine language – it's a hard-ass guy, it's no lambkin. Now, put a raft of hard-ass guys together and see what you get. There'll be a fight, for sure, there'll be a fight.'[20] He said this not in reference to the MWU of old but to Solidarity's current Head Council. Indeed, Jake and all of the men at the group interview were currently serving or had previously served as elected representatives on the council. Not only was Jake describing himself and his colleagues using characteristics typically attributed to the tough breed of unionists personified by Paulus and Ungerer, but he chose to use 'mine language' to do so. Such stories of continuity between the MWU and present-day Solidarity contradicted the leadership's sub-narrative that sought to distance the present organisation from its past. It also sat uneasily with the Movement's institutional framing. Although the official historical narrative extolled continuity between the MWU of old and the Movement in the present, it did so in declassed terms, portraying Afrikaners as a virtuous and homogeneous volk. This left little room for the thuggish tactics and coarse language that the men celebrated and with which they identified positively.

In fact, it was clear that these men consciously self-identified in class terms. The reason Jake signalled his use of 'mine language' at this point in the interview was because, a moment before, the men had been talking about how Solidarity's membership had been diversifying in recent years. They pointed specifically to the many professionals who were joining the union as individual members. As in Buys' and Hermann's personal narratives of joining the union, education and respectability functioned as markers distinguishing Solidarity's traditional from its new members. Werner spelled it out: 'A professor says, "Be quiet"; a miner says, "Shut your fucking trap."' Despite many allusions, this was the first profanity uttered during the interview and all four men erupted with laughter. Jake seized the opportunity. Turning to me, he pointed out: 'Already a few times today, [Neels] here has had to swallow his words in your company and look for a different word, because he struggles to speak this high-flown language.' 'It's true, really!' Neels confirmed, red-faced. It was clear how these men positioned themselves – and me – in class terms. They continued to chuckle under their breath, evidently relieved, and from that point in the interview they did not mince words. In no sense did they experience the continuity between themselves and their MWU predecessors or their working-class identification as shameful or disreputable. Rather, in contrast to the leadership's pejorative portrayals of

---

[20] Group interview, 14 September 2011, Kloofsig.

MWU 'culture', my blue-collar interviewees relished their identification as 'hard men'.

This positive identification also extended to the union's political stance. As mentioned, my interviewees all joined the MWU during or in the immediate aftermath of the Wiehahn Commission's investigation into labour legislation. Their statements indicate that they regarded subsequent labour reforms as essentially political in nature and thus as having far-reaching implications beyond the immediate labour sphere. This understanding corresponds with the arguments against labour reform articulated by union representatives and SACLA president Attie Nieuwoudt before the Wiehahn Commission. Thus, during interviews, trade union activities and political resistance often flowed together in the workers' narratives. Wouter explained excitedly that the MWU 'was an AWB organisation, a hot-headed organisation. You went and harassed mine managers because they were Jews and you've got to give them a thrashing and that kind of thing ... [W]e were militant ... Ungerer drilled us to resist, you must fight these people, you must oppose them, you should agree with nothing, it's about the whites.' Indeed, the MWU's role as a resistant organisation was also *their* role. Wouter frankly disclosed his enthusiasm for the AWB, spurred by the paramilitary extremists' connections with the MWU. Speaking about his own generation, he explained:

[Y]ou finish school, you join the army, they send you off to [military service on] the border and there you're taught that it's his life or yours. Then you get back from the army and you pass these AWB blokes ... [A]t one stage I thought, this is great, the AWB feels just like the border forces. Later when I joined the union, I found out that the union talks to Terre'Blanche, Terre'Blanche holds meetings with the union, you think, man, this is cool.[21]

Chapter 4 noted that, in 1993, the MWU and AWB were both among the founding members of the right-wing Afrikaner Volksfront. In his biography of the union, Visser addresses the nature of the MWU's relationship with the white supremacist and antisemitic AWB. Although the paramilitary organisation regularly made overtures towards the MWU leadership, both Paulus and Ungerer would not associate with the AWB, refusing to appear in public alongside its leader Eugene Terre'Blanche. Thus, no official ties existed between the organisations – yet a number of MWU members were involved in the AWB in their individual capacity, and the AWB claimed to have over 3,000 mineworkers among its members in the early 1990s. Visser notes that MWU

---

[21] Wouter, interviewed 20 September 2011, Kloofsig.

The good old days 275

Figure 7.4 MWU members protest at Telkom's head office about wage demands, 1995. Note the banners: 'White workers unite'.
Source: *MWU-News*, May 1995

organiser Krappie Cronje was involved in the AWB's June 1993 siege of the World Trade Centre outside Johannesburg, where the multiparty negotiations for South Africa's transition to democracy were taking place.[22] In a series of dramatic events, an armoured car was used to break through the building's glass doors, upon which the AWB and its supporters proceeded to occupy the main conference hall and harass delegates. After tense negotiations, the protestors eventually left the premises peacefully.[23]

At least four of the men I interviewed either disclosed directly or hinted at their involvement with the AWB. One interviewee confessed his involvement in the World Trade Centre siege and named a number of MWU colleagues alongside whom he had participated. Others offered stories of resistance to change that centred on the MWU. Eddie related one occasion when the union transported its Eskom workers to a rally at the electricity provider's headquarters with the intention of bringing all power stations to a halt.[24] Such actions were intended to frustrate democratising change within the company and act as a warning to government not to go through with political transformation. Other interviewees

[22] Visser, *Van MWU tot Solidariteit*, pp. 299–301.
[23] Heunis, *The Inner Circle*, pp. 180–9.
[24] Eddie, interviewed 18 August 2011, Kloofsig.

mentioned their involvement in more low-key incidents of resistance – 'small incidents that never even made the headlines' – and in efforts to intimidate blacks in the workplace or in neighbourhoods that were undergoing desegregation.[25] During one interview, Hugo recalled how, in 1993, he had 'pulled out 98 per cent of MWU members' in his workplace to participate in a rally in Potchefstroom, where they went to 'sit in the stands at political debates and make some noise'. He could not recall the details of the event and advised me to 'speak to Flip', who was 'more involved in the [event's] organisation than I was'.[26] Solidarity's current leadership was therefore not seen as separate from such initiatives, but regarded as part and parcel of the union's history of resistance. This again demonstrated the continuities the men perceived between the past and present of their organisation. Indeed, in many interviews there was an obvious slippage of terms as the men used 'MWU' and 'Solidarity' interchangeably across the decades they were talking about.[27] With memories and experience rooted in a working-class environment, they perceived no clear break between the MWU of old and the kind of men it cultivated, and Solidarity and the men they were. This, alongside the workers' positive evaluation of the old MWU and its 'hard mining culture', stood in clear contrast to the leadership's classist sub-narrative and its emphasis on discontinuity. And, while the workers' narratives in part supported the official institutional framing by stressing links between the MWU and the Solidarity Movement in terms of its resistance, these tactics and understandings hardly matched the organisation's self-representation in the present.

This is not to say that the men did not perceive any changes relating to their union throughout the decades of their membership. But here, too, their narratives ran counter to the Movement's institutional framing, which emphasised the political turning point of 1994, and to the leadership's anecdotes, which highlighted the shift from blue-collar to respectable, university-educated leadership in 1997. In contrast, the trade union veterans situated the most significant shifts in the late apartheid period. They identified the granting of industrial citizenship to black workers and the recognition of African trade unions as a major turning point. 'Lots of things changed since the early 1980s until the mid-1990s,' Hugo told me. 'The Wiehahn Commission gave [black workers] status and they started to organise. By [1985], our country was plagued by severe unrest, where

---

[25] For instance Eddie, interviewed 18 August 2011, Kloofsig.
[26] Hugo, interviewed 18 August 2011, Kloofsig.
[27] See, for instance, interviews with Frans, 22 September 2011, Bellville; Louis, 18 October 2011, Kloofsig; Gert, 27 October 2011, Kloofsig.

Figure 7.5 MWU members protest at the Duvha power station near Witbank against Eskom's decision to phase out housing, transport, water, and electricity allowances for employees in 1995.
Source: *MWU-News*, February 1995

they wanted to take up those rights by force, and [the MWU] just dug in our heels.'[28] Statements such as these testified to the close association these workers saw between political and workplace developments during the reform period. Paul offered a similar view from his position in the steel industry: 'The [Wiehahn] report said that all unions should be recognised, including black ones ... That was the first big transformation in Iscor ... and the whole bargaining process changed.' The government's labour reform programme required that employers and established unions negotiate the practicalities of the dismantling of race-based privilege in the workplace. 'We were all part of the negotiations for the new policies that were implemented, before 1994 – this whole transformation thing that we negotiated came about when job reservation was scrapped following the Wiehahn report,' Paul continued matter-of-factly.[29] Other men were not able to talk about the dismantling of the apartheid labour regime and the entrance of black workers to the bargaining arena quite so dispassionately.[30] Eddie became quite agitated as he told me about the repercussions of democratising change in his workplace: 'In Eskom, people already saw before 1994 what it would be like under a black government, people saw and felt it in the workplace. For instance, affirmative action was already being applied in Eskom

---

[28] Hugo, interviewed 18 August 2011, Kloofsig.
[29] Paul, interviewed 20 October 2011, Kloofsig.
[30] In addition to Eddie, quoted next, see also Anton, interviewed 28 October 2011, Kloofsig.

before it had even become policy, so many whites out and blacks in ... [P]eople started to experience it.'[31]

Clearly, the post-Wiehahn environment was remembered as one of dramatic and highly disruptive changes. But some men also identified positive consequences flowing from labour reform. Gert recalled: '[O]f their own accord [employers] started organising summits to improve the relationship between unions and management – that was still in the old Iscor days.' He recounted how representatives from white and African unions together engaged in talks with management. '[T]hose were still apartheid years,' remembered Gert, 'but the line, the trade unionism line we could talk about; white and black unions did agree on some things. And even then, we would support each other, against management.'[32] Wouter went further, claiming that in the post-Wiehahn workplace '[the African worker] wasn't my enemy; the employer was our enemy, not the black unions or other unions'.[33] According to Louis, pressures from African workers eventually brought greater power and recognition for all unions: 'before then unions didn't really play a role ... There were no COSATU unions with their demands and strikes and stuff that rocked the boat. Now things have changed.'[34] Frans similarly testified that the labour dispensation improved when 'unions started getting more of a say, when [employers] had to start negotiating with us as the law stipulated, when the structures were formed'. This facilitated 'loads of improvement, because you had a say, you knew what was going on. In the past you only knew what your manager told you, nothing more ... This [change] was in the early 1990s ... All the structures started to come together nicely, we had representation.'[35] These recollections stood in stark contrast to the chronology and ideological framing put forward by the institutional narrative, which sought to present any changes relating to democratisation as uniformly detrimental for Solidarity's members. This reveals how the union representatives' recollections presented a counternarrative in a further sense: while the Movement's official framing and the leadership's classist sub-narratives seemed to express very clear-cut – albeit sometimes contradictory or misleading – understandings of the past and the present, the union representatives displayed a much greater degree of ambivalence across a range of issues. In the case of the post-Wiehahn era discussed here, this period had engendered deep

---

[31] Eddie, interviewed 18 August 2011, Kloofsig.
[32] Gert, interviewed 27 October 2011, Kloofsig.
[33] Wouter, interviewed 20 September 2011, Kloofsig.
[34] Louis, interviewed 18 October 2011, Kloofsig.
[35] Frans, interviewed 22 September 2011, Bellville.

anxieties and resistance in the face of the deracialisation of industrial citizenship and the resulting shift in the status of white workers. At the same time, the men acknowledged and expressed their appreciation for the changes wrought by African unions' participation in industrial conciliation. Moreover, the men privileged their structural position when expressing solidarity with black unions vis-à-vis employers. This bore much closer resemblance to the anti-employer sentiments expressed by Paulus than to Buys' contemporary claim that Solidarity members 'feel closer to the manager'.[36]

Workplace experiences during this period were also remembered as stimulating positive shifts in my interviewees' personal attitudes. Hugo, for instance, related the unquestioned racism installed in him during his childhood in the 1950s. 'I grew up on a *plot* [smallholding], which meant we had a black family working there – the woman a servant in the house and the man milking cows and working in the garden and washing the car – a typical *baas–Klaas* relationship. They also addressed you as *baas* or *kleinbaas* – that's what South Africa was like back then.' He described how this was the only position in which he ever encountered Africans until he started work in 1975. 'Now you get to the factory and you're confronted with a different class of African ... who in some cases has had much broader political exposure than yourself, who conducts political debates, and you think, "Where's all this coming from?"' Although this experience challenged the young Hugo's prejudices and stereotypes, he related how apartheid – a context that propagated white supremacy and the importance of racial segregation – saw him hold fast to his established views. It was only when he became 'involved with the union' that a 'paradigm shift' occurred in his racist attitudes. Hugo became an MWU shop steward in 1989 and was promoted to full-time union representation in 1996. As a union representative:

you were kind of forced to share forums with other [racial] groups that you'd never done before, [then] you started gaining more insight into their right to existence. When his child dies, he's as heartbroken as I would be if my child died, whereas before, all these status levels and stuff meant it was almost unthinkable that [we] share the same emotions.[37]

Hugo's words presented a poignant illustration of the dehumanising distance created by apartheid's race-based system of inclusion and

---

[36] Flip Buys, interviewed 19 September 2011, Kloofsig.
[37] Hugo, interviewed 18 August 2011, Kloofsig. Similar narratives of shifting personal attitudes born of workplace experiences with black colleagues were told by Paul, interviewed 20 October 2011, and Eddie, interviewed 18 August 2011, both in Kloofsig.

exclusion. It was only in a democratising labour arena, when Hugo was 'forced' into contact with his black counterparts on an equal footing, that an awareness and appreciation of the humanity of the racial other could develop. By his own account, this experience is what stimulated the 'paradigm shift' in his racial attitudes. At the same time, recall Hugo's involvement with the AWB during this same period. Indeed, Hugo did relate that it was particularly as a full-time union representative from 1996 – that is, after the establishment of majority rule – that his convictions on race 'reach[ed] maturity' and 'modernise[d]'. He sought to demonstrate this change in his mindset by recounting his involvement, as union representative, in setting up new employment relations policies in the company where he worked, thus promoting employer–employee cooperation within the plant. Hugo explained how he now saw the importance of 'working together, we as whites and blacks sit in the same room, pursuing common goals. [That is when] you realise this [African] guy has the same rights as you do; he's just a man, like you, who wants and can have his place in the sun.'[38]

The process that narratives like this one revealed did not mean that men like Hugo no longer displayed racial prejudice, either explicitly or unknowingly, or that they were eager to see racial integration take place in their union or society. However, it did demonstrate how everyday experiences on the factory floor defied the simplistic characterisations about Africans inherited from working-class childhoods, or proffered by Solidarity's middle-class leadership. In his ethnography of white blue-collar lives in Pretoria West, John Sharp similarly provides evidence of the complexity of white working-class attitudes to and relations with their black compatriots, pointing to white workers' acknowledgement of black humanity, and their pragmatism in entering into mutually beneficial economic and social relationships with their black neighbours. As in the case of the union reps I interviewed, these views and strategies were products of the research subjects' class position, which placed them in close everyday interaction with blacks. This did not mean that these whites no longer displayed racial prejudice, but their working-class positionality produced complex views of and relationships with black South Africans. Sharp contrasts this with both the attitudes of many middle-class whites, who have little contact with blacks, and the established literature's simplistic portrayal of white workers as right-wing racists.[39]

Within the MWU itself, the men did identify important changes – but here, too, their emphasis differed from that of the leadership. Recall that

---

[38] Hugo, interviewed 18 August 2011, Kloofsig.   [39] Sharp, 'Market, race and nation'.

one of the positive consequences of labour reform identified by the union representatives was more effective communication with management and hence greater working-class bargaining power. Gert explained that 'management started to listen to what we were saying ... And that's where things started mellowing and relations improved.'[40] Like the 'mellowing' identified by Gert, the group of representatives I interviewed identified a shift in their union's approach to negotiations: '[Y]ou'd no longer go swear and shout ... we're now negotiating on a different level.'[41] While they connected this in part to the leadership of Flip Buys, they did not seek to delegitimise what had gone before, as in the case of the leadership's sub-narrative. Rather, they contended that the tactics of resistance and brinkmanship of Paulus and Ungerer were the 'right thing at the right time'[42] and explained that the union had now simply adapted to a new context. Schalk also identified a shift in the tenor of the MWU/Solidarity's negotiation tactics, attributing this to the diversification of the union's membership. Previously, the MWU had represented only 'the traditional blue-collar guy in his overall' who 'shaves once a week', Schalk explained, but it now included the 'nurse in her uniform, the guy wearing a tie'. He saw this shift in membership as underlying the change from 'traditional mining union-style' labour tactics to 'the new trade unionism', because 'these medical guys are much more moderate, [and] then you've got the guys with the degrees. So [the membership] has become very diverse.'[43] Not that new professional members were always welcomed. 'If you think that the prof at the LNR [Agricultural Research Council] has less problems at work than a miner, you're making a big mistake,' Kobus grumbled. 'They've got the same gripes, just on [a] higher level. And he will keep you ten times longer than a worker would, because he thinks he knows better.'[44]

Indeed, changes in union membership and structure were identified as much more significant shifts than Buys' appointment as general secretary. Hugo pointed to the reorganisation of the union in the late 1990s from a district- to industry-based organisation. He explicitly credited this shift to the initiative of his generation of union representatives, not the union's new graduate leadership. The reorganisation, he explained, put the union in a much stronger position, as union representatives could

---

[40] Gert, interviewed 27 October 2011, Kloofsig.
[41] Anton, interviewed 28 October 2011, Kloofsig.
[42] Group interview, 14 September 2011; Louis, interviewed 18 October 2011; Schalk, interviewed 18 October 2011, all in Kloofsig.
[43] Schalk, interviewed 28 October 2011, Kloofsig.
[44] Kobus, interviewed 18 August 2011, Kloofsig. Gert made a similar point; interviewed 27 October 2011, Kloofsig.

concentrate on a specific industry, thus becoming experts in the new labour legislation relating to it. This also allowed the MWU and later Solidarity to develop into a more effective counterweight to the COSATU trade unions, which in most cases were industry-specific and nationally organised. In this way, explained Hugo, the MWU/Solidarity was able to provide much more effective representation.[45] Gert, too, credited the late apartheid generation of trade union leaders and representatives with the positive changes he and his colleagues identified, and hence as laying the groundwork for the organisation's strength in the present. 'A house stays upright when its foundations are strong,' he told me solemnly. 'If the foundations are weak, it won't remain standing for long, it will collapse. And one should never overlook what these people did in this Movement.'[46]

The trade union representatives I interviewed therefore presented a number of counternarratives born of their blue-collar identities and experiences. These revealed how the Movement's institutional framing and the leadership's sub-narratives, constructed to serve certain agendas in the present, belied working-class realities and obscured the complexities of the shop floor. My interviewees articulated a nostalgic counternarrative of positive identification with the working-class culture and forceful union tactics of Arrie Paulus's MWU. They did not seek to discursively reinvent their organisation but spoke of continuities between the MWU and Solidarity. Similarly, they did not seek to recast themselves to conform to notions of middle-class respectability but celebrated their identity as 'hard men'. Indeed, they themselves embodied the continuities they identified – some had 'grown up with the union' in their families and communities, many had been members all their working lives, and several had been politicised under its auspices. While they recognised that changes had occurred within their union over the course of their membership, they did not evaluate these changes in moral terms, and pointed beyond the agency of new leaders such as Buys. For all of them, the MWU had long been their voice in the context of dramatic workplace and political change. Hence, they articulated a chronology that contradicted the Movement's official framing and the leadership's sub-narrative. Rather than the political transition of 1994 or the change in leadership when Buys was appointed in 1997, they located the most important transformation in the post-Wiehahn labour context. Reflecting on the past, these men spoke clearly of a long transition, starting in the labour arena in the late 1970s.

---

[45] Hugo, interviewed 18 August 2011, Kloofsig.
[46] Gert, interviewed 27 October 2011, Kloofsig.

'We whites are a strange bunch'   283

Figure 7.6 MWU members demand wage increases during a strike at Samancor Chrome in Krugersdorp in 1998.
Source: *MWU-News*, September 1998

'We whites are a strange bunch': racial ambivalence and working-class anxieties in the present

We have seen how the union representatives' accounts of the past often involved an ambivalence not evident in other narratives circulating within the Movement. For instance, the men identified the positive consequences of democratisation, they related instances of working-class solidarity across racial divides, and they expressed hostility towards employers rather than black workers. This contrasted sharply with the clear racialised dichotomy of white protagonists and black adversaries, and the irreconcilability of different 'trade union traditions', articulated in the Movement's official framing. Rather than absolutism, the workplace experiences of my blue-collar interviewees saw them express enthusiasm for the racist AWB even as they recognised the humanity of their fellow black trade unionists. This simultaneous upholding and contradiction of racial tropes was even more evident in stories about the present. It was most strikingly demonstrated in the group interview I conducted with Jake, Werner, Bertus, and Neels – not because their experiences differed markedly from those of the men I interviewed individually, but because the group setting facilitated a more natural conversation compared with a one-to-one interview. The fact that the four men all knew each other also meant that they were comfortable and frank in sharing their views.[47]

As the men related changes occurring in the workplace since the late 1970s, we stumbled onto some developments they found deeply disturbing – developments they connected unmistakably with the post-apartheid era. These started with the appearance of young white men in unskilled jobs: 'We're entering a new era – to think that I'd ever see little white faces sitting on tractors down in a mine. It was never like this.' Neels shook his head. The men attributed this development to a growing lack of education among whites. '[I]f you were to interview our whites at Sasol, you would see how many no longer have maths and science at matric level. It's shocking to see how many of our kids are leaving school at standard eight.'[48] They attributed this to a lack of discipline in the home, and in society at large. They swapped stories about how, when they were young, school was non-negotiable, and their parents forced them to do their homework, by candlelight if necessary. But nowadays, they said, parents have lost confidence in the future the country can offer their children, and discipline falls by the wayside. Bertus blamed a failing school system, Neels held parents personally responsible, while Jake pointed to new legislation forbidding corporal punishment, preventing parents from disciplining their children at home. Their explanations vacillated between laying responsibility at the feet of the new government and at those of parents of their own generation. 'I think [the problem lies with] the general enforcement of values in our lives today, in this country,' Neels continued animatedly. 'There are no value systems left and everything is being torn down ... Since this ANC came to power, things have changed completely – even us parents, it's as though we've thrown everything overboard.' The conversation became increasingly animated as the men discussed how 'our white boys have become the laziest little bums', how teachers are having 'more trouble with white children than with coloureds and blacks', how the youth ('White children! It's shocking!') were enrolling in university while lacking even basic reading skills, and how parents were to blame. The men were clearly uncomfortable with their negative portrayal of their white brethren, but they could not deny the social decline they perceived. The 'shock' of seeing whites,

---

[47] All subsequent quotations from group interview, 14 September 2011, Kloofsig.
[48] Standard eight corresponds to Grade 10, a level typically reached at 16 years of age, while matric corresponds to Grade 12, the qualification received upon completing secondary education and the minimum requirement to enter university. Current basic education legislation stipulates that children are compelled to attend school until the age of 15.

particularly white men, in positions that transgressed the norms of white supremacy – positions of menial labour, indolence, and illiteracy – clearly caused them great distress. This was compounded by not being able to unequivocally blame this on the advent of majority rule and the policies of the ANC government. Whites – even the men themselves, 'us parents' – were complicit in this social decline.

Perhaps inevitably, the conversation next turned to white poverty, demonstrating the men's familiarity with the fortunes of those whites who had fallen out of the formal economy and into unemployment and homelessness.[49] Neels was deeply disturbed by the growing incidence of whites living in informal settlements and shanty towns, describing their 'unbelievable circumstances' as 'shocking'. 'And there are millions of them!' he exclaimed more than once. The men attributed what they perceived as the rapid increase in white poverty to affirmative action policies and labour redundancies. But, as in the case of declining levels of education among white youth, they had mixed feelings. Speaking about whites begging at traffic intersections, Neels continued: 'It frustrates the living daylights [out of me]. This guy is my age and he *can* work, but if the system closes doors on you ...' His voice trailed off for a moment before he continued:

I don't know, I don't see myself in that kind of guy's position for ten minutes. And it's a kind of chain reaction ... [because] usually, my old man always said, the guy who is worst off – and now I'm speaking about whites specifically – always has the most children. I don't know why, perhaps he forgets ...

His words were drowned out as the other men howled with laughter, the tension briefly broken. 'But it's a fact!' Neels insisted with a sheepish grin. Their facetiousness again demonstrated that they could not and would not quite pin the responsibility for what they saw as rampant white impoverishment on the post-apartheid context alone. 'Are white squatter camps similar to black ones?' I asked. 'On the contrary, they're worse,' started Jake seriously, but then a grin played across his face again. 'Because it's almost like our poor whites can't even get the [sheets of corrugated] metal together to build a proper *khaya* [shack; literally 'house'],' he giggled. Neels returned the conversation to solemnity, speaking about the ANC government's lack of support for the white poor, and how 'Flip said' that workplace protection is not enough – Solidarity must 'see to civil rights', 'encourage education', and 'help those in need to help themselves'. 'Otherwise, I don't know what future

---

[49] See Sharp and Van Wyk, 'Beyond the market', pp. 120–36. For a more popular take on white poverty in South Africa, see E. Bottomley, *Poor White* (Cape Town: Tafelberg, 2012).

there is for us whites if we don't start standing up,' Neels said nervously, invoking the leadership's narrative of community autonomy and self-help. But Werner complicated the picture. Relating the experience of Gawie, a colleague, when visiting a white squatter camp, Werner drew the collective desire for 'standing up', and Afrikaners' ostensibly inherent propensity for it, into question:

At Bethal ... there's 64 families, also in similar conditions [to other white informal settlements] ... The one family has 11 kiddies, my friend. Now Gawie gets there, he says, 'Righto, I'll drive the tractor, I'll bring you shovels, pitchforks, we'll plough this piece of land.' That man tells him straight to his face, 'Listen, we're sitting here in the sun, smoking, we don't want to work.' Straight.

The story drew the usual cry of 'Unbelievable!' from Neels, who threw his hands in the air. 'It's because they no longer have that pride, that white pride,' said Jake contemptuously, wringing his large hands. His statement reflected an understanding of poverty and deprivation as contravening white racial identity, and the disdain for fellow whites that accompanied these observations. Jake seemed ready to abandon such 'bad whites' to their fate – but Neels was still clinging to the Movement's self-assigned mandate to help whites 'stand up' and to 'rebuild a future in which we [Afrikaners] can enjoy lasting freedom, security, and prosperity'.[50] 'How we'll manage to pull a guy like that out of the swamp, I don't know, it's not going to be easy,' he fretted. 'Some days I think we have to expose our children to this suffering ... I don't know, it's my personal feeling that we as parents just don't have the will any more to tell our children you *will* study, you *will* make matric. Finished.' Neels' choice of personal pronouns revealed how he was clearly haunted by the fact that the 'bad' whites under discussion – whether they were the parents of uneducated children or work-shy squatters – were his contemporaries, and thus uncomfortably close to him, even a foreshadowing of his own future.

The angst that pervaded the conversation now turned morbid, as the men returned to the topic of the white wage labourers they encountered in the mines. This time Werner shared his experience as a shop steward:

One of my members, my age, his kid also works on the mine as a wage labourer ... Yesterday morning this guy comes, he says, '[Werner],' and he closes the door. He says, 'I haven't slept a wink,' and he starts to cry. Big guy. He says, 'My child wants to commit suicide; last night I spoke to his mother, he doesn't want to live any more.' ... [It turns out] it's the white foreman who's belittling this child and cursing him all the way up the hem of his mother's dress, so much so that for the last four

---

[50] As Buys would later describe his vision (see Chapter 5).

months he no longer wants to live. He's made all kinds of plans, written letters. Now I must act to help this child and the father because they're looking to me. So I arrange things, talk to HR, get the kid out, transferred to another division, three days' leave, he's at home getting psychological help, that kind of thing ... But [the foreman] victimises the white kids; this is already the third case. The previous kid hanged himself underground, the other shop steward and I, and management, went to get him down, we went to cut the rope, he was hanging there.

This chilling tale silenced the room. This 'bad white' behaviour could not be attributed to black governance or economic change. 'We whites are a strange bunch,' Jake broke the silence bitterly, then drove the point home in the first person: 'I like being in a position where I can dominate others. But now I can't dominate the blacks – I can't do to them what I can do to these little white guys, because [the black worker] will give me hell ... [N]ow he does it to those white kids.' The other men all piped up in support of this view, adding how this kind of white-on-white victimisation had become 'a common trend' that 'you see all the time'. Jake continued his damning statement:

You know, we whites are like this – sorry, actually saying 'we whites' is wrong, we *Afrikaans* whites, because you won't see an Englishman doing this. Give a guy a little bit of status, and he becomes such a big-head that he has to turn sideways to fit through a door. That's one of our *boere* problems, I don't know why.

In stark contrast to the Movement's institutional narrative, Jake's words pointed to the dark side of 'Afrikaner DNA'. Where earlier comments about declining white education, slipshod parenting, and white poverty merely hinted at moral degeneracy, Jake now offered a universal condemnation of the Afrikaner character in which he actively implicated himself and his colleagues. There was no suggestion that this victimisation was, for instance, a symptom of white frustration at the loss of political power and social status brought about by the end of apartheid. Nor was there any indication – as in earlier statements – that such behaviour was part of 'hard mining culture' and specific to a certain class of whites. Rather, Jake seemed to suggest that the end of the racial state had exposed Afrikaners – all '*boere*' – for what they truly were. With racial oppression no longer sanctioned by the state, Afrikaners' inherent brutality now found other avenues of expression. This stood in stark contrast to the Movement's portrayal of Afrikaners as a virtuous volk being victimised by discriminatory policies in a black majority environment. Moreover, the manner in which Jake included himself and his colleagues – 'we Afrikaans whites' – in this pronouncement further suggested an awareness on the men's part of their generation's and their race's culpability in the sorry state of affairs in contemporary South Africa which they described. Indeed, the fact that my interviewees and such 'bad whites' were contemporaries made the spectre of their own material and moral precariousness loom large.

In contrast to the Movement's portrayal of Afrikaners, therefore, the conversation revealed much more profound ambiguities concerning the virtues of the volk and the nature of its ostensible victimhood in post-apartheid South Africa. Indeed, the men dared to go further, suggesting that blacks were in fact morally superior to whites. 'Let me tell you ... [S]ometimes it's almost better to work under a black than under a white,' Bertus picked up following Jake's statement. 'They're more humane!' interjected Neels. Jake agreed: 'You won't easily find [victimisation] among them.' Bertus concluded: 'My dad always said, if you want to make a pig out of a white man, make him a *baas*!' The others grunted in agreement. A simple 'bad black'–'good white' dichotomy – as offered in Hermann's anecdote about the two wolves and the sheep, or the Movement's portrayal of the differences between socialist and Christian trade unionism – therefore did not hold up in these men's personal and workplace experiences.

This was not to say that they did not readily demean black workers, managers, and politicians throughout the course of the interview. They were quick to comment on what they perceived as the militancy and corruption of COSATU and its affiliates, the cultural and developmental superiority of whites, and how South Africa's infrastructure and economy were failing under incompetent black management. 'These things, we whites are bottling it up, I'm telling you, especially us men, our age group,' Neels insisted. 'One day is one day,' he continued, again employing a revealing shift in pronouns, 'then these things will erupt, because I'm telling you, the whites have got to the point where I am sick and tired.' 'Do all whites feel this way?' I enquired. 'No!' came the answer, as they all started speaking simultaneously about 'high-rank guys' who were able to 'buy their security, their holidays, their apartheid, their exclusivity'. 'Everyone nowadays just worries about themselves,' said Bertus resentfully, still speaking about wealthy whites in comfortable managerial positions. 'As long as he's in this position, the *baas* who's up there ... as long as he can protect himself and the company, at whoever's or whatever cost, he worries only about himself.' And only the rich can afford to emigrate, Neels added: 'Guys like us are left to our own mercy.' Once again, the resentment and frustration articulated in such statements were not unambiguously directed at the black majority. Neels reflected the suppressed anger among white men of his age group.[51]

---

[51] On Afrikaner masculinity in apartheid and post-apartheid South Africa, see K. du Pisani, 'Puritanism transformed: Afrikaner masculinities in the apartheid and post-apartheid

But it was clear that my interviewees perceived and experienced these feelings not only in terms of race, gender, and generation, but also in terms of class: they resentfully identified 'high-rank' whites who were unperturbed by the end of the racial state because they could 'buy their apartheid'. Thus, the men pointed unambiguously to the role of class in shaping white experiences of South Africa's transition. In contrast to wealthy whites, they claimed, their generation of blue-collar whites who entered the workplace in the late apartheid years were struggling, in the absence of the racial state, to maintain their previous privilege, status, and security. Moreover, their statements about 'everyone just worrying about themselves' and being 'left to our own mercy' reflected their bitterness and sense of abandonment in the wake of the demise of the social contract and moral economy upon which the Afrikaner nationalist state had been founded. Despite the jesting and spontaneity that interspersed the interview, its overall tone was one of great negativity. The men's perceptions of social decline and of racial degradation, their ambivalence about the character of their own people, and their anger and anxiety about the loss of past certainties cast a dark shadow over their future. The vigour and volume with which they talked and the strength of their bodies contrasted sharply with the sense of vulnerability, loss, and helplessness they felt.

Only one thing offered them a glimmer of hope for the future. Throughout the conversation the men returned time and again to the role and work of their organisation. Whenever the ambivalence and anxieties born of their blue-collar experiences seemed to drive them to the edge of despair, they sought solace in Solidarity and found certainty in its clear racial and moral dichotomies and cultural nationalist agenda. Confronted with their own feelings of powerlessness and frustration, they saw the Movement as the vehicle with the collective muscle to address the issues troubling them. Crucially, they saw no political solution for whites and condemned all political parties, while looking to Solidarity as the 'only organisation in this country ... that does something for the white minority'. It struck me how closely this statement echoed the reason Eddie had offered in an interview for joining the MWU in the context of the Wiehahn reforms: 'there were no other institutions looking out for whites'.[52] Considering the future – their future – the men saw the Movement as their only hope. 'That Solidarity's vision, Flip's vision, is the right thing to do, is true – there's nothing else and no one else,'

---

period' in R. Morell (ed.), *Changing Men in Southern Africa* (London: Zed Books, 2001), pp. 157–75.
[52] Eddie, interviewed 18 August 2011, Kloofsig.

preached Jake. 'It's the only salvation!' Bertus joined in, and Neels continued: 'I too would dearly like to see, like Flip says, our own universities – white! Our own schools, own churches, own banks. I just wish we could do *this*' – he snapped his fingers – 'and next Monday we've got all these things right here in this black Africa.' Four years before the Movement's initiatives for community autonomy were announced at the *Toekomsberaad*, it seems that these union employees already had a clear idea of where the leadership was heading. Solidarity was perceived as the saviour organisation through which these ideals of separate development might be achieved, compensating not only for the loss of the racial state, but also for the loss of certainties the men suffered in the present. Hence, Neels concluded, with a mixture of resignation and grit: 'I feel like, this is the only thing that I still hang on [to]; there is nothing any longer that I support apart from Solidarity.'

These were precisely the sentiments that the leadership's interpretative framework sought to inculcate – indeed, in the case of the union representatives, the Movement could capitalise on their long-standing understanding of the MWU as the only institution 'looking out for whites'. But the interview showed further ways in the which the men had absorbed powerful elements of the Movement's official framing. 'Let me tell you, unionism isn't a job in the sense of a job – it's a *calling*,' Jake insisted. 'It's something that happens *in* you, and you feel in your heart, *this is it*.' The others murmured in solemn agreement, and Werner continued:

> This calling, right, it is for the sake of your fellow Afrikaner, and Solidarity is the only tool or thing for the future, for the survival of the Afrikaner, there's nothing else. That's the point, there's no alternative. And you must know in your heart, really, you must feel it, I'm doing it for the cause, not for anything else. If your heart isn't in the right place, you know, and you just want a nice cosy job, you won't be a good shop steward.

Throughout the interview, the men had expressed deep ambivalence about the state of post-apartheid South Africa, of white communities, and of themselves, and had struggled to know where to lay the blame for the decline and sense of loss they felt. Their blue-collar workplace experiences and specific working-class vulnerabilities and frustrations led to understandings of the past and present that contradicted the declassed narratives and clear-cut dichotomies proffered by Solidarity's leadership. Indeed, as in the case of Sharp's blue-collar interlocutors, the men's shared white Afrikaans identity was only one part of their experience[53] – their experiences in the industrial workplace and in working-class

---

[53] Sharp, 'Market, race and nation', p. 103.

communities amid the shifts of the long transition played a crucial role in shaping their perspectives and convictions, including about themselves and those around them. Now, however, they seemed to revert to the declassed framing and agenda of the leadership, invoking the cultural politics and nationalist rhetoric of the Movement's official narrative. Their invocation of 'calling' suggested an understanding of trade union work merging smoothly with service to the volk. Resentment of 'high-rank guys' who leave the working class 'to our own mercy' was replaced by talk of 'your fellow Afrikaner'; despair at the demise of the Afrikaner moral economy supplanted by the imperative of 'the survival of the Afrikaner'. In the face of their own precarity, the men responded with a longing for the race-based solutions with which they were presented – from 'uplifting' poor whites to founding white-only institutions. They longed for a new racial state and seemed ready to play their part in its establishment. But this, as many of my interviewees would divulge, came at a cost.

Keeping Solidarity's future white: racial gatekeeping and its working-class costs

Chapter 6 related how, after 1994, the MWU was compelled to remove racial membership definitions from its constitution. The union would in future 'maintain its character' in linguistic and cultural terms, as Buys had promised at the time. As it stood in 2011, the trade union's constitution made no mention of Afrikaans or Afrikaner identity as a core element of the union's character or membership. It stated only that the union was administered 'within the Christian faith', 'promotes an economic system of free enterprise', and 'believes in and accepts a system of true democracy in government and labour, in which the rights of minorities are recognised and protected'.[54] On the subject of organisational identity, Hermann told the *Solidariteitkunde* participants that:

> You just have to protect your [organisational] identity. If you don't, you'll simply become unspecific, and then at some stage you'll reach tipping point ... And before you know it, no one is standing up for the minority and you're no longer a true democracy, because all institutions are – because this is what people, they're increasingly saying, right, that an institution must be *representative* of South African society. Now, what does that mean in practice? It means black and English. It means there won't be a single institution left which can create space for our people ... And that's the risk that must be managed.[55]

---

[54] Solidarity constitution as approved by the National Council on 26 March 2009, courtesy of Hennie de Wet (10 August 2011), p. 3, 6.
[55] *Solidariteitkunde*, 13 September 2011 (his emphasis).

By implication, a 'true democracy' (Hermann echoed the exact wording in the union's constitution) had to contain spaces or institutions where 'the minority' could hold a majority, exercise power, and promote its own interests. It was such spaces that the Solidarity Movement was seeking to create through private initiatives in the civil society sphere, thereby restoring to whites the 'freedom' of which they were deprived by post-apartheid 'majority domination', as the official institutional framing held.

As Hermann's reference to a 'risk that must be managed' intimated, this agenda clearly held implications for recruitment and membership. Within Solidarity, the term *nismark* ('niche market') was used to characterise its target membership. The term's meaning was at once clear and opaque. As it was employed, *nismark* seemed to be a euphemism for 'white', or sometimes 'white Afrikaans-speakers'. I found there to be something distinctly surreptitious about the term. It was rarely used in conversations with me and was conspicuously absent from my interviews with Buys and Hermann. Yet I often heard it used throughout the organisation – it surfaced during *Solidariteitkunde* and was frequently used during my interviews with trade union representatives. In each setting, the term was invoked in a very natural way and functioned as a synonym for 'white' or 'white-Afrikaans'. It was consistently assumed that those present understood what the term signified – even during *Solidariteitkunde*, the participants, most of whom had only recently been appointed, seemed comfortable with the term and used it themselves. During his interview, Paul candidly explained that *nismark* 'really means purely Afrikaans and white, but because we can't say "white" – that would be wrong within the larger context – we say "Afrikaans". Remember, that's politically acceptable; you can do that, but that's not really what's meant.'[56] The ease with which the term was employed was disconcerting, as though it gave licence to Solidarity employees to use obviously racialised language among themselves, even if they used abstruse terms to do so. It is not a term I ever heard or saw printed in English. This strengthened my impression that it was used for internal communication only – a way of being clear about the organisation's objectives without overtly referencing race.

Yet despite his insistence on 'protecting organisational identity', Hermann did not explain *how* this was to be accomplished. When one *Solidariteitkunde* participant cautiously enquired how tipping point situations were managed, Hermann was evasive: 'That's a longer

---

[56] Paul, interviewed 20 October 2011, Kloofsig.

conversation. I can talk to you about it later, but it's a long – it's complicated.'⁵⁷ The issue was left there – the participants understood the *nismark* principle, and besides, very few of them would ever be directly involved in recruitment at shop-floor level.

I posed the question to the union representatives I interviewed. From their answers it was clear that the issue of *how* to manage the organisational identity was one they faced in practice – and saw them resort to questionable tactics on a daily basis. Wouter explained that, after the union's constitution was changed, 'you did start getting applications [from blacks]'. He chuckled nervously:

[S]ome of those things got mislaid, I personally mislaid the things, so in other words I didn't process [the applications]. And if [the African applicant] then later came by to ask, then you sent the application through to headquarters after all. And then they would get a [union] newspaper in Afrikaans, and the guy would phone HQ and say he wants it in English, and over there the guys would explain there is no English version, and then [the African member] would resign. So, personally, I didn't necessarily process the applications.⁵⁸

Gert offered a similar story. He explained that since he became an MWU shop steward in 1983, his members 'were and continue to be white, which is our *nismark* ... We do have African members [in my district],' he continued, 'and I'm actually quite proud of that ... [But] most of them, one tries to keep them out, and you can do so up to a point, but then, if you keep losing the [application] papers, it becomes too risky.'⁵⁹ Louis sighed at my question:

You can't refuse them, [but] we also don't go out looking to recruit them, because our goals are focused on whites with Christian norms and values. Affirmative action is aimed against the white – he's the one being forced out of the workplace by affirmative action, your language, culture, and religion, all those things, also in terms of security, it's mainly aimed against whites.⁶⁰

According to Anton, mainly 'Africans that aren't into politics' and 'skilled African workers who know what it's about' wanted to join Solidarity, because they recognised that 'the whole country has gone to the dogs', that COSATU unions are 'focused on money' and 'very corrupt'. There were 'loads' of African workers wanting to join Solidarity, he continued, adding, '[H]ow can I put it, you can't refuse him.'⁶¹

⁵⁷ *Solidariteitkunde*, 13 September 2011.
⁵⁸ Wouter, interviewed 20 September 2011, Kloofsig.
⁵⁹ Gert, interviewed 27 October 2011, Kloofsig.
⁶⁰ Louis, interviewed 18 October 2011, Kloofsig.
⁶¹ Anton, interviewed 28 October 2011, Kloofsig.

It was clear that, when it came to preserving a certain membership profile on the ground, the buck stopped with the union representatives and organisers. These men were aware that legally they 'could not refuse' Africans' applications, and they were nervous about revealing their strategies for excluding non-*nismark* workers. '[Solidarity's management] would skin me alive if they knew I was telling you this,' Frik started in response to my question. He had been a union organiser involved in the MWU/Solidarity's regional office in the Cape. Soon, many coloured workers wanted to join the union.

> When I saw it was becoming a problem ... I posed the question: should I let them join? And from their side, management never gave me a direct answer ... All I was told was, as Flip once told me, was 'manage it responsibly', and then they left it to me. By that I think he meant that I should just be careful, I should go about [it] in such a way that it doesn't become a problem.

But Frik's area was already 'a problem' as it was rapidly nearing 'tipping point'. He explained the dilemma:

> If too many [coloured] guys would join and they would outnumber the whites, they would be able to insist on representation, even representation on the General Council [now the National Council]. That would have caused an enormous problem at that stage, because the guys weren't ready for it, the union wasn't ready for it. I don't even know if nowadays there is one [coloured] guy sitting there [on the Council]. And that was always the danger, the crux of the matter.[62]

The Cape example clearly showed that the 'tipping point' dilemma was not about Solidarity ceasing to be an institution that protects the interests of the Christian, Afrikaans-speaking minority – after all, coloured South Africans were also a minority population group, and many were Afrikaans-speaking and identified with the Christian faith.[63] The real threat was that another racial group 'would outnumber the whites', make claims to representation, and threaten white power. The leadership's lofty formulations needed to be translated into practice on the shop floors

---

[62] Frik, interviewed 8 September 2011, Kloofsig.
[63] The relationship of white and so-called coloured Afrikaans-speakers in South Africa is marked by a long and uncomfortable history variously characterised by subjugation, tension, and rapprochement. Since 1994, there have been efforts to render 'Afrikaans' identity racially inclusive by acknowledging the heterogeneous nature of the language and those who speak it. It was clear, however, that coloured Afrikaans-speakers were not included in Solidarity's *nismark* target group. On post-1994 language politics, see C. S. van der Waal, 'Creolisation and purity: Afrikaans language politics in post-apartheid times', *African Studies* 71, no. 3 (2001), pp. 446–63; N. Alexander, 'Language politics in South Africa' in S. Bekker, M. Dodds, and M. Khosa (eds), *Shifting African Identities* (Pretoria: HSRC, 2001), pp. 141–52. For a broader historical view, see M. Adhikari, *Not White Enough, Not Black Enough: racial identity in the South African coloured community* (Athens OH: Ohio University Press, 2005).

and in the regional offices where union representatives had to manage this 'threat' at grassroots level. Frik was the only interviewee who spoke of receiving some direction from the executive, but the strategies he implemented closely resembled those described by other interviewees. He explained that he and his team of shop stewards were 'careful about where we went recruiting, choosing places where the majority of employees were still white ... I think sometimes application forms did get lost, but I think that's what we mean by managing responsibly ... And the guys [shop stewards] on the floor got that.'[64] Another interviewee, Frans, had worked alongside Frik on recruitment drives. He confirmed that 'the [management] guys always told us when we recruit, we should recruit *nismark*, that's what they pushed for. And we always told them it's not possible in the Cape – if you look at the companies' demography, the whites have decreased, so if you want to represent these guys, you can't just pick out the whites, because the guys work together.'[65]

The shop stewards I interviewed as a group spoke positively of their handful of black members, but confirmed employing similar exclusionary tactics. '[W]e currently have a black shop steward in the mine, I have a coloured in the factory, and we've had several blacks on the mine, and they do a pretty good job,' Jake explained. 'So now, [blacks] dearly want to come over to our side, and our union's policy' – he chuckled softly – 'is that we don't want too many of them, because we don't want things to end up with them dominating us and telling us how to run a union, because then Solidarity won't be itself any more. So you have to keep them to the minimum.' 'But what if many wanted to join?' I asked. Everyone answered simultaneously: 'consider his status in the company', 'lose the forms', 'if you have to go represent him, then just don't turn up', 'there are lots of tricks'. Jake's voice emerged clearly: '[You have to look at] whether he's a wage worker, or an artisan, or whether he's already in management, because the moment you move into those positions, his thinking changes, and then it's okay, he can join.' Bertus continued: '[T]he few individuals that do cross over, he's the same level as you are – I don't mean in the head, [I mean] in terms of position, you know. But he's already thinking differently ... and they are moderate.' No one blinked at this overt racism. 'What about other races?' I asked. Jake took the lead again: '[T]hey are the minority – they wouldn't be able to come and dominate you. It's the Africans who could do that, they are the only ones who could, if they *really* wanted to, if they wanted to be clever, take over Solidarity in the workplace and before we know it, [the union]

---

[64] Frik, interviewed 8 September 2011, Kloofsig.
[65] Frans, interviewed 22 September 2011, Bellville.

would be pitch black from top to bottom.' But whites were too smart to allow this, Jake's self-congratulatory tone seemed to say as he continued: 'Look, the easiest thing – it's something you learn ... when you do get one of those radicals, then you tell him, "Look, Solidarity is against affirmative action, are you still happy [to join]?" And then he's not happy.' He gave a pleased grin: 'So he says, "No thanks."'[66]

These conversations spoke of the grassroots work that went into maintaining Solidarity's racial profile through 'responsible management'. Despite the laughter that interspersed some testimonies, my interviewees were clearly nervous about their role as racial gatekeepers in the context of largely black workplaces and a legislative framework which forbade the restriction of membership in the manner required of them. Their uneasiness about the tactics they employed contrasted sharply with the apparent insouciance Flip Buys expressed during an interview when I asked how he saw Solidarity's identity and its maintenance. At first, Buys responded with abstract references to the importance of 'freedom of association' and the prerogative of an organisation to determine its own 'positioning'.[67] But when I pressed him to explain what this meant in practice, his answer resonated strongly with the ideas articulated by shop stewards on the ground:

[I]f a few want to join, there's no problem – but if it gets too much, then you have to start managing it and tell the guys [shop stewards], wait, our positioning is going to suffer ... Now we have to be straight with them [Africans]: listen, you can join ... but our constitution, like any organisation, has certain requirements and that means that you have to support our policy and our goals, that's the most important requirement. And we tell them, we are Afrikaans, that's what we operate in, we will try to help you in English, but no other language, we don't have that capacity. We tell them, this is our policy with regard to affirmative action, we don't agree with the way affirmative action is being managed. We tell them we don't agree ... we think the ANC and COSATU are damaging the country ... And then they can join.[68]

Although the trade union's constitution made no explicit mention of Afrikaner identity or opposition to affirmative action, the leadership and shop stewards alike utilised these elements to exclude racially undesirable members. In contrast to the nervousness displayed by union representatives, Buys seemed nonchalant, employing his now familiar emphasis on culture: 'Collective identity, you know, really determines who joins where, and it's the same when it comes to the union. What we

[66] Group interview, 14 September 2011, Kloofsig.
[67] Flip Buys, interviewed 19 September 2011, Kloofsig.
[68] Flip Buys, interviewed 19 September 2011, Kloofsig.

do find is that coloureds in the Western Cape are quite attracted to us, you know. And that's fine, [we] don't have a problem with that. The Indians are such a small group, they could never pose a ...' He broke off, suddenly aware of the incriminating formulation. 'And there are many of them that agree with us completely on affirmative action and so on,' he continued. 'So, we're very easy-going about these things, you know.'[69] Buys' placid approach was perhaps unsurprising – ensconced in the comfortable offices of Solidarity's headquarters, he was not involved in recruitment and membership management. He simply issued the directive – whether explicitly or implicitly – to 'manage responsibly', and left this up to the union's blue-collar shop stewards on the ground. It was, in this sense, up to them how they chose to manage this task. And it was clear that the pressure they felt saw them go to great lengths to restrict non-*nismark* membership – after all, a shop steward not turning up to represent a member's case, as Bertus had suggested, violated the very essence of trade union ethics and workers' protection.

A number of union representatives mentioned that higher-skilled African applicants were more readily considered for union membership because they 'thought differently' or were not 'into politics'. This would presumably render them less likely to challenge white dominance within Solidarity, or perhaps to be co-opted into it. Skills level, however, was not a requirement when it came to white workers. The group of union representatives testified that they rushed to recruit the young white wage workers they encountered in the mines, because 'they need support, a guy has to protect those kids'.[70] It seemed the identity marker 'Afrikaans' was also taken with a pinch of salt when recruiting whites: during the same interview, the men testified that their white members were 'Afrikaans, English, German, Dutch, many English [people]'.[71] One exclusion did apply to whites, I learned. One interviewee revealed that there was another way in which 'responsible management' was practised:

Most people [who] join [the union are] between 30 and 50 [years of age]. For 50 and older there was – I don't know if I should say this – a kind of block on them, not to let the guys join because of the benefits that would later have to be paid out to them. If you would calculate it, they would never have paid enough in membership fees to cover what you would have to give them in terms of funeral benefits and so on.[72]

[69] Flip Buys, interviewed 19 September 2011, Kloofsig.
[70] Neels, interviewed 14 September 2011, Kloofsig.
[71] Gert, interviewed 27 October 2011, Kloofsig.
[72] Frik, interviewed 8 September 2011, Kloofsig.

Such practices cast doubt on the union's commitment to workers' protection and well-being. Apparently, running a profitable business necessitated excluding the older members of the volk.

But 'responsible management' presented a dilemma to Solidarity's ambitions. While the union sought to attract new members by marketing itself as an effective service provider with attractive benefits, it simultaneously restricted its membership through practices of racial gatekeeping. (This was even more relevant with regard to other organisations in the Movement, such as AfriForum and Helping Hand, which explicitly communicated its appeal to white Afrikaans-speakers.) In the context of South Africa's overall demography, this imposed obvious limitations on membership growth, and hence on union recognition and power in the workplace, as well as on capital mobilisation through membership fees. As a result, there was immense stress on extending the organisation's reach within the white Afrikaans-speaking population in particular. Throughout my time at Solidarity, I was continuously struck by the pressure exerted by the leadership to recruit new members to both the union and the broader Movement. A target of 28,000 new members across the Movement was set for 2011. During a monthly staff meeting, a senior staff member encouraged HQ personnel to support the recruitment drive: 'Where do we find the right members? References! You must all send us your references for people we can recruit, your friends and family! ... Teamwork makes the dream work!'[73] Everyone present was white and Afrikaans – it was clear what was meant by the 'right' members. The 'dream' resonated strongly with Hermann's references to Solidarity's emulation of the Histadrut as a state within a state, and the goal of establishing 'own institutions' – 'white! Our own schools, own churches, own banks,' in Neels' words.[74] For the sake of the 'dream', the organisation set what seemed to be impossibly high and unsustainable recruitment targets. It is unsurprising that such pressure would result in dubious practices, such as asking employees to divulge friends' and relatives' personal data. And this went beyond personal connections. While conducting research at Solidarity's headquarters, I was present during an informal meeting of organisers working across a number of industries, including many professional job categories. During the meeting, one organiser enthusiastically produced a list of names of still unorganised employees at a major employer. He boasted that the list had been obtained via a Solidarity member who worked in the organisation's human resources department – a goldmine of potential

---

[73] Staff meeting, 9 September 2011, Kloofsig.
[74] Group interview, 14 September 2011, Kloofsig.

recruitment information. Peering over his shoulder, his colleagues scanned the list approvingly. 'Look at those surnames, this looks right,' one said, nodding. 'These are birds of our feather,' another concurred, pleased. Another *nismark* pool had been discovered, and the recruitment drive could continue. Such were the practices provoked by the policy of maintaining organisational identity by excluding non-*nismark* individuals amid pressure to keep membership numbers growing. Frik testified to this:

> The message from above was always very clear: 'recruit responsibly' ... But this made it very difficult for an organiser, because there is so much pressure to recruit. Loads. And I think the pressure is just growing due to affirmative action ... [T]here are much fewer white guys in the workplace, so who should we recruit, how should we recruit? It's an enormous problem, and I think with time it will only get worse.[75]

This dilemma led some union representatives to voice doubts about Solidarity's sustainability. Paul stated unequivocally that by formulating its 'ideology' in 'purely Afrikaans and white' terms, Solidarity was restricting itself to a very limited section of the population. 'There's a total of three million whites in South Africa, of which maybe one-eighth, if it's that many, are receptive for that ideology, maybe less, one-sixteenth,'[76] Paul said soberly. Frik also questioned the sustainability of Solidarity's ventures, particularly in the face of demographic and economic change:

> Flip will overwhelm you with positive information, about how we should do our own thing: our own hospitals, own clinics, own schools, own everything – we have to develop these things, and that's how we'll survive ... I look at how demography is changing, non-whites increasing, whites decreasing, and then I don't know how it will work and whether one can keep living in isolation.[77]

Louis also agonised over what would happen if Solidarity was to fail at its self-set task to 'protect our people':

> Because you need an alternative. If the one we have at the moment falls flat and the Malemas take over, what then? Do we wait for Australia to say, 'You can come over here' – would they do that? Or would New Zealand do it? Or who? England told Rhodesia[ns] they could come, but that was with English passports; we don't have those. Who is going to say, 'You can come'?[78]

The spectre of the potential failure of Solidarity's 'Plan B for Afrikaners' caused these men deep distress. To them, this threat was not abstract – in

---

[75] Frik, interviewed 8 September 2011, Kloofsig.
[76] Paul, interviewed 20 October 2011, Kloofsig.
[77] Frik, interviewed 8 September 2011, Kloofsig.
[78] Louis, interviewed 18 October 2011, Kloofsig.

the workplaces where they spent their days recruiting new members, and trying to exclude others, they were keenly aware of the reality of failure. For them, it was a double bind: if the Solidarity Movement failed to be an 'alternative state' for Afrikaners, to establish their 'own institutions' to 'protect the people', and 'rebuild a future' for them in South Africa, white workers like them would again find themselves without some form of protection. Unlike 'high-rank guys' who could emigrate, they would be 'left to [their] own mercy'. Yet, even as these men sought to support the Movement and its efforts to establish a privatised neo-racial state to protect their interests, they put themselves at risk by engaging in dubious practices in the workplace. While the leadership could be nonchalant and hide behind nebulous notions of 'responsible management' and *nismark*, trade union representatives and organisers were the ones responsible for enforcing this on the ground and bore the liability. The new racial state demanded its pound of flesh from those it claimed to protect.

Sharp and Van Wyk uncovered evidence of analogous dynamics as part of their study examining the fortunes of unemployed white Pretorians. They examined the fate of poor whites who had 'become embroiled in schemes to resuscitate the Afrikaner "volk"'[79] – that is, who receive support from 'upliftment' initiatives driven by members of the white Afrikaans middle class and offered exclusively to unemployed and homeless whites. Sharp and Van Wyk included initiatives by Solidarity's charity organisation Helping Hand in this category. They argue that racially exclusive schemes in fact render the poor whites 'entangled' in them *more* vulnerable by insulating them from the social contact and social capital that can be gained from interacting with 'the vast numbers of black South Africans who have ample experience in [being poor]'.[80] The authors contrast this with a multiracial settlement untouched by such Afrikaner nationalist philanthropy, where unemployed whites enter into diverse and mutually beneficial social and market relationships with blacks in positions similar to their own. Hence, they argue that it is precisely middle-class insistence that the white poor deserve 'special' treatment that exacerbates the vulnerability of the latter.[81] This argument resonates with the evidence presented above, and the manner in which

---

[79] Sharp and Van Wyk, 'Beyond the market', p. 122.
[80] Sharp and Van Wyk, 'Beyond the market', p. 122, 129. The authors remain somewhat opaque about the agency of the unemployed whites 'entangled' in these racially exclusive schemes, and so it is unclear whether we are dealing with chance, choice, or conviction.
[81] This is not just the authors' view, but is reflected in the hostility that some white residents of multiracial settlements displayed towards the charity efforts of the nationalist-minded middle class: '[W]e simply cannot afford [race-based separatism],' one commented, 'I say to hell with their volk.' Sharp and Van Wyk, 'Beyond the market', p. 133.

racial gatekeeping – Solidarity's middle-class leadership's determination to create spaces in which white Afrikaans-speakers can enjoy special, majority status – in fact renders working-class officials more precarious.

Conclusion

The testimonies presented in this chapter expose the persistent reality of class otherwise not readily visible within the white, Afrikaner population, and provide striking insights into how white workers experienced and sought to negotiate the demise of the racial state. This persistence of working-class identification sat uneasily with Solidarity's efforts to declass its history and cast Afrikaners as a homogeneous volk. Indeed, the union representatives' narratives often ran counter to those put forward by the leadership, and they articulated more complex subjectivities and varied experiences of South Africa's transition than the Movement's official framing. The chronology emerging from these narratives – of the Wiehahn period as marking significant shifts not only in workplaces but in working-class communities, politics, and world views – supports this book's argument surrounding the long transition since the 1970s. Viewing change from the shop floor, mineshaft, and negotiation room led these workers to express empathy and solidarity with black workers, to mock whites, and even to disdain their fellow Afrikaners. Crucially, they expressed profound apprehension about the fundamental nature of white society, and Afrikaners in particular. While the workers clearly ascribed to racist sentiments and ethnic identification, their narratives often privileged a working-class perspective above a clearly Afrikaner-centred interpretation. This saw them articulate resentment and perceptions of loss – of past ways of life, of once-certain values, and of an Afrikaner moral economy – which left them acutely aware of their inferior social position and vulnerability vis-à-vis their wealthier brethren.

These counternarratives and alternative perspectives suggest limitations to Solidarity's ability to shape the subjectivities and identities of its blue-collar members. At the same time, the men I interviewed also echoed elements of the language and meaning-making proffered by the Movement's official narrative. Clearly, these resonated with them and allowed them to make sense of their experiences of the demise of the racial state and the Africanisation of politics and society in the course of the long transition. Indeed, the men I interviewed all joined the MWU because, in the context of labour reform and the withdrawal of state support for working-class whiteness, they saw the union as the only institution committed to defending the interests of blue-collar whites.

In 2011, this continued to be how they understood Solidarity and its campaigns. Despite the ways in which it had changed under the leadership of Flip Buys, they regarded it as their 'saviour organisation'. And while they owned their explicitly working-class identities and articulated their resentment of whites with a higher social status, they nevertheless longed for the realisation of the neo-racial state envisioned by the Movement. Indeed, it was arguably their inability to resolve their disconcerting experiences and concerns that saw them revert to the Movement as their 'only hope' and express their commitment to its race-based and cultural nationalist agenda.

This returns us to the international literature that seeks to explain the recent political shift to the right by focusing on white workers and blue-collar communities. The South African evidence presented here exposes such approaches as simplistic and reductionist. In this sense, my findings concur with critiques such as those offered by Bhambra and Walley.[82] But whereas these authors harness electoral statistics and quantitative analyses, this chapter offers qualitative evidence that racism is not the preserve of the white working class. Indeed, it is clear that the growing popularity of the Solidarity Movement, its politics, and its initiatives cannot be attributed exclusively to white working-class interests. Solidarity has long ceased to be an exclusively blue-collar organisation and certainly does not present itself in this way. Likewise, the positionalities and perspectives articulated by the workers I interviewed resist simple categorisation as 'nationalist' or 'right-wing', testifying instead to complex subjectivities and ambivalent experiences. These findings contribute a white working-class perspective from the Global South to current debates on the insecurities, subjectivities, and politics produced by longer processes of the changing relationship between the state, capital, and labour as they emerge at the current historical juncture.

---

[82] As discussed in the Introduction.

Conclusion

Since the *Toekomsberaad*, the Solidarity Movement has continued its efforts to perform its self-appointed role as the champion of Afrikaner interests. Its most recent initiatives demonstrated how its state-like character was being extended beyond 'own institutions' and community-based projects. In 2017, AfriForum made headlines when it launched a private prosecutions unit headed by the prominent former state prosecutor Gerrie Nel. The establishment of the unit came amid accusations that the National Prosecuting Authority (NPA) was politically biased and selective in the cases it pursued. AfriForum explicitly presented its unit as an uncorrupted substitute for a failed state institution. It was no coincidence that the first person identified for private prosecution on charges of culpable homicide was Duduzane Zuma, son of Jacob Zuma, who was himself mired in controversy and corruption charges.[1]

In addition to extending its state-like initiatives at home, the Movement also increasingly sought to present itself as the voice of South Africa's white minority on the global stage. Chapter 5 noted its appeals to the UN and efforts to set up links with interest groups abroad. Another international campaign, which would attract much attention, followed in 2018. For some time, AfriForum had been campaigning around the issue of farm attacks, a crime it claimed disproportionally affected whites and which it accused the government of neglecting. When in 2018 the government reopened the national debate on land reform, raising the possibility of amending the Constitution in order to more readily facilitate land redistribution, the Solidarity Movement condemned this as yet another concerted attack on white farm owners, most of whom it claimed were Afrikaners. Combining the two issues, AfriForum representatives travelled to the USA with the goal of raising international support in order to place pressure on the South African

---

[1] Sesona Ngqakamba, 'Private prosecutions: this is how it works', *Huffington Post*, 19 April 2018, www.huffingtonpost.co.za/2018/04/19/private-prosecutions-this-is-how-it-works_a_23415246/ (accessed 6 August 2018).

government. In the US, AfriForum deputy CEO Ernst Roets was interviewed on the conservative Fox News channel, during which rural violence and land reform in South Africa were represented as an 'intentional campaign to crush the racial minority'.[2] The interview grabbed the attention of none other than president Donald Trump, an avid Fox News viewer, who subsequently took to the social media platform Twitter to express his concern about the 'large-scale killing of farmers' and seizure of land 'from white farmers' in South Africa.[3] With this, AfriForum's campaign was boosted to global prominence. Indeed, Maroela Media reported that AfriForum's US tour also enjoyed public support in Australia, the UK, and Europe.[4] In South Africa, however, both the government and opposition political leaders expressed dismay at Trump's reaction to AfriForum's campaign,[5] while a number of journalists, including whites and Afrikaners, accused the Solidarity Movement of inflaming local public debate and misrepresenting the facts in order to tap into international discourses of white anxiety and right-wing rhetoric around multiculturalism.[6] AfriForum was simply 'selling the

---

[2] 'Minority of farmers struggle for survival in South Africa', Fox News, 15 May 2018, http://video.foxnews.com/v/5785308294001/?#sp=show-clips (accessed 26 August 2018).

[3] 'Overview: "There's a black genocide in SA and US" – EFF hits back at Trump following Twitter storm', News24, 23 August 2018, www.news24.com/SouthAfrica/News/live-sa-reacts-to-donald-trump-comments-on-land-expropriation-farm-murders-20180823 (accessed 26 August 2018).

[4] 'AfriForum-hoës in VSA vir bewusmaking oor plaasmoorde en onteiening', Maroela Media, 2 May 2018, https://maroelamedia.co.za/nuus/sa-nuus/afriforum-hoes-in-vsa-vir-bewusmaking-oor-plaasmoorde-en-onteiening/ (accessed 1 June 2018).

[5] 'Trump tweet "based on false information": South African foreign minister', Reuters, 23 August 2018, www.reuters.com/article/us-safrica-usa-sisulu/trump-tweet-based-on-false-information-south-african-foreign-minister-idUSKCN1L813D; 'Ramaphosa's government delivers mature response to "misinformed" Trump, says analyst', TimesLIVE, 23 August 2018, www.timeslive.co.za/politics/2018-08-23-ramaphosas-government-delivers-mature-response-to-trump-says-analyst-fikeni/; 'Recap: Trump tweets and SA goes berserk – here's what was said and by whom', News24, 23 August 2018, www.news24.com/SouthAfrica/News/p2-trump-tweets-and-sa-goes-berserk-heres-what-was-said-and-by-whom-20180823 (all accessed 6 December 2018).

[6] 'AfriForum's US adventure: playing with fire, just like in Oz', *Huffington Post*, 4 May 2018, www.huffingtonpost.co.za/pieter-du-toit/afriforums-u-s-adventure-playing-with-fire-after-setting-australia-alight_a_23426470/ (accessed 31 May 2018); 'Trump's comment about South Africa is a reminder that race still matters', News24, 29 August 2018, www.news24.com/Columnists/GuestColumn/trumps-comment-about-south-africa-is-a-reminder-that-race-still-matters-20180829 (accessed 31 August 2018); 'Trump's South Africa tweet is a reminder that white supremacy is the original white-collar crime', *Washington Post*, 24 August 2018, www.washingtonpost.com/news/global-opinions/wp/2018/08/24/trumps-south-africa-tweet-is-a-reminder-that-white-supremacy-is-the-original-white-collar-crime/?arc404=true (accessed 4 December 2018); 'South Africa's white right, the Alt-Right and the alternative', The Conversation, 4 October 2018, https://theconversation.com/south-africas-white-right-the-alt-right-and-the-alternative-103544 (accessed 4 December 2018).

drama', some claimed, its scaremongering around white genocide no more than a sales pitch to boost its membership.[7]

In the late 1970s, the MWU under Arrie Paulus had sought to obstruct labour reform in order to maintain the workplace privilege – and hence the material status and social position – of semi-skilled white workers. Some 40 years later, the Solidarity Movement – in a variety of guises – was seeking to obstruct land reform, mobilising around the preservation of Afrikaans language and culture in public life, and pushing back against employment equity policies, while also setting up private institutions, community initiatives and market-based services for the white minority, and Afrikaners in particular. Beyond demonstrating how this organisation's scope, ambition, and reach have continued to grow over the period examined here, it is clear that a shift has occurred in the privileges to which it claimed entitlement and the precarities against which it sought to mobilise.

This book has sought to reinsert white workers into the historiography of South Africa's recent past. Instead of privileging race as the only salient feature and central analytic of the transition, I have highlighted class as an equally important logic that sees different experiences, motivations, and understandings reveal their presence and demonstrate their impact. From this vantage point, a much more nuanced understanding of white society and Afrikaner class formation and of South Africa's transition comes into view. Crucially, it also becomes clear how these processes intersect with broader global realities.

This book has emphasised the uneven nature of apartheid-era processes of embourgeoisement and the longevity of the structural and subjective vulnerabilities that had marked the white working class since its formation in the context of the late nineteenth-century mineral revolution. For a section of the white labour corps – particularly those labouring directly alongside black workers in older industries such as mining, who had a relatively low skills base or a craft, which, over time, had been eroded by technological advances and job fragmentation – the benevolence of the racial state and the commitment of white power wielders in politics and business to the Afrikaner nationalist social contract were the only things upholding white working-class privilege and partnership in racial citizenship. The Golden Age of post-war growth, marked by the hegemony of Afrikaner nationalism and the growing reach of separate development, obscured this precarity and kept the social

---

[7] 'AfriForum's land-reform sales pitch: "Help us stop the Commies"', *Huffington Post*, 12 April 2018, www.huffingtonpost.co.za/2018/04/12/selling-the-drama-the-land-debate-as-a-sales-pitch_a_23409707/ (accessed 31 May 2018).

tensions that had always characterised white society subdued under the veneer of white prosperity and power.

This changed in the 1970s. In South Africa, and across much of the Western world, the post-war social contract was upended by a crisis of capitalism. The policies which followed sought to revive economic growth by affecting a new balance of power between the state, capital, and workers. In this new configuration, the regulatory and protective role of the state would be scaled back and powerful labour movements disciplined in order to allow more freedom to the invisible hand to reinvigorate production and trade. This inaugurated a period of deregulation, globalisation, and internationalisation – the effects of which are widely regarded today as leading to the 2008 global financial crisis and preparing the ground for the deep social divisions and inequalities currently expressing themselves in national populist, xenophobic, and anti-globalisation politics. Across much of the globe, the weakening of labour movements and socialism and the diminishing appeal of class have affected a shift from inequality to identity as the main galvanising force in politics. Class was supplanted by culture even as inequality and social injustice grew more serious.

These processes had their own local inflection in South Africa, where the politics of race – in terms of a demographic reality coming up against the economic and political delusions of white supremacy – had always coloured politics. Here, too, the economic crisis of the 1970s stimulated a reconfiguration of existing balances of power. It is ultimately a moot question whether this reconfiguration would have taken a different shape if the economic slowdown had not coincided with – and, in fact, provoked – the resurrection of black labour power in South Africa, so that the white minority state and capital were faced not just with the workplace demands of a strategically powerful labour force but with the political demands of a frustrated, disenfranchised majority. The black workers' movement, as led by COSATU from the mid-1980s, made clear its understanding of the struggle for industrial and political citizenship as indivisible. White workers shared this understanding. As this book has shown, white labour recognised with sobering clarity that black industrial citizenship would be a milestone rather than a roadblock on the way to full political rights and black majority rule. To white workers such as those represented by SACLA, the political and business establishment's conviction that labour could be depoliticised and black workers mollified with industrial representation was a delusion that threatened the very existence of the racial state. And the main casualties would be white working-class power at the negotiation table, protection from job competition, and privilege in the workplace – that is, the very elements that, since the first battles for the colour bar, had undergirded white workers' identity, distinguishing them from and elevating them above the Africans alongside whom they laboured. Indeed, the government's acceptance of the Wiehahn reforms started to dismantle the established convergence between race and rights, with the withdrawal of state support for working-class whiteness annulling the social alliance on which the National Party had come to power. As Arrie Paulus's condemnation of the 'Wiehahn arsenic' demonstrated, this was seen as amounting to the effective ejection of white workers from the white body politic, reversing the full citizenship white workers had demanded from capital and the state in 1922, and had secured in 1924, and exposing them once more to structural and subjective vulnerability.

For white workers, this marked the beginning of the end of the racial state and the commencement of what I have designated the long transition. This term functions not simply to highlight a longer history prior to the negotiations of the 1990s, but also to acknowledge the ongoing nature of efforts to establish full non-racial citizenship and the continued impact of neoliberal policies. Indeed, in post-apartheid South Africa, this process remains contested and incomplete. This has become freshly apparent in recent years, as academic arguments around the 'limits of liberation' have been drowned out by a crescendo of public frustration with the unfulfilled promises of change, accompanied by dramatic forms of protest. For many, political freedoms remain hollow without economic opportunity, while the cronyism of the ruling ANC, growing inequality, and heightened social polarisation mock the one-time ideals of nation building and social justice.

The contemporary discursive and organisational strategies of the Solidarity Movement examined here present a response to the ongoing long transition. I have argued that, for white workers, the withdrawal of state support for working-class whiteness set in motion the search for a new patron. This is demonstrated by the flood of white workers from beyond the mining industry rushing to join the MWU in the course of the 1980s. This search for alternative avenues of protection in the wake of labour reform as black pressure gained pace is further borne out by the manner in which white workers were clearly attracted to the strategies of the right wing: recall that the MWU and the South African Iron, Steel and Allied Industries Union were founding members of the Afrikaner Volksfront, and white workers were well represented in the ranks of the white supremacist AWB. But neither the paramilitary right-wing nor conservative *volkstaat* apologists could provide an effective challenge or alternative to black majority rule. In the early years of the South African democracy, this demonstrated the futility of a political 'solution' to white workers as well as the broader white public. Racial demography as well as the fragmentation of white society in political and class terms in the wake of the demise of the hegemony of the racial state invariably meant that formal party politics could never afford meaningful power or influence to those wishing to pursue race- or ethnicity-based politics. In this context, the precarity long felt by the white working class intersected and merged with broader white experiences in material and subjective terms.

This convergence of working-class vulnerabilities with wider white experiences is crucial for understanding the relation between the long transition and post-apartheid white minority politics. It shifts the analytical focus away from the existing scholarship's overemphasis of 1994 as the genesis of white and Afrikaner 'cultural trauma' to bring the longer history and consequences of the dismantling of the racial state and racial capitalism into focus. This, in turn, facilitates an analysis that – while acknowledging the particularities and contingencies of the South African case – places the long transition and post-apartheid present in the context of global shifts in the relations between states, capital, and labour since the 1970s and the fallout of globalised neoliberalism as it is currently being revealed. In this way, the story of South Africa's transition shifts from being a tale of ostensible exceptionalism to a productive and meaningful case study of the recent history of capitalism and race from the South.

This holds important transnational lessons for present-day politics and debates around the future of the nation state, contestations surrounding citizenship, multiculturalism, and internationalisation, and the potential of nationalist populist politics in an interconnected and interdependent world. I have argued that the contemporary strategies of the Solidarity Movement present a response to the dismantling of the racial state and of racial capitalism – a response originating among structurally vulnerable white workers from the late 1970s and stretching into the present as a broader cross-class project. The processes and perceptions motivating this response are complex and varied, but they resonate globally: the retreat of once taken-for-granted state provision, the loss of work or workplace status, politics and power relations shifting to include those long regarded as outsiders, resultant feelings of marginalisation and resentment or anxiety as past certainties are seen to be replaced by new values and narratives. In the Global North, it is precisely these perceptions and experiences that are understood to underly the shift to the right. The Solidarity Movement demonstrates, first, that the mobilisation of such sentiments need not take the form of formal party politics, and, second, that they do not have to reflect or have the support of the majority of the population to gain prominence. Amid the hegemony of neoliberal logics of privatisation, freedom, and responsibilisation, a historically powerful minority – particularly one with the ability to mobilise capital – can create alternative avenues for autonomy and continued privilege in the civil society sphere. This can be facilitated and legitimised by tapping into broader global discourses and anxieties surrounding identity and appeals to the politics of rights. As popular disillusionment with formal politics grows, it is conceivable that similar extra-parliamentary efforts may emerge in other contexts. Consider, for instance, that population projections for the USA forecast a steady increase in racial and ethnic diversity over the next decades, so that within a generation the current white majority may become a numerical minority.[8]

As long as the politics of identity – focused on distinctions of race, ethnicity, nationalism, and culture – remains dominant, it is unclear what role class might play in such mobilisations. In the case of the white workers of the MWU, this book has demonstrated efforts to efface class alongside evidence of its continued salience. Despite shifting understandings and representations of precarity and privilege, despite historical blind spots and contemporary insistences to the contrary, class remains very much an 'Afrikaner thing'.

---

[8] US census reports acknowledge that racial (self-)classification is not clear-cut in the American context. Nonetheless, the US Census Bureau's 2009 projections estimated that between 2040 and 2050, the size of minority populations (including groups indicated as Hispanic, Black, and Asian) will increase to the point where they will represent the numeric majority. This estimation has been adjusted in more recent forecasts: although the overall trends stay the same, whites are still expected to form the numerical majority by 2060 – albeit by a small margin. See United States Census Bureau, 'United States population projections: 2000 to 2050' (Washington DC: US Census Bureau, 2009), www.census.gov/content/dam/Census/library/working-papers/2009/demo/us-pop-proj-2000-2050/analytical-document09.pdf (accessed 19 September 2019); United States Census Bureau, 'Demographic turning points – population projections for the United States: 2020 to 2060' (Washington DC: US Census Bureau, 2018), www.census.gov/content/dam/Census/newsroom/press-kits/2018/jsm/jsm-presentation-pop-projections.pdf (accessed 19 September 2019).

Bibliography

Archival collections

Afrikaner Broederbond Collection (AB), Erfenisstigting/Heritage Foundation, Pretoria.

Cabinet Minutes, CAB, SAB (National Archives Repository – Public Records of Government since 1910), National Archives of South Africa, Pretoria.

Commission of Inquiry into Labour Legislation – Wiehahn Commission, 1977–80, K364, SAB (National Archives Repository – Public Records of Government since 1910), National Archives of South Africa, Pretoria.

Finansiële bundels (Rekenmeester), MWU Archive, Solidarity Headquarters, Pretoria.

Marais Viljoen Collection, PV14, Archive for Contemporary Affairs (ARCA), University of the Free State, Bloemfontein.

National Party Caucus, PV408, Archive for Contemporary Affairs (ARCA), University of the Free State, Bloemfontein.

Pamphlet Collection, Archive for Contemporary Affairs (ARCA), University of the Free State, Bloemfontein.

S. P. Botha Collection, Erfenisstigting/Heritage Foundation, Pretoria.

Wiehahn Documentation (Commission of Inquiry into Labour Legislation, 1977–80), Naas Steenkamp private archive, Somerset West.

Interviews

Conducted by the author: general

Cor de Jager, telephone interview, 9 September 2011.
Dirk Hermann, interviewed 16 September 2011, Kloofsig.
 interviewed 17 October 2011, Kloofsig.
Flip Buys, interviewed 19 September 2011, Kloofsig.
 interviewed 25 October 2011, Kloofsig.
Naas Steenkamp, interviewed 6 December 2011, Somerset West.
 interviewed 23 August 2013, Somerset West.
Piet Nieuwenhuizen interviewed 11 August 2012, Bellville.

Conducted by the author: MWU veterans (pseudonyms)

Anton, interviewed 28 October 2011, Kloofsig.
Eddie, interviewed 18 August 2011, Kloofsig.

Frans, interviewed 22 September 2011, Bellville.
Frik, interviewed 8 September 2011, Kloofsig.
Gert, interviewed 27 October 2011, Kloofsig.
Group interview, 14 September 2011, Kloofsig.
Hugo, interviewed 18 August 2011, Kloofsig.
Kobus, interviewed 18 August 2011, Kloofsig.
Louis, interviewed 18 October 2011, Kloofsig.
Neels, interviewed 14 September 2011, Kloofsig.
Paul, interviewed 20 October 2011, Kloofsig.
Schalk, interviewed 28 October 2011, Kloofsig.
Wouter, interviewed 20 September 2011, Kloofsig.

Not conducted by the author
Dennis van der Walt, interviewed by Naas Steenkamp, 7 October 2008.
Fanie Botha, interviewed by Wessel Visser, 27 May 2002.
Nic Wiehahn, interviewed by Adam Ashforth, 10 October 1981. Interview: Nic Wiehahn, AG2738-152, Institute for Advanced Social Research Collection, Historical Papers Research Archive, University of the Witwatersrand, Johannesburg.
interviewed by Deborah Posel, 1 August 1984.
Piet van der Merwe, interviewed by Naas Steenkamp, 7 October 2008.
interviewed by Hermann Giliomee, 18 March 2009.

General titles

Adam, H. and H. Giliomee. *Ethnic Power Mobilized: can South Africa change?* New Haven CT and London: Yale University Press, 1979.
Adam, H., F. van Zyl Slabbert, and K. Moodley. *Comrades in Business: post-liberation politics in South Africa.* Cape Town: Tafelberg, 1997.
Adhikari, M. *Not White Enough, Not Black Enough: racial identity in the South African coloured community.* Athens OH: Ohio University Press, 2005.
Alexander, N. 'Language politics in South Africa' in S. Bekker, M. Dodds, and M. Khosa (eds), *Shifting African Identities.* Pretoria: HSRC, 2001.
Alexander, P. *Workers, War and the Origins of Apartheid: labour and politics in South Africa 1939–1948.* Oxford: James Currey, 2000.
'Rebellion of the poor: South Africa's service delivery protests – a preliminary analysis', *Review of African Political Economy* 37, no. 123 (2010): 25–40.
'Marikana, turning point in South African history', *Review of African Political Economy* 40, no. 138 (2013): 605–19.
Alsheh, Y. and F. Elliker. 'The art of becoming a minority: Afrikaner re-politicisation and Afrikaans political ethnicity', *African Studies* 74, no. 3 (2015): 429–48.
Appiah, K. A. *The Lies that Bind: rethinking identity.* London: Profile Books, 2018.
Arrighi, G. and J. S. Saul. *Essays on the Political Economy of Africa.* New York NY: Monthly Review Press, 1963.

Ashforth, A. *The Politics of Official Discourse in Twentieth-century South Africa*. Oxford: Clarendon Press, 1990.

Ballard, R. 'Assimilation, emigration, semigration, and integration: "white" peoples' strategies for finding a comfort zone in post-apartheid South Africa' in N. Distiller and M. Steyn (eds), *Under Construction: 'race' and identity in South Africa today*. Sandton: Heinemann, 2004.

Ballard, R., A. Habib, and I. Valodia (eds). *Voices of Protest: social movements in post-apartheid South Africa*. Durban: University of KwaZulu-Natal Press, 2006.

Barchiesi, F. *Precarious Liberation: workers, the state and contested social citizenship in postapartheid South Africa*. Albany NY: SUNY Press, 2011.

Baskin, J. *Striking Back: a history of COSATU*. Johannesburg: Ravan Press, 1991.

Bassett, C. 'Labour and hegemony in South Africa's first decade of majority rule', *Studies in Political Economy* 76 (2005): 61–81.

Beinart, W. *Twentieth-century South Africa*. Oxford: Oxford University Press, 2001.

Bentley, K. and A. Habib. 'Racial redress, national identity and citizenship in post-apartheid South Africa' in A. Habib and K. Bentley (eds), *Racial Redress and Citizenship in South Africa*. Pretoria: HSRC, 2008.

Beresford, A. 'Power, patronage, and gatekeeper politics in South Africa', *African Affairs* 114, no. 455 (2015): 226–48.

South Africa's Political Crisis: unfinished liberation and fractured class struggles. Basingstoke: Palgrave Macmillan, 2016.

Berger, I. *Threads of Solidarity: women in South African industry, 1900–1980*. Bloomington IN: Indiana University Press, 1992.

Betti, E. 'Historicizing precarious work: forty years of research in the social sciences and humanities', *International Review of Social History* 63 (2018): 273–319.

Bhambra, G. K. 'Brexit, Trump, and "methodological whiteness": on the misrecognition of race and class', *British Journal of Sociology* 68, no. S1 (2017): 214–32.

Bickford-Smith, V. *Ethnic Pride and Racial Prejudice in Victorian Cape Town: group identity and social practice, 1875–1902*. Cambridge: Cambridge University Press, 1995.

Blaser, T. *Afrikaner Identity after Nationalism*. Basel: Basler Afrika Bibliographien, 2006.

'"I don't know what I am": the end of Afrikaner nationalism in post-apartheid South Africa', *Transformation: Critical Perspectives on Southern Africa* 80 (2012): 1–21.

Blaser, T. and C. van der Westhuizen. 'Introduction: the paradox of post-apartheid "Afrikaner" identity: deployments of ethnicity and neo-liberalism', *African Studies* 71, no. 3 (2012): 380–90.

Blee, K. M. 'Evidence, empathy, and ethics: lessons from oral histories of the Klan', *Journal of American History* 80, no. 2 (1993): 596–606.

Blignaut, C. 'Untold history with a historiography: a review of scholarship on Afrikaner women in South African history', *South African Historical Journal* 65, no. 4 (2013): 596–617.

Boersema, J. R. 'Between recognition and resentment: an Afrikaner trade union's brand of post-nationalism', *African Studies* 71, no. 3 (2012): 408–25.
Bond, P. *Elite Transition: from apartheid to neoliberalism in South Africa*. Scottsville: University of KwaZulu-Natal Press, 2005.
'Neoliberalism, state repression and the rise of social protest in Africa' in B. Berberoglu (ed.), *The Palgrave Handbook of Social Movements, Revolution and Social Transformation*. Cham: Palgrave Macmillan, 2019.
Bond, P. and S. Mottiar. 'Movements, protests and a massacre in South Africa', *Journal of Contemporary African Studies* 31, no. 2 (2013): 283–302.
Bonner, P. 'South African society and culture, 1910–1948' in R. Ross et al. (eds), *The Cambridge History of South Africa*. Cambridge: Cambridge University Press, 2011.
Bonner, P. and E. Webster. 'Background', *South African Labour Bulletin* 5, no. 2 (1979): 1–12.
Bonner, P., J. Hyslop, and L. van der Walt. 'Rethinking worlds of labour: Southern African labour history in international context', *African Studies* 66, nos 2–3 (2007): 137–67.
Botha, J. 'Obituary: N. E. Wiehahn (1929–2006)', *South African Journal of Economics* 74, no. 2 (2006): 359–61.
Bottomley, E. *Poor White*. Cape Town: Tafelberg, 2012.
Bozzoli, B. (ed.), *Class, Community and Conflict: South African perspectives*. Johannesburg: Ravan Press, 1987.
'Interviewing the women of Phokeng' in A. Thomson and R. Perks (eds), *The Oral History Reader*. London: Routledge, 1998.
Breckenridge, K. 'Fighting for a white South Africa: white working-class racism and the 1922 Rand Revolt', *South African Historical Journal* 57, no. 1 (2007): 228–43.
Breman, J. and M. van der Linden. 'Informalizing the economy: the return of the social question at a global level', *Development and Change* 45, no. 5 (2014): 920–40.
Brenner, N., J. Peck, and N. Theodore. 'Variegated neoliberalization: geographies, modalities, pathways', *Global Networks* 10, no. 2 (2010): 182–222.
Brody, D. 'Reconciling the old labor history and the new', *Pacific Historical Review* 62, no. 1 (1993): 1–18.
Brown, J. *South Africa's Insurgent Citizens: on dissent and the possibility of politics*. London: Zed Books, 2015.
Brubaker, R. 'Between nationalism and civilizationism: the European populist moment in comparative perspective', *Ethnic and Racial Studies* 40, no. 8 (2017): 1191–226.
Buhlungu, S. (ed.). *Trade Unions and Democracy: Cosatu workers' political attitudes in South Africa*. Cape Town: HSRC Press, 2006.
A Paradox of Victory: COSATU and the democratic transformation of South Africa. Pietermaritzburg: University of KwaZulu Natal Press, 2010.
Bundy, C. 'Vagabond Hollanders and runaway Englishmen: white poverty in the Cape before poor whiteism' in W. Beinart, P. Delius, and S. Trapido (eds), *Putting a Plough to the Ground: accumulation and dispossession in rural South Africa, 1850–1930*. Johannesburg: Ravan Press, 1986.

Poverty in South Africa: past and present. Auckland Park: Jacana, 2016.
Burawoy, M. 'The functions of migrant labour: comparative material from Southern Africa and the United States', *American Journal of Sociology* 81 (1976): 1050–87.
Charney, C. 'Class conflict and the National Party split', *Journal of Southern African Studies* 10, no. 2 (1984): 269–82.
Cheru, F. 'Overcoming apartheid's legacy: the ascendancy of neoliberalism in South Africa's anti-poverty strategy', *Third World Quarterly* 22, no. 4 (2001): 505–27.
Childs, D. *Britain since 1945: a political history.* London: Routledge, 2006.
Chipkin, I. '"Functional" and "dysfunctional" communities: the making of national citizens', *Journal of Southern African Studies* 29, no. 1 (2003): 63–82.
Clapson, M. *The Routledge Companion to Britain in the Twentieth Century.* Abingdon: Routledge, 2009.
Clark, N. L. and W. H. Worger. *South Africa: the rise and fall of apartheid.* Harlow: Pearson: 2011.
Clawson, D. and M. A. Clawson. 'What has happened to the US labor movement? Union decline and renewal', *Annual Review of Sociology* 26 (1999): 95–119.
Comaroff, J. and J. L. Comaroff (eds), *Millennial Capitalism and the Culture of Neoliberalism.* Durham NC: Duke University Press, 2001.
Comaroff, J. and J. L. Comaroff *Ethnicity, Inc.* Scottsville: University of KwaZulu-Natal Press, 2009.
  The Truth about Crime: sovereignty, knowledge, social order. Chicago IL: University of Chicago Press, 2016.
Conway, D. 'Struggles for citizenship in South Africa' in E. F. Isin and P. Nyers (eds), *Routledge Handbook of Global Citizenship Studies.* New York NY: Routledge, 2014.
Cooper, C. 'The mineworkers' strike', *South African Labour Bulletin* 5, no. 3 (1979): 4–29.
Cooper, F. *Decolonization and African Society: the labor question in French and British Africa.* Cambridge: Cambridge University Press, 1996.
  'Possibility and constraint: African independence in historical perspective', *Journal of African History* 49, no. 2 (2008): 176–96.
Coupe, S. 'Labour relations by authoritarian regimes since 1945: South Africa in international perspective', Wits History Workshop, 13–15 July 1994, http://wiredspace.wits.ac.za/bitstream/handle/10539/7760/HWS-72.pdf?sequence=1 (accessed 29 January 2013).
Crankshaw, O. *Race, Class and the Changing Division of Labour under Apartheid.* London and New York NY: Routledge, 1997.
Crankshaw, O. and C. White. 'Racial desegregation and inner city decay in Johannesburg', *International Journal of Urban and Regional Research* 19, no. 4 (1995): 622–38.
Crush, J., Jeeves, A., and Yudelman, D. *South Africa's Labor Empire: a history of black migrancy to the gold mines.* Cape Town: David Philip, 1991.
Curless, G. 'Introduction: trade unions in the Global South from imperialism to the present day', *Labor History* 57, no. 1 (2016): 1–19.

Darnton, R. *The Kiss of Lamourette: reflections in cultural History*. New York NY and London: W. W. Norton & Company, 1990.
Davie, G. *Poverty Knowledge in South Africa: a social history of human science, 1855–2005*. New York NY: Cambridge University Press, 2015.
Davies, R. 'The white working-class in South Africa', *New Left Review* 82 (November–December 1973): 40–59.
'Mining capital, the state and unskilled white workers in South Africa, 1901–1913', *Journal of Southern African Studies* 3, no. 1 (1976): 41–69.
Capital, State and White Labour in South Africa 1900–1960: a historical materialist analysis of class formation and class relations. Atlantic Highlands NJ: Humanities Press, 1979.
Afrikaners in the New South Africa: identity politics in a globalised economy. London: Tauris Academic Studies, 2009.
Davis, D. 'Narrating the mute: racializing and racism in a neoliberal moment,' *Souls* 9, no. 4 (2007): 346–60.
De Beer, F. C. 'Exercise in futility or dawn of Afrikaner self-determination: an exploratory ethno-historical investigation of Orania', *Anthropology Southern Africa* 29, nos 3–4 (2006): 105–14.
Della Porta, D. and M. Diani (eds). *The Oxford Handbook of Social Movements*. Oxford: Oxford University Press, 2015.
Dorman, S., D. Hammett, and P. Nugent (eds). *Making Nations, Creating Strangers: states and citizenship in Africa*. Leiden: Brill, 2007.
Doxey, G. V. *The Industrial Colour Bar in South Africa*. Cape Town: Oxford University Press, 1961.
Dubow, S. 'Afrikaner nationalism, apartheid and the conceptualization of *"race"'*, Journal of African History 33 (1992): 209–37.
'South Africa and South Africans: nationality, belonging, citizenship' in R. Ross et al. (eds), *The Cambridge History of South Africa*. Cambridge: Cambridge University Press, 2011.
Apartheid 1948–1994. Oxford: Oxford University Press, 2014.
'Closing remarks: new approaches to high apartheid and anti-apartheid', *South African Historical Journal* 69, no. 2 (2017): 304–29.
Dubow, S. and A. Jeeves (eds). *South Africa's 1940s: worlds of possibilities*. Cape Town: Double Storey Books, 2005.
Du Pisani, K. 'Puritanism transformed: Afrikaner masculinities in the apartheid and post-apartheid period' in R. Morell (ed.), *Changing Men in Southern Africa*. London: Zed Books, 2001.
Du Plessis, I. 'Living in "Jan Bom": making and imagining lives after apartheid in a council housing scheme in Johannesburg', *Current Sociology* 52, no. 5 (2004): 879–908.
Du Toit, D. *Capital and Labour in South Africa: class struggle in the 1970s*. London: Kegan Paul, 1981.
'Boers, Afrikaners, and diasporas', *Historia* 48, no. 1 (2003): 15–54.
Du Toit, M. A. *South African Trade Unions: history, legislation, policy*. Johannesburg: McGraw-Hill Book Company, 1976.
Edgar, D. 'The politics of the right: a review article', *Race and Class* 58, no. 2 (2016): 87–94.

Editors. 'Introduction', *New Left Review* 82 (November–December 1973): 38–9.
Ehlers, A. 'The Helpmekaar: rescuing the "volk" through reading, writing and arithmetic, *c.*1916–1965', *Historia* 60, no. 2 (2015): 87–108.
   Die Kaapse Helpmekaar, *c.*1916–*c.*2014: bemiddelaar in Afrikaner opheffing, selfrespek en respektabiliteit. Stellenbosch: SUN Media, 2018.
Eksteen, T. 'The decline of the United Party, 1970–1977'. MA thesis, University of Cape Town, 1982.
Eley, G. and K. Nield. 'Farewell to the working class?', *International Labor and Working-class History* 57 (2000): 1–30.
Ellis, S. 'The ANC in exile', *African Affairs* 90, no. 360 (1991): 439–47.
Ellis, S. and I. van Kessel. 'Introduction: African social movements or social movements in Africa?' in S. Ellis and I. van Kessel (eds), *Movers and Shakers: social movements in Africa*. Leiden: Brill, 2009.
Enck-Wanzer, D. 'Barack Obama, the Tea Party, and the threat of race: on racial neoliberalism and born again racism', *Communication, Culture and Critique* 4, no. 1 (2011): 23–30.
Feinstein, C. H. *An Economic History of South Africa: conquest, discrimination and development*. Cambridge: Cambridge University Press, 2005.
Field, G. and M. Hanagan. 'ILWCH: forty years on', *International Labor and Working-class History* 82 (2012): 5–14.
Fine, R. with E. Davis. *Beyond Apartheid: labour and liberation in South Africa*. Johannesburg: Ravan Press, 1990.
Fisher, F. 'Parliamentary debate on labour', *South African Labour Bulletin* 2, no. 1 (1975): 47–50.
Ford, R. and M. Goodwin. *Revolt on the Right: explaining support for the radical right in Britain*. Abingdon: Routledge, 2014.
Freund, B. *The African Worker*. Cambridge: Cambridge University Press, 1988.
   'Labour studies and labour history in South Africa: perspectives from the apartheid era and after', *International Review of Social History* 58 (2013): 493–515.
   Twentieth-century South Africa: a developmental history. Cambridge: Cambridge University Press, 2019.
Friedman, G. 'Is labor dead?', *Interational Labor and Working-class History* 75 (2009): 126–44.
Friedman, S. *Building Tomorrow Today: African workers in trade unions 1970–1984*. Johannesburg: Ravan Press, 1987.
Geschiere, P. *The Perils of Belonging: autochthony, citizenship, and exclusion in Africa and Europe*. Chicago IL: University of Chicago Press, 2009.
Gidron, N. and P. A. Hall. 'The politics of social status: economic and cultural roots of the populist right', *British Journal of Sociology* 68, no. S1 (2017): 57–84.
Giliomee, H. '"Broedertwis": intra-Afrikaner conflicts in the transition from apartheid', *African Affairs* 91, no. 364 (1992): 339–64.
   '"Survival in justice": an Afrikaner debate over apartheid', *Comparative Studies in Society and History* 36, no. 3 (1994): 527–48.
   The Afrikaners: biography of a people. London: Hurst & Co., 2003.
   '"Allowed such a state of freedom": women and gender relations in the Afrikaner community before enfranchisement in 1930', *New Contree* 59 (May 2004): 29–60.

The Afrikaners: biography of a people. Cape Town: Tafelberg, 2011 [expanded and updated edition].
The Last Afrikaner Leaders: a supreme test of power. Cape Town: Tafelberg, 2012.
Goldberg, D. T. *The Threat of Race: reflections on racial neoliberalism*. Oxford and Malden MA: Wiley-Blackwell, 2009.
Greenberg, S. *Race and State in Capitalist Development: South Africa in comparative perspective*. Johannesburg: Ravan Press, 1980.
Legitimating the Illegitimate: state, markets, and resistance in South Africa. Berkeley CA: University of California Press, 1987.
Grundlingh, A. '"Are we Afrikaners getting too rich?" Cornucopia and change in Afrikanerdom in the 1960s', *Journal of Historical Sociology* 21 nos. 2–3 (2008): 143–65.
Habib, A. 'State–civil society relations in post-apartheid South Africa', *Social Research: An International Quarterly* 72, no. 3 (2005): 680–1.
Habib, A. and K. Bentley (eds). *Racial Redress and Citizenship in South Africa*. Cape Town: HSRC Press, 2008.
Habib, A. and P. Opoku-Mensah. 'Speaking to global debates through a national and continental lens: South African and African social movements in comparative perspective' in S. Ellis and I. van Kessel (eds), *Movers and Shakers: social movements in Africa*. Leiden: Brill, 2009.
Hart, G. 'The provocations of neoliberalism: contesting the nation and liberation after apartheid', *Antipode* 40, no. 4 (2008): 678–705.
Harvey, D. *The Condition of Postmodernity: an enquiry into the origins of cultural change*. Cambridge MA: Blackwell, 1992.
A Brief History of Neoliberalism. Oxford: Oxford University Press, 2007.
Hayem, J. 'From May 2008 to 2011: xenophobic violence and national subjectivity in South Africa', *Journal of Southern African Studies* 39, no. 1 (2013): 7–97.
Hermann, D. *Basta! Ons voetspore is in Afrika*. Pretoria: Kraal Uitgewers, 2011.
Heunis, J. *The Inner Circle: reflections on the last days of white rule*. Johannesburg: Jonathan Ball, 2007.
Hlatshwayo, M. 'NUMSA and Solidarity's responses to technological changes at the ArcelorMittal Vanderbijlpark plant: unions caught on the back foot', *Global Labour Journal* 5, no. 3 (2014): 238–305.
'Neo-liberal restructuring and the fate of South Africa's labour unions: a case study' in P. Vale and E. H. Prinsloo (eds). *The New South Africa at Twenty: critical perspectives*. Pietermaritzburg: University of KwaZulu-Natal Press, 2014.
Hoagland, J. *South Africa: civilisations in conflict*. London: George Allen & Unwin, 1973.
Hobsbawm, E. *Labouring Men: studies in the history of labour*. London: Weidenfeld and Nicolson, 1964.
'Artisan or labour aristocrat?', *Economic History Review* 37, no. 3 (1984): 355–72.
Age of Extremes: the short twentieth century, 1914–1991. London: Michael Joseph, 1994.
Hochschild, A. R. *Strangers in their Own Land: anger and mourning on the American right*. New York NY: The New Press, 2016.

Horrell, M. *South Africa's Workers: their organizations and the patterns of employment*. Johannesburg: South African Institute of Race Relations (SAIRR), 1969.
Hunter, C. W. and T. J. Power. 'Bolsonaro and Brazil's illiberal backlash', *Journal of Democracy* 30, no. 1 (2019): 68–82.
Hunter, M. A. 'Racial physics or a theory for everything that happened', *Ethnic and Racial Studies* 40, no. 8 (2017): 1173–83.
Hyslop, J. 'Why was the white right unable to stop South Africa's democratic transition?' in P. F. Alexander et al. (eds), *Africa Today: a multi-disciplinary snapshot of the continent in 1995*. Canberra: Humanities Research Centre, Australian National University (ANU), 1995.
'The imperial working class makes itself "white": white labourism in Britain, Australia and South Africa before the First World War', *Journal of Historical Sociology* 12, no. 4 (1999): 398–421.
'The world voyage of James Keir Hardie: Indian nationalism, Zulu insurgency and the British labour diaspora 1907–1908', *Journal of Global History* 1 (2006): 343–62.
'The British and Australian leaders of the South African labour movement, 1902–1914: a group biography' in K. Darian-Smith, P. Grimshaw, and S. Macintyre (eds), *Britishness Abroad: transnational movements and imperial cultures*. Victoria: Melbourne University Press, 2007.
'The strange death of liberal England and the strange birth of illiberal South Africa: British trade unionists, Indian labourers and Afrikaner rebels, 1910–1914', *Labour History Review* 79, no. 1 (2014): 95–118.
'Workers called white and classes called poor: the "white working class" and "poor whites" in Southern Africa 1910–1994' in D. Money and D. van Zyl-Hermann (eds), *Rethinking White Societies in Southern Africa, 1930s–1990s*. Abingdon: Routledge, 2020.
Isenberg, N. *White Trash: the 400-year untold history of class in America*. New York NY: Penguin Books, 2016.
Jackson, W. 'Dangers to the colony: loose women and the "poor white" problem in Kenya', *Journal of Colonialism and Colonial History* 14, no. 2 (2013).
James, D. 'Citizenship and land in South Africa: from rights to responsibilities', *Critique of Anthropology* 33, no. 1 (2013): 26–46.
Jansen, J. D. *Knowledge in the Blood: confronting race and the apartheid past*. Stanford CA: Stanford University Press, 2009.
Jeeves, A. H. *Migrant Labour in South Africa's Mining Economy: the struggle for the gold mines' labour supply, 1890–1920*. Johannesburg: Witwatersrand University Press, 1985.
Jessop, B. 'Liberalism, neoliberalism and urban governance: a state-theoretical perspective', *Antipode* 34, no. 3 (2002): 458–78.
Johnstone, F. A. *Class, Race and Gold: a study of class relations and racial discrimination in South Africa*. London: Routledge and Kegan Paul, 1976.
Katz, E. 'White workers' grievances and the industrial colour bar, 1902–1913', *South African Journal of Economics* 42, no. 2 (1974): 84–105.
A Trade Union Aristocracy: a history of white workers in the Transvaal and the general strike of 1913. Johannesburg: African Studies Institute, 1976.

The White Death: silicosis on the Witwatersrand gold mines, 1886–1910. Johannesburg: University of the Witwatersrand Press, 1994.

'Revisiting the origins of the industrial colour bar in the Witwatersrand gold mining industry, 1891–1899', *Journal of Southern African Studies* 25, no. 1 (1999): 73–97.

Kenny, B. 'Servicing modernity: white women shop workers on the Rand and changing gendered respectabilities, 1940s–1970s', *African Studies* 67, no. 3 (2008): 365–96.

King, D. and S. Wood. 'The political economy of neoliberalism: Britain and the United States in the 1980s' in H. Kitschelt et al. (eds), *Continuity and Change in Contemporary Capitalism*. Cambridge: Cambridge University Press, 1999.

Koorts, L. '"The Black Peril would not exist if it were not for a White Peril that is a hundred times greater": D. F. Malan's fluidity on poor whiteism and race in the pre-apartheid era, 1912–1939', *South African Historical Journal* 65, no. 4 (2013): S555–76.

Kraus, J. (ed.). *Trade Unions and the Coming of Democracy in Africa*. Basingstoke: Palgrave Macmillan, 2007.

Kriel, M. 'A new generation of Gustav Prellers? The Fragmente/FAK/Vrye Afrikaan Movement, 1998–2008', *African Studies* 71, no. 3 (2012): 426–45.

Krikler, J. 'Lessons from America: the writings of David Roediger', *Journal of Southern African Studies* 20, no. 4 (1994): 663–9.

The Rand Revolt: the 1922 insurrection and racial killing in South Africa. Johannesburg and Cape Town: Jonathan Ball, 2005.

'Re-thinking race and class in South Africa: some ways forward' in W. D. Hund, J. Krikler, and D. Roediger (eds), *Wages of Whiteness and Racist Symbolic Capital*. Berlin: Lit Verlag, 2010.

Lake, M. and H. Reynolds. *Drawing the Global Colour Line: white men's countries and the question of racial equality*. Cambridge: Cambridge University Press, 2008.

Lange, L. *White, Poor and Angry: white working class families in Johannesburg*. Aldershot: Ashgate Publishing, 2003.

Langner, D. (ed.). *Gebroke Land: armoede in die Afrikaanse gemeenskap sedert 1902*. Centurion: Kraal Uitgewers, 2009.

Leach, G. *The Afrikaners: their last great trek*. London: Macmillan, 1989.

Levy, N. *The Foundations of the South African Cheap Labour System*. London: Routledge and Kegan Paul, 1982.

Lewis, J. *Industrialisation and Trade Union Organisation in South Africa, 1924–55: the rise and fall of the South African Trades and Labour Council*. Cambridge: Cambridge University Press, 1984.

Lichtenstein, A. '"The hope for white and black"? Race, labour and the state in South Africa and the United States, 1924–1956', *Journal of Southern African Studies* 30, no. 1 (2004): 133–53.

'Making apartheid work: African trade unions and the 1953 Native Labour (Settlement of Disputes) Act in South Africa', *Journal of African History* 46, no. 2 (2005): 293–314.

'"A measure of democracy": works committees, black workers, and industrial citizenship in South Africa, 1973–1979', *South African Historical Journal* 67, no. 2 (2015): 113–38.

'"We do not think that the Bantu is ready for labour unions": remaking South Africa's apartheid workplace in the 1970s', *South African Historical Journal* 69, no. 2 (2017): 215–35.

'"We feel that our strength is on the factory floor": dualism, shop-floor power, and labor law in late apartheid South Africa', *Labor History* 60, no. 6 (2019): 606–25.

Lipton, M. *Capitalism and Apartheid: South Africa, 1910–1984*. Aldershot: Gower, 1985.

Lodge, T. 'The Zuma tsunami: South Africa's succession politics', *Representation* 45, no. 2 (2009): 125–41.

'Resistance and reform, 1973–1994' in R. Ross et al. (eds), *The Cambridge History of South Africa*. Cambridge: Cambridge University Press, 2011.

'Neo-patrimonial politics in the ANC', *African Affairs* 113, no. 450 (2014): 1–23.

Louw, P. E. 'Political power, national identity, and language: the case of Afrikaans', *International Journal of the Sociology of Language* 170 (2004): 43–58.

The Rise, Fall, and Legacy of Apartheid. Westport CT: Praeger, 2004.

Mantashe, G. 'The decline of the mining industry and the response of the mining unions'. MA research report, University of the Witwatersrand, 2008.

Marais, H. *South Africa Pushed to the Limit: the political economy of change*. Claremont: UCT Press, 2010.

Maree, J. 'The emergence, struggles and achievements of black trade unions in South Africa from 1973 to 1984', *Labour, Capital and Society* 18, no. 2 (1985): 278–303.

Mariotti, M. and D. van Zyl-Hermann. 'Policy, practice and perception: reconsidering the efficacy and meaning of statutory job reservation in South Africa, 1956–1979', *Economic History of Developing Regions* 29, no. 2 (2014): 197–233.

Marks, S. 'War and union, 1899–1910' in R. Ross et al. (eds), *The Cambridge History of South Africa*. Cambridge: Cambridge University Press, 2011.

'Class, culture, and consciousness in South Africa, 1880–1899' in R. Ross et al. (eds), *The Cambridge History of South Africa*. Cambridge: Cambridge University Press, 2011.

Mawbey, J. 'Afrikaner women of the Garment Union during the Thirties and Forties' in E. Webster (ed.), *Essays in Southern African Labour History*. Johannesburg: Ravan Press, 1978.

McCulloch, J. *Black Peril, White Virtue: sexual crime in Southern Rhodesia, 1902–1935*. Bloomington IN: Indiana University Press, 2000.

McDermott, M. and F. L. Samson. 'White racial and ethnic identity in the United States', *Annual Review of Sociology* 31 (2005): 245–61.

Meeks, E. V. 'Protecting the "white citizen worker": race, labor, and citizenship in south-central Arizona, 1929–1945, *Journal of the Southwest* 48, no. 1 (2006): 91–113.

Meyiwa, T., M. Nkondo, M. Chitiga-Mabugu, M. Sithole, and F. Nyamnjoh (eds). *State of the Nation: South Africa 1994–2014*. Cape Town: HSRC Press, 2014.

Money, D. and D. van Zyl-Hermann (eds). *Rethinking White Societies in Southern Africa, 1930s–1990s.* Abingdon: Routledge, 2020.
Montgomery, D. *Citizen Worker: the experience of workers in the United States with democracy and the free market during the nineteenth century.* Cambridge: Cambridge University Press, 1993.
Moodie, T. D. *The Rise of Afrikanerdom: power, apartheid, and the Afrikaner civil religion.* Berkeley CA: University of California Press, 1975.
Moodie, T. D. with V. Ndatshe. *Going for Gold: men, mines and migration.* Berkeley CA: University of California Press, 1975.
Morrell, R. (ed.). *Changing Men in Southern Africa.* Durban: University of Natal Press, 2001.
Mosoetsa, S. *Eating from One Pot: the dynamics of survival in poor South African households.* Johannesburg: Wits University Press, 2011.
Mosoetsa, S., J. Stillerman, and C. Tilly. 'Precarious labor, South and North: an introduction', *International Labor and Working-class History* 89 (2016): 5–19.
Mudde, C. *Populist Radical Right Parties in Europe.* Cambridge: Cambridge University Press, 2007.
Munck, R. 'The precariat: a view from the South', *Third World Quarterly* 34, no. 5 (2013): 747–62.
Muro, D. 'Ethnicity, nationalism, and social movements' in D. Della Porta and M. Diani (eds), *The Oxford Handbook of Social Movements.* Oxford: Oxford University Press, 2015.
Narsiah, S. 'Neoliberalism and privatisation in South Africa', *GeoJournal* 57, nos 1–2 (2002): 29–38.
Neilson, B. and N. Rossiter. 'Precarity as a political concept, or, Fordism as exception', *Theory, Culture and Society* 25, nos 7–8 (2008): 51–72.
Nelson, B. 'Class, race and democracy in the CIO: the "new" labor history meets the "wages of whiteness"', *International Review of Social History* 41 (1996): 351–74.
Norval, A. 'Reinventing the politics of cultural recognition: the Freedom Front and the demand for a volkstaat' in D. Howarth and A. Norval (eds), *South Africa in Transition.* New York NY: St Martin's Press, 1998.
O'Meara, D. 'Analysing Afrikaner nationalism: the "Christian-National" assault on white trade unionism in South Africa, 1934–1948', *African Affairs* 77, no. 306 (1978): 45–72.
Volkskapitalisme: class, capital and ideology in the development of Afrikaner nationalism. Johannesburg: Ravan Press, 1983.
Forty Lost Years: the apartheid state and the politics of the National Party, 1948–1994. Randburg: Ravan Press, 1996.
Palmer, B. D. 'Reconsiderations of class: precariousness as proletarianization', *Socialist Register* (2014): 40–62.
'"Mind forg'd manacles" and recent pathways to "new" labor histories', *International Review of Social History* 62 (2017): 279–303.
Panitch, L. and G. Albo (eds). *The Politics of the Right: Socialist Register 2016.* London: Merlin Press, 2015.
Piketty, T. *Capital in the Twenty-first Century.* Harvard MA: Harvard University Press, 2014.

Pilkington, H. *Loud and Proud: passion and politics in the English Defence League*. Manchester: Manchester University Press, 2016.

Pillay, D. 'Between social movement and political unionism: COSATU and democratic politics in South Africa', *Rethinking Development and Inequality* 2 (2013): 10–27.

Pilossof, R. 'The unbearable whiteness of being: land, race and belonging in the memoirs of white Zimbabweans', *South African Historical Journal* 61, no. 3 (2009): 621–38.

'"For farmers, by farmers"', *Media History* 19, no. 1 (2013): 32–44.

Polletta, F. and J. M. Jasper. 'Collective identity and social movements', *Annual Review of Sociology* 27 (2001): 283–305.

Polletta, F. and B. G. Gardner. 'Narrative and social movements' in D. Della Porta and M. Diani (eds), *The Oxford Handbook of Social Movements*. Oxford: Oxford University Press, 2015.

Posel, D. 'Rethinking the "race–class debate" in South African historiography', *Social Dynamics* 9, no. 1 (1983): 50–66.

'Language, legitimation and control: the South African state after 1978', *Social Dynamics: A Journal of African Studies* 10, no. 1 (1984): 1–16.

'Whiteness and power in the South African civil service: paradoxes of the apartheid state', *Journal of Southern African Studies* 25, no. 1 (1999): 99–119.

'The apartheid project, 1948–1970' in R. Ross et al. (eds), *The Cambridge History of South Africa*. Cambridge: Cambridge University Press, 2011.

Powell, D. *British Politics and the Labour Question, 1986–1990*. London: Macmillan, 1992.

Ramphele, M. 'Citizenship challenges for South Africa's young democracy', *Daedalus* 130, no. 1 (2001): 1–17.

Reynolds, D. *One World Divisible: a global history since 1945*. London: Penguin Books, 2000.

Roberts, D. J. and M. Mahtani. 'Neoliberalizing race, racing neoliberalism: placing "race" in neoliberal discourses', *Antipode* 42, no. 2 (2010): 248–57.

Robins, S. 'Introduction' in S. Robins (ed.), *Limits to Liberation after Apartheid: citizenship, governance and culture*. Oxford: James Currey, 2005.

From Revolution to Rights in South Africa: social movements, NGOs and popular politics after apartheid. Woodbridge: James Currey, 2008.

Roediger, D. *The Wages of Whiteness: race and the making of the American working class*. New York NY: Verso, 1991.

Roos, N. 'South African history and subaltern historiography: ideas for a radical history of white folk', *International Review of Social History* 61, no. 1 (2016): 117–50.

Ross, A. *Nice Work If You Can Get It: life and labor in precarious times*. New York NY: New York University Press, 2009.

Ross, R. *A Concise History of South Africa*. Cambridge: Cambridge University Press, 2008.

Ross, R., A. K. Mager, and B. Nasson. 'Introduction' in R. Ross et al. (eds), *The Cambridge History of South Africa*. Cambridge: Cambridge University Press, 2011.

Rutherford, B. A. *Working on the Margins: black workers, white farmers in postcolonial Zimbabwe*. London: Zed Books, 2001.
Sadie, J. L. *The Fall and Rise of the Afrikaner in the South African Economy*. Stellenbosch: University of Stellenbosch Annale, 2002.
Satgar, V. 'Beyond Marikana: the post-apartheid South African state', *Africa Spectrum* 47, nos 2–3 (2012): 33–62.
Saul, J. S. and P. Bond. *South Africa – The Present as History: from Mrs Ples to Mandela and Marikana*. Auckland Park: Jacana, 2014.
Saunders, C. *The Making of the South African Past: major historians on race and class*. Cape Town and Johannesburg: David Philip, 1988.
Seekings, J. '"Not a single white person should be allowed to go under": *swartgevaar* and the origins of South Africa's welfare state, 1924–1929', *Journal of African History* 48, no. 3 (2007): 375–94.
'The National Party and the ideology of welfare in South Africa under apartheid', *Journal of Southern African Studies*, 46, no. 6 (2020): 1145–1162.
Seekings, J. and N. Nattrass. *Class, Race, and Inequality in South Africa*. New Haven CT: Yale University Press, 2005.
Serfontein, J. H. P. *Brotherhood of Power: an exposé of the secret Afrikaner Broederbond*. London: Rex Collings, 1979.
Sharp, J. 'Market, race and nation: history of the white working class in Pretoria' in K. Hart and J. Sharp (eds), *People, Money and Power in Economic Crisis: perspectives from the Global South*. New York NY: Berghahn Books, 2015.
Sharp, J. and S. van Wyk. 'The most intractable whites in South Africa? Ethnography of a 'Boere-Afrikaner' settlement'. Paper presented to the 5th ECAS Conference, Lisbon, 2013.
'Beyond the market: white workers in Pretoria' in K. Hart (ed.). *Economy for and against Democracy*. New York NY: Berghahn Books, 2015.
Shefer, T., K. Ratele, and A. Strebel (eds). *From Boys to Men: social constructions of masculinity in contemporary society*. Cape Town: UCT Press, 2007.
Simon, H. 'The myth of the white working class in South Africa', *African Affairs* 4, no. 2 (1974): 189–203.
Simons, H. J. and R. E. Simons. *Class and Colour in South Africa, 1850–1950*. Harmondsworth: Penguin, 1969.
Simson, H. 'The myth of the white working class in South Africa', *African Affairs* 4, no. 2 (1974): 189–203.
Smuts, J. 'Male trouble: independent women and male dependency in a white working-class suburb of Pretoria', *Agenda* 20, no. 68 (2006): 80–7.
South African Democracy Education Trust. *The Road to Democracy in South Africa. Volumes 1–7*. Cape Town: Zebra Press, 2004–17.
Southall, R. 'Understanding the "Zuma tsunami"', *Review of African Political Economy* 36, no. 121 (2009): 317–33.
'Democracy at risk? Politics and governance under the ANC', *Annals of the American Academy of Political and Social Science* 652 (2014): 48–69.
The New Black Middle Class in South Africa. Auckland Park: Jacana, 2016.
'The coming crisis of Zuma's ANC: the party state confronts fiscal crisis', *Review of African Political Economy* 43, no. 147 (2016): 73–88.

Southern, N. 'The Freedom Front Plus: an analysis of Afrikaner politics and ethnic identity in the new South Africa', *Contemporary Politics* 14, no. 4 (2008): 463–78.
Standing, G. *The Precariat: the new dangerous class*. London: Bloomsbury, 2011.
Stedman Jones, G. 'Class struggle and the industrial revolution', *New Left Review* 90 (1975): 35–69.
Sternhell, Z. *The Founding Myths of Israel: nationalism, socialism and the making of the Jewish state*. Princeton NJ: Princeton University Press, 1998.
Stewart, C. J., C. A. Smith, and R. E. Denton. *Persuasion and Social Movements*. Long Grove IL: Waveland Press, 2012.
Steyn, M. *'Whiteness Just Isn't What It Used to Be': white identity in a changing South Africa*. Albany NY: SUNY Press, 2001.
'Rehabilitating a whiteness disgraced: Afrikaner *white talk* in post-apartheid South Africa', *Communication Quarterly* 52, no. 2 (2004): 143–69.
Steyn, M. and D. Foster. 'Repertoires for talking white: resistant whiteness in post-apartheid South Africa', *Ethnic and Racial Studies* 31, no. 1 (2008): 25–51.
Stoler, A. 'Sexual affronts and racial frontiers: European identities and the cultural politics of exclusion in colonial Southeast Asia', *Comparative Studies in Society and History* 34, no. 3 (1992): 514–51.
'Colonial archives and the arts of governance', *Archival Science* 2 (2002): 87–109.
Along the Archival Grain: epistemic anxieties and colonial common sense. Princeton NJ: Princeton University Press, 2009.
Super, G. *Governing through Crime in South Africa: the politics of race and class in neoliberalizing regimes*. Burlington VT: Ashgate, 2013.
Tayler, J. '"Our poor": the politicisation of the poor white problem, 1932–1942', *Kleio* 24, no. 1 (1992): 40–65.
Terreblanche, S. *A History of Inequality in South Africa*. Pietermaritzburg: University of Natal Press, 2003.
Lost in Transformation? South Africa's search for a new future since 1986. Johannesburg: KMM Review Publishing Company, 2012.
Thompson, L. M. 'Afrikaner nationalist historiography and the policy of apartheid', *Journal of African History* 3, no. 1 (1962): 125–41.
The Political Mythology of Apartheid. New Haven CT: Yale University Press, 1985.
Todd, S. *The People: the rise and fall of the working class, 1910–2010*. London: John Murray, 2014.
Valentine, G. and C. Harris. 'Strivers vs skivers: class prejudice and the demonization of dependency in everyday life', *Geoforum* 53 (2014): 84–92.
Vance, J. D. *Hillbilly Elegy: a memoir of a family and culture in crisis*. New York NY: HarperCollins, 2016.
Van der Linden, M. 'Labour history: the old, the new and the global', *African Studies* 66, nos 2–3 (2007): 169–80.
Van der Waal, C. S. 'Creolisation and purity: Afrikaans language politics in post-apartheid times', *African Studies* 71, no. 3 (2001): 446–63.
Van der Waal, K. and S. Robins. '"De La Rey" and the revival of "Boer heritage": nostalgia in the post-apartheid Afrikaner culture industry', *Journal of Southern African Studies* 37, no. 4 (2011): 763–79.

Van der Westhuizen, C. *White Power and the Rise and Fall of the National Party.* Cape Town: Zebra Press, 2007.
Sitting Pretty: white Afrikaans women in postapartheid South Africa. Durban: University of KwaZulu-Natal, 2018.
Van Onselen, C. *New Babylon, New Nineveh: everyday life on the Witwatersrand 1886–1914.* Johannesburg: Jonathan Ball, 1982.
Van Rooyen, J. *Hard Right: the new white power in South Africa.* London: I. B. Tauris, 1994.
The New Great Trek: the story of South Africa's white exodus. Pretoria: Unisa Press, 2000.
Van Vuuren, H. *Apartheid, Guns and Money: a tale of profit.* Auckland Park: Jacana, 2017.
Van Wyk, S. 'Buying into Kleinfontein: the financial implications of Afrikaner self-determination'. MSocSci thesis, University of Pretoria, 2015.
Van Zyl-Hermann, D. 'White workers and South Africa's democratic transition, 1977–2011'. PhD thesis, University of Cambridge, 2014.
'White workers in the late apartheid period: a report on the Wiehahn Commission and Mineworkers' Union archival collections', *History in Africa* 43 (2016): 229–58.
'Make Afrikaners great again! National populism, democracy and the new white minority politics in post-apartheid South Africa', *Ethnic and Racial Studies* 41, no. 15 (2017): 2673–92.
'Race, rumour and the politics of class in late and post-apartheid South Africa: the case of Arrie Paulus', *Social History* 43, no. 4 (2018): 509–30.
'White workers and the unravelling of racial citizenship in late apartheid South Africa' in D. Money and D. van Zyl-Hermann (eds), *Rethinking White Societies in Southern Africa, 1930s–1990s.* Abingdon: Routledge, 2020.
Van Zyl-Hermann, D. and J. Boersema. 'The politics of whiteness', *Africa* 87, no. 4 (2017): 651–61.
Veracini, L. 'Afterword: Orania as settler self-transfer', *Settler Colonial Studies* 1, no. 2 (2011): 190–6.
Verwey, M. and C. Quayle. 'Whiteness, racism and Afrikaner identity in post-apartheid South Africa', *African Affairs* 111, no. 445 (2012): 551–75.
Vestergaard, M. 'Who's got the map? The negotiation of Afrikaner identities in post-apartheid South Africa', *Daedalus* 130, no. 1 (2001): 19–44.
Vincent, L. 'A cake of soap: the *Volksmoeder* ideology and Afrikaner women's campaign for the vote', *International Journal of African Historical Studies* 32, no. 1 (1999): 1–17.
'Bread and honour: white working-class women and Afrikaner nationalism in the 1930s', *Journal of Southern African Studies* 26, no. 1 (2000): 61–78.
Visser, W. 'From MWU to Solidarity – a trade union reinventing itself', *South African Journal of Labour Relations* 3, no. 2 (2006): 19–41.
'Post-hegemonic Afrikanerdom and diaspora: redefining Afrikaner identity in post-apartheid South Africa', *New Contree* 54 (2007): 1–30.
Van MWU tot Solidariteit: geskiedenis van die Mynwerkersunie 1902–2002. Centurion: Solidariteit, 2008.

'Die vestiging van Solidariteit se Helpende Hand as 'n suksesvolle gemeenskapsgebaseerde welsynsorganisasie', *Tydskrif vir Geesteswetenskappe* 51, no. 1 (2011): 21–35.

A History of the South African Mine Workers' Union, 1902–2014. Lewiston NY: Edwin Mellen Press, 2016.

Von Holdt, K. 'Social movement unionism: the case of South Africa', *Work, Employment and Society* 16, no. 2 (2002): 283–304.

Von Schnitzler, A. 'Citizenship prepaid: water, calculability, and techno-politics in South Africa', *Journal of Southern African Studies* 34, no. 4 (2008): 899–917.

Walley, C. L. 'Trump's election and the "white working class": what we missed', *American Ethnologist* 44, no. 2 (2017): 231–6.

Waterman, P. 'The "labour aristocracy" in Africa: introduction to a debate', *Development and Change* 6, no. 3 (1975): 57–74.

Webster, E. (ed.). *Essays in Southern African Labour History*. Johannesburg: Ravan Press, 1978.

Cast in a Racial Mould: labour process and trade unionism in the foundries. Johannesburg: Ravan Press, 1985.

'The rise of social-movement unionism: the two faces of the black trade union movement in South Africa' in P. Frankel, P. Pines, and M. Swilling (eds), *State Resistance and Change in South Africa*. New York NY: Croom Helm, 1988.

'South African labour studies in a global perspective, 1973–2006', *Labour, Capital and Society* 37 (2004): 268–70.

Webster, E. and K. von Holdt (eds). *Beyond the Apartheid Workplace: studies in transition*. Scottsville: University of KwaZulu Natal Press, 2005.

Weide, R. and S. Weide. *Die Volledige Verkiesingsuitslae van Suid-Afrika, 1910–1986*. Pretoria: Private Publication, 1987.

Werbner, P. 'Rethinking class and culture in Africa: between E. P. Thompson and Pierre Bourdieu', *Review of African Political Economy* 45, no. 155 (2017): 7–24.

Wilkins, I. and H. Strydom. *The Super-Afrikaners: inside the Afrikaner Broederbond*. Johannesburg and Cape Town: Jonathan Ball, 2012.

Willoughby-Herard, T. *Waste of White Skin: the Carnegie Corporation and the racial logic of white vulnerability*. Oakland CA: University of California Press, 2015.

Wilson, F. *Labour in the South African Gold Mines, 1911–1969*. Cambridge: Cambridge University Press, 1972.

Witz, L. 'A case of schizophrenia: the rise and fall of the Independent Labour Party' in B. Bozzoli (ed.), *Class, Community and Conflict: South African perspectives*. Johannesburg: Ravan Press, 1987.

Wolpe, H. 'Capitalism and cheap labour power in South Africa: from segregation to apartheid', *Economy and Society* 1, no. 4 (1972): 425–56.

'The "white working class" in South Africa', *Economy and Society* 5, no. 2 (1976): 197–240.

Race, Class and the Apartheid State. London: James Currey, 1988.

Yudelman, D. *The Emergence of Modern South Africa: state, capital and the incorporation of organized labour on the South African goldfields, 1902–1939*. London: Greenwood, 1983.

Newspapers and online sources

Newspapers and magazines
Mail and Guardian (2011)
MWU-Nuus/MWU-News (1991–2000)
Die Mynwerker/The Mineworker (1977–91)
Rand Daily Mail (1972–3)
Solidariteit/Solidarity (2001–15)
Die Vaderland (December 1975)

Websites
www.afriforum.co.za
www.afriforumjeug.co.za
https://blog.solidariteit.co.za
https://boufonds.solidariteit.co.za
www.fak.org.za
https://finansies.solidariteit.co.za
https://helpendehand.co.za
www.krisisberaad.co.za
www.maroelamedia.co.za
https://solidariteit.co.za/
https://solidariteit.co.za/solidariteit-beweging
https://tydskrif.solidariteit.co.za
https://vrae.solidariteit.co.za

Online articles
www.bbc.co.uk/news/world-africa-14878102 (accessed 2 August 2014)
www.bdlive.co.za/national/2016/07/21/afriforum-is-selfish-and-use-of-constitutions-preamble-is-ironic-mogoeng-says (accessed 22 July 2016)
www.corruptionwatch.org.za/corruption-becoming-endemic/ (accessed 5 December 2016)
www.dailymaverick.co.za/article/2014-02-05-analysis-bonfires-of-discontent-in-horrifying-numbers#.WEU_WvmGPIU (accessed 5 December 2016)
www.dailymaverick.co.za/article/2015-10-12-back-to-the-future-afrikaners-unveil-r3.5-billion-plan-to-secure-future-autonomy/#.VuZhRPmGPIU (accessed 14 March 2016)
http://video.foxnews.com/v/5785308294001/?#sp=show-clips (accessed 26 August 2018)
www.fwdeklerk.org/index.php/afr/nuus/474-artikel-plan-b-se-kritici-bly-in-kammaland (accessed 4 February 2016)
www.huffingtonpost.co.za/2018/04/19/private-prosecutions-this-is-how-it-works_a_23415246/ (accessed 6 August 2018)
www.huffingtonpost.co.za/pieter-du-toit/afriforums-u-s-adventure-playing-with-fire-after-setting-australia-alight_a_23426470/ (accessed 31 May 2018)
www.huffingtonpost.co.za/2018/04/12/selling-the-drama-the-land-debate-as-a-sales-pitch_a_23409707/ (accessed 31 May 2018)

https://lareviewofbooks.org/article/whos-afraid-of-the-white-working-class-on-joan-c-williamss-white-working-class-overcoming-class-cluelessness-in-america/# (accessed 28 January 2019)
http://mg.co.za/article/2009-11-17-saps-affirmative-action-policies-under-scrutiny (accessed 9 August 2016)
http://mg.co.za/article/2014-06-04-renate-barnard-resigns-from-saps-over-race-discrimination (accessed 9 August 2016)
https://monthlyreview.org/2014/04/01/south-africas-resource-curses-growing-social-resistance/ (accessed 5 November 2017)
www.netwerk24.com/nuus/2015-10-04-ons-plan-b-vir-sa (accessed 9 October 2015)
www.netwerk24.com/Stemme/Menings/5-redes-waarom-Solidariteit-se-Plan-B-sleg-is-vir-Suid-Afrika-en-Afrikaners-20151008 (accessed 4 February 2016)
www.netwerk24.com/Nuus/Politiek/ANC-kap-Solidariteit-20150507 (accessed 7 May 2015)
www.news24.com/SouthAfrica/News/Former-minister-Fanie-Botha-dies-20100904 (accessed 17 September 2015)
www.news24.com/Columnists/MaxduPreez/afriforum-hijacking-the-afrikaner-mainstream-20160726 (accessed 26 July 2016)
www.news24.com/SouthAfrica/News/live-sa-reacts-to-donald-trump-comments-on-land-expropriation-farm-murders-20180823 (accessed 26 August 2018)
www.news24.com/SouthAfrica/News/p2-trump-tweets-and-sa-goes-berserk-heres-what-was-said-and-by-whom-20180823 (accessed 6 December 2018)
www.news24.com/Columnists/GuestColumn/trumps-comment-about-south-africa-is-a-reminder-that-race-still-matters-20180829 (accessed 31 August 2018)
www.nytimes.com/2016/11/10/books/6-books-to-help-understand-trumps-win.html (accessed 29 January 2019)
www.politicsweb.co.za/contact/fw-de-klerks-tribute-to-late-fanie-botha (accessed 17 September 2015)
www.reuters.com/article/us-safrica-usa-sisulu/trump-tweet-based-on-false-information-south-african-foreign-minister-idUSKCN1L813D (accessed 6 December 2018)

Published sources

Chamber of Mines of South Africa. *96th Annual Report: 1985*. Johannesburg: Chamber of Mines, 1986.
97th Annual Report: 1986. Johannesburg: Chamber of Mines, 1987.
Department of Labour and of Mines. *Report of the Commission of Inquiry into Labour Legislation Part 1 (Key Issues)*. Pretoria: Government Printer, RP49/1979.
Department of Manpower Utilisation. *Report of the Commission of Inquiry into Labour Legislation Part 5 (Industrial Relations)*. Pretoria: Government Printer, RP27/1981.
Report of the Commission of Inquiry into Labour Legislation Part 6 (Industrial Relations in the Mining Industry). Pretoria: Government Printer, RP28/1981.
Hansard (1970–93)

Open Society Foundations. *Europe's White Working Class Communities. At home in Europe: a report on six European cities*. New York NY: Open Society Foundations, 2014.

SAIRR. *A Survey of Race Relations in South Africa 1973*. Johannesburg: South African Institute of Race Relations (SAIRR), 1974.

A Survey of Race Relations in South Africa 1976. Johannesburg: South African Institute of Race Relations (SAIRR), 1977.

A Survey of Race Relations in South Africa 1977. Johannesburg: South African Institute of Race Relations (SAIRR), 1978.

Southern African Migration Project. '*The perfect storm: the realities of xenophobia in contemporary South Africa*'. Migration Policy Brief no. 50. Cape Town: Idasa, 2008, http://samponline.org/wp-content/uploads/2016/10/Acrobat50.pdf (accessed 13 October 2020).

Statistics South Africa. *Census 2011: census in brief*. Report no. 03-01-41. Pretoria: Statistics South Africa, 2012.

United States Census Bureau. 'United States population projections: 2000 to 2050'. Washington DC: US Census Bureau, 2009, www.census.gov/content/dam/Census/library/working-papers/2009/demo/us-pop-proj-2000-2050/analytical-document09.pdf (accessed 19 September 2019).

'Demographic turning points – population projections for the United States: 2020 to 2060'. Washington DC: US Census Bureau, 2018, www.census.gov/content/dam/Census/newsroom/press-kits/2018/jsm/jsm-presentation-pop-projections.pdf (accessed 19 September 2019).

Other sources

Solidariteitkunde, 13 September 2011.

'Solidariteit Lede-inligting 2000–2008', courtesy of Dawid Durie (10 November 2011).

Solidarity constitution as approved by the National Council on 26 March 2009, courtesy of Hennie de Wet (10 August 2011).

Index

Page numbers in italics relate to figures

affirmative action
  AfriForum and, 236
  MWU and, 164–5, 185, 190–1, 193, *271*
  Solidarity and, 218, 221, 296–7
  white poverty and, 185, 285
African labour; *see also* black labour
  advancement of, 146–7
  as competition for white workers, 47–8, 51
  industrial rights of, 78–9, 89, 114–15, 117–18, 152
  migrant workers, 38–41, 118
  role in liberation struggle, 20–2, 35
African National Congress (ANC); *see also* Tripartite Alliance
  COSATU and, 197
  in government, 22–5, 170
  industrial rights and, 93
  liberation struggle, 21, 152
  MWU and, 185
  Solidarity and, 199–200, 203, 210, 233
African National Union of Clothing Workers, 131
African unions, 20, 60–1, 117–18, 144, 149–50
African urbanisation, 58, 60
AfriForum
  affirmative action and, 236
  community work of, 231, 233, 235
  farm attacks, 303–5
  funding, 224
  hate speech case against Julius Malema, 199, 204, 218, 241
  international campaigns of, 303–5
  membership of, 241, 298
  private prosecutions unit of, 303
AfriForum Youth, 222
Afrikaans language, 9, 57, 123, 165, 185, 225

Afrikaner Broederbond
  background to, 57–8
  economic growth and, 226
  labour reforms, 97–100, 105–7, 110
  National Party and, 68, 104
  trade unions and, 58–9
  Wiehahn Commission and, 112–13, 122–3
Afrikaner nationalism, 9, 50, 55–60, 216–17, 265–6
Afrikaner Volksfront, *163*, *184*, 251, 274, 307
Afrikaner Weerstandsbeweging (AWB), 163, 251, 274–5, 280, 283, 307
Afrikaners
  as classless volk, 1, 5, 9, 46–7, 70–1, 74, 262–3, 273–4, 288–9, 301–2
  history of, 56–7, 68, 201–10
  as miners, 45
  MWU and, 186
  Solidarity and, 225–6, 303
  white poverty, 54
agricultural sector, 60, 66, 68–9, 169, 183, 214; *see also* farm attacks
Akademia, 221, 224, 231, 234, 241
alternative government *see* Solidarity Movement, as 'state' for Afrikaners
Amalgamated Engineering Union, 131–2
Amalgamated Union of Building Trade Workers, 133–4
American Federation of Labor and Congress of Industrial Organizations (AFL-CIO), 168
Anglo American, 73
Anglo-Boer War *see* South African War
antiracialism, 217
antiracism, 217
antisemitism, 72, 274
apartheid
  economic growth and, 80, 89
  impact of, 279–80

Index

National Party and, 58
organised labour movement, 60–6
Solidarity and, 203, 205–7, 238, 240, 258
white workers and, 1–2
ArcelorMittal South Africa, 170; *see also* Mittal Steel
armaments industry, 10
Artisans Staff Association, 131
Australia, 38, 41

baas–Klaas relationships, 177, 279
Bantu Labour Act (1964), 110–15; *see also* Native Labour Act (1953)
Bantu Labour Relations Amendment Act (1973), 97
Bantustans *see* homelands
Basson, Adriaan, 233
Basta! Ons voetspore is in Afrika, 207–8
Beech, Richard, 130, 133–4
black labour
  as competition for white workers, 1–2
  industrial rights of, 98, 107
  role in liberation struggle, 152, 168, 306
  threat of, 93
black oppression, 2, 36
black trade unions, 102–3, 112–13; *see also* Congress of South African Trade Unions (COSATU)
blasting certificates, 44, 73–5, 147–8, 162, 174–5, 177, 179
Bodenstein, P., 92
Boilermakers' Society, 135–6
Bond, Fred, 181, 245
Boraine, Alex, 96, 102, 110–11
Bornman, Wessel, 87, *104*, 126, 128, 153
Botes, Chris, 122, *123*, 138–53
Botha, Fanie
  Afrikaner Broederbond and, 107
  blasting certificates, 148
  labour reforms, 125–6, *127*, 129
  as Minister of Labour, 101–5, *104*
  MWU and, 106, 113, *173*
  TUCSA and, 141
  Wiehahn Commission, 108–12, *133*, *143*
Botha, Louis (General), 40
Botha, P. W., 108, 115, 134, *143*, 169–70
Brexit, 17–19, 265
Britain
  Brexit, 17–19, 265
  colonial regime of, 119, 152, 226
  elections in, 69, 94–5
  immigration to, 299
  industrial action in, 86
  labour movements in, 167
  migrants from, 38, 41, 56

Broederbond *see* Afrikaner Broederbond
bursaries, 189–97, 221, 234, 238; *see also* education
Buys, Flip
  affirmative action, *192*
  on class, 1, 9, 164, 175–95, 245–7, 249–55, 262
  on community work, 227–32, 234
  editorship of MWU newspapers, 161
  hate speech case against Julius Malema, *215*
  on membership, 223, 296–7
  on MWU, 181–97, 244–50, 252, 254–6, 271
  as MWU general secretary, 164, *187*, 188–90, 195, 261, *270*
  partnerships with employers, 190–1
  on Solidarity, 179, 206–39
  on strikes, 260–1
  'super white union' and, 180–2
  on values, 210, 213–14
  on white victimhood, 194

'calling' concept, 212, 216, 218, 242, 247, 290–1
capitalism, 19, 45, 66–71, *69*, 77–8, 127–8, 168, 306; *see also* late capitalism; neoliberalism
Carnegie Commission, 54–5, 71
Chamber of Mines
  background to, 37–8
  blasting certificates, 147–8, 174
  industrial action and, 42
  MWU and, 105, 113, 172, 198
  racial division of labour, 43, 49, 71–2
  Rand Revolt (1922), 45–6
  statistics of, 7
Christian Nationalism, 56, 204, 212, 215–16
Christian trade unionism, 210, 212, 216
Christianity, 72, 246–7, 254
Cilliers, Jaap, *133*
citizenship, 7–8, 20, 27, 40–1, 47, 65, 118–19, 127, 129, 135, 152–3, 172, 208, 306; *see also* industrial rights; political rights
civil service, 67–8
'civilised labour' 48–9, 51–5, 57, 128, 172
class
  black labour and, 175, 177, 279
  classless volk, 1, 5, 9, 46–7, 70–1, 74, 262–3, 273–4, 288–9, 301–2
  middle-class whites, 6, 11, 18–19, 261–2, 280, 300
  MWU/Solidarity and, 243–61, 301–2
  race and, 22, 45, 186
Cold War, 4, 58, 168

colonial regimes, 44, 53, 119, 152, 226
colour bar, 41–2, 46, 48, 52
coloured voters, 49, 118, 134–5
coloured workers, 51, 61, 96, 133–4, 139, 144, 294
Commission of Inquiry into Labour Legislation *see* Wiehahn Commission
commodification of culture, 222, 224–5
communism, 58, 93, 167, 169, 210, 259–60; *see also* Suppression of Communism Act (1950)
compounds, 39–41
Confederation of Metal and Building Unions, 124
Congress of South African Trade Unions (COSATU), 20–1, 152, 168, 170, 197, 210, 282, 306; *see also* Tripartite Alliance
Conservative Party (CP), 81, 109, 162, 177–8, 180
conservative politics *see* right-wing politics
Constitution Act (1983), 135
Constitution of South Africa (1996), 303–5
Co-ordinating Council of South African Trade Unions, 63, 87
corruption, 24–5, 199–200
Cronje, Krappie, 181, 244, 246, 275
crony capitalism, 23–5
cultural identity, 8–9, 165, 247–50
cultural turn, 4
culture, institutional, 243–50, 271–4, 282

De Beers Mining Company, 192
De Jager, Cor
 Afrikaner Volksfront and, *184*
 on *baas–Klaas* relationships, 176–7
 background and role, 251–2
 Conservative Party and, *181*
 as HNP candidate, 162
 on MWU, 175–6, 185, 188
 National Party and, *73*, *173*, 174–5
 opposition to labour reform, 172, 175
De Jager, P. R., 92
De Klerk, F. W., 87, 92, 97–100, 160–2, 180
De Villiers, Wim, 97, 123
De Wet, Carel, 73
Deacon, Jan, 246
deindustrialisation, 11, 16
Department of Labour, 50–1, 79
Department of Manpower Utilisation, 117
desegregation, 162, 182, *183*, 198, 268, *269*, *270*, 276
Drummond, Errol, 122, *123*, *133*, 133, 138
Du Toit, Chris, 122, *123*, *133*, 138–53
Durban strikes, 90–101, *93*, 103, 114, 135

economic growth
 1970s, 2, 20, 76–8, 114, 151, 306
 Afrikaner Broederbond and, 97–8, 100
 after Second World War, 69–70
 ANC and, 199–200, 210
 financial crisis of 2008, 14, 25, 264–5, 306
 Golden Age, 66, 69, 76–7, 305–6
 Great Depression, 52, 54
 National Party and, 66, 68, 80–1, 83–4, 89, 101, 104–5, 169–70
 PRP and, 102
 recessions, 106, 168, 172
 state intervention and, 52, 118
 United Party and, 83–4, 88, 177
 Wiehahn Commission, 119
education, 67, 185–6, 220–1, 231, 234, 238, 245, 284–5
elections
 1924 general, 48
 1948 general, 50, 58–60, 188
 1974 general, 94–5
 1981 general, 162, 175
 1987 general, 177–8
 1989 general, 177–8
 in Britain, 69
 by-elections, 101, 162, 174
 European Parliament, 16
electronic communications, 161
Elisio, Alfieri, 130
Eloff, Theuns, 233
embourgeoisement, 5–6, 8–9, 26, 67–8, 70, 121, 130, 305; *see also* social mobility
employers
 baas–Klaas relationships, 177
 black workers and, 91–2, 144, 149
 class compromise with state and unions, 14
 conflict with white labour, 42, 47–8, 71, 89
 job reservation and, 49, 51, 67, 108, 142
 MWU attitude towards, 161, 165, 173, 177, 179–80, 190–1, 270
 negotiations with white workers, 72, 78–9, 103, 111
 Solidarity attitude towards, 196, 260–1, 277–9, 283
 Wiehahn Commission and, 124, 129, 131, 141–2, 144, 149
employment equity, 10, 223; *see also* affirmative action
Engels, Friedrich, 35
English
 dominance, 58, 67, 228, 291
 language, 56, 123, 160, 191, 228, 291–3, 296
 -speakers, 160, 287, 297

Index

Eskom
  Afrikaner business and, 68
  MWU and, 191, 268–9, 275, 277–8
  protests against, *183*, *269*, *277*
ethnicity, 182, 184, 188–9, 194–5, 226, 318–29
European Parliament, 16, 236
exceptionalism of South African transition, 3, 308

farm attacks, 303–5
farming *see* agricultural sector
Federasie van Afrikaanse Kultuurvereniginge (FAK), 57, 222, 231–9
Federation of Salaried Staff Associations, 124
financial crisis of 2008, 14, 25, 264–5, 306
First World War, 44, 231
five-day working week, 105–6
flexibilisation, 15
Fortune magazine, 76
Fox News, 304
France, 119
franchise *see* voting rights
free market system, 22–3, 77–8, 118, 169–70, 260
Freedom Front (FF), 163–4, 190
freedom of association, 142, 145

Gemeenskap Volk en Arbeid (GVA), 99
gender, 4, 19, 30, 175, 249
gold mining, 33, *34*, 37–41, *39*, 79–80
Golden Age, 66, 69, 76–7, 305–6
Government of National Unity, 168–9
governmentality, 235–6
Graaff, De Villiers, 83, 86
Great Depression, 52, 54
Great Trek, centenary of, 56–7
Grobbelaar, Arthur, 122, *123*, 124, 135–6, 138–41
Grobler, Wally, 122, *123*, 131–2, 138
Grobler, W. S. J., 84
Growth, Employment, and Redistribution (GEAR), 23, 170

Hartzenberg, Ferdi, 143
hate speech case against Julius Malema, 117–53, 199, 204, *220*, 241
Hechter, Nic, 105, 112, 122, *123*, 138
Helping Hand, 221, 234, 300, 326–9
Helpmekaar 2020, 230–4, 237
Henning, Jood, 95, 102–3, 108–9
Hermann, Dirk; *see also Basta! Ons voetspore is in Afrika*
  on Afrikaner DNA, 216
  on apartheid, 258
  on community work, 228, 238
  on funding, 223–4, 241
  on legal action, *192*, 218–21
  on Maroela Media, 222
  on MWU, 188–9, *192*, 243–8, 250
  on Rand Revolt (1922), 258–60
  on socialism, 211–12, 260
  on Solidarity, 203–7, *230*, 238–9
  on tipping point dilemma, 291–3
Herstigte Nasionale Party (HNP), 81, 162
Hertzog, J. B. M., 51
Hickman, Tony, 91
Histadrut, 164, 226–7
Hoagland, Jim, 33, 36–7
homelands, 65–6, 91, 104, 142–3
homogenising views of white society, 8, 12
Human Rights Commission, 164

identity
  crisis, 8, 46, 84, 165–7, 195
  cultural, 8–9, 165, 247–50
  economy, 224–5
  inequality and, 12–20
  literature on, 4, 9
  MWU and, 186
  politics, 168, 306
  Solidarity and, 216–18
immigrant communities, 16–18
Indian South Africans, 51–61, 118, 134–5, 144
Industrial Conciliation Act (1924), 48, 51
Industrial Conciliation Act (1956)
  impact of, 61, 64
  Section 77 of, 61, 82–3, 95–6, 108, 131–2, 142
  TUCSA and, 62–3
  Wiehahn Commission, 124
industrial relations *see* works committees; Bantu Labour Act (1964); Bantu Labour Relations Amendment Act (1973); Industrial Conciliation Act (1924); Industrial Conciliation Act (1953); Native Labour Act (1953)
industrial rights, 22, 108, 117–19, 129–30, 134, 141, 143, 145–6, 152–3, 172, 175, 306–7
Industrial Tribunal investigation, 108–9, 126
inflation, 77–80, 84, 101, 175
influx control, 66, *see also* pass laws
informal economy, 10
informal settlements *see* squatter camps, white
Information Service, 86–7
International Labour Organization (ILO), 138, 140–53, 236

334   Index

interviews by author, 12, 28–9, 264–7
Iron and Steel Industrial Corporation (Iscor)
  employment by, 64, 68, 128
  history of, 10, 49
  MWU and, 269–70
  privatisation of, 169
  protests against, 192–3, *271*
  workers at, *65*
Iron and Steel Union *see* South African Iron, Steel and Allied Industries Union

Jacobs, Gideon, 85–101
Jewish role in business, 56; *see also* antisemitism
job creation, 222–3, 235
job reservation
  Afrikaner Broederbond and, 112
  history of, 43, 82–3
  MWU defense of, 174–9
  National Party and, 89–90, 94–6, 103, 108–11, 125, 174–5
  United Party and, 88, 109–10
  Wiehahn Commission, 113, 119, 126, 128, 131, 142, 174–5
Johannesburg, 53, 198
Joint Committee Representing All Organised Labour in the Republic of South Africa, 124–5, 130–5, 144, 151

Kagan, Morris, 130
Kraal Publishers, 224, 231–2
Kriel, Kallie, 228
Krisisberaad (Crisis Summit), 227–9
Kruger, Paul, 40, 230

labour aristocracy, 35–7, 73–5
Labour Party, 42, 49–72
labour reforms, 108–15, 150–2, 274–8
labour shortages, 69, 72, 77–80, 82–94, 108
labour, relations with state and capital *see* states, capital and labour, relations between
Lamont, Colin, 204
land redistribution, 303–5
Langner, Danie, 228
late capitalism, 3, 15, 20, 27–30, 200; *see also* capitalism; neoliberalism
Le Roux, Francois, 109
Le Roux, Frederick, 90–1
legal action, 218, 223, 231; *see also* Solidarity Movement
Lenin, Vladimir, 35–75
living standards, 171–2, 179–80

long transition, 2–3, 11, 20, 153, 158, 171, 189, 196–7, 240, 262, 267, 282, 291, 301, 307

Malan, D. F., 56–7
Malema, Julius, 199–228, 241
Mandela, Nelson, 22
Mantashe, Gwede, 213–14, *215*
manufacturing industry, 79, 90
Marikana massacre, 24
Maroela Media, 221–2, 232, 241, 304
Marxism, 3, 12, 75, 210
masculinity, 30, 175, 265
Metal and Boilermakers' Union, 268
middle-class whites, 6, 11, 18–19, 261–2, 280, 300
mineral revolution, 33–5, 37–41, 305; *see also* mining industry
Mines and Works Act (1911), 42–3
Mines and Works Amendment Act (1926), 49, 71
Mineworker, The, 157, 172–4, 176–8, 180–2, 246–7
Mineworkers' Union (MWU)
  constitution of, 255–6, 291–2; *see also* Solidarity trade union
  Dirk Hermann on, 188–9, 243–8, 250
  Flip Buys on, 244–50, 252, 254–6, 271
  headquarters of, 198–9
  history of, 71–3, 188–9
  membership of, 157–8, 161, 165–93, 246, 268–82
  militancy, 173, 270
  political alignment of, 184–5, 274–6
  'reinvention' of, 158–9, 161–71, 195
  rough institutional culture of, 243–50, 271–4, 282
  services of, 193
  Wessel Visser biography of, 158–9, 164, 167, 187, 195, 198, 249, 252, 274–5
  white workers on, 267–82
mining industry
  economic growth and, 79–80
  impact of, 33–5
  labour reforms, 147–8
  racial order and, 37–41
  work processes, 33, *34*, *43*, *50*
  workers of, *34*, *39*, *43*, *50*, *62*, 148
minorities; *see also* immigrant communities
  MWU and, 179
  neoliberalism and, 19
  Solidarity and, 2, 236, 291–2
  Wiehahn Commission, 132, 134–5, 137–8, 145–9

Mittal Steel, 10; *see also* ArcelorMittal South Africa
Mokoatle, Ben, 122, *123*, 138–53
Mulder, Connie, 178
Muller, Helgaard, 108
municipal service delivery, 24, 231, 233
Munsook, Gopi, 122, *123*, 138–53
MWU-News, 182, 184–5, 188, 190–1, 254–6

National Manpower Commission (NMC), 139, 146
National Party (NP)
  Afrikaner nationalism and, 56–60
  apartheid and, 60–6
  capitalism and, 66, 70
  disbanding of, 166
  Durban strikes, 91–7
  HNP and, 161–2
  labour reforms, 80–3, 101–3, 108–12, 114–15, 151
  MWU and, 72, 174, 178–80, 185, 188, 205, 258
  negotiations for transition to democracy, 22, 180
  TUCSA and, 141
  white workers and, 1, 5–6, 48–52
  Wiehahn Commission, 125–6, 157
National Prosecuting Authority (NPA), 303
National Union of Clothing Workers (NUCW), 135, 140
National Union of Furniture and Allied Workers, 136
National Union of Metalworkers of South Africa (NUMSA), 169
National Union of Mineworkers (NUM), 162, 192–3, 213–14
National Union of Motor Assembly and Rubber Workers of South Africa (NUMARWOSA), 136
nationalisation, 58
Native Labour Act (1953), 60–1, 92
Neethling, Tommie, 122, *123*, 131–3, 138
negotiations for transition to democracy, 2, 7, 23, 162, 180, 182–3, 195, 208–9, 274–6
Nel, Gerrie, 303
neoliberalism, 14, 19, 169–71, 200, 212–13, 217–18, 235–40; *see also* capitalism; late capitalism
New York Times, 17–18
Nicholson, Ben, 130–1
Nieuwoudt, Attie
  Afrikaner Broederbond and, 97, 112
  labour reforms, 64–75, 125, *127*

National Party and, 104
Wiehahn Commission, 112, 122, *123*, 125, 128–30, 152
nismark, 292–5, 297, 299

O'Okiep copper mine, 113–14
Open Society Foundations, 16

Pact government, 53–4, 59, 71, 128, 258
Pan-South African Language Board (PANSAB), 191
pass laws, 41, *see also* influx control
Paulus, Arrie
  AWB and, 274
  background of, 247–9, 271–2
  Conservative Party and, 178
  on history of MWU, 188
  on labour reforms, 72–3, 78, 100, 177, 182
  media coverage of, 270
  membership of MWU, 172–4
  as MP, 162
  National Party and, *73*, 96, 113, 172, *173*
  Wiehahn Commission, 125–6, 153, 157
  political rights, 117–19, 129–30, 134–5, 141, 143, 145–6, 152–3, 172, 175, 306–7
politics of race, 171, 306–7
poor white problem *see* white poverty
Population Registration Act (1950), 65
populism, 3, 16–19, 204, 208, 215–16, 238–9, 265–6, 306, 308
postcolonial theory, 4, 12
poverty, 41, 212–13, 265; *see also* white poverty
precarity, 14–16, 22, 37, 41–8, 73–5, 265, 305–6
Pretoria, 9–11, 199
private sector, 49, 66, 68, 115, 119
privatisation, 169, 178, 235
Progressive Party (PP), 87, 89, 96
Progressive Reform Party (PRP), 80, 102, 109–11
Promotion of Bantu Self-Government Act (1959), 65
protests, 80, 132–3, *183*, *269*, *271*, *275*, *277*, 307; *see also* Soweto uprising
Public Service Association, 67

race
  -based order, 19, 40–1, 48–52, 55, 59–60, 120, 171–8
  class and, 22, 45, 186
  culture and, 194–5, 262
  labour and, 33, 39

race (cont.)
  MWU/Solidarity membership and, 255–6, 267, 291–301
  neoliberalism and, 217–18, 240
  as social construction, 12–13
  racial capitalism, 3, 119, 308
  racial degeneracy, 53–5
  racism, 42, 217–18, 279–80
Railroads and Harbours Staff Associations, 63, 124
railways, 49
rainbow nation, 22
Rand Revolt 1922
  history of, 44–8
  impact of, 48, 50
  murders of Africans during, 45
  MWU and, 71, 113, 157, 173–4, 179, 183, 188, 202
  photographs of, 46–7, 257–60
  Solidarity and, 257–61
  white poverty and, 55
rebellion of 1914–1915, 231
recessions, 168, 172
Reconstruction and Development Programme (RDP), 23, 169
redundancies, 10, 285
Reyneke, J. P. A., 83
Riekert Commission, 112
right-wing politics, 16–19, 244–6, 265–6, 302, 307–8
Roets, Ernst, 304

Sasol, 68
Schoeman, Ben, 61
scholarships *see* bursaries
Second World War, 58, 60, 66
self-help, 212–14, 218, 221, 231, 238
separate development, 126–7, 240, 290
seven-day working week, 182
skilled workers, 43–4, 50, 78–80, 82–3, 88, 94; *see also* labour shortages
Smuts, Jan (General/Prime Minister), 40, 45, 48, 51, 59
social Darwinism, 53
social mobility, 67–71, 69, 147; *see also* embourgeoisement
social movement unionism, 20–2, 197
social movements, 3, 25, 27, 159, 168, 171, 197, 199–201, 209, 216, 219, 237–8
socialism, 210–12, 218, 260
Solidariteitkunde seminar, 204–17, 220–1, 223–4, 227, 242–4, 250, 257, 259, 262, 266, 291–3; *see also* Hermann, Dirk
Solidarity Building Fund, 223–4

Solidarity Financial Services, 224
Solidarity Investment Company (SIC), 223–4
Solidarity magazine, 161, 192, 203, 261
Solidarity Movement
  1922 as founding myth, 256–61
  articulation of 'calling' concept, 212, 216, 218, 242, 247, 290–1
  as civil society organisation, 194–5, 199, 237–8
  coloured members of, 165, 297
  counternarratives in, 240, 267–83, 301–2
  cradle-to-grave approach of, 234–5
  discursive strategies of, 200–18, 241–2
  global campaigns by, 236, 303–5
  graduate appointments at, 252–3
  headquarters of, 198–9, 223, 241, 257
  historical narrative about, 201–10, 239–42, 276
  history of, 2, 262
  magazine of, 161
  media coverage of, 165, 232–3, 304–5; *see also* Maroela Media
  membership of, 223–4, 240, 292
  organisational strategies of, 200, 218–40
  'own institutions' strategy, 220–7, 235, 239–40
  as political actor, 229, 236–7, 289, 300, 308–9
  populism of, 204, 208, 215–16, 238–9, 265–6
  services of, 207–8, 222, 234–6, 303–5
  as social movement, 2, 27–30, 199, 236–8, 248
  as 'state' for Afrikaners, 199–200, 227–39
  strategies of, 303, 307–8
  sub-narratives in, 240, 242–63
  sustainability of, 299
Solidarity Property Company, 224
Solidarity Research Institute, 222
Solidarity trade union
  as civil society organisation, 162–3, 185–6, 190, 194–7, 199, 209–10
  historical narrative about, 201–10, 216–17, 239–40
  history of, 158–9, 165, 175–93, 214, 253
  media coverage of, 165, 232–3
  membership of, 195–7, 250–6, 291–301
  neo-racism hearings, 190
  services of, 234–6
  as social movement, vii–xvi, 159, 195, 197, 199
  as social movement union, 27, 158, 200
  working-class whites and, 251–61, 301–2
Solidarity World (online platform), 235

Solidariność, 193
SolTech, 221, 224, 231, 234
South African Communist Party (SACP), 21, 259; *see also* Tripartite Alliance
South African Confederation of Labour (SACLA)
  history of, 63–4
  labour reforms, 87, 95, 100, 150–1
  membership of, 149, 157
  National Party and, *104*, 109, 111, 114, 141, 143
  Wiehahn Commission, 124–30, 152
South African Congress of Trade Unions (SACTU), 63–4
South African Co-ordinating Council of International Metal Workers Federation, 124, 131
South African Electrical Workers' Association, 130
South African Iron, Steel and Allied Industries Union (Iron and Steel Union), 63–75, 87, 95, 128, 163
South African Party (SAP), 48, 53, 56
South African War, 40, 45, 183–4, 188, 201–2
Soweto uprising, 106–8, 110, 114, 134
Spies, Willie, *220*
squatter camps, white, 53, 285–6
state capture, 57
state employment, 8, 10
state intervention, 16, 19, 52, 60, 146, 169–70, 212–14, 235–6
state retreat, 16, 23, 30, 78, 146, 168–9, 171, 212–13, 236–8, 308
states, capital, and labour, relations between, 14, 26, 35, 50, 66, 306
steel industry, 50, 269–70
Steenkamp, Naas, 122–3, *123*, 138–41, 146, 149, 153
Steyn, Marais, 82
Stilfontein mine closure, 213–15
Stofberg, Louis, 178
strike of 1922 *see* Rand Revolt (1922)
strikes
  decline in, 51, 167–8
  Durban strikes, 90–101, *93*, 103, 114, 135
  MWU, 113–14, 173, 191–3, *283*
  National Party and, 77, 85
  on Rand, 42
  Solidarity, 260–1
  'super white union', 162, 180, 182, 187, 195, 256, 264
Suppression of Communism Act (1950), 61–2, 64

Sutton, Dick, 122, *123*, 138–53
Suzman, Helen, 89

Telkom, *187*, 275
Terre'Blanche, Eugene, 274
tipping point dilemma, 291–5
Toekomsberaad (Future Summit), 230–3
Trade Union Council of South Africa (TUCSA)
  coloured president of, 136
  decline of, 157
  Durban strikes, 92
  history of, 62–3
  National Party and, 88, 109, 111
  Wiehahn Commission, 124, 131, 135–41, 149, 151
trade unions
  Afrikaner Broederbond and, 58–9, 98–100
  growth of, 21, 47–8, 168–9
  Industrial Conciliation Act (1924), 51
  international context, 14, 35
  labour reforms, 102–3
  National Party and, 87, 94–5
  Wiehahn Commission, 121, 126–7, 145, 149–51
training *see* education
Transkei, 65–6
Transvaal (Zuid-Afrikaansche Republiek), 40
Transvaal Agricultural Union, 163, 183
Transvaal Miners' Association (TMA), 41–2, 44
Treurnicht, Andries, 109, 143, *181*
tricameral parliament, 135
Tripartite Alliance, 21–2, 72–3, 168, 197
Trump, Donald, 17–19, 304
Truth and Reconciliation Commission, 166

unemployment
  economic growth and, 80
  growth of, 24
  National Party and, 86, 94
  power and, 22, 78
  privatisation and, 169
  white poverty and, 10–11, 41, 300–1
Ungerer, Peet
  Afrikaner Volksfront and, *184*
  AWB and, 274
  Conservative Party and, *181*
  as MWU general secretary, 162, 178–86, 246, *270*, 272, 274
  retirement of, 164
  on white poverty, 185
Union of South Africa, 40–1

unions *see* trade unions
United Kingdom *see* Britain
United Nations (UN), 76, 108, 236
United Party (UP)
　Afrikaners and, 72
　agricultural sector, 60
　history of, 56
　labour reforms, 83–95, 101–2, 109–10
　MWU and, 113–14
　urbanisation, 58
　Wiehahn Commission, 96
United States of America (USA), 17–19, 77, 86, 167–8, 303–5, 309
unskilled jobs, 39, 128, 283–91
urbanisation, 58, 60, 117–18, 142–4, 150–1, 175

Van der Merwe, Piet, 81–115, 122, *123*, 138, 144, 148, 153
Van der Walt, Dennis, *123*, *133*, 139
Van der Watt, Abel, 130
verkramptes, 81, 109
verligtes, 81, 109
Verwoerd, H. F., 65
victimhood, 9, 203, 209, 219, 258
victimisation, white-on-white, 286–8
Viljoen, Constand, 163–4, *184*
Viljoen, I. J., 71
Viljoen, Marais
　Durban strikes, 91–2
　on economic growth, 83–4
　labour reforms, 76, 86–9, *88*, *93*, 101, 113
　retirement of, 101–2
Volksblad, 165
Volksfront *see* Afrikaner Volksfront
volkstaat, 163, 190, 217, 233–4, 307
Voortrekker monument, 56
Vorster, John, 80, 92, 106–8, 112, 121, *127*
voting rights, 23, 40–1, 52, 61, 152, 306

wages, 33, 40, 58, 67, 77, 84, 91–2
Webb, Ronnie, 136–7, 141
welfare states, 66, 70
Wenplan 2002, 189–90, 193, 197, 221
white poverty
　'civilised labour' and, 49, 52–7
　end of, 5, 61, 69
　history of, 44
　MWU/Solidarity and, 185–6, 213–14, 285–6, 300–1
　white working class and, 11–12
　Wiehahn Commission, 128–30

white workers; *see also baas–Klaas* relationships
　citizenship, 9, 18, 56, 59, 167, 194, 209
　conflict with employers, 42, 47–8, 71, 89
　as labour aristocracy, 35–7, 73–5
　mine language, 273–4
　National Party 1948 victory, 5, 50, 60, 72, 85, 174–97, 205–39
　power, 52–3, 72–3, 78, 84–8, 93, 112–13, 129, 188–9
　as privileged precariat, 73–5
　state dependence of, 55, 66, 74–5
　struggle for recognition of, 168, 180, 194
　wages of whiteness, 75
　white labourism, 42
Wiehahn Commission
　Afrikaner Broederbond and, 107, 112
　aftermath of, 141–50, *148*
　appointment of, 80, 110, 114–15, 121–4
　black members of, 122–3
　impact of, 150–1
　Joint Committee testimony at, 130–5
　members of, 116–17, 120–53, *123*
　MWU and, 115, 172–4, 206, 251
　recommendations of, 114
　reforms, 157, 168–70, 197, 276–7, 281–2, 301, 307
　report of, 141–50
　SACLA testimony at, 125–30
　TUCSA testimony at, 135–41
　white labour and, 124–41, 151–3
　White Paper following, 142–4
Wiehahn, Nic
　Afrikaner Broederbond and, 105, 112–13
　background of, 80, 121–2
　Commission of Inquiry into Labour Legislation, 112, 116, 120, *123*, *133*, 134, 139, *143*, 151
　as labour adviser, 109–10
women, 4, 19, 52, 123, 165, 204
works committees, 60–1, 91, 96, 98, 101, 105, 107
World Trade Centre, 1993 storming of, 251, 275
World War I *see* First World War
World War II *see* Second World War

Zuid-Afrikaansche Republiek (Transvaal), 40
Zuma, Duduzane, 303
Zuma, Jacob, 23–4, 199, 210, 228–9, *230*

Titles in the Series

63. DANELLE VAN ZYL-HERMANN *Privileged Precariat: White Workers and South Africa's Long Transition to Majority Rule*
62. BENEDIKT PONTZEN *Islam in a Zongo: Muslim Lifeworlds in Asante, Ghana*
61. LOUISA LOMBARD *Hunting Game: Raiding Politics in the Central African Republic*
60. MARK HUNTER *Race for Education: Gender, White Tone, and Schooling in South Africa*
59. LIZ GUNNER *Radio Soundings: South Africa and the Black Modern*
58. JESSICA JOHNSON *In Search of Gender Justice: Rights and Relationships in Matrilineal Malawi*
57. JASON SUMICH *The Middle Class in Mozambique: The State and the Politics of Transformation in Southern Africa*
56. JOSÉ-MARÍA MUÑOZ *Doing Business in Cameroon: An Anatomy of Economic Governance*
55. JENNIFER DIGGINS *Coastal Sierra Leone: Materiality and the Unseen in Maritime West Africa*
54. HANNAH HOECHNER *Quranic Schools in Northern Nigeria: Everyday Experiences of Youth, Faith, and Poverty*
53. HOLLY PORTER *After Rape: Violence, Justice, and Social Harmony in Uganda*
52. ALEXANDER THURSTON *Salafism in Nigeria: Islam, Preaching, and Politics*
51. ANDREW BANK *Pioneers of the Field: South Africa's Women Anthropologists*
50. MAXIM BOLT *Zimbabwe's Migrants and South Africa's Border Farms: The Roots of Impermanence*
49. MEERA VENKATACHALAM *Slavery, Memory and Religion in Southeastern Ghana, c.1850–Present*
48. DEREK PETERSON, KODZO GAVUA, and CIRAJ RASSOOL (eds) *The Politics of Heritage in Africa: Economies, Histories, and Infrastructures*
47. ILANA VAN WYK *The Universal Church of the Kingdom of God in South Africa: A Church of Strangers*
46. JOEL CABRITA *Text and Authority in the South African Nazaretha Church*
45. MARLOES JANSON *Islam, Youth, and Modernity in the Gambia: The Tablighi Jama'at*
44. ANDREW BANK and LESLIE J. BANK (eds) *Inside African Anthropology: Monica Wilson and Her Interpreters*
43. ISAK NIEHAUS *Witchcraft and a Life in the New South Africa*
42. FRASER G. MCNEILL *AIDS, Politics, and Music in South Africa*
41. KRIJN PETERS *War and the Crisis of Youth in Sierra Leone*
40. INSA NOLTE *Obafemi Awolowo and the Making of Remo: The Local Politics of a Nigerian Nationalist*
39. BEN JONES *Beyond the State in Rural Uganda*
38. RAMON SARRÓ *The Politics of Religious Change on the Upper Guinea Coast: Iconoclasm Done and Undone*
37. CHARLES GORE *Art, Performance and Ritual in Benin City*

36. FERDINAND DE JONG *Masquerades of Modernity: Power and Secrecy in Casamance, Senegal*
35. KAI KRESSE *Philosophising in Mombasa: Knowledge, Islam and Intellectual Practice on the Swahili Coast*
34. DAVID PRATTEN *The Man-Leopard Murders: History and Society in Colonial Nigeria*
33. CAROLA LENTZ *Ethnicity and the Making of History in Northern Ghana*
32. BENJAMIN F. SOARES *Islam and the Prayer Economy: History and Authority in a Malian Town*
31. COLIN MURRAY and PETER SANDERS *Medicine Murder in Colonial Lesotho: The Anatomy of a Moral Crisis*
30. R. M. DILLEY *Islamic and Caste Knowledge Practices among Haalpulaar'en in Senegal: Between Mosque and Termite Mound*
29. BELINDA BOZZOLI *Theatres of Struggle and the End of Apartheid*
28. ELISHA RENNE *Population and Progress in a Yoruba Town*
27. ANTHONY SIMPSON *'Half-London' in Zambia: Contested Identities in a Catholic Mission School*
26. HARRI ENGLUND *From War to Peace on the Mozambique–Malawi Borderland*
25. T. C. MCCASKIE *Asante Identities: History and Modernity in an African Village 1850–1950*
24. JANET BUJRA *Serving Class: Masculinity and the Feminisation of Domestic Service in Tanzania*
23. CHRISTOPHER O. DAVIS *Death in Abeyance: Illness and Therapy among the Tabwa of Central Africa*
22. DEBORAH JAMES *Songs of the Women Migrants: Performance and Identity in South Africa*
21. BIRGIT MEYER *Translating the Devil: Religion and Modernity among the Ewe in Ghana*
20. DAVID MAXWELL *Christians and Chiefs in Zimbabwe: A Social History of the Hwesa People c.1870s–1990s*
19. FIONA D. MACKENZIE *Land, Ecology and Resistance in Kenya, 1880–1952*
18. JANE I. GUYER *An African Niche Economy: Farming to Feed Ibadan, 1968–88*
17. PHILIP BURNHAM *The Politics of Cultural Difference in Northern Cameroon*
16. GRAHAM FURNISS *Poetry, Prose and Popular Culture in Hausa*
15. C. BAWA YAMBA *Permanent Pilgrims: The Role of Pilgrimage in the Lives of West African Muslims in Sudan*
14. TOM FORREST *The Advance of African Capital: The Growth of Nigerian Private Enterprise*
13. MELISSA LEACH *Rainforest Relations: Gender and Resource Use among the Mende of Gola, Sierra Leone*
12. ISAAC NCUBE MAZONDE *Ranching and Enterprise in Eastern Botswana: A Case Study of Black and White Farmers*
11. G. S. EADES *Strangers and Traders: Yoruba Migrants, Markets and the State in Northern Ghana*

10. COLIN MURRAY *Black Mountain: Land, Class and Power in the Eastern Orange Free State, 1880s to 1980s*
9. RICHARD WERBNER *Tears of the Dead: The Social Biography of an African Family*
8. RICHARD FARDON *Between God, the Dead and the Wild: Chamba Interpretations of Religion and Ritual*
7. KARIN BARBER *I Could Speak Until Tomorrow: Oriki, Women and the Past in a Yoruba Town*
6. SUZETTE HEALD *Controlling Anger: The Sociology of Gisu Violence*
5. GUNTHER SCHLEE *Identities on the Move: Clanship and Pastoralism in Northern Kenya*
4. JOHAN POTTIER *Migrants No More: Settlement and Survival in Mambwe Villages, Zambia*
3. PAUL SPENCER *The Maasai of Matapato: A Study of Rituals of Rebellion*
2. JANE I. GUYER (ed.) *Feeding African Cities: Essays in Social History*
1. SANDRA T. BARNES *Patrons and Power: Creating a Political Community in Metropolitan Lagos*

CPSIA information can be obtained
at www.ICGtesting.com
Printed in the USA
LVHW011048030821
694401LV00005B/348